the sourcebook of decorative stone

AN ILLUSTRATED IDENTIFICATION GUIDE

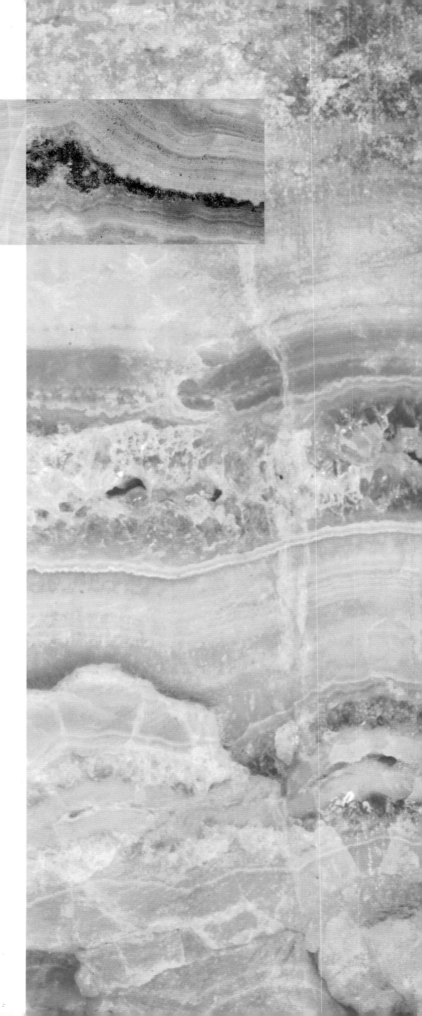

Dedication
For my wonderful parents, Sheila and David Price

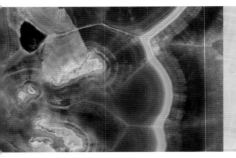

A FIREFLY BOOK

Published by Firefly Books Ltd. 2007

First printing

Publisher Cataloging-in-Publication Data (U.S.)

Price, Monica T. The sourcebook of decorative stone : an illustrated identification guide / Monica T. Price ; photographs by Gary Ombler
[288] p. : col. photos. ; cm. Includes bibliographical references and index.
Summary: A visual sourcebook of stones and marbles, accompanied by description, location, geological and topographical source, and history of usage in architecture, interiors, decorative items.
ISBN-13: 978-1-55407-254-5
ISBN-10: 1-55407-254-9
1. Building stones—Identification. 2. Marble—Identification. 3. Building stones—Pictorial works. 4. Marble—Pictorial works. 5. Building stones—History. 6. Marble—History. I. Ombler, Gary. II. Title.
691.2 dc22   TN950.P753 2007

Library and Archives Canada Cataloguing in Publication

Price, Monica T., 1956-
The sourcebook of decorative stone : an illustrated identification guide / Monica T. Price ; photographer: Gary Ombler.
Includes bibliographical references and indexes.
ISBN-13: 978-1-55407-254-5
ISBN-10: 1-55407-254-9.--
1. Building stones—Identification. 2. Marble—Identification.
3. Building stones—Pictorial works. 4. Marble—Pictorial works.
5. Building stones—History. 6. Marble—History. I. Ombler, Gary
II. Title.
1 TN950.P85 2007   691'.2   C2006-906522-5

Published in the United States by
Firefly Books (U.S.) Inc.
P.O. Box 1338, Ellicott Station
Buffalo, New York 14205

Published in Canada by
Firefly Books Ltd.
66 Leek Crescent
Richmond Hill, Ontario L4B 1H1

Designed and produced by Quintet Publishing Limited
Project Editor: James Harrison
Designer: Miranda Harvey
Photography: Gary Ombler, Monica T. Price
Picture Researchers: Joanne Forrest Smith, Jo Walton
Editor: Marianne Canty
Creative Director: Richard Dewing
Publisher: Gaynor Sermon

Manufactured in Singapore by Pica Digital Pte Ltd.
Printed in China by SNP Leefung Printers Ltd.

the sourcebook of decorative stone

AN ILLUSTRATED IDENTIFICATION GUIDE

Monica T. Price

contents

Introduction

There are thousands of different decorative stones, and they are used in every country of the world. Look around and you'll see them adding color to store fronts. They form the practical, hard-wearing cladding of many architectural interiors and exteriors of company offices and public buildings. Enter a church, synagogue or mosque and you will see them, often in beautiful patterns, cladding walls and floors, lecterns and altars. Memorials are carved into them, graves are marked with them, and they make superb raw material for sculptors to carve. Beautiful, natural rocks have a functional place inside our homes, too, forming practical surfaces for kitchens and bathrooms, or made into the vases, tealight holders and other ornaments so popular with contemporary interior designers. Of course decorative minerals are widely used in jewelry too. Stone has a timeless quality, and some of the most exquisite ornamental stones are found in the decoration of precious antique furniture. The tradition of using polished stone for decoration is shared among civilizations all over the world, going well back into antiquity.

TURNING ROCK INTO A THING OF BEAUTY

It has to be admitted that most natural rocks are not particularly attractive to look at. Even the stones in this book, when roughly hewn from the ground, are generally rather dull. It is when they are polished, buffed to a bright reflective luster, that colors are enriched and patterns and structures sharpened, and their inherent natural beauty is revealed. Not all rocks have decorative value. They must have a compact and cohesive structure that enables them to be sawn or shaped without splitting or breaking up, and they must have an attractive appearance. They also need to occur

LEFT AND BELOW Marbleworkers in the town of Teignmouth, on the South Devon coast of England, used to carve the local *madrepore marble* (a coral limestone) into gifts such as this little box. They were sold mainly to visiting tourists.

in nature in sufficient quantities. Some semiprecious minerals are so valuable that quite small deposits are commercially viable. For "dimension stone"—that is, slabbed and polished for architectural use—much larger quantities of stone must be available. A huge global quarrying and processing industry supplies the polished stone we see all around us.

DETECTIVE WORK

Decorative rocks can reveal evidence of ancient life forms, and great global processes—from earthquakes to the formation of great mountain chains. When identifying stones, it helps to understand a little about the geological processes that formed them and gave them their various characteristics. Traditionally, marble is defined as any rock composed of calcite or dolomite (two common carbonate minerals) that takes a good polish. The stone trade still uses this definition, comparing marbles to limestones that have similar compositions but do not take a polish. Modern geologists are much more specific: they classify limestones as sedimentary rocks, and marbles as limestones that have been "metamorphosed" that is, altered—by heat and pressure. In a similar way, the trade uses the term granite to encompass a wide

variety of rock types composed of silica or silicate minerals (but not as specifically as geologists in their definition). This "jungle of names" is explained more fully in the opening "All about decorative stones" section of this book, as are the "earth-shattering" processes by which rocks form, and the broad range of different rock types and how they are classified by the trade and by geologists.

This sourcebook describes and illustrates close to 300 decorative rocks and minerals, and introduces many others. This may be just a tiny proportion of the many different kinds used globally, but it includes those that are particularly popular or of special historic interest. The photographs show the stones in actual size, as they appear when polished. Each entry gives a short summary of the stone's source, history and use, and a brief geological description to help with identification. It will be an invaluable reference for archaeologists, architects, artists, antique restorers, auction houses, museum curators, the stone trade and geologists, and indeed for anyone who delights in the beautiful natural stones that are used to decorate the world around us.

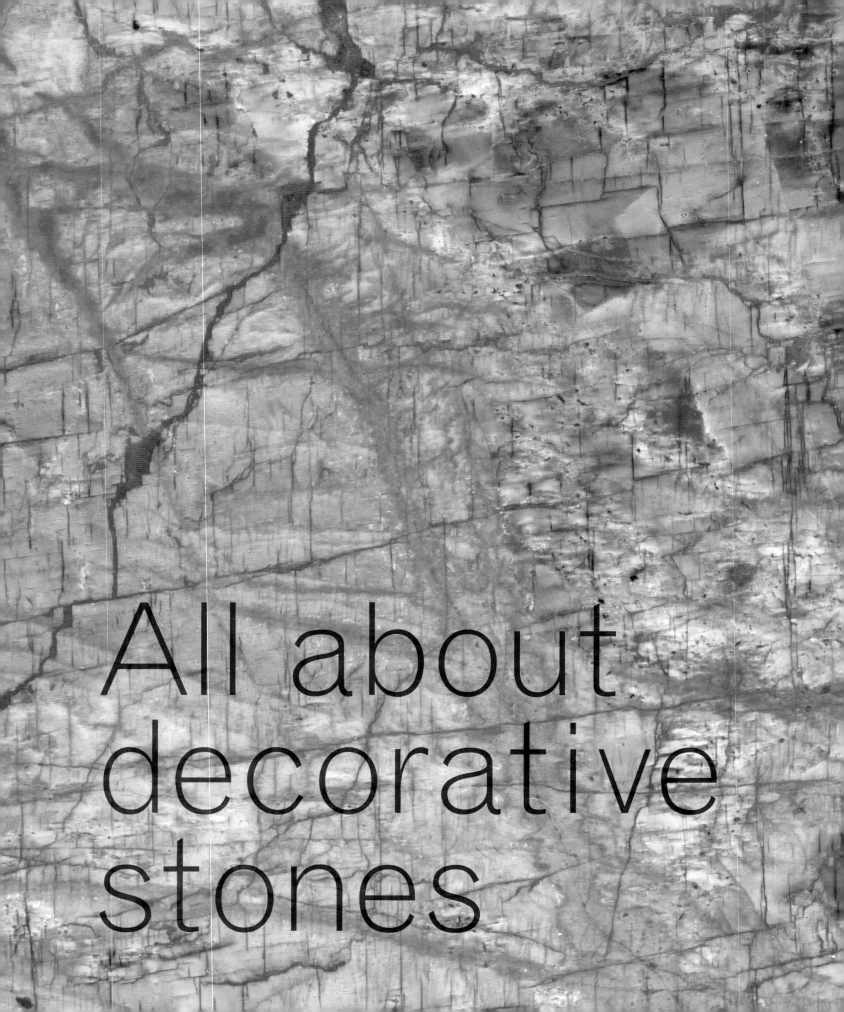

All about decorative stones

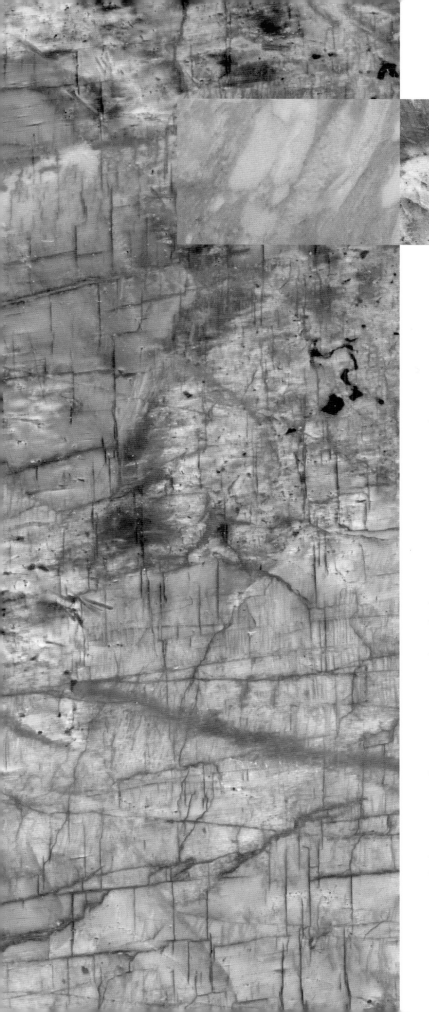

Inspirational stone

There is no doubt that January of 1827 was freezing cold, but this did not deter a young student from setting out on a long and inclement overland journey across Europe, to visit a Roman lawyer and avid stone collector by the name of Faustino Corsi. He had heard that something special was for sale.

The Oxford student, Stephen Jarrett, had heard that Signor Corsi was to sell his remarkable collection of polished stone slabs. Corsi, a respected citizen of Rome, was fascinated by the history of his native city. He had collected large samples of all the polished marbles, granites, serpentinites and other decorative stones to be found in the ruins of Rome. To these he added stones from contemporary Italian quarries. Finally, he included samples from farther afield, decorative minerals from England, Russia, Afghanistan, Madagascar and Canada. Some of his stones came from the scalpellini (stonecutters, see page 15) of the city who had a long tradition of reworking pillars and slabs found in the ancient ruins. Others were tracked down for him by his agents, and yet others were sent to him by foreign visitors who had seen and admired his collection—the learned Professor of Geology at Oxford University, William Buckland, was one admirer. By 1827, Corsi had acquired 900 different slabs of stone, each measuring 6 x 3 x 1½ inch (15 x 7 x 4 cm) and weighing about 2¼ pounds (1 kg)—a heavy load for the floors of his second floor apartment.

COVERT NEGOTIATIONS

Stephen Jarrett knew he had competition. An architect working for the British Museum had been undertaking covert negotiations to buy the collection for the museum, and was attempting to drive a hard bargain. The Museum Trustees deliberated. Meanwhile, Jarrett arrived in Rome to buy the collection, a gift for his alma mater, the famous University of Oxford in England.

Jarrett had ample funds of his own from properties in the sugar plantations of Jamaica, and he proceeded to charm the marble collector with his offer to pay a generous price for the collection and all remaining copies of the printed catalog, and to commission more specimens to bring the total to 1,000 samples. By the time the British Museum Trustees had agreed to proceed with the purchase, the collection had already been sold to the student. In November 1827 it was installed in Oxford University's Radcliffe Library, and for his efforts, Stephen Jarrett earned an extension to his period of study in the University and an honorary Master of Arts degree.

THE REDOUBTABLE SIGNOR CORSI

Faustino Corsi was a true pioneer in the study of decorative stone. In his printed *Catalogo ragionato* he attempted to record where each stone had been quarried. He interpreted the writings of the ancient authors, drew on the literature of contemporary scientists, recorded the observations and traditional names of the scalpellini, and arranged his collection according to geological principles. The observations in his *Catalogo ragionato*, and in his book *Delle Pietre Antiche* (1828, 1833, 1845) have been hugely influential in the study of ancient stone, and still inform visitors to Rome of some of the best examples of ancient marbles to be seen there.

Corsi's collection is housed in the Oxford University Museum of Natural History, where for me a routine curatorial exercise turned into a major research project, as I started verifying his names and localities and updating his catalog with the location of quarries rediscovered since his time. Meanwhile, my colleague Lisa Cooke has translated and researched his catalog.

THE FARNBOROUGH HALL TABLE

About 30 miles (50 km) north of Oxford, in the Warwick village of Farnborough, is Farnborough Hall. It is the beautiful old National Trust home of the Holbech family (open to visitors in the summer months). Entering the grand entrance hall, you will see a rocking horse and grand piano, but there in the middle of the room is an exquisite round table, the top inlaid with samples of 166 different decorative stones. Marbles, serpentinites, granites, fossiliferous limestones, agates and other decorative minerals and rocks radiate out from a central roundel of vivid blue *lapis lazuli*. Some sparkle and glint in the light, while others have curious patterns, the fossil remains of ancient sea creatures. Visitors invariably spend time admiring the stones and choosing their favorites, seeing something new at each angle.

Tables of this kind were manufactured for the wealthier travelers doing the Grand Tour of Europe in the 18th and early 19th centuries. This one, with its white *Carrara marble* rim, was typical of the handiwork of the scalpellini of Rome. They used thin veneers of different, often rare, stones. Some were originally quarried in Roman times, others came from quarries opened in the baroque period of the 17th and 18th centuries, and yet others were from contemporary quarries. Small scraps of stone could be converted into a work of great beauty and some educational merit for the purchaser. The inlaid tabletop at Farnborough Hall is a beautiful family heirloom, purchased and brought to England around 1830.

I was invited to see if I could identify the stones so that the volunteer guides could tell visitors more about the table. Without Corsi's collection, this would have been very difficult. There are some illustrated Italian books on ancient marbles but hardly any featuring more recent stones. A few years earlier, a grant from the Jerwood Foundation had enabled us to photograph all of Corsi's stone slabs, and armed with pictures, his catalog and our research notes, I was able to recognize nearly all the stones in the table. Now the guides can tell visitors how one stone came from the remote Labrador coast, another from the Ural Mountains of Russia, while yet another was quarried by convict labor in

LEFT Faustino Corsi's collection of 1,000 different polished slabs of decorative stone was an amazing reference collection in his own time and is even more important today.

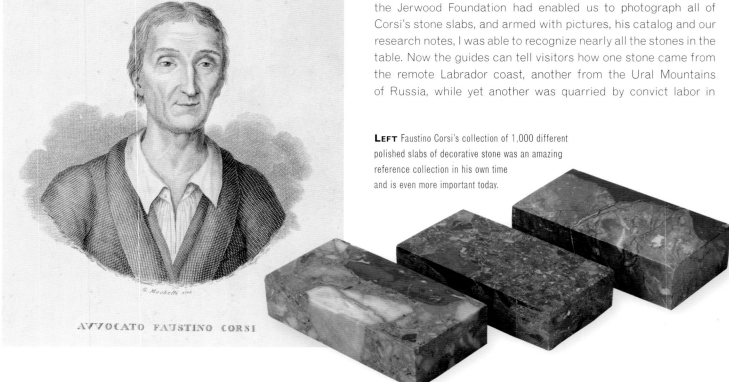

G. Mochetti inc.

AVVOCATO FAUSTINO CORSI

the heat of the Egyptian desert nearly 2,000 years ago. Stones can have extraordinary stories to tell.

The stones in the Farnborough Hall table are the same ones employed to make all sorts of ornaments and items of furniture, quality souvenirs of the Grand Tour that can be found in private collections and museums all over the world today. They are also the decorative rocks and minerals used in antiquity and routinely found in archaeological excavations all across Europe and north Africa. The recycling of stone for inlaid furniture continues a long tradition in which beautiful stones have been used and reused for the decoration of palaces, public buildings, churches and cathedrals. Now that we know more about Faustino Corsi's collection, we can use it as a reference for the identification of decorative stone in many different places.

THE OXFORD CONNECTION

But what about the decorative stones discovered since Corsi's time? The Oxford University Museum of Natural History was completed in 1860 to a design much influenced by the Neo-Gothic movement, in which a central glazed court is surrounded on all four sides by two stories of galleries. A recurring theme of the building is that all elements of the architecture should be educational, and the pillars surrounding the galleries are no exception. They form a collection of 127 different British and Irish decorative stones, each carefully selected by John Phillips, the Professor of Geology and labeled with its name. To me, they are part of the reason why

the Oxford University Museum of Natural History is such a special building, a jewel in the university's architectural heritage.

Faustino Corsi's superb collection, the beautiful Farnborough tabletop, and the fine museum pillars are together the inspiration behind this book. Corsi's collection can be viewed by prior arrangement, and I warmly welcome visitors to see and use it. But how convenient it would be to take the best known Corsi samples, add to them a selection of the stones used in our museum building, and some of the most important of the stones used in the 20th and 21st centuries from our mineral and decorative rocks reference collections, and publish them in an informative, illustrated book. That is the intention of this book. It is further enhanced by the inclusion of several specimens from the beautifully documented John Watson Collection of building and decorative stones in the Sedgwick Museum of the University of Cambridge, which is worldwide in scope and dates from the early 20th century. It complements our Oxford holdings particularly well. I hope this book will help you to recognize many different decorative stones, understand a little better how they formed and discover some of their more remarkable histories.

A very ancient history

The use of stone for decoration and adornment began in prehistoric times. People first learned the skills to manufacture essential tools and weapons from stone, and soon applied the same skills to the creation of items of beauty and symbolism. Softer stones could be cut by harder ones, brittle stones could be chipped and split. A bamboo stick charged with abrasive sand could, with patience, be used to cut intricate designs, carve figurines and personalize jewelry. Carnelian, amethyst, turquoise, jade and *lapis lazuli* are among the first stones to have been used for purely decorative purposes by ancient civilizations in Egypt, Mesopotamia, India, China, central Asia and the Americas. Artifacts such as beads, seals and figurines are found in archaeological excavations of sites that date back thousands of years.

In Europe, the ancient Greeks worked white marble into fine classical buildings and dramatic lifelike sculptures, but it was the Romans who loved colored stones.

THE ROMAN INFLUENCE

The ancient Romans' desire for colored marbles and granites became an obsession as they opened quarries all across their growing empire, introducing decoration to homes and public buildings, and shipping huge slabs and columns back to Rome for the embellishment of the city. Small pieces and cut slabs were arranged as mosaics and patterned inlays for floors and walls, and all manner of stones were carved into sarcophagi, fountain basins and vases, or sculpted into busts and figurines. The finest stones were so highly valued that the quarries came under direct Imperial control, and the finest red and purple stones were reserved for the use of the Emperor. The importance of stone in ancient culture is made very clear by the writings of authors such as Theophrastus (370–285 BCE), Strabo (63/64 BCE–24 CE), and perhaps most importantly by the observations and detailed descriptions of Pliny the Elder (23–79 CE) in his *Naturalis Historia*. Curiously, the Romans spurned most of the beautiful stones to be found in Italy, preferring those from more exotic locations and transporting them to the *marmorata* (ancient marble yards in Rome and Ostia). Inscriptions in the *marmorata* and quarries, the writings of ancient authors, and the distribution of the stones themselves around the empire have enabled archaeologists to build a fascinating picture of this hugely important ancient trade.

THE BYZANTINE ERA

The value of decorative stone in the Byzantine era is undeniable. Indeed the marbles used in the opulent decoration of Sancta Sophia (Hagia Sophia) in Istanbul (Constantinople) were the subject of highly evocative verse by the court poet, Paul the Silentiary in about 563 CE. But political instability and the dangers of piracy on the seas meant that most of the ancient quarries closed. Instead of importing new stone, Byzantine stoneworkers reworked the ample supply of stone already existing in Roman buildings and stockyards, recutting it according to contemporary fashions, and employing it in the ornamentation of new buildings.

BELOW The ancient Romans decorated their villa floors with mosaics made up from small squares of decorative stones. This well-preserved mosaic is from a villa in Kourion, Cyprus.

Churches and public buildings were richly decorated with spoliated stone. Over time the locations of many ancient quarries were completely forgotten. New ways were being discovered to use the stones quarried in ancient times, for example the extraordinarily complex Cosmati pavements of the 12th, 13th and 14th centuries.

WEALTHY PATRONS AND DESIRABLE STONES

Every skilled artist and artisan needed a patron in medieval Europe, and the wealthiest patrons were very powerful people indeed. Just as the millionaire media moguls and Hollywood stars commission luxurious mansions today, so the wealthy rulers of Renaissance times had lavish new palaces and churches built for their comfort and spiritual edification. Constructing such ostentatious displays of wealth kept large workforces in gainful employment and helped bond their loyalty. These great building projects also demanded huge quantities of the most desirable decorative stones. Marble from Carrara had been used for building right through medieval times, but the Tuscan quarrying industries expanded dramatically under the patronage of the Medici dynasty of Florence, and Michelangelo himself was despatched to Seravezza to organize the opening of quarries on Montaltissimo.

The popes and cardinals of medieval and baroque times also brought great secular wealth, which they employed in the construction of many excessively elaborate churches and basilicas. St. Peter's Basilica in Rome in the 16th century was one of the greatest of these projects. When Roman marble began to run out, the search began for new colorful decorative stones from Italian quarries. Many fine stones were first used in Rennaissance times and the 16th- and 17th-century baroque period, and the famous marble quarrying industry in Italy largely has its origins not in the Roman use of decorative stone, but in these later times.

Another enterprise which made heavy demands for the choicest decorative stones was the *Opificio delle Pietre Dure* in Florence, founded by Ferdinando I de' Medici in 1588. These famous workshops produced exquisite inlaid furniture and sculptures using colorful hard stones. The stones were sourced from many different countries, and new quarries were opened to obtain stones such as Monterufoli chalcedony, Sicilian jasper and Corsican smaragdite.

ART-LOVING ROYALTY

The French marble industry flourished during the reign of King Louis XIV in the 17th and 18th centuries. He had large amounts of the most beautiful stones from France, Belgium and Italy quarried for use in the decoration of the palaces of Versailles and St. Cloud, the Hospital des Invalides, the Louvre and his other building projects, making the ancient quarries in the Pyrenees famous all across Europe. Many of the finest examples of marble-topped chests and tables, and most beautifully carved chimneypieces use stones from France and date from this time.

THE SCALPELLINI OF ROME

Time and time again, you will see the name "scalpellini" of Rome mentioned in this book. The name scalpellini (formerly scarpellini) comes from the Italian *scalpello* meaning chisel, and this indicates an important part of their work. They were responsible for all the general stonecutting work, whether for buildings or memorials. All the major cities in Italy had guilds of scalpellini, and the profession was commonly passed from father to son. As so often happens when many generations of a family are employed in the same occupation, a whole body of knowledge is passed down through the generations. This is precisely what had happened in Rome. The scalpellini had their own names for the different stones, some dating back to medieval times. They held stocks of decorative stones including the rare, ancient stones that were salvaged from archaeological digs, from engineering work such as road-widening in the city, or from demolition of ancient villas. Undoubtedly they were early masters at the art of recycling, as can be seen in the vast quantity of ancient marble reused in churches and basilicas since medieval times. Their expertise was, and still is, important in the restoration of historic decorative stone in architecture. When Faustino Corsi was building his collection in the early 19th century, he obtained his samples of ancient stones from the scalpellini of Rome, and recorded the names that they used. Many of their names are still in common use today.

BELOW The scalpellini supplied the stone used in the decoration of churches and palaces throughout Italy. This illustration of a palace under construction is from a 16th-century manuscript of Antonio Averlino's 25-volume *Trattato d'Architettura,* completed around 1465.

ABOVE The most expensive piece of furniture ever sold at auction is an absolutely superb example of Florentine pietre dure work. "The Badminton cabinet" was commissioned by 19-year-old Henry Somerset, the third Duke of Beaufort, in 1726. It took some five years to make, and resided at the Beaufort family home, Badminton House in Gloucestershire, England, until it was sold in 1990. It returned to the auction room in 2004 when it was bought for over £19 million (almost $36 million) for the Museum of Liechtenstein in Vienna, Austria.

CATHERINE THE COLLECTOR

Russia also had its champions of decorative stones, notably the 18th-century Empress of Russia, Catherine the Great. She was one of the greatest art collectors of her time, establishing the remarkable collections of the Hermitage in St. Petersburg. The great lapidary works at Ekaterinburg and Peterhof in the Ural Mountains, and Kolyvan in the Altai Mountains carved beautiful vases and other decorative items from local stones, and were funded by a succession of art-loving czars. The colossal Kolyvan vase that took 11 years to manufacture from a 16-foot (5-m) block of Revnevskaya jasper was installed in the Hermitage in 1843.

Thriving decorative stone industries throughout Europe owed their success to the patronage of royalty and the aristocracy. This was to change as decorative stone became accessible to the nouveau riche of society, and from the 18th century onward quarries and tradesmen began to operate a more open commercial market.

THE CRAZE FOR COLLECTING

Gorgeous furniture and ornaments with inlaid decoration in colored stones are found today in private collections and museums all over the world. They were manufactured in the workshops of Rome, Florence and other marble-working centers of Europe for travelers on the Grand Tour of the cultural centers of Europe, the mobile finishing school for the aristocratic young people of the 17th, 18th and early 19th centuries. Marbles from the ruins of Rome could also be purchased as sets of small squares, often marked with the stones' names, from the scalpellini. These little tablets of stone turn up in the collections of museums and country houses and are popular with modern marble collectors. The more discerning collectors might acquire small round or oval samples each with a gilded collar around it.

Indeed a growing craze for studying and collecting ancient marbles spread across Europe during the first half of the 19th century, hand-in-hand with a huge and often dubious international trade in antiquities. The geological museum of the University of Rome "La Sapienza" has one of a number of collections made by the brothers Tomasso and Francesco Belli in the 1840s. Monsieur De Ravestein's collection in the Museum Cinquantenaire, Brussels, Belgium is another. In Berlin, Alceo Feliciani's fine collection in the Antikenmuseum also dates from this time. A fine old collection of ancient stones in the Capitoline Museums of Rome is illustrated in Caterina Napoleone's beautiful book which reproduces in facsimile parts of Corsi's *Delle Pietre Antiche*. Faustino Corsi continued to collect marbles, and his two tabletops inlaid with small squares of ancient and modern stones were purchased by the husband of art historian Fanny Palliser, and are now in the Natural History Museum, London. In the Naturhistorisches Museum of Vienna, an excellent collection of ancient stones was acquired from the Bellini Brothers of Rome, and documented in Felix Karrer's catalog of 1892. The collection of the natural history museum of the Accademia dei Fisiocritici in Siena is informatively illustrated on the Internet.

While some collectors noted which excavations the stone had come from, and many recorded the names used by the scalpellini, few collectors made any attempt to establish where the different stones had been quarried, and few indeed seemed to have concerned themselves with the collection of contemporary stones. Corsi's collection is a very important exception in both these respects, as are the mid-19th century collections of F. Pescetto and Pio De Santis in the Italian Geological Survey's offices in Rome. The Survey also has a fine regional decorative stone collection which would be a superb resource for researchers were it not consigned to storage in sealed packing crates.

Collections of ancient marbles are readily snapped up in auctions today, and samples are always sought by collectors in flea markets, especially in Italy. Most museums welcome visitors to enjoy these historic collections and use them as research resources. It is marble museums and natural history museums around the world that largely hold collections of 20th- and 21st-century marbles that will be important historical collections for future generations.

ANCIENT STONES REDISCOVERED

Two great movements that started in the 18th century and peaked in the 19th kept the stones of antiquity in the limelight. Neoclassicism strongly influenced the architecture of the period, not only in Europe but in North America too. Proportions and styles were modeled on Greek and Roman architecture, and decorative stones were fundamentally important to the ornamentation—the more "authentic" the better. The second movement that emerged strongly in the mid-19th century was the Gothic revival in which architects looked to the romantic palaces of medieval times for their inspiration. Again, authentic decorative stones were desired. But there was a problem. Although Corsi and other authors had predicted where various stones had come from, many of the quarries were still lost. When the new Opera House in Paris was being built in the 1860s, the architect, Charles Garnier was obliged to compromise and use the modern Italian *cipollino Apuano* instead of the famous *cipollino verde* of antiquity. This was one of the spurs that prompted the enterprising sculptor and marble merchant William Brindley, of the London firm Farmer & Brindley, to seek out the ancient quarries and reopen them. This he did with huge commercial success, and being so widely traveled and well informed on the subject of decorative stones, he was hailed as the marble expert of the late 19th and early 20th centuries.

The fashion for classical marble in the United States resulted in the import of large quantities of stone from Europe, and there persisted an unfounded view that the native American decorative stones were in some way inferior to those from Italy and Greece. The strategic marketing of green serpentinite from Vermont as *verde antique* no doubt helped encourage its use in situations where the Greek *verde antico* would have been preferred.

Decorative stones became massively popular in both Europe and North America, and huge quantities were used in the decoration of buildings until World War I saw the loss of of men from the workforce and crushed the building industries. The Great Depression of the 1930s provided the final blow—luxury products such as marble and granite had no market in times of economic hardship. The memorial amphitheater at the Arlington National Cemetery, Virginia, completed in 1921, the Lincoln Memorial constructed from American stones in 1922, and the Jefferson Memorial built in 1943 were all showcases for American ornamental stone, but too late. The great stone trade was at rock bottom, and remained so throughout the mid-20th century.

MODERN FADS AND FASHIONS

Traditional building materials including natural stone, wood and brick rarely featured in the new skyscrapers and urban landscapes of the 1960s and 1970s. Inside, chrome plate, stainless steel and plastics replaced the traditional wood, china and glass for furniture and kitchenware.

This was a difficult time for the dimension stone industry and many quarries resorted to crushing equipment for the production of aggregate, the bulk stone used in the production of concrete. While the dimension stone industry remained at a painfully low ebb, the demand for granite and marble gravestones remained constant, and this at least kept some quarries in business.

There was much better news for the lapidary trade. Gaudily colored decorative minerals suited the bold craft jewelry of the 1960s and 1970s, and innumerable tumble polishers rumbled away in workshops and garden sheds, buffing up pebbles to a high polish. The more serious enthusiasts got to grips with rock saws, laps and lathes, learning to cut and polish gemstones. Lapidary was becoming a very popular new hobby hand-in-hand with the popular pastime of mineral collecting. Magazines explained where to find decorative minerals and how to cut them, and clubs were formed to bring enthusiasts together. New discoveries, such as the American landscape jaspers and the beautiful Russian charoite were snapped up at the growing number of mineral and gem fairs. Big shows such as those in Tucson, Arizona, Munich in Germany and Ste. Marie-aux-Mines in France, and the many smaller shows in other towns and cities across the world, continue to be rich sources of beautiful decorative stones and great places for amateur rockhounds to meet together.

It was not until the 1970s that architects started introducing polished stone into new building projects again. Fresh eyes saw ways to incorporate this practical and attractive facing material into the very new styles of construction. As demand for stone grew again, so the technologies for producing, handling and fixing very large sheets of stone also evolved. Traditional white marble was passé. A slick modern look could never be achieved using the old-fashioned colorful breccias. Tastes turned to the granites and the neutral-colored polished limestones, and it is these stones that continue to be the height of fashion today.

LEFT *Tennessee pink marble* is used for the staircase in the Clinton Presidential Library in Little Rock, Arizona, opened in November 2004.

Taking a global view

Changing fashions and emerging nations have forced major changes in the huge global market in ornamental stone. Put very simply, there are "producing nations," "processing nations" and "consuming nations." The producing nations supply rough quarried blocks. The processing nations do the fabricating—cutting, polishing and finishing—of stone. This may be their own stone or it may be stone imported from other countries. The consuming nations buy and install the end product. Italy, for example, has a long history as a major stone-producing nation, and over the centuries it built up a reputation as the premier country for stone processing. Rough stone blocks were and still are shipped from all over the world to Italy to be fabricated. They are then exported again to the end users, which incidentally may be the country where the stone was originally quarried.

But fabricated stone sells for premium prices, and an increasing number of stone-producing nations are investing in the technologies to process their own stone so they can capitalize on that premium. The economics of the ornamental stone industry are now remarkably complex as different countries work in partnership, buying stone from one to be fabricated in another, either for domestic use or for re-export. Similarly there is a healthy trade in machinery and expertise from traditional processing nations to develop new fabrication centers in developing countries. Trade fairs take place all over the world to bring together the suppliers, fabricators, machinery manufacturers, end users and others engaged in different aspects of the stone industry. New products are launched and partnerships are forged. An increasing number of companies can now be considered multinational.

The stone trade may be complex but the overall trends can be distilled much more easily. Today's major producers of "granites"

(in the broad sense of the stone trade) are China, India, Brazil and Spain. Those of "marbles" include Iran, Egypt, Turkey, Portugal and Italy. Overall the quantity of stone being quarried and used around the world is growing. Italy is still increasing its output of marbles and granites but it is no longer the top producer or processor. As with so many other products, China has become a major producing nation since the 1990s, and a major processing nation relatively recently. Where does the stone go? China uses vast quantities of its own stone but still needs to import stone from other countries to satisfy its internal market. But it also exports stone, especially to the United States. The United States is the top consuming nation. It is a major producer and processor, supplying mainly to the domestic market, but it also imports huge quantities of stone from other countries. India is an important producing nation too, consuming the greater part of its own stone production. Taiwan is now a major processing country, both of its own stone and raw blocks imported from other countries. South Korea, Japan and Germany are following the United States, the top consumers of decorative stone products.

Never before has natural stone been so widely used, but there is much more to this boom industry than at first meets the eye. Anyone buying natural stone may wish to take into account the environmental and human cost of its production.

HERITAGE AND HIDDEN COSTS

The number of different decorative stones has grown exponentially in the latter half of the 20th century. It is true that the trade introduces new names for even slight variants of a single stone, but to a considerable extent this growth reflects the ease with which stone is transported many thousands of miles from one country to another. The extent to which a decorative stone industry has become part of local culture varies considerably. Countries in which there is a long tradition of quarrying can see the fruits of their productivity incorporated in the building heritage, and when that heritage extends beyond their national borders, they can feel well justified in extolling a stone as "famous" or "important." Adnet in Austria, Älvdalen in Sweden, and Vermont in the United States are among a growing number of quarrying areas that have capitalized on their stone heritage by opening museums that celebrate their historic stone industries.

For some of the world's most important stone producers today, the transition from a product intended for purely local consumption to a major international industry has come in a sudden leap in the last few decades, but also at a time when heritage pride has been tarnished by a growing awareness of the environmental impact of stone quarrying. Spain, for example, is Europe's leading producer of granites and a major source of limestones and marbles. These stones have a long history of local use, but their launch on the

LEFT The Friedrichstadtpassagen, a modern shopping mall in Berlin, Germany, is decorated with a colorful mixture of classic European "marbles," *noir St. Laurent* from France, and *calacatta d'oro* and *giallo di Siena* from Italy.

international market came just when quarries were increasingly perceived as blots on the landscape. There is little celebration of the stone heritage here, few references to the history of their stones or where they can be seen and admired.

Concerns about environmental and human impact are well justified all across the world. Stone quarrying strips productive vegetation and opens large holes in the ground. The process of quarrying and fabricating stone is noisy, dirty and consumes large amounts of water, an increasingly precious commodity. Slurries can pollute waterways, and waste heaps of stone can scar the landscape. The transportation of such a heavy bulky material is a major user of precious energy reserves.

Quarries and mines are dangerous places to work, and human life is often valued too low. Falling rocks and flying splinters account for innumerable injuries, and each year many lives are lost and workers are left permanently disabled, all for the lack of proper training, protective clothing, correct maintenance of equipment and proper risk management. Fabricating stone can be dangerous too, and unprotected workers who inhale stone dust are very vulnerable to silicosis, a fatal lung disease. Child labor in both quarries and fabricating plants is a serious social problem, particularly in Asia.

ABOVE Workers in this marble quarry in Makrana, India, have no protective clothing or footwear. Many quarry owners in developing countries show little regard for the health and safety of their workforce, which includes women and children. Serious injuries and deaths are all too common. Initiatives are being introduced to try to improve working conditions.

The modern stone trade is working to meet the challenge of working in an environmentally sensitive way. Use of diamond wire saws can substantially reduce waste. Water can be recycled, filtered, cleaned. If fabrication is carried out at, or close to, the quarry, then demand for fossil fuels for transportation is reduced, and with it, the damaging carbon emissions that promise to be so costly to our planet. Land can be filled and restored to agriculture or vegetation, or it can be redeveloped as quality wetland habitat. Increasingly, stone is mined underground to avoid the environmental impact of surface quarrying.

The decorative stone industry is a big employer, but far greater attention to the training and protection of workers is needed in many countries. A number of initiatives are being introduced to improve working conditions particularly in India and China, and to label stone that has been produced in quarries that meet minimum standards for the care of workers, including such basics as the supply of drinking water and shelter from the sun.

A jungle of names

There are thousands of names used for decorative stones. The fact that a stone can have several different names makes identification all the more confusing. Some were given at different times in a stone's history, others were to accommodate different languages. A short word of explanation may help to clarify the nomenclature jungle.

Today, decorative stone names can be divided into four main categories, all actively used depending on the context:
- those used in antiquity;
- historical names;
- modern trade names, and;
- those used in the scientific literature.

NAMES USED IN ANTIQUITY

These are primarily of interest to archaeologists. Hardly any names used by the ancient Egyptians and Greeks are known or in use today. The Egyptian *Bekhen-stone* and the Greek name *lithos pyrrhopoecilos* for pink Aswan granite are rare examples. On the other hand, names in Latin used by the Romans are widely quoted in archaeological literature. Latin names are recorded in ancient literature such as Pliny the Elder's books on natural history of the first century CE, or the descriptive verse of the Byzantine poet Paul the Silentiary in the fourth century. Another important source is the Emperor Diocletian's edict of maximum prices of 301 CE which listed the highest price for all sorts of commodities, including the different kinds of marble and granite. Usually, stones were named after the location of the quarries or the nearest city (*marmor Docimenium*, *lapis Syenites*)—a logical consequence of the need to manage the transportation and trade of the stone. Rarely, stones were named to honor a person (*marmor Claudianum*, *marmor Lucullaneum*) or after the stones' physical appearance, such as the snakeskinlike *lapis ophytes*.

NAMES INTRODUCED BY THE SCALPELLINI

By the time the scalpellini of Rome were reusing ancient stone in medieval times, the source of these stones was largely forgotten and they had introduced their own names. These are still very widely used today, particularly for stones that are no longer commercially available or are found in historical contexts. They often allude to the appearance and antiquity of the stone (*giallo antico*, *porfido serpentino antico*, *cipollino rosso*). New stones discovered in archaeological excavations were sometimes called after the place they were found (*breccia di Settebasi*, *breccia bruna del Testaccio*) or used (*portasanta*, *granito del foro*). Faustino Corsi, at the beginning of the 19th century, was one of the first to attempt to correlate the ancient names with those of the scalpellini, and the process continues to this day.

As new Italian stones were introduced into architecture, the scalpellini would usually call them after the place where the stone was obtained, sometimes referring to appearance too (*Cottanello*, *broccatello di Siena*).

TRADITIONAL NAMES IN OTHER COUNTRIES

Similarly, the usual tradition in other countries has been to name a stone after the place it was quarried, or a combination of terms which describe the appearance too. French marbles such as *Sarrancolin*, *Campan melangé* and *rouge Languedoc* are good examples. *Rouge griotte* was named after appearance rather than locality. In England, a stone which was used for decorative purposes would usually be denoted by the term "marble" whether or not this was geologically correct (*Purbeck marble*, *madrepore marble* and *Sussex marble*—all limestones).

There is considerable scope for confusion where stones are named after different places but actually come from the same bed of rock and appear indistinguishable. It means that a stone to all intents and purposes identical in appearance, may have been given several different names in the past.

MODERN TRADE AND LAPIDARY NAMES

But the converse is also true, a single location can yield stones that vary in appearance or properties, and the modern tendency is to give each variant its own trade name. The use of place names for naming decorative stones has seen a rapid decline since the 1960s in both the lapidary and dimension stone trades. One that suggests an appealing appearance (*spectrolite*, *crema marfil*, *verde tropicale*) is a more effective marketing tool. It also addresses the issue that the same stone may be quarried over a large geographical area, and a variety of different names would not help the stone obtain a clear market identity.

Many stones have established a fine reputation for excellent physical properties, and consistent high quality. A common marketing ploy in recent years is to give a new stone from a very different locality, the same or a very similar name to the well-known "classic" stone. *Verde Guatemala* is a green serpentine marble that does indeed come from Guatemala but most of the stone of this name on the market today is from India. *Rosso lepanto* is not a typographical error for the famous red *serpentinite rosso Levanto* from Liguria, in Italy, but a stone of similar appearance from Turkey.

Some of these "lookalike" stones are very good indeed, but many are decidedly inferior. The warning goes to anyone purchasing stone that, just because the name is similar to that of a stone with an established high reputation, it does not mean that the new stone in any way matches its qualities.

Names are often shared too. *Giallo antico*, for example, is a very modern gneiss from Brazil as well as the traditional name for ancient limestones from Tunisia and Algeria. *Forest green* can be a serpentine marble from India, or a coarse-grained igneous rock from India, Brazil or Australia.

SCIENTIFIC NAMES

Scientific names are the formal terms used by the international scientific community for minerals (quartz, turquoise, charoite, malachite, pectolite), and rocks (marble, gneiss, serpentinite). These terms do not indicate any place of origin but they are fundamentally important for the petrographical descriptions used by geologists. Other scientific terms are informal but often used within the scientific literature. They include mineral variety names (amethyst, agate, thulite) and informal rock names (*lapis lazuli*, larvikite, unakite, orbicular granite).

It should be remembered that when the stone trade uses the terms "marble," "limestone" and "granite" it uses the criteria of hardness and ability to take a polish to classify these stones, and not the composition or geological history.

ORDER OUT OF THE CHAOS?

The European Union has introduced new standards for the naming of dimension stones as part of a series of standards relating to the dimension stone industry. According to EN12440 a stone is given an identifier consisting of the traditional name, the petrographical family, geological age, the typical color, and the place of origin. A list of these terms is given in EN12670. This means that popular trade names can be retained, but the petrological description and locality give an unambiguous statement of exactly what the stone is and where it is from. Stones meeting these standards are tagged accordingly.

There is another trend in the naming of stones which gives a unique identifying alpha-numeric code to a stone rather than a descriptive name. Many Chinese and most Iranian stones use this system, and it has to be said that while a name like "G5150" or "M235" may be consistent in all languages, it does make the stone sound singularly unalluring!

QUARRY VARIATION

Because decorative stone is a natural material, it will always tend to show some variability in its color, mineral or fossil content, quantity of veining or fracturing, degree of deformation, and so on. This may be evident when comparing stone from different quarries in the same area, or even from different levels or areas in the same quarry. It is often referred to as "quarry variation."

For some stones, and especially the coarser breccias (which are composed of fragments of different rocks naturally cemented together), considerable variation may be evident even within the same commercial-sized slab of stone, so that several small samples of very different appearance may be cut from a single slab of stone. Anyone trying to identify small slabs of decorative stones such as fragments from archaeological excavations or veneers in inlaid furniture, should always bear this in mind.

Stone from the same location can also have a very different appearance depending on whether it is sawn parallel or perpendicular to the bedding.

In this sourcebook, where stones are shown which often display significant quarry variation, a number of samples will be illustrated. Anyone choosing decorative stone should be aware that the sample seen here, or in catalogs or on websites can only give a very general idea of the stone's appearance.

LEFT Different parts of a standard 6½ foot (2 m) slab of *breccia Medici di Siena* have furnished three samples that look very unalike. When stones are able to show considerable variation in appearance like this, identifying small samples can be particularly challenging.

Out of the ground

It is extraordinary to think how in ancient times, massive obelisks and huge granite columns could be cut out of the ground and shaped with great accuracy long before the invention of explosives. Of course an endless supply of slaves was a huge asset, but the whole process of quarrying was, and still is, only possible because nature has provided a helping hand.

When the first blocks were cut from solid bedrock in prehistoric times, some simple methods proved surprisingly effective. Wooden wedges would be hammered along joints—natural planes of weakness in the stone. Then they would be soaked with water, making them swell enough to force the rock apart. Another technique was to heat the stone with fires and then douse it with cold water. The thermal shock would be enough to weaken the stone and make it easier to break.

There is one fundamental property of stone that was exploited in ancient times and is just as important for quarrying industries today. A softer stone can always be cut by a harder one. In prehistoric Mexico or India, for example, a hard stone such as jade would be carved with sticks and quartz, garnet or emery sands. The Romans made saws out of strips of bronze charged with the same abrasives that they used along with various chisels and points for working stone. In more recent times, steel shot and carborundum have also been employed, but the abrasive of choice today is the hardest one of all, diamond.

QUARRYING TODAY

The modern quarry is a muddy, dusty, noisy place where stone must be extracted in a cost-effective way but always to a consistently high quality. All sorts of factors influence the way this is done. It will depend, for example, on the kind of stone being worked and how it is sited in the quarry; the setup costs of the machinery and availability of labor; and how fast stone must be produced to meet purchase orders.

The traditional method has been to fire explosive charges to release blocks of stone. Little expensive equipment is needed and so this method is still widely used in developing countries and by many small quarrying companies. But it is difficult to predict the consequences of running explosive

LEFT One of the characteristic features of a decorative stone quarry is the flat sawn faces.

INSET Diamond wire machines are often used to cut granite and marble from the quarry face. Holes are drilled and a steel wire charged with diamonds is threaded through, tensioned, and revolved at rapid speed. The diamonds cut cleanly through the stone.

ABOVE In smaller limestone, travertine and marble quarries, all the cutting of a stone block can be carried out using a giant chain saw. Hydraulic cushions are then inserted into the slots left by the saw blade and filled with water at high pressure, dislodging the block from the face. Chain saws, mounted on steel tracking, are also used to saw the base of blocks cut from a face using diamond wire.

RIGHT The traditional way to split stone blocks from the quarry face is to drill holes with a pneumatic hammer drill at 6–12 inch (15–30 cm) intervals along where the block is to split. The holes are charged with explosives, and detonated to release the block.

BELOW Squaring off and any further trimming is carried out with a small diamond wire saw (as shown here), a chain saw, single-blade gang saw or circular saw.

charges through a naturally variable material, and fractures can easily be generated through a whole block of stone. The true costs lie in the amount of waste stone generated, which usually exceeds the quantity of marketable stone.

DIAMOND WIRE

Much less waste is generated when giant chain saws are employed in marble, travertine and limestone quarries, but it is the use of diamond wire that has revolutionized ornamental stone quarrying in the last 20 to 30 years. Heavy wire fitted at regular intervals with beads impregnated with industrial diamonds can be used to saw through granite or marble surprisingly quickly. It gives a clean, accurate cut with minimum wastage, and it can be employed in underground mines as well as in open-air quarries. Diamond-wire machines can be left to operate on their own, so fewer employees are needed. The initial start-up costs may be high. but quarries using this technology can expect to reap huge rewards in terms of productivity.

With concern growing about the environmental impact of quarrying and the need to reduce wastage and pollution, the search continues for even better technologies. High-power water jets, for example, are proving very effective for cutting granites.

ABOVE Stone blocks may be cut into slabs using a single-blade saw or a multiblade saw that can cut several slabs at once. A variety of different saws and moldcutters are used to create other profiles in stone.

RIGHT The final touches must often be done by hand.

FINISHING THE SURFACE

Stone can be used rough, with no final finishing, but this is unusual. Polishing shows the colors and patterns of a stone to best advantage, but other finishes are also available. The choice depends on the desired appearance and on how and where the stone is to be used.

POLISHING

Most decorative stone is polished. In the modern processing works, this is carried out on a sophisticated computer-controlled line marble polishing machine. Sheets of stone are carried on a conveyer under a series of rotating spindles charged with sequentially finer grades of abrasive. First, any undulations in the stone are leveled. It then hones the stone to a very smooth surface, and finally buffs it to a glossy finish.

HONING

Honed stone is ground smooth, but it does not receive the final buffing that brings out the shine of a polished stone. This means it is not very reflective and its color is not so strong, but it still shows any natural patterning very clearly.

SANDBLASTING

If a jet of water charged with sand, carborundum or steel shots is passed over a stone, it roughens the surface slightly. The color and pattern is dulled, but not to the same extent as a bush-hammered

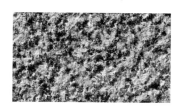

ABOVE Different finishes create different appearances. Here, balmoral granite is polished (top left), honed (top right), sand-blasted (bottom left), and bush-hammered (bottom right).

surface. Selective sandblasting can be used to create lettering and patterns on the surface of a polished stone, very suitable for some monumental work.

BUSH-HAMMERING

The bush hammer indents the surface of the stone, either randomly or in definite patterns, giving a distinct texture. It forms a good nonslip surface but is difficult to clean, and the texture obscures much of the natural color and pattern of the stone. Bush-hammering is more time-consuming and costly than flaming or water finishing.

FLAMING AND WATER FINISHING

Flaming of stone is restricted mainly to granites. A very hot oxy-propane flame is passed from side to side over the surface of the stone as it moves on a conveyer belt. This shatters some crystals, leaving a granular nonslip surface. The flame also oxidizes iron in the stone, turning it red. The color is subdued and may have distinctive red tints. A similar texture is achieved by passing a very high pressure water jet over the surface of the stone, which washes out softer minerals. Water finishing is suitable for marbles as well as granites, and for yellow stones where a color change is not desirable. Flamed or water-finished surfaces may be brushed to give a smoother velvety surface.

A FINAL COATING

Many stones are impregnated with a polymer filler to strengthen the stone and fill gaps, a procedure carried out under vacuum between honing and final polishing. A fiberglass or plastic mesh may be applied to the back of the slab to provide extra strength. Final polishing of the front surface can then be carried out. The stone is now ready for installation.

LEFT AND INSET At the end of the conveyer, the slabs or tiles have a mirrorlike finish.

The evolving Earth

Look at a decorative stone and what do you see? It may be a single color or a mixture of colors. Some show individual grains clearly, others do not. Some have patches of a single color, others are mottled with grains of different colors mixed together. Some are patterned with veins cutting across a stone, others are made of fragments of stone cemented together. It is possible to identify many stones just by looking at their colors and patterns, but for an accurate identification it helps to know a little petrology— that is, the branch of geology involved with the study of rocks. We may have been using rocks and minerals for decoration for thousands of years, but the stones themselves are much, *much* older. A little bit of geological detective work can reveal stories about how they formed millions or even billions of years ago.

A VERY RESTLESS EARTH

It is easy to think of the Earth as a ready-made package of continents and oceans, but our planet has some scary ways to remind us that it is constantly evolving and changing. Earthquakes, tsunamis and volcanic eruptions signal a melting pot of activity below the surface, while landslides and floods make catastrophic changes to the landscape around us. We hear much about rising sea levels today, but sea levels have been rising and falling since the primordial oceans formed. Geological catastrophe is nothing new to planet Earth, although it is a potentially terrifying reality for some of its youngest inhabitants: humans. The Earth has been in existence for some 4,570 million years, but imagine if the history of the Earth was compressed down to one year. Say it formed on January 1: then the first animals with preserved hard parts didn't

SAME NAME, DIFFERENT MEANING

Geologists name a rock according to its mineral composition and the environment in which it formed. The size of the grains is often important, too. The stone trade uses just a few of the same names— marble, limestone, travertine, granite, slate, sandstone and sometimes quartzite but with very different meanings.

When is a marble not a marble? ...
If a rock is composed mainly of calcite (a comparatively soft carbonate mineral), geologists call it limestone, if it is unmetamorphosed, and marble, if it has been metamorphosed. The stone trade says a rock of this composition is "marble" or "limestone" depending on whether it will take a good polish or not. This means that many of the "marbles" of the trade are, in petrological terms, limestones. Serpentinites that polish well are also classed as "marbles."

... and a granite not a granite?
Furthermore, geologists use the term "granite" for igneous rocks that formed within the crust of the Earth, which are made up mainly of quartz, feldspars and mica. *But* the stone trade defines most hard rocks composed mainly of silicon minerals (such as quartz and feldspar) as "granite" irrespective of whether the rock is igneous, metamorphic or sedimentary. This means that "granites" in the trade can include metaconglomerates (metamorphosed sedimentary rocks), gneisses (metamorphosed igneous or sedimentary rocks) and basalts (volcanic igneous rocks) as well as "true" granites.

GEOLOGICAL TIMELINE

This timeline—from the formation of the Earth around 4,570 million years ago to the present day—shows the divisions of geological time referred to in this book and some of the organisms that were alive at the time. Some decorative stones are remarkably young, such as travertines actively deposited by hot springs today. Others are thousands of millions of years old and, as the examples show, there are decorative stones of just about any age in geological time.

Eon	ARCHEAN	PROTEROZOIC		PHANEROZOIC						
	PRECAMBRIAN		Era		PALEOZOIC					
Subperiod Period				CAMBRIAN	ORDOVICIAN	SILURIAN	DEVONIAN	Pennsylvanian	Mississippian	
								CARBONIFEROUS		

Boogardie orbicular granite
Azul Macaubas
Tennessee pink marble
Madrepore marble
Irish fossil marble

Million years before present	4,570	2,500	542	488	444	416	359

Not to scale

appear until late November, and the first humans evolved at about 11:35 p.m. on December 31.

WHEN PLATES COLLIDE

Most geological processes happen so slowly that they are barely perceptible. The crust and solid upper mantle of the Earth is broken up into a number of plates that are constantly drifting, powered by heat from the Earth's core. As the plates move apart, the gap is filled by new rock spewed out by mid-ocean volcanoes. The Atlantic Ocean is widening by about 1 inch (2.5 cm) each year. The crust under the oceans is heavier than that under the continents. If the two collide, the oceanic crust sinks, pushing the continent up to form a mountain chain and generating a line of volcanoes. Where one plate of oceanic crust sinks below another, volcanoes form along island arcs. If the plates are both continental crust, they crumple together pushing up great ranges of mountains. The Himalayas are still growing as the Indian continental plate pushes ever northward, crashing into the great Eurasian plate. The line where two plates pass each other is a fault that sometimes moves smoothly, and sometimes in a jerky way. When energy is released and the two sides of the faults move in different directions, it generates a massive earthquake. The San Andreas Fault, on which San Franscisco lies, is just such a boundary.

All the edges of the great crustal plates are areas of great geological activity, where earthquakes are very common. It is only in the middle of the great continents that conditions have remained stable for billions of years. This is where some of the oldest rocks on Earth—and some fine ornamental stones—are found. But here too, geological activity occurs as rivers and glaciers erode the rock, breaking it up and carrying fragments to the sea. Larger boulders are not carried far, but finer particles may drift for very long distances before sinking to the bottom.

Each geological process, whether it is a sudden catastrophe or a slow creeping change, results in the formation of a particular kind of rock. Geologists classify rocks into three groups:

Igneous rocks form from the molten rock beneath the Earth's surface (magma) that has cooled and solidified. The magma may reach the surface of the Earth and erupt as volcanic lava. Often, however, it does not reach the Earth's surface, instead cooling and solidifying deep underground.

Sedimentary rocks are made from sediments, fragments of pre-existing rocks that have been broken down by weathering and erosion, or crushed during earthquakes and other tectonic events. When the sediments are deposited by rivers, lakes and seas, they are often mixed up with, or even made entirely from, the remains of living organisms such as corals and seashells preserved as fossils. Sedimentary rocks can also be made up of sediments deposited by chemical means, such as the beds of travertine laid down by hot springs.

Metamorphic rocks form where heat, pressure or a combination of both alters an already existing rock. Before metamorphism, the rock can be sedimentary, igneous or indeed metamorphic. Minerals are the building blocks of all rocks. After metamorphism they may be reconstituted into new minerals, or simply recrystallized into a different form of the same mineral.

The most accurate way to identify a decorative stone is by examining a thin section, a polished slice of rock no more than 30 microns (0.03 mm) thick, using a petrological microscope. This uses polarized light to help identify the minerals and reveal how they are bonded together. But it is not necessary to have any specialist equipment to recognise most of the rocks used for ornamental purposes because they are often coarse-grained, and with a bit of practice the important minerals can be identified just using a magnifying glass.

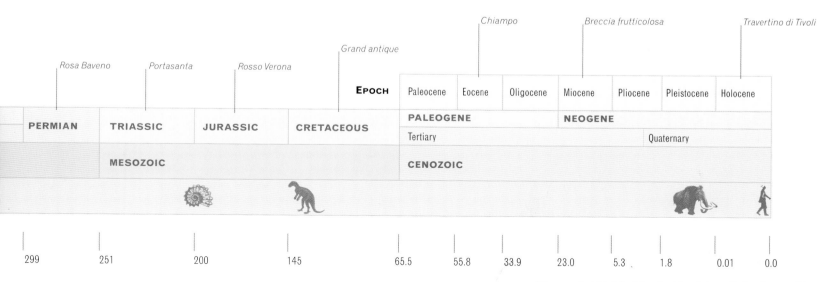

Minerals—the basic building blocks

All rocks are made up of minerals, and as minerals are the basic building blocks of rocks, a little explanation about what minerals are, and how to identify them may help anyone trying to identify rocks. Each different mineral is a naturally formed inorganic substance with a particular chemical composition. There are over 4,500 different minerals, but only a small number of these are major constituents of rocks. Others occur, for example, in ore veins, and some of the most decorative of these are shown in the "Other minerals" section of this book.

Nearly all minerals are crystalline because their atoms are arranged in a very regular pattern. Two minerals can have the same composition but very different crystal structures; for example, calcite and aragonite are both composed of calcium carbonate but they form differently shaped crystals. A small number of minerals never form crystals. They have atoms arranged in a random way and so they are amorphous like glass.

To be able to identify a rock accurately it is necessary to identify its constituent minerals. Each mineral has its own particular properties—color, luster, hardness and so on, which give clues to its identity. Many can be distinguished with the aid of a magnifying glass; a binocular microscope is particularly helpful.

IDENTIFYING MINERALS

Color: Some minerals are always the same color, for example malachite is always green. But many minerals can be more than one color. Perfectly pure quartz is colorless, but most quartz is white, pink, purple, yellow or brown, depending on what natural flaws or trace chemical elements it contains. Some chemical elements are responsible for particular colors, and this is explained in the box below. When a mineral can be various different colors, it always shows its true color (usually colorless or white) if it is powdered. This color is known as the streak, and it can be tested by drawing the mineral across the back of an unglazed tile, known as a streak plate.

Transparency: Most of the important rock-forming minerals are transparent or translucent, so some light will pass through them, but often they are so dark they appear to be opaque.

Luster: The luster is the way a mineral reflects light, and varies from the very bright "adamantine" luster shown by diamond, to pearly, silky or earthy lusters for the softer minerals. Most of the minerals in rocks have a vitreous luster—in other words, they look glassy. Some may have a dull luster. Certain opaque minerals have a metallic luster: they look like metals.

Crystal habit: The general shape of crystals or the way they

WHERE DO THE COLORS IN DECORATIVE ROCKS COME FROM?

WHITE Some of the most common and important rock-forming minerals, such as quartz, feldspar, calcite and dolomite are colorless or white when pure. Statuary white marble is composed almost entirely of pure white calcite or dolomite. Usually other minerals are present and they can impart a variety of different colors.

GRAY OR BLACK In marbles, grays and blacks are due to the presence of graphite (*bardiglio*) or bitumen derived from organic matter. Bitumen and other carbonaceous matter (*Belgian black*) or goethite (*king gold*) turn limestones black or dark brown. Manganese oxides are also black but tend to be concentrated in veins and coatings (*rosso Montecitorio*) or tree-like aggregates called dendrites.

VIOLET TO RED TO PINK, YELLOW OR BROWN Coarse-grained hematite can impart a gray or violet color to various different kinds of rock (*pavonazzetto*), and the uncommon manganese-bearing mineral piedmontite also gives a violet-red color (*imperial porphyry*). Finer-grained hematite tints a stone red or pink (*duke's red, marmo carnagione*). If other iron oxides, particularly goethite, are mixed with the hematite, the stone is salmon-pink or orange (*rosso Verona*), and goethite on its own can color a stone yellow or brown (*giallo antico*). Siderite also imparts a yellow coloration.

GREEN The green in decorative stones is usually due to the presence of iron-bearing silicate minerals such as chlorite and actinolite (*cipollino verde*). Serpentine normally has some iron, too, making it green (*Vermont verde antique*). Epidote gives a distinctive yellowish green color (unakite). Just as ferric iron tends to color minerals yellow or red, and ferrous iron colors them green (*diaspri di Sicilia*), so other chemical elements impart strong colorings when they are present. Minerals containing copper either as an essential constituent or an impurity, are usually green or blue (malachite, turquoise), those bearing chromium are green or red (*smaragdite di Corsica*, anyolite), manganese minerals are either black or pink (Inca rose), and nickel-bearing minerals are typically apple-green (chrysoprase).

BLUE Some of the brightest blue stones are colored by the feldspathoids sodalite, and lazurite. Blue feldspars (larvikite, labradorite) are usually colored as a consequence of their internal structures and often show iridescence. Dumortierite and lazulite together contribute to the color of certain quartzites (*azul Macaubas*). Blue minerals are relatively uncommon as coloring agents, and this is why so many blue stones are at the luxury end of the decorative stone market.

cluster together is known as the "habit" of a mineral. For example, leucite forms rounded crystals, while the crystals of feldspar in Cornish granite (see page 217) have a blocky habit. The crystals in larimar (see page 260) have a radiating fibrous habit. Hornblende crystals such as those seen in *granito della colonna* (see page 230) have an elongate habit. But many minerals in rocks are granular or massive (showing no crystal shape at all).

Hardness: One of the most important properties of a mineral is its hardness, and this influences just how tough a rock can be, and also how high a polish it will take. Harder minerals will take—and more easily keep—a higher polish. Hardness is measured by comparing the mineral with Mohs' scale, which consists of 10 standard minerals each harder than the next—the softest is talc and the hardest is diamond. If the unknown mineral is scratched by topaz but scratches orthoclase then it has a hardness of about 7. If it scratches calcite and is scratched by fluorite, it has a hardness of 3.5. For quick tests it is useful to know that a fingernail is 2.5 on the scale, a copper coin is 3, and a steel penknife blade is 5.5.

MOHS' SCALE

1	Talc	6	Orthoclase
2	Gypsum	7	Quartz
3	Calcite	8	Topaz
4	Fluorite	9	Corundum
5	Apatite	10	Diamond

Cleavage and fracture: Some minerals cleave, that is they break along flat planes. The shape formed can give a useful clue to the mineral's identity. Calcite and dolomite, for example, have a rhombohedral cleavage, breaking into diamond-shaped fragments. Pyroxene minerals have cleavages at roughly right angles, while in amphiboles, this is about 120°. (This is one of the easiest ways to tell amphiboles and pyroxenes apart.) Not all minerals have cleavages. Some break in a rough, irregular way. Others have a conchoidal fracture, with a curved surface a bit like a seashell. Quartz has this kind of fracture.

Spot acid tests: Acid tests are used to distinguish minerals that contain the carbonate group -CO_3 in their chemical formula. If a tiny drop of weak acid is placed on the surface and it fizzes, this is because carbon dioxide is being given off, showing that the mineral is a carbonate. Some carbonate minerals react more vigorously than others. This test particularly helps identify marbles and limestones. Calcite fizzes very fast while dolomite fizzes only very slowly. Dilute hydrochloric acid (dil.HCl) is normally used in industrial laboratories, colleges and museums but it is dangerous and not suitable for home use. Safe alternatives are lemon juice and vinegar, which are both weakly acidic. They will remove the polish from a decorative stone—very fast if it is composed of calcite (and fizzing may sometimes be seen), but slowly if it is dolomite. Always test an inconspicuous part of a stone sample because the damage cannot be reversed.

THE MAIN MINERALS IN ORNAMENTAL ROCKS

Only the most useful properties for identifying these minerals in hand specimens of decorative stones are described here. For details of their chemical compositions see the table on page 31. All these minerals can be granular or massive, and all have a vitreous luster unless otherwise stated.

QUARTZ is usually colorless or gray but can be many other colors; elongate crystals, hexagonal in section; chalcedony is a very fine-grained (cryptocrystalline) variety; conchoidal fracture; hardness 7.

CALCITE is colorless, gray or yellow but also tinted other colors; short or elongate crystals with rhombohedral cleavage; fizzes vigorously in dil.HCl; hardness 3. Aragonite (having the same composition) is found in recent travertines and limestones, but alters to calcite over time; it lacks rhombohedral cleavage.

FELDSPARS (family of silicate minerals) are hugely important rock-forming minerals, and are rather complicated.

Potassium feldspars are microcline (above), orthoclase or sanidine; sodium feldspar is called albite and calcium feldspar is anorthite. Potassium and sodium feldspars often occur together and are referred to as "alkali feldspars." Anorthoclase is intermediate between the two.

Plagioclase feldspars have compositions between those of albite and anorthite.

Feldspars are usually colorless, white or gray and can show iridescence. Potassium feldspars are often pink or red. Tabular or blocky crystals have good cleavages; uneven or conchoidal fracture; hardness 6–6.5.

DOLOMITE is usually white, cream or gray; rhombohedral crystals have good rhombohedral cleavage, and may appear to have curved faces; fizzes weakly in dil.HCl; hardness 3.5–4.

GYPSUM is colorless, white or tinted with other colors; pearly luster; short, curved or elongate crystals; three excellent cleavages; hardness 2. It may be mixed with anhydrite, which is anhydrous calcium sulphate and is harder at 3–3.5.

FELDSPATHOIDS (family of silicate minerals) include nepheline (which often has a greasy luster), sodalite, leucite (above) and lazurite; usually colorless, white, gray or bright blue; rounded or blocky crystals; conchoidal or uneven fracture; hardness 5–6.

MICAS (family of silicate minerals) include muscovite (usually colorless) and biotite, above, (very dark brown or green); vitreous or pearly luster. Hexagonal crystals cleave perfectly into flexible thin sheets; hardness 2.5–4.

AMPHIBOLES (family of silicate minerals) include tremolite-actinolite, above, (white-green), riebeckite (grayish blue) and "hornblende" (black); elongate or fibrous crystals with cleavages at roughly 120°; uneven fracture; hardness 5.5–6.5.

PYROXENES (family of silicate minerals) include augite (above), diopside, jadeite, and the orthopyroxenes enstatite and ferrosilite; green, white, gray and other colors; blocky to elongate crystals with cleavages at roughly right angles; uneven fracture; hardness 5.5–6.5.

SERPENTINES (family of silicate minerals) are green; fine-grained, and sometimes occur as fibrous or asbestos veins; hardness 2.5–3.5.

CHLORITES (family of silicate minerals) includes clinochlore; usually green; vitreous or pearly luster. Hexagonal crystals cleave well into non-flexible thin sheets; hardness 2.5–4.

EPIDOTE forms yellowish green, elongate crystals with perfect cleavage and uneven fracture; hardness 6–7. Zoisite and piemontite are closely related with similar properties but different colors.

CLAYS (certain extremely fine-grained silicate minerals); white, brown, gray, pink and other colors; earthy luster; crystals are only visible at high magnification; hardness 1–2.5.

GARNETS (family of silicate minerals) include pink or red almandine (above). Other garnets can be brown, green and many other colors; rounded crystals with no cleavage; uneven or conchoidal fracture; hardness 6.5–7.5.

MAGNETITE is opaque metallic lead-gray and strongly magnetic; crystals are octahedral with uneven fracture; hardness 5.5–6.5. Chromite looks similar but is only weakly magnetic.

HEMATITE is metallic gray, but compact masses of crystals are red; the streak is red; in decorative stones it occurs mainly as minute grains and coatings; hardness 5–6.

GOETHITE is opaque earthy yellow-brown to dark brown; the streak is yellow-brown; in decorative stones it occurs mainly as minute grains and coatings; hardness 5–5.5.

COMPOSITIONS OF THE MINERALS REFERRED TO IN THIS BOOK

NAME	FORMULA
Actinolite-tremolite (amphibole group)	$Ca_2(Mg,Fe^{2+})_5Si_8O_{22}(OH)_2 - Ca_2Mg_5Si_8O_{22}(OH)_2$
Albite (feldspar group)	$NaAlSi_3O_8$
Almandine (garnet group)	$Fe_3^{2+}Al_2(SiO_4)_3$
Amphibole group see actinolite-tremolite, hornblende, riebeckite	
Anorthoclase (feldspar group)	$(Na,K)AlSi_3O_8$
Aragonite	$CaCO_3$
Augite (pyroxene group)	$(Ca,Na)(Mg,Fe,Al,Ti)(Si,Al)_2O_6$
Azurite	$Cu_3^{2+}(CO_3)_2(OH)_2$
Barite	$BaSO_4$
Biotite (mica group)	Dark colored mica without lithium
"Bitumen"	Hydrocarbon compound of variable composition
Calcite	$CaCO_3$
Charoite	$K(Ca,Na)_2Si_4O_{10}(OH,F)\cdot H_2O$
Chlorite group	Commonly clinochlore $(Mg,Al)_5(Si,Al)_4O_{10}(OH)_8$
Chromite	$Fe^{2+}Cr_2O_4$
Chrysocolla	$(Cu,Al)_2H_2Si_2O_5(OH)_4\cdot nH_2O$
"Clay"	Various extremely fine-grained hydrated silicate minerals
Corundum	Al_2O_3
Diopside (pyroxene group)	$CaMgSi_2O_6$
Dolomite	$CaMg(CO_3)_2$
Dumortierite	$Al_7(BO_3)(SiO_4)_3O_3$
Enstatite (pyroxene group)	$Mg_2Si_2O_6$
Epidote	$Ca_2Al_2(Fe^{3+},Al)Si_3O_{12}(OH)$
Eudialyte	$Na_{15}Ca_6(Fe^{2+},Mn^{2+})_3Zr_3(Si,Nb)(Si_{25}O_{73})(O,OH,H_2O)_3(Cl,OH)_2$
Feldspar group see albite, anorthoclase, labradorite, microcline, orthoclase, plagioclase	
Feldspathoid group see lazurite, leucite, nepheline and sodalite	
Ferrosilite (pyroxene group)	$(Fe^{2+},Mg)_2Si_2O_6$
Fluorite	CaF_2
Garnet group see almandine	
Goethite	alpha-$Fe^{3+}O(OH)$
Graphite	C
Gypsum	$CaSO_4\cdot 2H_2O$
Hematite	alpha-Fe_2O_3
"Hornblende" (amphibole group)	approximately $Ca_2[(Fe^{2+},Mg)_4(AlFe^{3+})](Si_7Al)O_{22}(OH)_2$
Hydromagnesite	$Mg_5(CO_3)_4(OH)_2\cdot 4H_2O$

NAME	FORMULA
Jadeite (pyroxene group)	$Na(Al,Fe^{3+})Si_2O_6$
Labradorite (feldspar group)	$Na_{0.5-0.3}Ca_{0.5-0.7}Al_{1.5-1.7}Si_{2.5-2.3}O_8$
Lazulite	$MgAl_2(PO_4)_2(OH)_2$
Lazurite (feldspathoid group)	$(Na,Ca)_8Si_6Al_6O_{24}[(SO_4),S,Cl,(OH)]_2$
Leucite (feldspathoid group)	$KAlSi_2O_6$
Magnetite	$Fe^{2+}Fe_2^{3+}O_4$
Malachite	$Cu_2^{2+}(CO_3)(OH)_2$
Mica group see biotite, muscovite	
Microcline (feldspar group)	$KAlSi_3O_8$
Molybdenite	MoS_2
Muscovite (mica group)	$KAl_2AlSi_3O_{10}(OH)_2$
Nepheline (feldspathoid group)	$(Na,K)AlSiO_4$
Olivine	Mg_2SiO_4 (forsterite) $- Fe_2^{2+}SiO_4$ (fayalite)
Opal	$SiO_2\cdot nH_2O$
Orthoclase (feldspar group)	$KAlSi_3O_8$
Pectolite	$NaCa_2Si_3O_8(OH)$
Piemontite	$Ca_2(Al,Mn^{3+},Fe^{3+})_3Si_3O_{12}(OH)$
Plagioclase (feldspar group)	$NaAlSi_3O_8$ (albite) $- CaAl_2Si_2O_8$ (anorthite)
Pyrite	FeS_2
Pyroxene group see augite, diopside, enstatite, ferrosilite, jadeite	
Quartz	SiO_2
Rhodochrosite	$Mg^{2+}CO_3$
Rhodonite	$CaMn_4Si_5O_{15}$
Riebeckite (amphibole group)	$Na_2(Fe_3^{2+}Fe_2^{3+})Si_8O_{22}(OH)_2$
Schorl (tourmaline group)	$NaFe_3^{2+}Al_6(BO_3)_3Si_6O_{18}(OH)_4$
Serpentine group	Typically $Mg_3Si_2O_5(OH)_4$
Siderite	$Fe^{2+}CO_3$
Sodalite (feldspathoid group)	$Na_8Al_6Si_6O_{24}Cl_2$
Sugilite	$KNa_2(Fe^{2+},Mn^{2+},Al)_2Li_3Si_{12}O_{30}$
Talc	$Mg_3Si_4O_{10}(OH)_2$
Tourmaline group see schorl	
Turquoise	$Cu^{2+}Al_6(PO_4)_4(OH)_8\cdot 4H_2O$
Zoisite	$Ca_2Al_3(Si_3O_{12})(OH)$

Igneous rocks

Igneous rocks are formed when hot magma cools. They are composed of a mixture of different minerals. In igneous rocks used for decorative purposes, most minerals are siliceous (containing silicon) and they tend to be hard and durable. This is why these stones can take a good long-lasting polish.

Igneous rocks are further subdivided according to the composition of the magma, into acid, intermediate, basic and ultrabasic. Acid magmas form the rocks of continents, intermediate magmas are formed where continental and oceanic plates collide, while basic magmas form the floors of the oceans. Ultrabasic magma comes from deep in the mantle of the Earth.

HOW THEY ARE ORGANIZED

Igneous rocks are divided into plutonic rocks (also called intrusive rocks), which cooled and solidified in intrusions underground without reaching the Earth's surface, and volcanic rocks (also called extrusive rocks), which erupted to the Earth's surface from volcanoes before cooling and solidifying. Sediments deposited from ash and other volcanic debris are called pyroclastic rocks.

WHAT TO LOOK OUT FOR

Mineral composition varies. Acid rocks are usually light colored, and rich in quartz and feldspars. Basic rocks are usually darker colored, with heavier magnesium- and iron-bearing minerals. The main mineral constituents of igneous rocks are mentioned in the guide below.

IGNEOUS ROCKS MOST OFTEN USED FOR DECORATIVE PURPOSES

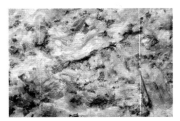

SYENITE, NEPHELINE SYENITE Coarse-grained intermediate plutonic rock composed mainly of alkali feldspar, with minor quartz or feldspathoids (but never both), plagioclase, biotite, hornblende and other dark minerals. Larger amounts of nepheline make the stone a nepheline syenite (examples: larvikite, page 226; sodalite, page 261).

GRANITE Coarse-grained acid plutonic rock composed of quartz; potassium and plagioclase feldspars, mica and often hornblende. One of the most important rocks that make up continental masses (examples: *blanco perlina*, page 218; *granito rosso antico*, page 220).

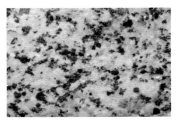

DIORITE, GRANODIORITE Coarse-grained intermediate plutonic rock composed of plagioclase feldspar and hornblende, with minor biotite and augite. If quartz is present it is quartz diorite (above), if both quartz and alkali feldspar are present it is a granodiorite (examples: *granito della colonna* page 230; *granito nero antico*, page 234).

GABBRO, NORITE Coarse-grained basic plutonic rock, a mixture of plagioclase feldspar and augite with some magnetite. Orthopyroxene can replace augite, making it a norite (examples: *granito verde antico* page 231; *Rustenburg*, page 234).

RHYOLITE Fine-grained acid volcanic rock of the same composition as granite. It is a light-colored rock formed from thick viscous lava, and flow structures are sometimes preserved (example: *leopardskin jasper*, page 251).

ANDESITE Fine-grained intermediate volcanic rock of the same composition as diorite. Rocks intermediate between andesite and rhyolite are called dacite. Andesite and dacite are dark colored and often porphyritic (examples: *imperial porphyry*, page 202; *porfido verde antico*, page 206).

DOLERITE Medium-grained basic plutonic rock, of the same composition as gabbro and basalt, formed in small intrusions and dikes, which is why the grain size is smaller (example: *nero Zimbabwe*, page 235).

BASALT Fine-grained basic volcanic rock, of the same composition as gabbro and dolerite, it may have phenocrysts of leucite or olivine, or gas bubbles (amygdules) lined with crystals. The most common kind of lava, it forms the ocean floors (example: *lava di Borghetto*, page 212).

Grain size usually depends on how fast the magma cools. Volcanic rocks cool very quickly making them very fine-grained or even glassy. The grains can only be identified in thin sections under a petrological microscope. Conversely, large crystals can grow if the cooling is slow as in a large intrusion. Volatile elements such as boron and fluorine can also allow large crystals to grow. Very coarse-grained igneous rocks are known as pegmatites, and crystals can be many yards in size.

Porphyritic rocks can be of any composition but they have one feature in common: they contain large crystals, known as "phenocrysts" in a finer-grained groundmass. Igneous rocks that form small intrusions or that start to cool and solidify before being extruded by a volcano often show a porphyritic texture.

Layering and foliation is sometimes present. Igneous rocks that are rich in heavy, dark colored minerals sometimes show layering where heavier minerals have crystallized and sunk. If the layers are of less dense minerals such as mica, this is because crystals were aligned by physical pressures on the rock as it formed. This is termed foliation.

Hydrothermal veins are formed where hot water rich in chemical elements, circulated by igneous activity, has deposited minerals along fractures in rocks. Weathering of hydrothermal veins creates some of the colorful minerals in the "Other decorative minerals" section of this book.

RIGHT Lava ejected from volcanoes cools and solidifies to form extrusive igneous rocks. New rocks are constantly being formed in this way at the margins of the great plates that creep across the surface of the Earth.

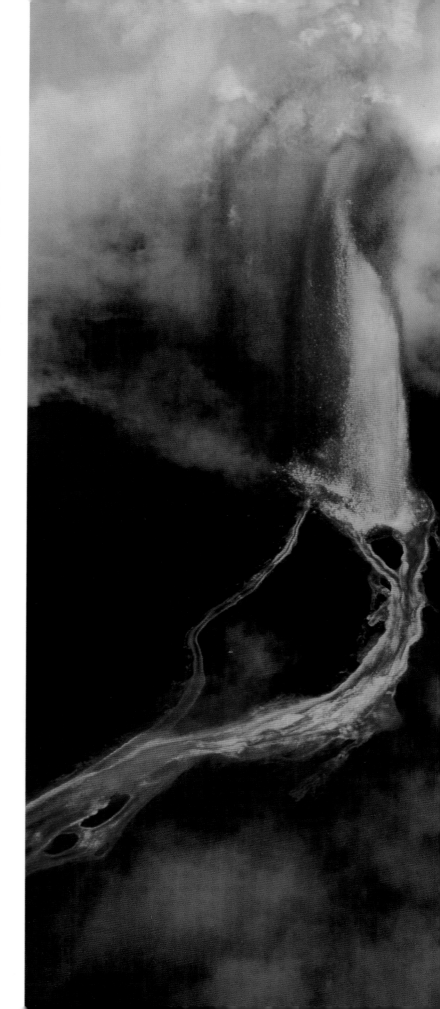

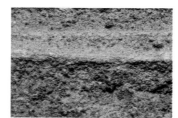

TUFF Fine- to coarse-grained pyroclastic rock of acid or intermediate composition consisting of rock fragments, ash and volcanic glass. It shows graded bedding and other sedimentary structures especially when the eruption was over water (examples: *peperino*, page 212; *pietre del Vesuvio*, page 214).

CHARNOCKITE Coarse-grained acid plutonic rock composed mainly of plagioclase feldspar and orthopyroxene. It is formed by metamorphism of granites and gneisses at extremely high temperatures and may be classified as an igneous or metamorphic rock (example: *verde Ubatuba*, page 236).

Sedimentary rocks

RIGHT A muddy tropical seafloor is the kind of environment where sedimentary rocks are forming today. Clay eroded from rocks on land, combines with calcium carbonate from fossils and seawater, to form marls and marly limestones.

Sedimentary rocks are made up of recycled fragments from existing rocks, the fossil remains of plants and animals, and chemically precipitated minerals. As the sediment is buried more deeply, it is compacted, driving out water and compressing the grains, welding them together. When crystals grow to fill pore spaces between the grains, the sediment is cemented to form a hard rock. Most sedimentary rocks are still too soft or poorly cemented to take a polish and wear well. There are some important exceptions, and they are shown below.

HOW THEY ARE ORGANIZED

Sedimentary rocks composed of detrital fragments that have been carried by wind, ice or water are called clastic rocks. They are distinguished from those composed of sediments that actually formed where they were deposited, the non-clastic rocks. Clastic rocks are subdivided according to the size of their fragments, known as "clasts," from very fine-grained claystones to siltstones, sandstones and pebbly conglomerates and breccias. Non-clastic rocks are organized according to their compositions and the ways they formed. They include travertines, and evaporites such as alabaster, as well as the limestones.

WHAT TO LOOK OUT FOR

The important minerals in sedimentary rocks are relatively few. Weathering converts feldspars into soft clays, but quartz is particularly durable. Calcite is the main mineral in limestones, and some calcite may alter to dolomite.

Fossils help to identify the rock type and give clues to its age.

Clasts and matrix are the terms used to describe the fragments that make up a sedimentary rock and the cement that bonds them together. Clasts can be fragments of any kind of rock, mineral grains or fossils. Gaps between the clasts are usually filled with matrix. This is composed either of fine-grained sediment or a newly crystallized mineral such as calcite. Compaction underground or very low-grade metamorphism can improve the cementation of clasts in many sedimentary rocks making them more suitable for ornamental use.

Size of clasts in a sedimentary rock can vary from clay-sized particles too small to see without a microscope, to large boulders, yards across. Larger clasts are normally deposited close to their original source but smaller particles can be carried much farther away. Currents sometimes winnow fragments, sorting them according to size.

Bedding can give attractive patterns to sedimentary rocks. Cross bedding occurs in sediments deposited on slopes where bedding planes wedge out against each other. Graded bedding is found in rapidly deposited sediments where larger, heavier grains have settled before lighter ones, so the grain size gets progressively smaller going upward.

Stylolites are wiggly lines that form as part of the changes that take place in a rock after it is buried and compacted (see *Tennessee pink marble*, page 107). Some of the calcium carbonate is dissolved away and redeposited in pore spaces, helping to cement the rock. The insoluble residue, which can include clay minerals and iron oxides, is left behind in the form of stylolites. They are common in certain decorative rocks.

SEDIMENTARY ROCKS MOST OFTEN USED FOR DECORATIVE PURPOSES

 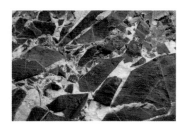  

CONGLOMERATE Clastic deposit of rounded pebbles from a river, beach or shallow sea deposit. They can be from a single source or a mixture of different rock types. The cement can be calcareous or siliceous. Low-grade metamorphism helps cement the clasts more strongly, making these rocks more suitable for decorative use (examples: *breccia frutticolosa*, page 146; *verde Marinace*, page 195).

BRECCIA Clastic deposit of angular clasts in a finer-grained cement, either formed close to the breakdown of the parent rock or where movement of a fault has shattered a rock. The clasts can be from a single source or a mixture of different rock types. The cement can be calcareous or siliceous (example: *africano*, page 136).

SANDSTONE Clastic deposit of sand-sized grains of quartz often with feldspar, mica and other minerals; formed by weathering of quartz-rich rocks, and deposited by water or in deserts by the wind. Sandstones do not take a polish but are used unpolished for example as floor tiles.

MARL Clastic deposit of calcareous mud, composed of a mixture of calcite and clay minerals. Marls are rarely used for decoration but marly limestones can be important (examples: Alberese, page 99; *pietra paesina*, page 102).

LIMESTONE Non-clastic rocks formed in lakes and seas, composed of calcium carbonate both from living organisms and chemically precipitated from seawater. Fossils and small, rounded particles known as ooliths and pelloids, are cemented together by calcite crystals or by chemically precipitated calcareous mud known as micrite (examples: *crema marfil*, page 98; *astracane di Verona*, page 161).

TRAVERTINE Non-clastic deposit of calcium carbonate, precipitated from supersaturated water in limestone caves to form stalagmites and stalactites (speleothems) or by hot springs, where bacterial action may also be an agent (examples: Egyptian alabaster, page 48; *travertino di Tivoli*, page 58).

EVAPORITE Non-clastic deposit, formed by evaporation of ancient enclosed seas. Gypsum (alabaster) is a typical evaporite deposit, which may also contain anhydrite and clay minerals (example: English alabaster, page 47).

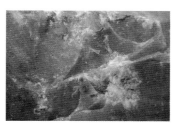

CHERT Non-clastic deposit of very fine-grained quartz, often colored by iron oxides, either derived from siliceous fossils or by chemical alteration of existing sediments. Many jaspers are technically chert deposits (examples: *diaspro di Sicilia*, page 246; *diaspro di barga*, page 247).

Fossils

Sedimentary rocks, especially those deposited by rivers, lakes and seas, can often contain fossils. These are the remains of ancient living organisms. The soft parts of a plant or animal normally decay away, and it is the hard parts—shells, "skeletons" of corals and sponges, bones and teeth of vertebrate animals and woody parts of plants—that are preserved. Trace fossils, which include burrows and other forms of what is called "bioturbation," where sediments have been stirred up by animal movements, are common. They are often seen in decorative stones.

As life has evolved on Earth, so different kinds of fossils have been preserved through geological time. Many are now extinct, for example the ammonites, and of course the dinosaurs. Some fossils evolved rapidly, changing their physical appearance over quite a short period of time. They are known as "index fossils" and can be used to correlate rocks of the same age from different geographic areas. This provides geologists with an important tool to work out the relative ages of rocks.

The most common fossils found in decorative rocks are composed of calcium carbonate. Some are preserved as calcite, others as aragonite, but most aragonite changes to calcite as the rock gets older. Fossils are hugely important constituents of many limestones, and those rich in seashells are traditionally referred to as lumachella from the Italian for "little snail." Fossils with shells or skeletons composed of silica can occur in decorative stones (such as the Australian *mookaite*) but the individual constituents are not readily visible.

The fossils described below are those that are readily visible in decorative rocks. They are all composed of calcite or aragonite, and can help in the identification of decorative stones.

HOW FOSSILS ARE NAMED

Simple names such as cockle or starfish may be easy to remember, but it is impossible to give each of the millions of different animals and plants a unique name that could be understood anywhere. Instead, scientists use a "family tree" of Latin names based on a strict, internationally agreed system initiated by a Swedish naturalist named Carolus Linnaeus in the 1700s. It applies to fossils and to living organisms.

For example, the ammonite shown below is called *Asteroceras obtusum* where "Asteroceras" is the genus name and "obtusum" is the species name. Going up the family tree, ammonites belong to the order "Ammonitida" of the subclass "Ammonoidea" (the ammonoids), which in turn belong to the class known as "Cephalopoda" (the cephalopods). Other members of this class include squids and octopuses. All cephalopods are mollusks, which means they belong to the phylum "Mollusca." The Mollusca belong to the kingdom "Animalia." Other mollusks include bivalves and gastropods. If a new fossil is discovered, its Latin name and a description are published in a scientific journal, and the original specimens preserved in a museum. Linnaean names may seem complicated but they uniquely identify each organism on the tree of life.

FOSSILS MOST OFTEN USED FOR DECORATIVE PURPOSES

BRACHIOPODS Marine animals living between two hinged shells; known as "lamp shells" because they can be shaped like ancient oil lamps; first evolved in early Cambrian period and are particularly common in Paleozoic rocks; some still live in oceans today (example: *Kilkenny fossil marble*, page 155).

BIVALVES Marine and freshwater mollusks with two hinged shells, such as oysters, clams and mussels; first evolved in Cambrian period; particularly abundant since late Permian times; rudists are late Jurassic and Cretaceous reef-forming bivalves with bizarre conical shells (examples: *astracane di Verona*, page 161; *occhio di pavone*, page 162).

GASTROPODS Marine, freshwater and land mollusks which include snails, winkles and whelks. They have a single shell which is usually coiled and lacks separate chambers; first evolved in late Cambrian times; more common in the Mesozoic era (examples: *Purbeck* and *Sussex marbles*, page 159; *Pakistan fossil stone*, page 158).

CEPHALOPODS Marine mollusks with tentacles such as octopus, squid and nautilus. Ammonoids are fossil cephalopods that first evolved in the Silurian period; ammonites and belemnites were common in the Mesozoic era then became extinct. They had coiled or straight shells divided into chambers which they filled or emptied with water to control buoyancy and propulsion (example: *Jura marble*, page 167).

ECHINODERMS Marine animals including echinoids (sea urchins), starfish and crinoids (sea lilies); echinoid spines, pentagonal plates from echinoid shells and disklike ossicles from the "stems" of crinoids are the most common fossils; first evolved in Ordovician times and also found today (example: *Derbyshire fossil limestone*, page 170).

CORALS Organisms that build up skeletons of calcite; internal divisions (septa) may give a starlike appearance; solitary corals each form a separate skeleton; colonial corals cluster together, forming clumps or branching masses; first evolved in Cambrian period; still important today (examples: *stellaria*, page 172; *Frosterley marble*, page 171).

SPONGES AND BRYOZOANS Sponges (above) secrete silica, calcite or protein skeletons made up of spiky spicules with numerous pores; first evolved in Cambrian times; still common today. Bryozoa are tiny colonial marine animals living in calcareous tubelike structures; important in Ordovician times; abundant in seas today (example: *Tennessee cedar*, page 164).

FORAMINIFERA ("FORAMS") Single-celled organisms with shells of various shapes; most are microfossils under 1/30 inch (1 mm) across; may look like tiny gastropods; first evolved in early Cambrian period; nummulites have disk-shaped shells and can be more than 1/2 inch (12 mm) across; very common in Eocene times (examples: *Chiampo*, page 169; *lumachella rosea*, page 163).

Metamorphic rocks

Metamorphic rocks are formed when the minerals in an existing rock are altered by the effects of heat and pressure. Either a mineral has recrystallized, or entirely new minerals have formed. The mineral composition depends on the nature of the original rock. Recrystallization during metamorphism can strengthen a decorative stone so it is more durable and takes a better polish. Some metamorphosed rocks develop a tendency to split along flat planes, a property exploited in slates.

HOW THEY ARE ORGANIZED

These rocks are subdivided as to whether the metamorphism has a regional cause such as the crushing of continental masses together to form mountains, or whether it is a more local contact effect, for example where the intrusion of an igneous body has baked the surrounding rocks. They are further subdivided according to the grade of metamorphism. Low-grade metamorphism recrystallizes some minerals so the grains lock more tightly together and converts others to new minerals, such as epidote, chlorite and actinolite. If the original rock type is still clearly recognizable, the name is given the prefix "meta," for example metaconglomerate, meta-greywacke and meta-gabbro. As the grade increases, different minerals form, and the texture changes completely.

WHAT TO LOOK OUT FOR

The minerals in metamorphic rocks give clues as to what grade of metamorphism has occurred. For example, epidote is found in low- to medium-grade rocks while jadeite only forms at high grades. The panel below refers to the principal minerals in each of the metamorphic rocks most often used for decorative purposes but other minerals are normally present as well.

Foliation is present when pressure on the rock causes the grains of a mineral to grow aligned in one plane. It is referred to as cleavage in slates and schistosity in their medium-grade counterparts, the schists. In higher-grade rocks called gneisses, very distinct layering is also visible. Foliation can be exploited when stones are split to form floor or roof tiles, but it can limit the use of the stone where overall strength is important.

Folding of rocks occurs when they buckle and fold in a plastic way under pressure. It may be evident within individual grains, over scales of a few inches, yards or greater. Folded rocks such as the cipollini can be very atttractive, but a combination of folding and strong foliation creates considerable weaknesses in a stone.

Shearing is the stretching of individual grains or clasts in the rock during metamorphism. It can be used to analyze the forces that caused the metamorphism, and is a property that can help distinguish certain stones, such as breccia di Skyros.

RIGHT Regional metamorphism occurs when continental plates collide to form mountains. Enough heat and pressure is generated to deform the rock and create entirely new minerals.

METAMORPHIC ROCKS MOST OFTEN USED FOR DECORATIVE PURPOSES

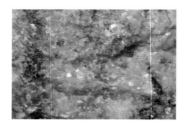   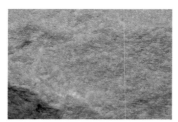

MARBLE Fine- to coarse-grained metamorphic rock composed of calcite and/or dolomite, formed by low- to high-grade metamorphism of limestones or limestone breccias and conglomerates. White when pure, impurities impart different colors (examples: imperial Danby, page 68; pavonazetto, page 130).

SERPENTINITE Fine-grained metamorphic rock composed of serpentines, usually with chromite or magnetite, and often veined with talc, calcite or dolomite. They form by low-grade metamorphism of basic and ultrabasic igneous rocks and are usually green or red (examples: Cornish serpentine, page 180; Tinos green, page 181).

SLATE Fine-grained metamorphic rock which splits easily along the foliation, composed mainly of quartz and mica, and formed by low-grade regional metamorphism of fine-grained clays, mudstones and volcanic ash deposits (example: Cumbrian slate, page 190).

QUARTZITE Medium-grained metamorphic rock (also called metaquartzite) composed mainly of quartz, formed by metamorphism of sandstones (orthoquartzite). Metamorphism cements the grains more strongly together and so quartzites can take a good polish (examples: aventurine, page 192; azul Macaubas, page 193).

GNEISS Fine to coarse-grained regional metamorphic rocks with a distinctly layered texture, either of different compositions or grain sizes, composed of quartz and feldspar, usually with mica and garnet. Large crystals, called "augen," can form during metamorphism. Gneisses form by high-grade metamorphism of acid igneous rocks or quartz-rich sediments (example: *verde tropicale*, page 200).

MIGMATITE Essentially a gneiss in which parts have melted to form granite. This is the highest grade of metamorphism a rock can have before it melts completely and cools to become an igneous rock (example: *Kinawa*, page 197).

GRANULITE Coarse-grained regional metamorphic rocks composed of quartz, plagioclase feldspar and pyroxene, formed by high-grade metamorphism of basic igneous rocks deep in the Earth's crust (example: *Kashmir white*, page 197).

TECTONITE A deformed metamorphosed rock formed by squeezing to develop foliation, or stretching to cause folding and shearing. Tectonites are often deformed gneisses, marbles, and marble breccias (example: *greco scritto*, page 73)

What makes a good decorative stone?

What makes a good decorative stone? Obviously color and pattern are important, but if a stone is to be used in architecture, it needs to meet a number of technical specifications. First, it must be established what minerals give the stone its durable composition and structure, and whether there are any harmful minerals that could weaken it or react in an adverse way. For example, tiny pyrite crystals in a stone can cause rust spots if the stone gets wet, making it unsuitable for bathroom tiles. The identities and structures of constituent minerals in thin sections of the stone are examined using a petrological microscope, and at higher magnification using an electron microscope.

COPING OUTSIDE AND IN

The density of a stone depends on both its mineral constituents and on its "porosity": the amount of empty pore space inside the stone. When the pore spaces are interconnected so that fluids can penetrate, the stone is said to be permeable. Lots of tiny interconnecting pore spaces can make a stone weather badly, but larger cavities such as those in travertines, tend to have few adverse effects. Permeability is an important factor in discovering how well a stone can resist the repetitive freezing and thawing cycles of winter weather. Freezing makes water expand and can shatter a weaker stone. This is why many stones are unsuitable

for external use except in warm dry climates. The absorbency of a stone is also important for tables and kitchen countertops where grease and cooking oil could ruin the stone's appearance.

STRONG AND SAFE

An engineer or architect will need to know how much pressure a stone can take before it shatters, how much it will bend and how easily it will break. Properties referred to as "flexural strength," "modulus of rupture," "compressive strength" and "modulus of elasticity" are measured in the laboratory by applying forces to the stone in different ways and measuring the point at which it bends or breaks. Stones also vary in how easily they are abraded. Marbles, limestones and travertines cannot hold a high polish in exterior situations, and are much more easily scratched than most "granites," but even granites can vary in how well they resist abrasion.

For polished or honed floors, there is another important property that needs to be evaluated. How slippery is the stone? Just because a stone is polished does not mean it is slippery. Some stones are more slippery than others, a property that can be measured when the stone is either dry or wet.

LASTING WELL

All these properties will influence how durable a stone will be as the years pass by. Other factors may be important, too. How will it respond to acid rain or spray by chemical salts? Did the processes of quarrying, fabrication or installation generate stresses and microscopic fractures in the stone that might accelerate its aging? It should be remembered, too, that a stone is only as strong as the fixing method used. If fixtures rust or adhesives and cements deteriorate, an otherwise sound stone may become very dangerous.

The composition and various physical properties of a stone are all established by laboratory examination and testing, and should meet industry benchmarks such as those of the American Society for Testing and Materials (ASTM), the British Standards Institute (BS) and the Comité Européen de Normalisation (EN). It cannot be overstressed that anyone wanting to use decorative stones in the home or workplace should always seek professional advice to ensure that the stone is suitable for the intended use. When a durable and beautiful surface is needed in architecture, carefully selected natural stone is hard to beat!

LEFT It is important to choose stones that are not slippery if they are to be used for paving, either in the home or in a public place.

Checklist for identifying decorative stones

This checklist is an at-a-glance reminder of the different properties and features that are most important when trying to identify decorative stones. A good starting point is to establish whether the stone is a soft calcareous rock such as limestone or marble, or a hard siliceous rock such as a granite or gneiss, remembering always to test hardness (see page 29) on an inconspicuous place on a sample. If the mineral constituents can be recognized, this makes identification much easier. There are so many different granites, marbles and limestones that the smaller details become particularly significant in telling one from another. What are the phenocrysts composed of? Does it have stylolites? How rounded are the clasts and are they deformed? This checklist can be used to note down the key features of any decorative stone.

The context in which the stone is found is always important too, for example, stones first quarried in modern times will not be found in ancient artifacts.

If the stone is made up of a random mixture of different crystals
o How many different kinds of crystals are there?
o What color are they?
o Do any of the crystals have a play of light or other optical effect?
o How big are they? Are they all roughly the same size?
o How hard are they? Can they be scratched with a pocketknife?
o Do they have a distinctive shape?
o Are some of the crystals much larger than the others? Could they be phenocrysts?
o Are the crystals aligned, or does the stone appear to be layered?
o Can you recognize any of the crystals?

If the bulk of the stone appears to composed of a single mineral
o What color is it?
o How hard is the mineral? Can it be scratched with a fingernail? A pocketknife?
o Can individual grains be seen and how big are they?
o What shape are the grains?
o Can you recognize what the mineral is?
o Are there any traces of fossils?

If the stone is composed of larger pieces or pebbles of rock cemented together
o How hard are the fragments and cement? Can either be scratched with a penknife?
o Are the fragments rounded or angular?
o How big are the fragments?
o Are they all much the same size or a mixture of different sizes?
o Are they all the same kind of rock or a mixture of different rocks?
o Are the edges sharp and clear? Zigzagged? Diffuse and hard to distinguish?
o Are the fragments deformed in any way?
o Is the cement a single mineral or a mixture?
o How fine-grained is it?
o Can you recognize what the fragments or cement are made of?

If there are fossils
o Can you recognize what the fossils are?
o How much of the total rock is made of fossils?
o How broken up are the fossils?
o How are they cemented together? Is the cement a single mineral or a mixture?
o How fine-grained is it?
o Can you recognize what the fossils or cement are made of?

If there are any veins or stylolites (zigzag lines like a graph chart) crossing the stone
o If there are stylolites, what color are they?
o If there are veins, what color are they?
o Are there different generations of veins, some crossing others?
o Are veins straight? Curved? Irregular?
o Do the veins run parallel to each other? En echelon (see page 81)? Arranged randomly?
o Are they narrow or wide?
o What minerals are they filled with?
o Are the crystals filling veins granular, elongate or fibrous?

If there is a distinctive pattern to the stone
o Is there banding or layering?
o Are the bands linear or circular?
o Are the layers composed of the same mineral or of different minerals?
o Are the layers composed of different grain sizes?
o Are there any treelike or shrublike patterns?
o Are there empty cavities or pores?

The
stones

Introduction

Every stone tells a story; and with several thousand different ornamental stones to choose from, making a selection for this book has been a fascinating challenge. Many are ancient stones going back thousands of years and are of obvious interest to archaeologists, historians and collectors, as are those quarried for the beautiful buildings and furniture of the Renaissance. There are also rocks and minerals used in more recent times. Some are very modern stones that have become popular in the home, and others are widely employed in the decoration of public buildings. Special features in the different sections tell more about how decorative stone is identified and used.

HOW THE STONES ARE ARRANGED

The stones are organized into sections according to their geological nature, beginning with the "calcareous" rocks, composed mainly of calcium minerals (see pages 34–38). The first section contains stones known as **alabaster and travertine**, both the true scientific alabasters of geologists and those that are called alabaster or onyx marble, but are actually composed of calcium carbonate (for a fuller understanding of the minefield that is the naming of these stones see page 45).

The **marbles and limestones** follow. They are composed of carbonate minerals, calcite and dolomite. There is no sharp boundary between a limestone and a marble for geologists; one grades into the other as their characteristics change through heat and pressure. If there are no fossils, it can be hard to tell the two kinds of stone apart. To make identification easier, entries for marbles and limestones are mixed together. Because there are so many varieties, they are subdivided simply by color and pattern. So, this section starts with the pure white marbles, followed by marbles and limestones that are gray or black.

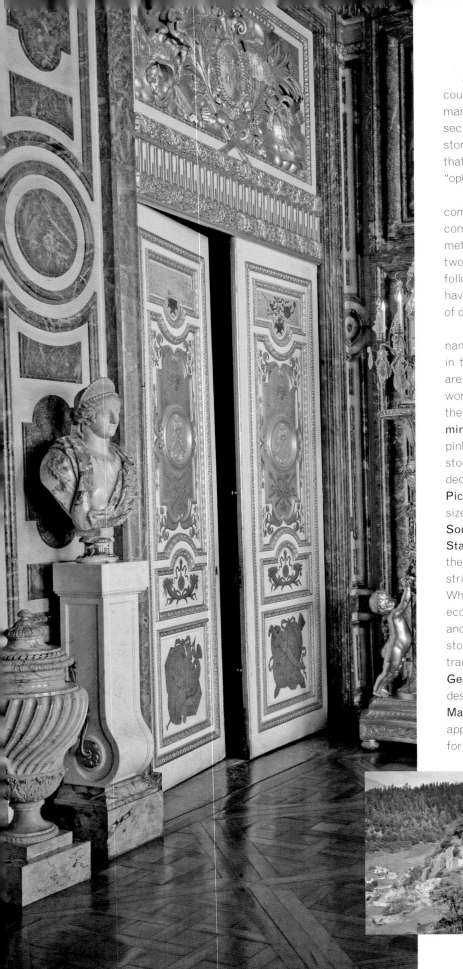

After gray and black come the yellow and brown, and so on. Of course some stones defy color classification by being a mixture of many different colors. They are placed together in a "multicolor" section. Where fossils are the main decorative feature, these stones, too, are placed together. The last of the marbles are those that mix with green silicate minerals to form green marbles and "ophicalcites," and they are put with the serpentinites.

The next sections are "siliceous" stones: harder stones composed of silica and silicate minerals. The first of these contains all the **other metamorphic rocks**, including quartzites, metaconglomerates and gneisses. Igneous rocks are divided into two sections. The so-called **"porphyries" and volcanic rocks** are followed by the **granites and other plutonic rocks**. These always have a mottled appearance because they are made up of crystals of different minerals mixed together.

The last two sections focus on decorative stones that are named after a mineral, or are best known for one of the minerals in their composition. All the stones in the penultimate section are composed of silica, either **quartz** or **opal**. They are so wonderfully varied in appearance that they deserve a section to themselves. The final section includes all the **other decorative minerals**. With vibrant green malachite, rich blue sodalite, pretty pink rhodochrosite and classy purple fluorite, the selection of stones in this book ends with some of the most colorful of all the decorative stones.

Pictures of stone samples show the polished stones at actual size (unless otherwise specified).

Source gives the location of the quarries.

Status indicates whether a stone was actively quarried or mined at the time this book was written. Unless a quarry has been entirely stripped of stone, it can be closed and reopened at any time. Whether this happens depends on the geological feasibility and economic costs of extracting the stone, the state of the stone market and, increasingly, environmental issues. When a quarry is closed, stone is often stockpiled and still commercially available, or in the tradition of the Italian scalpellini (stonecutters) it can be recycled.

Geological description uses modern geological terminology to describe the stone and includes identifying details.

Major usage indicates the kind of uses to which the stone is applied and where it is most likely to be seen. Before using a stone for a particular purpose, you are advised to check its suitability with experts in the professional stone trade.

LEFT Marble used extensively for the decoration of the Chateau of Versailles, France, includes beautiful multicolored stones quarried in the Campan Valley of the French Pyrenees *(inset)*.

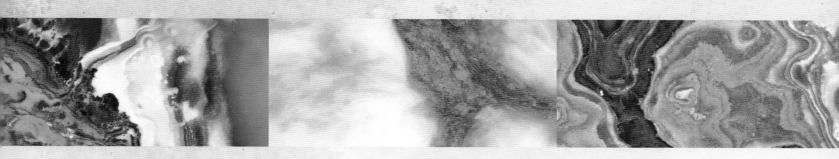

Alabasters and travertines

The name "alabaster" causes no end of confusion. Modern geologists use it for compact fine-grained gypsum, a soft mineral composed of hydrated calcium sulfate that occurs in thick beds formed by evaporation of seawater. Archaeologists, in the tradition of the Italian scalpellini, use the same word for compact banded rocks composed of calcium carbonate (usually the mineral calcite) with two rather different origins. Some are "speleothems," structures such as stalagmites and stalactites found in limestone caves—they grow from dripping water that is saturated with calcium carbonate leached out of surrounding rocks. Others are close-grained, banded forms of travertine deposited by hot springs. The name "oriental alabaster" is sometimes used for both these carbonate rocks. To muddle things further, the modern stone trade calls them "onyx marble," despite the fact that they are neither onyx nor marble in the eyes of geologists. This section includes examples of the different kinds of stone referred to as alabaster, onyx marble or travertine.

Alabastro di Volterra

SOURCE: Volterra and Castellina Marittima, Tuscany, Italy
STATUS: Actively mined

Soft, snowy-white and slightly translucent, the alabaster of Volterra is a beautiful but fragile ornamental stone.

There are various colors and grades of alabaster, some banded or mottled gray, others with a yellowish tint. The finest "Volterra alabaster" (shown above) is pure snowy-white and very translucent with faint delicate veins. It is known as *scaglione* and comes not from Volterra, but Castellina Marittima, 15 miles (25 km) west.

There are many gypsum mines and quarries in the region of Castellina Marittima and Volterra. The Etruscans in the eighth century BCE were the first to exploit this stone, using it to decorate buildings and make funerary urns. In medieval times this long tradition of alabaster working died out. It was revived again in the 17th and early 18th centuries, and today many of the skills of alabaster working have, in time-honored tradition, been passed down from generation to generation.

The soft nature of alabaster greatly constrains its use in architecture, but makes it a superb medium for sculpture—easy to work yet challenging to achieve perfect results without bruising the stone. The range of objects made today in the back streets of Volterra panders to every taste: intricate sculptures nestle among chess sets, lamps and vases.

GEOLOGICAL DESCRIPTION

Alabaster (compact fine-grained gypsum) found as nodules in Miocene evaporite deposits. Measures only 2 on Mohs' scale.

MAJOR USAGE

Monuments, sculptures and a diverse range of ornamental items.

LEFT The skills of alabaster working continue in the back streets of Volterra.

46

English alabaster

SOURCE: Derbyshire, Staffordshire, Nottinghamshire, England
STATUS: No longer quarried as an ornamental rock

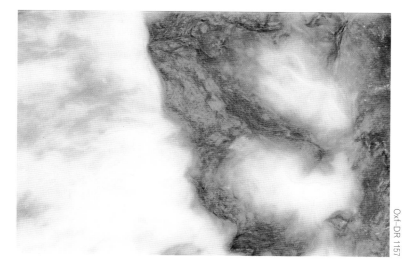

Oxf-DR 1157

In the nearest thing to a medieval mass-production line, monuments and statues made of English alabaster were carved for export all across Europe.

The thick gypsum beds of the Midlands of England are the source of the alabaster quarried during medieval times at Fauld in Staffordshire, Newark in Nottinghamshire and Chellaston in Derbyshire. The pure white gypsum was regarded as the finest stone (lower quality stone has cloudy orange staining). The stone was supplied to workshops in Nottingham, Burton on Trent, York and London where, in the 14th and 15th centuries, many thousands of monuments and figurines were carved that can now be seen in churches and museums all over the world. This highly prosperous industry foundered at the time of the English Reformation.

In the 19th century, English alabaster was used in interior marble decoration of many public buildings. The best stone was reserved for architecture and sculptural work, but smaller blocks were supplied to cottage industries in Whitwick, Thringstone and Coleorton where "Derbyshire spar" was turned on lathes to make trinkets. They were sold mainly in English vacation resorts, but each year, a consignment was sent out for sale at Niagara Falls.

GEOLOGICAL DESCRIPTION

Alabaster (compact fine-grained gypsum) found as nodular beds and spheroidal masses in Triassic evaporite deposits. Finely disseminated iron oxides impart a patchy orange coloration.

MAJOR USAGE

Church monuments, ornamental claddings, vacation souvenirs.

RIGHT English alabaster is famously used in the marble hall of Holkham Hall, Norfolk.

Egyptian alabaster

SOURCE: Eastern Desert, Egypt
STATUS: Intermittent small-scale extraction

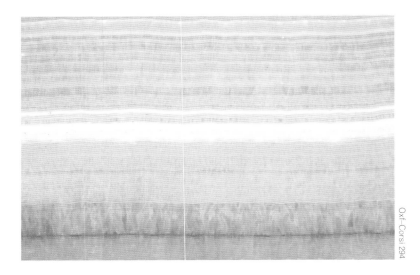

Oxf-Corsi 294

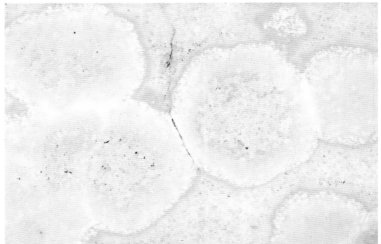

Oxf-Corsi 325

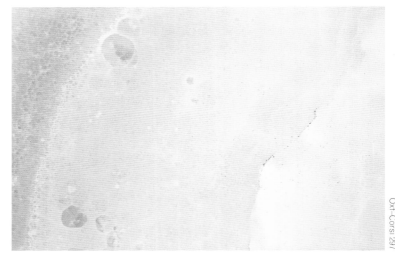

Oxf-Corsi 297

Which came first, a place called Alabastron, the little pots known as *alabastri* or the decorative stone known as alabaster?

The answer is lost somewhere in history. It is known that there was an ancient town called Alabastron in the Nile Valley of Egypt where a beautiful creamy-white banded calcite deposit was quarried as early as 4000 BCE. This stone was named alabaster. It was first worked for making small vases, bowls and handleless pots or *alabastri* that were considered to be the best storage receptacles for perfumes and precious oils. It was cut into slabs for construction and decoration, and by the time of the pharaohs it was being carved to make figurines, sarcophagi, canopi and votive dishes. Some of the most notable examples to be seen today are the huge sarcophagus of Seti I in Sir John Soane's Museum in London, the alabaster sphinx at Memphis, and the statue of Amenhotep III and the crocodile god Sobek in Luxor. The ancient Romans enthusiastically adopted this stone when they subsumed Egypt into the Roman Empire, using it for columns, wine vessels and many other purposes. The scalpellini of Rome named it *alabastro Egiziano*, *alabastro onice* or *alabastro cotognino* and reused it extensively.

Egyptian alabaster was extracted at many locations in the Eastern Desert, all within 15 miles (25 km) of the Nile Valley. Of these, the quarries at Hatnub are particularly well documented. The stone is colored creamy-white to pale honey-yellow with occasional slender orange bands. When cut parallel to the bedding, the patterning is in the form of concentric circles, but cut across the bedding it shows a series of undulating bands of greater or lesser translucency.

Extraction of Egyptian alabaster has continued sporadically right up to the present day. Stone from Beni Suef (Bani Suwayf) was used extensively in the decoration of the Muhammed Ali mosque in Cairo, completed in 1857, appropriately dubbed the "Alabaster Mosque." Egyptian alabaster columns and windows were employed in 19th-century restorations of the Basilica of San Paolo fuori le Mura in Rome. In the 20th century alabaster has been obtained from Wadi Assiut. Most deposits are now exhausted and little stone is extracted today.

GEOLOGICAL DESCRIPTION

Compact banded calcite in veins and pods, formed as speleothemic deposits infilling cavities in Eocene limestones.

MAJOR USAGE

Pots, vases and decorative items; construction and facing stone.

ABOVE Stonecutters in modern-day Egypt carving decorative products in the traditional way.

RIGHT Examples of ancient Egyptian alabaster pots dating back thousands of years.

Alabastro a giaccione

SOURCE: Capo Circeo, Lazio, Italy
STATUS: No longer quarried

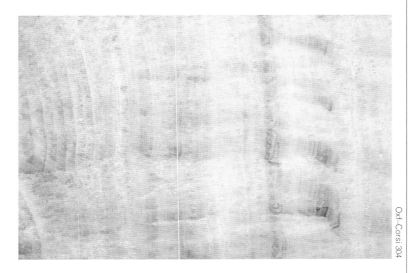

"Ghiaccio" means "ice" and it is easy to see why the scalpellini of Rome gave the name *giaccione* to the more transparent, coarsely crystalline alabasters.

Several well-documented examples of *alabastro a giaccione* match the banded calcite quarried at La Batteria on the southwest tip of Cape Circeo, halfway between Naples and Rome. Other quarries on the Cape have yielded yellow and brown varieties, but the beautiful white or pale yellow-tinted stone has only come from La Batteria. The *giaccione* quarry was active in the 16th century but was particularly busy in the 18th and early 19th centuries, supplying stone for projects under the patronage of popes Pius VI and Leo XII. The doorways of the sacristy of St. Peter's Basilica and the small balusters of the balustrade that surrounds the baptismal font in the Church of Santa Maria Maggiore in Rome are examples that can be seen today. By 1873 there was little market for the stone and the quarry was more or less exhausted.

When Faustino Corsi cataloged his sample (shown above) he reminded readers of the fine column of the same stone to be seen in the Room of the Dying Gladiator in the Capitoline Museums. This appears to be one of very few items made from *alabastro a giaccione* that show the stone was also extracted in ancient Roman times.

GEOLOGICAL DESCRIPTION

Bands of rather coarse-grained columnar and granular calcite, forming speleothemic deposits in limestone cavities.

MAJOR USAGE

Columns, slabs and windows.

Pakistan onyx marble

SOURCE: Chagai, Baluchistan, Pakistan
STATUS: Actively quarried

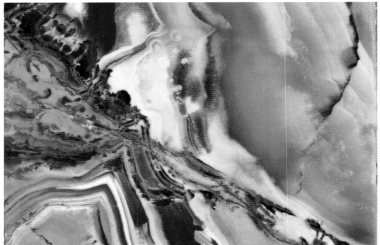

Trinkets made of green onyx marble can be found for sale right across the world, yet few people know where this popular stone comes from.

Zard Kan, Patkok, Juhli, Butak, Mashki Chah, Tozghi and Zeh: these villages lying south of the sparsely populated Chagai Mountains are the centers of the Pakistan onyx marble industry. This colorful stone was first quarried in the 1950s, and huge quantities of inexpensive decorative pieces have flooded the overseas markets. Volcanic activity created the mountains during late Miocene and Pleistocene times, and supplied the geothermal heat for the hot springs that deposited huge quantities of onyx marble in a broad band across northwestern Baluchistan, crossing the borders into Afghanistan and Iran.

Pakistan onyx marble is very fine-grained, and ranges in color from milky-white to translucent green. Darker green shades are particularly highly prized. The stone has a fairly high iron content and when it is oxidized by circulating groundwater, red and orange-brown iron oxides form in agate-like bands, enhancing its beauty. There are huge reserves of Pakistan onyx marble available for quarrying.

GEOLOGICAL DESCRIPTION

Compact banded travertine composed of very fine-grained calcite. Bands of orange-brown to red iron oxides may in part result from cyanobacterial growth, but also result from oxidation by penetrating groundwater.

MAJOR USAGE

Vases, candle holders and other trinkets; larger slabs available for decorative cladding, paving and other architectural uses.

Mexican onyx marble

SOURCE: Puebla, Oaxaca and Baja California, Mexico
STATUS: Actively quarried in Puebla and Oaxaca

Oxf–Min 30614

Curious monkey-shaped jugs were carved out of *tecali*, the Mexican onyx marble, long before the Spanish conquistadors arrived in Mexico.

Mexican onyx marble is often called by its Náhuatl name *tecali* and this is also the name of a town south of Mexico City that has become a center for the production of onyx marble artifacts. Masks were carved from this stone as early as the first century CE, and fascinating jars in the shape of a monkey, its tail held over its head for a handle, were made by the Mixtec people between the 10th and 16th centuries. When the Spanish conquistadors arrived, they too appreciated this beautiful stone, using it particularly for church windows, fonts and altar fronts.

Most Mexican onyx marble is white, and when embellished with random streaks of bright orange or red, it is a gorgeous sight. More richly colored varieties are the most popular. Notable sources are the famous La Pedrara quarry and other places near Tecali (Puebla), San Antonio Texcala (Puebla), Etla (Oaxaca) and El Marmol (Baja California). The quarry at El Marmol, worked by the New Pedrara Onyx Company, was also called La Pedrara. It opened in 1890 and closed in 1958. Nearly all onyx marble used in the United States before the 1880s came from Mexico. It was exported to other countries in the early 20th century.

GEOLOGICAL DESCRIPTION
Compact banded travertine deposited by hot springs, composed of very fine-grained white or pale green calcite stained orange or red by iron oxides.

MAJOR USAGE
Ecclesiastical decoration and various decorative objects.

Yava onyx

SOURCE: Yavapai County, Arizona, United States
STATUS: Actively quarried

Oxf–DR1630

In the late 1880s, the American hero William "Buckey" O'Neill spent $150 on a third share in a quarry of onyx marble at Mayer's Station. His fortune was made when the partners sold their business in 1893 for $200,000.

Arizona onyx marble was first discovered in the 1880s at two locations in Yavapai County. The first was at the western end of Big Bug Creek in the town of Mayer. The second was farther south, at Cave Creek. The onyx marbles from both locations were translucent creamy-white or green, typically veined with orange-brown and red. Both deposits were quickly put to commercial use, but it was the Mayer enterprise, in which O'Neill had bought his stake, that was particularly successful. The stone was called *Yava onyx* and it was widely used for decorative work in the United States, including the interior décor of the new automobiles made by Henry Ford's motor company. It was exported to other countries including the United Kingdom. The success was halted by the Great Depression of the 1930s, when all quarrying ceased. The quarry was reopened in 2003 after drilling had revealed that the onyx deposit, at more than 180 feet (55 m), was exceptionally thick. The modern Arizona onyx marble is a swirling mixture of honey-brown, white, orange and black. It is mainly sold as tiles and slabs.

GEOLOGICAL DESCRIPTION
Compact banded travertine composed of very fine-grained calcite. Orange-brown to red iron oxides result from oxidation by penetrating groundwater.

MAJOR USAGE
Architectural decoration, smaller decorative items such as paperweights and candlesticks.

Alabastro a tartaruga

SOURCE: Iano, Montaione, Tuscany, Italy

STATUS: No longer quarried

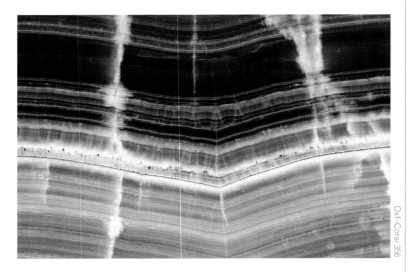

OxF-Corsi 356

Tortoise shells are marked with bands of light and dark brown, which makes the name *alabastro a tartaruga* (tortoise alabaster) seem especially apt.

The scalpellini of Rome would find small pieces of this attractive brown "alabaster" in the archaeological excavations of Rome, and named it *alabastro a tartaruga* because it had markings like a tortoise's shell. It is seen in small panels, decorating buildings and furniture and, according to Faustino Corsi, the scalpellini used it to make snuff boxes.

It seems that much of this stone had come from the vicinity of Iano, near Montaione. Hot springs rising at a farm called La California had formed travertine deposits a little south of Iano, and fractures in the travertine were filled with the fine-grained translucent *alabastro a tartaruga*. Quarries were opened after World War II to extract the travertine for use in construction, but it was apparent that large quantities of the alabaster had been extracted in past times. More recently, this attractive stone was supplied to workshops in Iano and Montaione where it was fabricated into various small decorative items. The cost of extracting the stones and a lack of ready markets resulted in the quarries closing again.

GEOLOGICAL DESCRIPTION

Secondary speleothemic deposits of very fine-grained compact banded calcite hosted in fractures in a travertine deposit.

MAJOR USAGE

Small decorative panels in buildings and furniture; snuff boxes and other small decorative items.

Alabastro di Busca

SOURCE: Busca, Piedmont, Italy

STATUS: No longer quarried

OxF-Corsi 359

The gray limestone from Busca was burned to make lime, but the beautiful honey-colored "alabaster" from the same quarry was used to decorate the palaces of Turin.

Busca is a small town in the Piedmont region of Italy lying north of Cuneo. From the 17th century until the early 20th century, a quarry over a mile (2 km) outside Busca on the road to Dronero supplied limestone for burning to make lime. It also yielded a very beautiful "oriental alabaster," filling fractures 6–8 feet (2–3 m) thick in the limestone. This stone is a glowing orange-brown to honey-yellow color with bands of a granular pure white calcite. The deposit was speleothemic, formed by dripping water in a cave environment, and cavities in the stone were lined with yellowish calcite crystals.

Alabastro di Busco is seen decorating churches, palaces and houses in Italy, notably the Royal Palace in Turin and the Church of San Filippo Neri in the same city. It seems that it was admired by the scalpellini of Rome as well, for they used it in tabletops and collections of marble samples sold to travelers on the Grand Tour of Europe.

GEOLOGICAL DESCRIPTION

Speleothemic calcite deposit.

MAJOR USAGE

Interior decoration of churches and public buildings; inlaid tables and other furniture.

Alabastro di Palombara

SOURCE: Uncertain
STATUS: Quarried in antiquity

Oxf-Corsi 311

The story of the beautiful and distinctive *alabastro di Palombara* highlights the difficulties in identifying alabasters and travertines.

Alabastro di Palombara is fine-grained, compact and unusually opaque. Bands of pure white and rich brown are straight or curved depending on which direction the stone is cut. It is the most distinctive of the many alabaster fragments found in the grounds of the Villa Palombara on the Esquiline Hill of Rome. This was the residence of the eccentric 17th-century alchemist Marquis Massimiliano Palombara, built on the Hortus Lamiani, the pleasure gardens of Imperial Rome. When the archaeologist Rodolfo Lanciani organized excavations between 1773 and 1776, he discovered the relics of a palace that once had floors and walls richly decorated with oriental alabaster.

Opinions have varied as to where the stone was quarried. Marble expert Raniero Gnoli suggested it came from Asia Minor but specimens in the Borromeo collection in Milan indicated that it may have come from Iano, near Montaione in Tuscany, the source of *alabastro a tartaruga*. Then, in 2000, ancient quarries of *alabastro fiorito* were rediscovered near the ruins of Hierapolis in Turkey that also yielded samples closely resembling *alabastro di Palombara*. The same techniques used to distinguish white marbles will be needed to confirm the provenance of the Palombara stone.

GEOLOGICAL DESCRIPTION
Compact banded travertine deposited by hot springs.

MAJOR USAGE
Paving and other architectural decoration, small pieces in inlaid tables, historic collections of ancient stones.

Gibraltar stone

SOURCE: Gibraltar
STATUS: No longer quarried

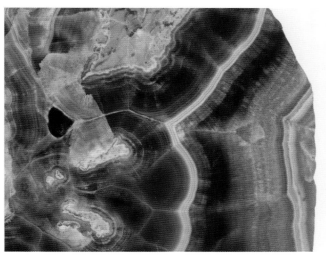

Oxf-Min15746

Hidden within the famous Rock of Gibraltar is a huge network of more than 150 caves that, in times gone by, would supply the stone for tourists' souvenirs.

The Rock of Gibraltar is a huge outcrop of Jurassic limestone. Rainwater percolating through fractures in the stone has worn huge caverns, and the sea has played its part, too, in eroding the rock. More than 150 natural caves and caverns have been discovered so far and more certainly lie below sea level. The caves have sheltered humans since Neanderthal times, and are famous for the skeletons and artifacts that have been discovered since the 19th century. Stunning stalactites have flowed down and in places meet stalagmites inching upward. These amazing structures used to be cut and polished, and made into inkstands, cups, candlesticks, models of cannons and other souvenirs. They were sold as *Gibraltar onyx*, or simply *Gibraltar stone*.

Some of the stunning caves of Gibraltar are open to tourists, but they will no longer be able to take home trinkets made of *Gibraltar stone*. The stalagmites and stalactites are now protected.

GEOLOGICAL DESCRIPTION
Compact banded brown calcite from a speleothemic deposit in Jurassic limestone caves.

MAJOR USAGE
Small gifts and souvenirs.

Alabastro a pecorella

SOURCE: Oran, Algeria
STATUS: No longer quarried

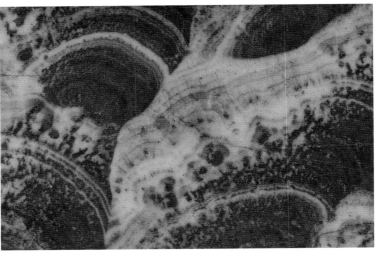

Oxf-Corsi 331

The "pecorella" or "little sheep" in this easily recognized stone are puffy spots and bands of white calcite, gathered in flocks on red or brown "hills."

Of all the travertines and alabasters used in ancient times, *alabastro a pecorella* is the most richly colored—the type of patterning and markings varying according to the direction in which the stone is cut. It is a travertine, laid down by hot springs at Aïn Tekbalet in the Oran district of Algeria. Modern research has shown that the bushlike dendritic growths of yellow, red and black metal oxides seen in travertines were most probably formed by bacteria that thrived in the hot springs long ago. It is not unusual for these colored oxide minerals to give *alabastro a pecorella* a curiously three-dimensional appearance.

LEFT A bust of Marcus Aurelius clad in *alabastro a pecorella*, a much favored stone among the ancient Roman emperors.

FAR LEFT The exquisite contoured banisters are made of white Algerian alabaster in the Garnier Opera House in Paris.

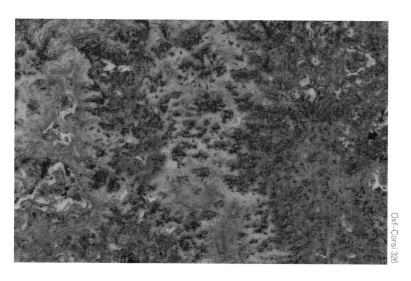

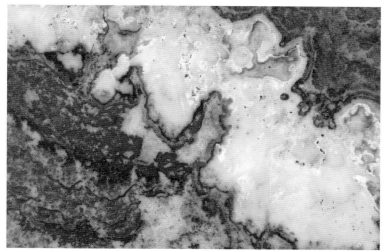

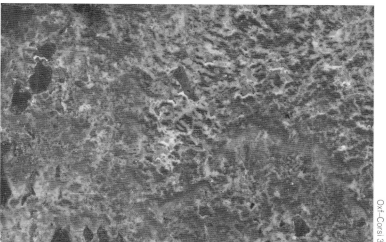

Alabastro a pecorella is the most striking of the various compact travertines to come from the province of Oran. It was used extensively in north Africa, and first brought to Rome around the beginning of the second century CE. Since then it has been extensively recycled in the decoration of churches, in pillars and plinths and in pietre dure inlay work.

Not all oriental alabaster from Oran is so richly colored. The more translucent varieties are still quarried today. They became extremely fashionable when the quarries were reopened in the latter half of the 19th century, and were used for windows in churches and mosques, the decoration of buildings, manufacture of vases and other decorative pieces, and to make lampshades. Fine examples of translucent creamy-white Algerian alabaster can be seen forming the banisters of the grand staircase of the

Garnier Opera House in Paris. Translucent green stone similar to the modern Pakistan onyx marble (see page 50) was used so excessively for all manner of decorative items in the 20th century that it is generally considered rather kitsch.

GEOLOGICAL DESCRIPTION

Fine-grained compact banded travertine containing dendritic brown goethite, red hematite and black manganese oxides.

MAJOR USAGE

Paving, wall cladding and other architectural elements; inlay work, sculpture.

Alabastro fiorito

SOURCE: Pamukkale area, Denizli, Turkey
STATUS: Some quarrying still takes place

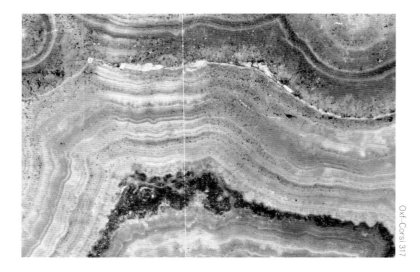

The name Pamukkale means "cotton castle," quite apt for the gleaming white travertine terraces that so many tourists visit.

In the early years of the first century CE, the geographer and historian Strabo described new stones that were being brought to Rome, and listed one that came from the city of Hierapolis in Phrygia. The ruins of this ancient city are close to the modern spa resort of Pamukkale in an area of extensive hot spring activity. Two ancient travertine quarries were discovered not far from the ruins of Hierapolis in 2000. The larger and more important lay beyond the village of Gölemezli, and was evidently the source of much of the stone that the Roman scalpellini called *alabastro fiorito*. They used this name rather loosely for compact travertines that are subtly banded white and many shades of yellow, buff and brown. Slender dark red lines can enhance the patterning, and darker bands often have a dendritic appearance. Depending on the direction of cut, the bands are either straight or swirled in a convoluted way. Chips of other alabaster varieties were also found at the newly discovered quarries, including some resembling *alabastro di Palombara* (see page 53) and *giaccione* (see page 50).

GEOLOGICAL DESCRIPTION

Compact banded travertine deposited by hot springs. The dendritic growths of iron oxides were most probably deposited by colonies of cyanobacteria living in the warm mineral waters.

MAJOR USAGE

Floor and wall cladding; vases and urns; sculpture.

BELOW The hot springs at the modern spa resort of Pamukkale, Turkey.

Travertino di Civitavecchia

SOURCE: Civitavecchia, Lazio, Italy

STATUS: No longer quarried

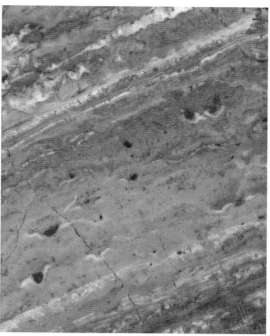

Oxf–Corsi 368

Most of the travertine quarried in the area around Rome is creamy-white or pale gray, but some varieties from the ancient seaport of Civitavecchia can be much more colorful.

The hot springs of Lazio formed the famous Tivoli travertine deposits of which much of Rome is built, but they deposited travertines in other areas too. Near Civitavecchia, northwest of Rome, the travertines are generally grayish white and were considered to be good quality building stones that were easy to work. Less commonly, they were colored with bands of yellow, pink and red and, taking a fair polish, these varieties were used for ornamental purposes. They are found in 18th and 19th century furniture, particularly marble sample tabletops, and in historic collections of ornamental stones.

Travertine was quarried to the east of the town at Bagni di Traiani and Ficoncella. It was also extracted farther south, at Pian Sultano, north of Santa Severo, and at the Guglielmi quarry owned by the wealthy family of that name living in Civitavecchia. All the quarries were still being worked at the end of the 1880s, but which one supplied the colored travertines is not known.

GEOLOGICAL DESCRIPTION

Porous banded travertine colored by iron oxides.

MAJOR USAGE

Furniture and small decorative slabs.

Persian travertine

SOURCE: East Azerbaijan, Iran

STATUS: Actively quarried

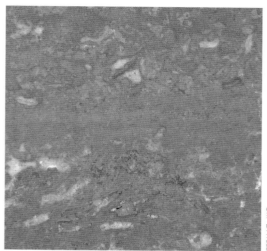

Oxf–DR1682

In the past, Persian travertine could be obtained that was remarkably transparent and milky-white. Today, it is the opaque varieties in rich colors that are most often seen.

There are numerous thermal springs in the provinces of Ardebil and East Azerbaijan in far northwest Iran, and some are traditional tourist destinations and health resorts. Between the city of Tabriz and Lake Orumiyeh, the springs have deposited travertines that have been quarried for centuries. The most beautiful stone is compact, banded and a very translucent milky-white or delicately tinted pink or green. It often has red or copper-colored veins. It was known as *Tabriz marble* or *Maragha marble* and its use was at one time reserved for the Persian nobility. Thin slices were used for windows; thicker slabs were worked for paving and wall coverings.

A second kind of travertine has also been obtained in this region. It is opaque and richly colored red, yellow or brown by iron oxides. Cut along the grain it shows the typical banding and porous structure of travertine, but parallel to the bedding the patterning is much more subtle. It is actively quarried today. The red variety, shown here, is marketed as *Persian red travertine* or *Azarshahr travertine* because it comes from near the town of Azarshahr about 18 miles (30 km) south of Tabriz.

GEOLOGICAL DESCRIPTION

Travertine deposits. Varieties are either compact, fine-grained and translucent, or porous and opaque, colored by disseminated iron oxides.

MAJOR USAGE

Flooring, wall cladding and other architectural uses.

Travertino di Tivoli

SOURCE: Tivoli, Lazio, Italy
STATUS: Actively quarried

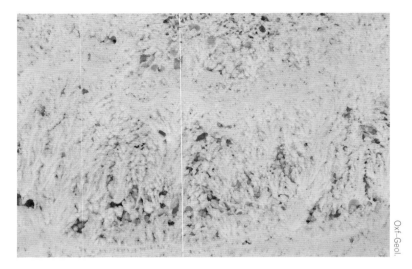

Oxf-Geol.

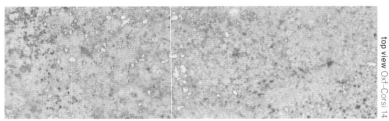

top view Oxf-Corsi 14

The word "travertine" is often linked to the creamy-white stone from Tivoli that was used extensively to build the city of Rome.

The hills around Rome are ancient volcanoes, and they heated hot springs that flooded large areas of land, depositing the well-known travertine. The ancient Romans called it *marmor Tiberinus*, after the ancient town of Tibur, now called Tivoli. The stone was first used in ornaments, then by the first century CE it became a staple in construction because newly quarried it is relatively soft and easy to work, but exposure to the elements makes it harder and more durable. Such durability is admirably demonstrated by that landmark of Rome, the Colosseum, built between 70 and 80 CE. It was constructed using more than 131,000 cubic yards (100,000 m³) of travertine obtained from the quarry of Barca, on the banks of the river Aniene near Bagni di Tivoli. From the 16th century, much stone was obtained from the nearby La Fosse quarry, and used in the construction of St. Peter's Basilica. Now there are many quarries extracting travertine near Bagni di Tivoli and Guidonia.

The stone is creamy-white to buff colored and, depending on the direction of cutting, can show distinct layering. It can be quite compact, but usually it has a spongy appearance. The little cavities are gas bubbles or where plant material once trapped in the mud of the hot springs has decayed. Today, the cavities are usually infilled with epoxy resin to give a more durable surface for polishing.

It is a much traveled stone, cladding the Getty Center in Los Angeles and extensively used in New York's Lincoln Center. The lower walls of the foyer and staircases of the new British Library, opened in 1998, are also lined with this stone, contributing to the light and spacious appearance of this building.

GEOLOGICAL DESCRIPTION

Opaque cream or buff-colored travertine deposited by hot springs,

Tartaro di Tivoli

SOURCE: Tivoli, Lazio, Italy
STATUS: Actively quarried

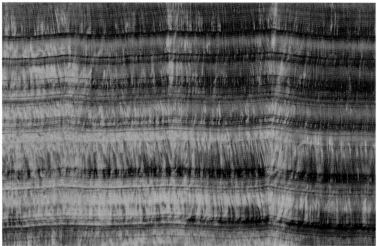

Oxf–Corsi 377

The tartari have a delicate fibrous structure—they interested collector Faustino Corsi so much he dedicated a special section of his catalog to them.

Corsi's *tartaro* is a very distinctive travertine consisting of sprays of fibrous crystals of calcite, tightly bonded together in layers, typically creamy-white to mid-brown in color. He explains that it was deposited from the aerial spray thrown up by waterfalls, and that masses of *tartaro* can be seen where the Aniene falls at the Grotto of Neptune in Tivoli. His specimens came from Tivoli (shown above) and Terni, near Rome and from the Bagni di San Philippo in Tuscany. These stones take a beautiful polish. They were used in furniture and inlays, and are found in historic stone collections of the 18th and 19th centuries.

The name "tartaro" is interesting. Today it is sometimes used for porous, spongy travertine deposits, and for the decoration applied to grottoes to give this naturalistic look. It is so called because it resembles in appearance the potassium tartrate deposits that form on the walls of wine casks. In Corsi's time (the early 1800s) there was a Lake Tartarus near Tivoli that was fed by hot springs. Some have suggested this was the source of Corsi's specimens but contemporary accounts record that travertine from the lake was spongy and full of plant material, quite unlike the attractive banded stones belonging to Corsi.

GEOLOGICAL DESCRIPTION

Compact banded travertine deposits of fine fibrous calcite crystals, probably deposited by the aerial spray of supersaturated water.

MAJOR USAGE

Inlaid tabletops and historic collections of decorative stones.

ABOVE The Getty Center in Los Angeles is clad with *travertino di Tivoli*.

variably banded with abundant small cavities. Shrubby structures are the relics of bacterial activity in the warm spring water. Fossils, especially preserved plant material, are quite common.

MAJOR USAGE

Pillars, paving, wall cladding and many other interior and exterior architectural applications; sculpture.

Travertino oro

SOURCE: Albox, Almeria, Spain
STATUS: Actively quarried

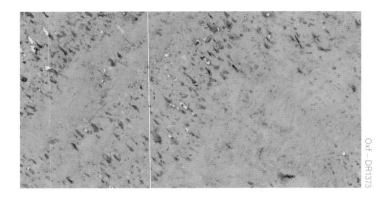

Oxf – DR1373

Albox in Almeria is best known for its vacation villas, and some of them will be furnished with its rustic local stone.

Travertino oro comes from two quarries in Albox, and occurs in a couple of layers each 10–13 feet (3–4 m) thick, interbedded with conglomerates. It has a long history of use in Spain and Portugal but it is only in recent decades that this stone has been exported to other countries, traded either as *travertino oro* or *travertino amarillo*. It can be beautifully colored, either a deep, even golden-yellow as shown here, or more delicately tinted, in streaks of yellow, gray and white. Whether the banding is clearly seen depends on whether the stone is cut perpendicular or parallel to the bedding.

It is a very typical travertine, full of small holes left behind by gas bubbles and fragments of decaying plant material. When stone is prepared for sale, these are usually filled with plaster or epoxy filler to level the surface for polishing. Surface treatments are often applied to seal and protect the stone, and when suitably treated, it makes an attractive rustic-looking paving stone and is particularly ideal for hard surfaces in bathrooms. Stones of similar appearance come from east Azerbaijan, Iran, and from Belen, in New Mexico.

GEOLOGICAL DESCRIPTION
Porous banded travertine deposited by hot springs during Pliocene times.

MAJOR USAGE
Flooring, wall cladding, and other architectural applications; mosaics.

LEFT Bathroom with yellow travertine tile floor and shower.

Other alabasters and travertines

Large deposits of true alabaster, the variety of gypsum, are mined and carved in Spain, at Fuentes de Ebro, in Zaragoza Province, and Albalate del Arzobispo in Teruel Province.

Compacte banded travertines are known from many other places. Of the various deposits found in California, that of Musick in San Luis Obispo County was one of the more commercially successful. The so-called *Brazilian onyx* was actually quarried in San Luis, Argentina, and is white or green with gold veining. It was popular in both North and South America and in France in the early 20th century for fireplaces and tabletops. The compact banded travertine from the hot springs of Karlovy Vary (Carlsberg) in the Czech Republic has a long history of use in Europe.

All kinds of ornamental objects were made in the town of Bagnères-de-Bigorre from speleothemic deposits of calcite obtained from caverns in the Hautes Pyrénées.

A speleothemic deposit at Arbolow in Derbyshire, England, is known as *Derbyshire oakstone*. To all appearances it could be a brown-banded cave deposit from Italy or Gibraltar, but when handled, it is surprisingly heavy. This is because it is composed of barite (barium sulfate), a mineral that is much more dense than calcite. It was used for inlays in Ashford marbleware. More conventional calcite speleothems were also quarried in the Derbyshire Peak District, including a beautiful yellow calcite from Pool Hole.

The more opaque, spongy-looking travertine deposits are quarried in many other places in Italy, particularly in Tuscany. In the United States, the yellowish-brown travertine quarried at Belen, New Mexico, and marketed today as *desert gold*, is one of the most attractive and commercially successful of these stones.

White marbles

To most people, the word "marble" brings to mind the pure white stone so prized
for sculpture since ancient times. Michelangelo's *David* and Rodin's *The Kiss*
are both carved in white marble; the Acropolis in Athens and the Taj Mahal in
Agra are both built of it. White marble sets off the beautiful colors and patterns
of other decorative stones and has dramatic uses in interior architecture. This
section shows marbles that are predominantly white in color. In strict geological
terms they are described as true marbles—metamorphic rocks with a fine
to coarse granular texture. The earliest sources in the Western world were in
Greece and the Apuan Alps of Italy, but excellent quality stones have also been
obtained from the United States, especially in the Appalachian Mountains.
Pure white marbles are virtually impossible to distinguish by eye. The context in
which they are used may give some clues, but often sophisticated technologies
such as neutron activation analysis and mass spectroscopy, are needed to
establish where a stone was quarried (see pages 66–7).

Pentelic marble

SOURCE: Mount Pentéli, Attica, Greece

STATUS: Ancient quarries are now closed; active quarrying is near Dionysos

Oxf-DR1657

It is remarkable to think that individually shaped blocks of stone were rolled out of the Pentéli quarries on tree trunks, then carried on huge carts to the foot of the Acropolis in Athens, to be hauled up this steep hill, and used to build the Parthenon.

The famous pure white *Pentelic marble* was most famously used in the construction of the Parthenon, the magnificent temple dedicated to Athena built on the Acropolis of Athens. The labor, which started in 447 BCE, took nine years to complete. The ancient Greeks particularly valued white marble, and used stone from Pentéli extensively for building and for sculpture during Hellenistic and Roman times. The Elgin Marbles, the now somewhat controversial sections of the frieze that once graced the façade of the Parthenon, are sculpted from *Pentelic marble*. The Romans too valued the stone they called *marmor Pentelicum*, using it for sculpture, sarcophagi and architecture. It has often been found in the ruins of Rome, and was known to the scalpellini (stonecutters) as *marmo Greco fino*.

After the fall of the Roman Empire, the quarries were worked sporadically. The most recent period of quarry working began in the 1830s when marble was extracted for new public buildings in Greece. The Panathenaic Stadium, extensively refurbished with huge quantities of *Pentelic* marble under the orders of Herodes Atticus between 140 and 144 CE, was restored with the same stone to host the first modern Olympic Games in 1896. It is perhaps no coincidence that soon after, the Marmor Company started exporting pure white *Pentelic statuary* and the bluish gray *Pentelic blue* to a worldwide market.

In 1976, the quarries on the southern side of Mount Pentéli were closed. Since then, marble from a different geological horizon has been extracted from underground workings on the north

ABOVE The Parthenon in Athens was built of *Pentelic marble* and is currently undergoing major restoration work using marble from nearby Dionysus.

side of the mountain at Dionysos. It is used for restoration of the Parthenon, and traded as *Dionysos Pentelikon white*.

GEOLOGICAL DESCRIPTION

Fine-grained calcitic marble formed in late Cretaceous or Tertiary times. Weathering of trace iron minerals imparts a slight yellow coloration; organic matter metamorphosed to graphite tints the stone gray.

MAJOR USAGE

Architectural, sculpture.

Parian marble

SOURCE: Island of Paros, Cyclades, Greece

STATUS: Quarried in antiquity; nowadays sporadic and small scale

Oxf-Corsi 1

If a marble is considered to be the finest stone for sculpture—and pure white *Parian marble* is exceptional—then even in ancient times it was worth opening underground mines to obtain the finest blocks.

The Greek island of Paros is almost entirely formed of marble, and the finest is pristine white and fine-grained, and has a remarkable translucency. It is statuary marble *par excellence*. It has been extracted since the sixth century BCE from mines running into the side of Mount Marpesso (now Capresso) near the village of Marathi. In the first century BCE, the mines came under Roman Imperial control. Pliny tells us that the marble was known as *lychnites*, from the Greek word for a lamp, because it was quarried by the light of oil lamps. *Parian marble* was used by Praxiteles, a master sculptor in Attica in the fourth century BCE. His figure of Hermes bearing the infant Dionysus was discovered in the excavations of the Temple of Hera at Olympia in 1877, and is among the best known of ancient marble statues.

Parian marble was used for roof tiles of temples because it allowed light to penetrate. It was employed in such prestigious projects as the Temple of Apollo in Delphi on the Greek mainland. Open quarries near Lakkoi in the Chorodaki valley, southwest of Marathi, yielded a coarser-grained, slightly grayer marble commonly found in archaeological excavations.

GEOLOGICAL DESCRIPTION

Fine- to medium-grained calcitic marble; small amounts of dolomitic marble have also been quarried on Paros.

MAJOR USAGE

For statues, but also used as a construction and facing stone.

Thasian marble

SOURCE: Island of Thásos, Kaválla, Greece

STATUS: Actively quarried

Oxf-Corsi 5

"We think ourselves poor and mean ... if our swimming pools are not lined with Thasian marble, once a rare and wonderful sight in any temple," commented the Roman philosopher Seneca.

He gave the name *marmor Thasium* to the marbles that were first quarried on the Greek island of Thasos in the fifth century BCE. The stone shown here is pure white and coarse-grained, with resplendent crystals. It was quarried at Cape Vathy on the southern tip of the island. Extraction of marble on this headland in ancient times slowly brought it down to the level of the sea, where the stone was easily carried away by ship. Large blocks could be obtained, and they were particularly favored for sarcophagi and statuary. What makes it different from most other white marbles quarried at that time around the Mediterranean is that it is a dolomitic marble. The presence of substantial quantities of dolomite means that it is a little more durable and more resistant to acid attack. The scalpellini called it *marmo Greco duro*.

Grayish white marbles, sometimes veined, were extracted at Aliki and other smaller quarries on Thasos. They were semi-formed into columns, blocks and slabs and transported all over the Roman Empire for finishing at their final destinations. Political instability forced the closure of the quarries by the seventh century CE. Commercial extraction on Thasos recommenced in the late 1900s and it is now traded under the name *Thasos snow white marble*.

GEOLOGICAL DESCRIPTION

Medium- to coarse-grained dolomitic (Cape Vathy) or calcitic (Aliki) marbles, formed during the Tertiary period.

MAJOR USAGE

Flooring, wall cladding, bath lining; sarcophagi and statuary.

White marbles of Tuscany

SOURCE: Apuan Alps, Tuscany, Italy
STATUS: Actively quarried

To many people, the name "Carrara" is synonymous with pristine white marble, but fine white marbles have been quarried from other places in Italy's Apuan Alps, every bit as exquisite as those from Carrara.

The first to open quarries in the Apuan Alps were the ancient Romans who in the late first century BCE started to extract marble near the ancient Etruscan city of Luna (Luni), close to the modern Carrara. They used the marble for buildings, sarcophagi and statuary, and called it *marmor lunense*. By the third century CE, the quarries had fallen into disuse. In the 14th century, marble was being worked again, for example in the decoration of the cathedral of Florence. Through the Italian Renaissance, the fame of the quarries grew. The Crestola, Cavetta and Poggio Silvestro

LEFT Quarries in the mountains near Carrara, Italy, are now highly mechanized.

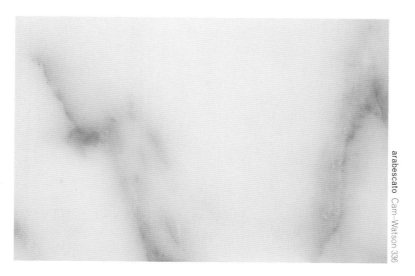

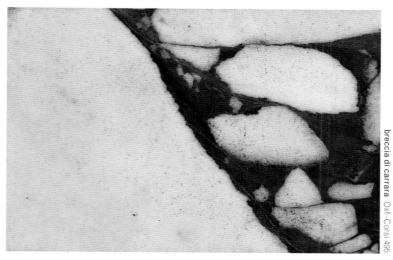

how marble from the new Massa quarries was traded as *Carrara marble*, happy to thrive on the illustrious reputation of its neighbor. He paints a vivid picture of the precipitous faces and dangerous quarrying methods, and the remarkable bravery of the quarry workers, sometimes hanging from ropes over huge crevasses to cut the stone. Bull-hauled carts carried the marble to the sawmills of Carrara and Seravezza until the arrival in the late 1800s of the Ferrovia Marmifera railroad. Today, the quarries are highly mechanized and road transportation is used again.

There are many different grades and varieties of "white" marble from the Apuan Alps. The finest is referred to as *statuario*. It is fine-grained, free from veins and stains of other minerals, and has a pleasing translucent quality. Some *statuario* has a distinctly waxy appearance. By comparison, *ordinario* is opaque, and sometimes a little gray or mottled. *Sicilian* is, rather confusingly, a white or pale gray variety with veins or flecks of gray, and has been particularly popular in England. Perhaps it was at one time shipped via Sicily or carried on a ship called *Sicilia*; no one is sure. Both the Victoria Memorial opposite Buckingham Palace and the Marble Arch in London are made of *Carrara Sicilian*. *Bianco venato* has distinct darker veins; *calacatta* has subtle golden-yellow or pale gray veining or brecciation, while in *arabsescato* the markings are darker. The most clearly brecciated white marbles, with veins of dark gray or dark purple, are referred to as *pavonazzo* or *pavonazzetto* (not to be confused with the ancient stone of the same name; see page 130).

GEOLOGICAL DESCRIPTION

Triassic or early Jurassic limestones metamorphosed during the Tertiary period to form fine-grained white calcitic marbles. The gray and black flecks and veins are rich in graphite derived from organic matter in the limestones.

MAJOR USAGE

Used extensively in statuary; inlay work; ecclesiastical, domestic and commercial architecture.

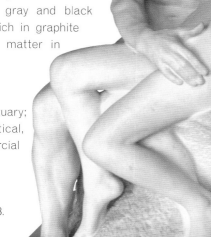

RIGHT Rodin's world-famous statue *The Kiss (Le Baiser)*, 1898.

quarries produced the finest statuary marble but Polvaccio quarry could supply large blocks with few imperfections. This was the quarry that Michelangelo Buonarroti visited to select marble for many of his larger works, including the famous *David*, finished in 1504. In 1518, Pope Leo X ordered him to use the fine white statuary marbles of Seravezza in preference to *Carrara* stone, and for many years the quarries of Monte Altissimo outside Seravezza supplied all the statuary marble for the Medici family projects. These quarries, too, fell into eventual disuse.

The Tuscan quarries had a virtual monopoly on the supply of white marble to world markets when quarrying recommenced at the end of the 18th century. New quarries opened in Carrara and Seravezza, and interest turned to the deposits of statuary marble near Massa. English geologist William Jervis recorded in 1862

"This white marble looks like all the others" is the exasperated cry of many a student trying to identify white marble fragments from archaeological digs. And make no mistake, it is tough to distinguish white marble without having to run a variety of scientific tests.

One piece of white marble on its own does not show the whole picture, but a whole armory of different analytical tests can. Each one adds another piece to the puzzle, and just two or three pieces may help reveal where the stone was quarried.

Unfortunately not all marbles can be identified with certainty; after all, not all ancient quarries have yet been discovered. But scientific tests can sometimes be so precise it is possible to say where a stone came from within an individual quarry. It is important that marbles are correctly identified for conservation and restoration projects, and the scientific information gleaned means that if the original quarry is worked out, the best matching alternative can be used instead.

GETTING CLOSE UP

Techniques that work for white marbles can be used to identify colored marbles too. Nearly always a small amount of marble has to be destroyed, and to get reliable results, several different samples are taken from the same "mystery" stone. The results can then be compared with data for samples field-collected from named quarries, to try and find the best match.

The simplest test measures the maximum grain size; this varies from locality to locality. This and more is revealed by petrographic examination. A slice of marble mounted on a glass slide is ground to about $\frac{1}{1000}$ inch (0.03 mm) thickness—so thin that light passes easily through it. Using a petrological microscope, the researcher can see the shape of the grains, the way they bond together, and identify flakes of mica, crystals of pyrite and other mineral grains.

White marbles are composed of calcite, a mixture of calcite and dolomite or more rarely, just dolomite on its own. But even the purest white marble is not as pure as it looks, for it contains minute traces of other chemical elements. Which elements, and in what concentration, correlate to a certain degree with where the stone was quarried. It takes some highly sophisticated machinery coupled with hi-tech-sounding techniques to measure trace elements in a sample of marble. Neutron activation analysis has often been used; inductively coupled plasma mass spectroscopy is a newer and particularly sensitive method that only requires the smallest scrape of a sample. Measurements of carbon and oxygen isotopes using a mass spectrometer has been a growth area of research in recent years. Isotope levels depend on the geological history of the marble.

When plotted on a graph, results for each quarry or quarry area cluster together. But some clusters overlap, and other tests are needed to decide which is the correct provenance for the "mystery" marble.

Other techniques available to researchers include measuring calcium:strontium ratios, laser absorption, cathodoluminescence and electron spin resonance spectroscopy. Not one of these techniques will, on its own, reveal where a marble originally came from – but each can fill in a puzzle piece.

The completed puzzle has helped archaeologists and art historians discover where marbles were quarried, the many places they were used, and the amazing networks of trade and transportation that carried this highly valued cargo across the ancient world.

RIGHT Inductively coupled plasma mass spectroscopy enables very accurate chemical analyses of minute samples of stone.

RIGHT Thin sections (in cross-polarized light) at the same magnification of *Carrara marble* (above right) and *Parian marble* (right) showing fields of view about $\frac{6}{100}$ inch (1.5 mm) across. *Carrara marble* has small polygonal grains with rather straight margins. Those of *Parian marble* are larger on average, and join with more convoluted margins.

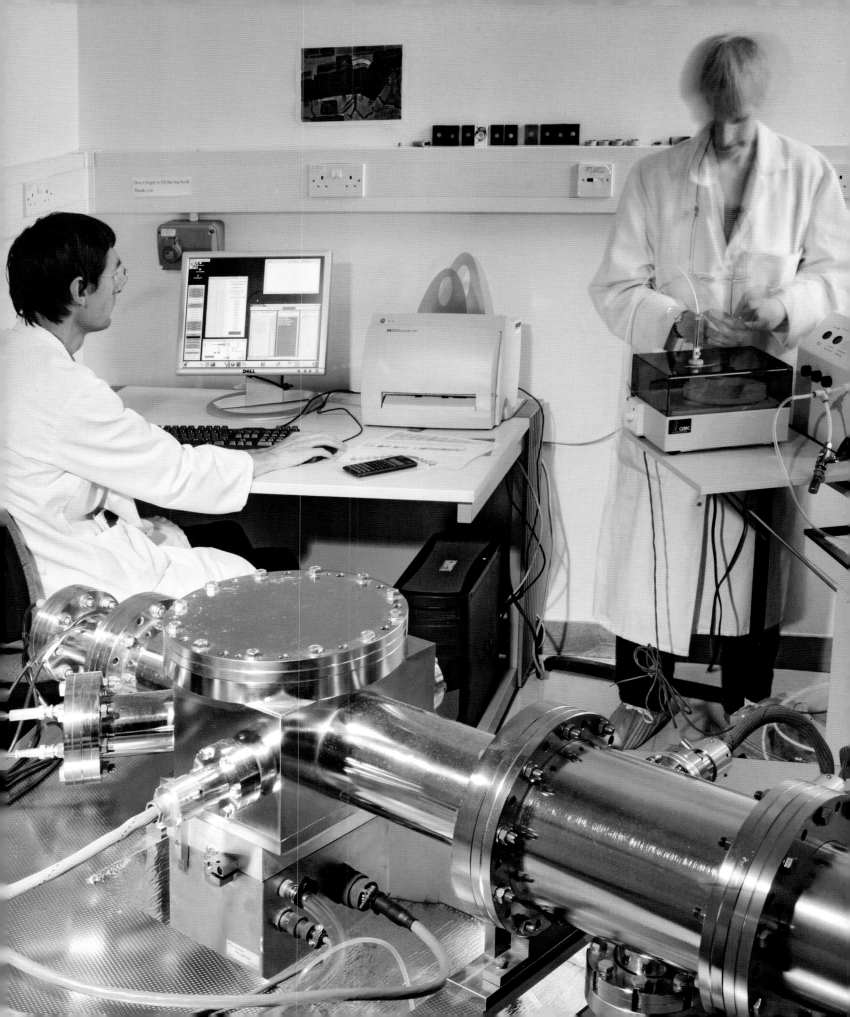

Alabama white marble

SOURCE: Talladega County, Alabama, United States
STATUS: Actively quarried

Cam–Watson 588

In the early 1900s near the town of Sylacauga in Talladega County, a huge belt of very fine white and veined marble awaited exploitation.

The Herd brothers from Scotland had started quarrying marble for gravestones in the 1830s. Dr. Edward Gantt, a surgeon and sculptor, had also opened a quarry in the early 19th century, but after his death, the quarry was abandoned. Around 1904–05, the quarrying industry began to burgeon. The creamy-white sample shown here is from Gantt's quarry that was reopened by the Alabama Marble Company. *Alabama marble* was used extensively in the interior decoration of the U.S. Supreme Court, and in the ceiling of the Lincoln Memorial, where it is soaked in paraffin to make it more translucent. The memorial to jazz musician Al Jolson in Culver City, California, is built of *Alabama marble*. The marble can of course be seen in many places in the state.

The prolific sculptor Giuseppe Moretti liked the marble so much, he purchased a quarry of his own. His *Head of Christ*, one of many works he carved from *Alabama marble*, is now in the Alabama Department of Archives and History in Montgomery.

Today, the marble is still extracted in huge quantities and is available for building and sculpture, but most of it is ground down for use as a filler in papers and many other products.

GEOLOGICAL DESCRIPTION

Calcitic marble of Paleozoic age; white, cream or gray, or veined in various colors.

MAJOR USAGE

Interior paving, wall claddings, stairways and other architectural features; a good stone for sculpture.

Danby marble

SOURCE: Dorset Mountain, Vermont, United States
STATUS: Actively quarried

Cam–Watson 650

In western Vermont there is a doorway in the side of Dorset Mountain that leads down six huge levels into one of the largest underground marble quarries in the world. This is where the famous *Danby marble* is quarried.

Commercial quarrying commenced in 1785 near the towns of Dorset and Danby to get stone for buildings, fireplaces, horse troughs and gravestones. Working was sporadic, partly reflecting fashions in the use of marble, but also the stiff competition from quarries in West Rutland and other towns farther north along the "marble belt" that runs the length of western Vermont.

The modern quarry has operated since 1903. In the 1920s and 1930s *Danby marble* was used for the amphitheater at the Arlington National Cemetery in West Virginia, and for projects designed by architect Cass Gilbert such as the Detroit Public Library and the U.S. Supreme Court. It was also famously used for the Thomas Jefferson Memorial in Washington, D.C. (1943). Not much Vermont marble was exported outside the United States until recently, with *Danby marble* used in the Saudi Arabian Monetary Agency and the Singapore Stock Exchange.

Danby marble is fine-grained and delicately veined. Varieties are named according to the color of the veining; for example, *imperial Danby* has golden veins, those in *royal Danby* are bluish gray, and in *montclair Danby*, they are green.

GEOLOGICAL DESCRIPTION

Ordovician fine-grained calcitic marble with veins of iron oxide and silicate impurities.

MAJOR USAGE

Flooring, wall cladding and worktops; memorials; sculpture.

Colorado Yule

SOURCE: Yule Valley, Gunnison County, Colorado, United States
STATUS: Sporadic quarrying takes place

Avalanche, bankruptcy and war have all checkered the history of America's most famous white marble.

The *Colorado Yule* marble was discovered by prospector George Yule in the late 1870s. Samples exhibited at the 1893 Colombia Exposition were greatly admired for their quality and purity, and in 1907 quarrying commenced under the management of the Colorado Yule Marble Company. A huge quarry mill was built to process the stone and the town of Marble grew up.

But a series of mishaps followed: the company founder died in a quarrying accident in 1912, and the mill was destroyed by an avalanche the same year. During World War I, the skilled Italian workers returned to Europe. The construction of the Lincoln Memorial in Washington using *Colorado Yule* should have signaled a revival in fortunes, but the quarries closed soon after completion in 1917. They reopened in 1930, supplying an enormous 56 ton (62 tonne) block for the Tomb of the Unknown Soldier in Arlington National Cemetery, Virginia. By 1941, they had shut down again. Extraction of *Yule* recommenced in 1990, cutting underground into the mountainside where huge reserves are available.

GEOLOGICAL DESCRIPTION

Fine- to medium-grained calcitic marble; a Carboniferous limestone metamorphosed by intrusion of a granite in the Tertiary period. The statuary white variety is particularly pure; veined varieties contain quartz and amphibole minerals.

MAJOR USAGE

Popular for monuments and sculpture, also a construction stone.

RIGHT *Sophisticated Lady* by Reno Carollo carved from *Colorado Yule.*

White Makrana

SOURCE: Makrana, Rajasthan, India
STATUS: Actively quarried

ABOVE *White Makrana* marble was used to build the Taj Mahal in Agra.

There are several hundred marble quarries at the western edge of the Aravalli mountain range near the town of Makrana, for this is the source of India's best known marble.

White Makrana marble was chosen as the building stone for the Taj Mahal in Agra, India. This extraordinarily beautiful mausoleum, constructed between 1631 and 1648, was for Mumtaz Mahal, commissioned by her husband Emperor Shah Jahan. It is a combination of Islamic, Hindu, Persian and Mughal architecture, and since 1983 has been a UNESCO World Heritage Site. Makrana marble was used to build the central tomb with its domed roof and minarets. The same stone was carved and inlaid with semiprecious stones for much of the interior decoration.

The finely crafted ornamentation of the Taj Mahal has been the inspiration for the many marble boxes, dishes and other trinkets that are manufactured in Makrana from local stone, and sold to tourists all across India. Often they are inlaid with patterns of mother of pearl, carnelian, aventurine and other gems. Makrana marble is also used to make "jali," screens with pierced geometric patterns, sometimes cut so delicately that they look like lace.

White Makrana is a fine- to medium-grained marble that can be cut in quite large blocks. Pink and gray marbles are also quarried near the town, and Rajasthan supplies more marble to the stone trade than any other province of India.

GEOLOGICAL DESCRIPTION
Precambrian fine- to medium-grained white calcitic marble.

MAJOR USAGE
Construction stone, pavings, wall claddings; monuments; gifts and souvenirs, often with semiprecious inlays.

Other white marbles

The Greek islands of Delos, Naxos, Skyros and Tinos supplied white marble in ancient times, while much modern stone comes from Naxos and the area of Macedonia around Volakas, Drama and Kavala. In Turkey, Aphrodisias, near Karakasu, was a center for sculpture in ancient Roman times, with marble quarries close by. These are now protected sites but *Aphrodisias* marble is still quarried in the area. Marble from Iscehisar in the province of Afyon was also worked in ancient times and is traded today as *Afyon white*.

The finest of the French white marbles, *blanc de St. Béat*, was quarried near the village of that name in Haute-Garonne, and used extensively in the churches and palaces of France. *Blanco Macael* is a well known, coarse-grained white marble from Macael in Andalucia, in Spain. *Estremoz branco* is one of the best Portuguese white marbles.

Other Italian white marbles are from Crevola d'Ossola (still worked) and Pont Canavese in the Piedmont region, and from the island of Elba. This was worked at the time Napoleon was exiled on the island (in 1814).

In the United States, the white marble of South Dover, New York, was used mainly for construction in New York City and nearby towns during the 19th and early 20th centuries. The quarries were exhausted around the time of World War II. *Penna white* marble from Chester County, Pennsylvania, has been used extensively in buildings of that state. Other white marbles come from Iran, Malaysia, Brazil and Australia.

Gray and black marbles and limestones

The marbles and limestones in this section range from pale silvery gray to darkest pitch black. Until they are polished, black stones are dark gray or brown, and it is the polishing process that brings out the black color. Interesting tonal effects can be achieved by combining polished and unpolished stone in a single design. Black marbles and limestones are a traditional choice for funerary monuments, but they also make superb backing stones for colorful marble inlays such as those fabricated in Florence, Italy, and Ashford in England. Brecciated and veined black stones can be particularly striking, whether the *negro Marquina* or *noir St. Laurent* fitted in public buildings and private homes today, or the *grand antique* and *portoro* of historic times. These are some of the most popular choices of stone to be replicated as faux marble and scagliola, handcrafted imitations of the natural stones.

Bardiglio

SOURCE: Apuan Alps, Tuscany, Italy
STATUS: Actively quarried

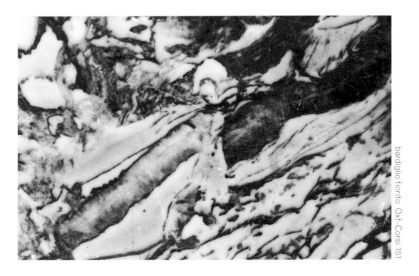

bardiglio fiorito Oxf–Corsi 151

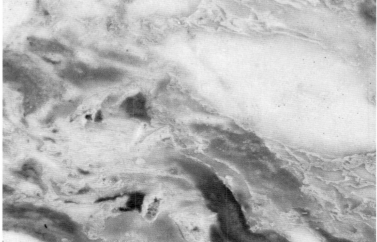

bardiglio nuvolato Oxf–Corsi 156

Though widely used, the gray *bardiglio* marbles of Tuscany rarely attract the same kind of attention as their white counterparts.

The traditional Italian name for gray marbles taken from the same quarries in the Apuan Alps that are worked primarily for white marbles, is *bardiglio*. They have sometimes been called *dove marble* in English-speaking countries because the color resembles the bluish gray of a pigeon's wing.

Like their white counterparts, the *bardiglio* are fine-grained true marbles with a sugary texture, but they are colored a bluish gray, often with lighter or darker flecks, lines, bands and streaks. Some *bardiglio* is pale gray, an inexpensive stone that understandably was never regarded highly. Others are a silvery-gray with very beautiful markings, and make an excellent foil for more brightly colored stones. *Bardiglio fiorito*, also called *bleu fleuri*, has slender dark gray veins. *Bardiglio Cappella*, the *bleu turquin* of the French, has soft parallel bands of paler gray running through it.

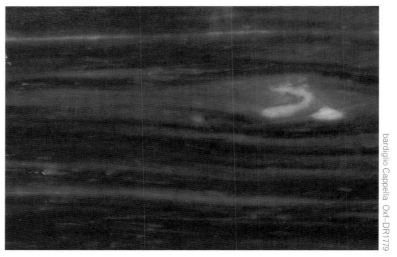

bardiglio Cappella Oxf–DR1779

The *bardiglio* marbles were first used in ancient Roman times, probably in the first century BCE, and were employed mainly for lining baths and for sidewalks. The modern period of quarrying in the Apuan commenced in the late 18th century, and since then, *bardiglio* has been used a great deal for architectural purposes.

GEOLOGICAL DESCRIPTION

Fine-grained calcitic marble colored by disseminated graphite.

MAJOR USAGE

Paving, wall cladding and other architectural applications; furniture; chimneypieces.

RIGHT Detail from a 19th-century *bardiglio* chimneypiece.

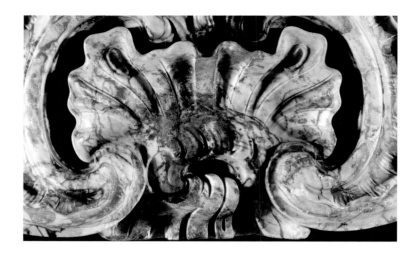

Greco scritto

SOURCE: Capo de Garde, Annaba, Algeria
STATUS: Quarried in antiquity

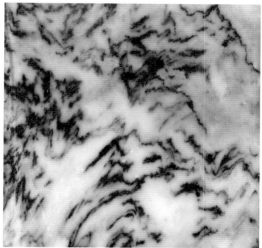

Oxf–Corsi 99

It looks like someone has been scribbling with a black pen on this white marble, and it looked as unintelligible as Greek script to the scalpellini of Rome.

The groundmass of *Greco scritto* is a medium- to coarse-grained white marble and it is covered in small black markings. Sawn at other angles, the black markings are seen to join together to form long convoluted black lines. The scalpellini of Rome found this marble in the ruins of Rome and, thinking the black squiggles looked like Greek characters, they named the stone *Greco scritto*.

Greco scritto was quarried at Capo de Garde near the ancient Hippo Regius, now called Annaba. The quarries were so close to the sea, the marble could easily be shipped to Rome, Ostia and other places around the Mediterranean. *Greco scritto* was extracted mainly between the first and third centuries CE, and as the quarries were not under Imperial control, it was used mainly in private houses and minor public buildings.

Similar stones, generally of finer grain size, have come from Carrara and elsewhere in the Apuan Alps.

GEOLOGICAL DESCRIPTION
A tectonite; a deformed veined calcitic marble.

MAJOR USAGE
Slabs and paving; furniture.

Ashburton marble

SOURCE: Ashburton, Devon, England
STATUS: No longer quarried

Oxf–DR 1125

A rainy day in south Devon can be brightened up by the sight of curbstones made of *Ashburton marble*, gleaming dark gray with brilliant pink veins.

The marble once quarried at Ashburton in south Devon is an unusual combination of colors, a light or dark mottled gray groundmass with bright pink and white veins. It is a limestone, containing fossil remains of creatures that lived in the Devonian sea some 360–380 million years ago. During Carboniferous times, tectonic movements and the emplacement of the Dartmoor granite just a few miles away caused the crushing and deformation that give this stone its attractive brecciated appearance.

Ashburton marble has been used locally for stone walls and curbstones. Although expensive to transport from Devon during Georgian and Victorian times, it was often made into fireplaces and used for stairs and skirtings in buildings. Original fireplace moldings in the historic Wren building of William and Mary College, Virginia, were restored with the same stone in 1967. The staircase of Hornsey Town Hall, London, built in the 1930s, is made of *Ashburton marble*; it was used in Guildford Cathedral in the 1950s, and in many other churches. In 1967, *Ashburton marble* was employed for the decoration of the central staircase and lobby of the Canadian National Library in Ottawa.

GEOLOGICAL DESCRIPTION
Brecciated, deformed fossiliferous limestone of mid-Devonian age. Fossils are predominantly corals, stromatoporids, crinoids and brachiopods. Fractures are filled with pink and white calcite.

MAJOR USAGE
Chimneypieces and tabletops; store fronts; columns, staircases.

Cherokee, solar grey

SOURCE: Tate, Pickens County, Georgia, United States
STATUS: Actively quarried

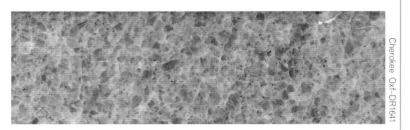

Cherokee Oxf-DR1641

Solar grey Oxf-DR 1640

As long ago as 800 CE, Native North Americans carved boulders of marble into ornaments—this stone is now named *Cherokee*.

The marble belt of the southern Appalachians of Georgia runs from Fannin County southwest, ending in Cherokee County. A little marble was worked by settlers as early as the 1830s, but large-scale extraction started in 1884 in Pickens County. Here, the Georgia Marble Company was set up, exploiting the new railroad extension to transport the marble to new markets.

Cherokee is coarse-grained pale gray with a few darker streaks; *white Cherokee* is virtually white. A marble with heavy dark gray or black streaking was quarried nearby. It was called *Creole marble* until political correctness prevailed in the 1970s, when it was renamed *solar grey*. Today, *white Cherokee* and *solar grey* are quarried from different levels in the same huge quarry.

Although used extensively in the United States for interior and exterior cladding, these stones are not often seen overseas. The statue in the Lincoln Memorial, Washington, D.C., is carved out of *Cherokee*, and the U.S. Capitol Building is faced with it. *Creole* is mixed with pink *Etowah marble* (see page 107) in the wonderfully quirky Bok Singing Tower, a 205-foot (62 m) tall carillon tower constructed in the late 1920s in Lake Wales, Florida.

GEOLOGICAL DESCRIPTION

Limestones metamorphosed in Cambrian times to form coarse-grained calcitic marbles colored by disseminated black graphite.

MAJOR USAGE

Paving, wall cladding, bathtub surrounds and other interior and exterior architectural uses; monuments and memorial stones.

Proconnesian marble

SOURCE: Island of Marmara, Balıkesir, Turkey
STATUS: Actively quarried

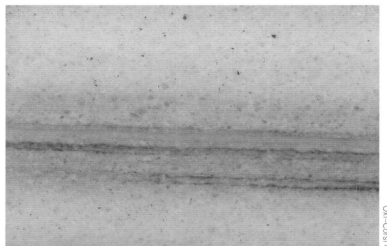

Oxf-Corsi 4

A sense of smell is not often useful when identifying marbles but this marble has a rather distinctive feature—a fetid aroma of rotten eggs when it is crushed.

The scalpellini of Rome called this stone *marmo cipolla*, the onion marble, because it emitted the pungent smell of hydrogen sulfide as they cut it. Tiny amounts of this gas are trapped inside the crystals. *Proconnesian marble* was employed as early as the fourth century BCE for the palace of Mausolus, the King of Halicarnassus. The Romans began to use it in the first century CE, calling it *marmor Proconnesium* after the island of Proconnesus (now called Marmara). The quarries are near Saraylar and other places on the island. The kind of *Proconnesian marble* most widely used in architecture and for sarcophagi is a medium-grained white stone with straight gray bands running though it. A monochrome grayish white variety was preferred for sculpture.

The Marmara quarries continued to be worked through the Byzantine and Ottoman eras and were an important source of marble in Turkey and north Africa. In the late 19th century and early 20th century, the stone was being used for paving, baths and tombstones in Istanbul. In England, it was used to clad the wall behind the altar of St. Paul's Chapel in Westminster Cathedral. The marble is currently traded as *Marmara white* or *gray*.

GEOLOGICAL DESCRIPTION

Medium- to coarse-grained calcitic marble with bands of finely disseminated graphite, magnetite and pyrite.

MAJOR USAGE

Slabs, paving, pillars and architectural decoration; sarcophagi.

Cipollino nero

SOURCE: Island of Euboea, Greece

STATUS: Used in antiquity

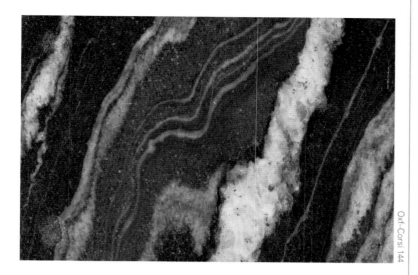

Oxf–Corsi 144

When a marble has an appearance like the layers of an onion, the Roman stonecutters called it *cipollino*. The *cipollini* can be various different colors.

All the *cipollini* are impure marbles, the impurities concentrated in colored bands. A gray and white *cipollino* was sometimes obtained from near the town of Karystos on the mountainous island of Euboea, an uncommon and very attractive variant of the better known *cipollino verde* (see pages 174–5). Like its green counterpart, *cipollino nero* would have been known to the ancient Romans as *marmor Carystium*, and small quantities were found in the ruins of Rome.

The *cipollini* of Euboea originally formed as beds of limestone, silt and clay in Permian times. This part of Greece has been an area of considerable tectonic activity since Cretaceous times, and the collision of crustal plates has resulted in extensive metamorphism of the sediments. Limestone was converted to marble, clays altered to chlorite and mica, and organic matter from the original marine fauna has changed to graphite. Further movements compressed the banded marble until it buckled and folded, forming the *cipollini* we see today.

GEOLOGICAL DESCRIPTION

Medium-grained folded marble containing bands rich in mica and graphite.

MAJOR USAGE

Small paving slabs, inlays; samples in historic marble collections.

Bigio antico

SOURCE: Greece, Turkey and France

STATUS: Quarried in antiquity

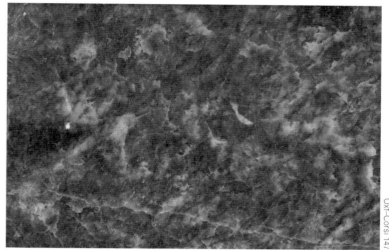

Oxf–Corsi 147

In the time of Faustino Corsi, it was not known where gray marbles had been quarried in antiquity. Now we know there are many different sources.

The name *bigio antico* is a generic term for the various gray marbles used in ancient times. They are medium- to coarse-grained, and have mottling or waves in different shades of gray or white. They were found in the ruins of Rome dating mainly from the first to the third century CE, and were among the less expensive marbles of the time. It is now known that these stones came from several locations. Ancient quarries have been found east of Moria, on the island of Lesbos, Greece, and on other islands of the eastern Aegean. In Turkey, they have been located at Teos (Sığacık), in Izmir, and at Aphrodisias, near Karakasu. Gray marble from St. Béat in France has also been recognized, and no doubt other sources will be discovered.

Pillars of *bigio antico* flank the nave of the Church of San Giovanni Evangelista in Ravenna, and the marble is carved as drapes hanging from the huge holy water stoups in St. Peter's Basilica in the Vatican. The Getty Center in California has a white marble medallion of Pope Alexander III mounted on a plinth of *bigio antico* that was carved in the 1690s. The plinth was sculpted in the form of a double-headed eagle, the emblem of the pope's Ottoboni family.

GEOLOGICAL DESCRIPTION

Medium- to coarse-grained calcitic marble containing finely disseminated graphite. Relics of fossils may be evident.

MAJOR USAGE

Pillars, slabs and paving; sculpture.

Nero antico, bigio morato

SOURCE: Greece and Tunisia
STATUS: No longer quarried

Oxf-Corsi 71

GEOLOGICAL DESCRIPTION

Black or dark gray fine-grained limestones or marbles, sometimes with veins of white calcite. Some limestones are fossiliferous, depending on the source.

MAJOR USAGE

Small columns, panels and veneers; *bigio morato* was employed in statuary.

Just as gray marbles were known as *bigio antico*, so the black ones were called *nero antico*. In between, there was *bigio morato*, of a very dark gray color.

The division between the black *nero antico* and dark gray *bigio morato* is very ambiguous. For a very long time it was believed that all *nero antico* was Pliny's *marmor Taenarium*, quarried at Cape Matapan (Taenarium) on the Mani Peninsula of Greece. The marble found on Cape Matapan is rather gray, and correlates more closely with *bigio morato* or *bigio antico*. More feasible sources are ancient quarries near Chemtou and at Gebel Aziza in Tunisia. Faustino Corsi's sample, with its slender straight white veins (shown above), most probably came from Gebel Aziza. Going by the size of the quarries discovered in the 1990s, large amounts of *nero antico* or *bigio morato* must also have been extracted on the Margaritis Peninsula of the Greek island of Chios. Teos, the modern Sığacık, in Izmir, Turkey, is just one more of the various other sources of ancient dark gray stones discovered in recent times.

Nero antico was used mainly in Rome and other locations in Italy from the first to the third century CE, and was much desired for funerary monuments in the 17th and 18th centuries. Some of the best examples of *bigio morato* are sculptures that were found in Hadrian's Villa during excavations in 1736, and include two carved centaurs, now to be seen in the Capitoline Museums in Rome.

RIGHT A sculpture of a centaur found in the ruins of Hadrian's Villa is made of *bigio morato*.

Ashford black marble

SOURCE: Ashford-in-the-Water, Derbyshire, England
STATUS: No longer quarried

Oxf-Corsi 72

When Faustino Corsi described *Ashford black marble*, he likened the color to that of coffee, and as this picture shows, the comparison is very apt.

The first examples of the working of *Ashford black marble* are the fireplaces in Hardwick Hall, Derbyshire, made about 1590. The stone was obtained from the estates of the Duke of Devonshire, and quarried first at Sheldon Moor, west of Ashford. Later it was mined at two locations, Arrock and Rookery Plantation. Blocks no thicker than about 12 inches (30 cm) could be extracted, and they were made into mantelpieces and tabletops, with small offcuts used to make paperweights, candlesticks, vases and the like. The Ashford Marble Works were set up in 1748, the first water-powered marble mill in England.

Fine examples of *Ashford black marble* can be seen at Chatsworth House where it forms pillars and steps in the chapel. The floor of the Painted Hall is checkered with Ashford stone and white Carrara marble, and there are pillars here too. *Ashford black marble* does not tolerate high light levels well, and the sides of pillars facing windows have tended to fade.

Among early tourist souvenirs made of *Ashford marble* were "moonlit" pictures of Chatsworth House and other views etched or engraved into the stone. In around the 1830s the stone was first used as a backing for colored stone inlays. The stone inlay industry continued until about 1939.

GEOLOGICAL DESCRIPTION

Fine-grained, dark brown, bituminous Carboniferous limestone.

MAJOR USAGE

Pillars, floors and other architectural decoration; inlay work.

Irish black marble

SOURCE: Galway and Kilkenny, Ireland
STATUS: Minor quarrying, mainly for restoration work

Oxf-DR1164

Black fine-grained limestones, virtually free of fossils, used to come in abundance from the Emerald Isle.

Ireland has been a rich source of black limestones, collectively termed *Irish black marble*, with quarries in several counties. The most important sources were in Galway and Kilkenny.

The Angliham and Menlough quarries, a short distance north of Galway, supplied some of the best *Irish black*. Angliham had three beds, the second of which was 12 inches (30 cm) thick and, being the most economic to cut, was reserved for the London market. Stone was also sent to the United States, traded as *London black*. Black marble was also extracted at the Merlin Park quarry, which was active before the 1830s and only closed in the 1970s. It has been proposed as a National Natural Heritage Area.

Kilkenny black marble was worked at Archer's Grove, now on the outskirts of the city of Kilkenny, from as early as the 17th century until the 1930s. It was also extracted at Butler's Grove, east of the city. Hamilton Palace in Lanarkshire had huge chimneypieces and door frames that were made from *Kilkenny black marble* in the 1830s. Examples of this stone can also be seen in Brompton Oratory, London, and forming columns that were erected in Wells Cathedral during restoration in 1869.

GEOLOGICAL DESCRIPTION

Black fine-grained limestones of Carboniferous age.

MAJOR USAGE

Floors, wall cladding, stairways and chimneypieces; sculpture; jewelry and souvenirs.

Belgian black marble

SOURCE: Hainault and Namur, Belgium
STATUS: Actively quarried

ABOVE *Patience* (2005), a sculpture by Marian Sava, is 100 x 30 x 16 inches and shows gray unpolished and black polished *Belgian black* marble.

Chocolate may be the first Belgian specialty to come to mind, but a superb quality black marble ranks a very close second among stone experts!

The quarries of black marble are in two areas of Belgium. In Hainault, stone has been quarried in the region of Tournai since at least the 11th century. It is often referred to as *Tournai marble* and used extensively for fonts and memorial slabs in the churches of Belgium. By the 12th century they were being exported to England too. The carved font in Winchester Cathedral, the Abbot slab in Westminster Abbey and the Memorial to Bishop Roger in Salisbury Cathedral all date to this period. The black *marble of Golzinne*, also called *Mazy black*, has been exploited since the 19th century northwest of Namur, and is an older stone of Devonian age. It is considered one of the most pure of the Belgian black marbles.

Belgian black marble was often called *touch marble* by the marble workers because it was used as a touchstone (paragon) for testing precious metals. In the *Opificio delle Pietre Dure*, it was referred to as *paragone di Fiandra* (*paragon of Flanders*) and was the preferred backing stone for inlays of colored marble. Toward the end of the 19th century, checkerboard designs of *Belgian black* and *Carrara Sicilian* white marble were very widely used for hallways in offices and public buildings, part of the fashion for marble decoration that was sweeping Europe and the United States.

Belgian black is extremely fine-grained and breaks with a curved conchoidal fracture just as glass does. Like glass, *Belgian black* can form viciously sharp edges. Sculptors who work this stone always advise caution and the use of eye protection against flying splinters. The rewards are huge, for the stone will hold very intricate detail, and although it is gray when unpolished, it polishes to a brilliant pitch black finish. Small amounts are still quarried, and it remains a highly regarded medium for sculptors.

GEOLOGICAL DESCRIPTION

Black fine-grained limestones or siliceous limestones of Devonian or Carboniferous age; the black is due to inclusions of bitumen. Fossils such as crinoids occur, but are uncommon and the best quality stone lacks any white veins of calcite.

MAJOR USAGE

Ecclesiastical items including fonts and memorials; paving and other architectural applications; Florentine pietre dure work; sculpture; furniture and clocks.

OxF-DR1793

Above *Belgian black* and *Carrara Sicilian* marble are commonly used together in checkerboard floors of the late 19th and early 20th centuries. This floor is in the Queen's House, Greenwich, London.

Right Detail from the 12th-century font in Winchester Cathedral.

Champlain black

SOURCE: Isle La Motte, Vermont, United States
STATUS: Occasional small-scale quarrying

Oxf-DR1637

Radio black is one of several names this stone has been known by in its long and illustrious history.

The mountains of Vermont are a rich source of different colored marbles, and the best black comes from quarries on Isle La Motte, an island in Lake Champlain. When Ichabod Fisk came to Isle La Motte in 1788, he opened a marble quarry and sold the stone as *Fisk black* or *Fisk gray*. In recent times, it has been called *Champlain black*. It was used in the flooring of the State Capitol of Maine, first in 1889–90 and then in 1909–11. It was also employed in the decoration of the famous Radio City Music Hall in New York's Rockefeller Center, which opened in 1932, and this earned the stone yet another name, *radio black*.

Champlain black is actually a limestone, and fossils are often present. They can include a rather characteristic gastropod, appearing like a white spiral, an inch or so in diameter. It is called *Maclurites* and is common in certain limestones deposited in the Champlain basin in Ordovician times, some 475 million years ago.

Attempts were made to reopen the Fisk quarry in 1995, but local opposition prevailed, and it is now preserved as an environmental interpretation center, famed for its fossils and wetland habitats. Other quarries are occasionally worked on a small scale.

GEOLOGICAL DESCRIPTION
Ordovician limestone rich in carbonaceous material from a reef deposit; fossils are common and include crinoids, corals, bryozoa and gastropods.

MAJOR USAGE
Floors, wall panels, chimneypieces, furniture.

Negro Marquina

SOURCE: Marquina and Aulestia, Vizcaya, Spain
STATUS: Actively quarried

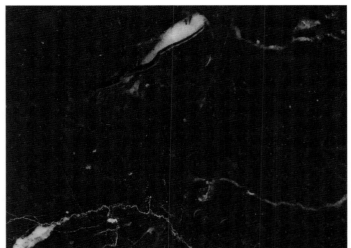

Oxf-DR1753

Not so many years ago, the black marble of Marquina was unknown outside Spain. Now it is one of the popular black decorative stones.

This black "marble" comes from the Basque Country, and has sometimes been sold as *negro Bilbao* or *Spanish black* marble. It is quarried near the town of Marquina (Markina in Basque) and the village of Aulestia. A recrystallized reef limestone, *negro Marquina* contains relics of fossils and white calcite veins. Some stone has just a few flecks of white, while other examples are very heavily veined. Strings of "en echelon veins," like those of *marmo Portoferraio*, are not uncommon.

This attractive stone was used in the Bilbao region for many years before it reached an international market. Today it is one of the most popular of black marbles, suitable for a wide range of domestic and business uses. It is routinely exported to many other countries including the United States. An excellent example is the Thomas V. Mike Miller, Jr., Senate Office Building in Annapolis, Maryland. When the building was renovated in 2001, *negro Marquina* was used in a checkerboard pattern with white *Carrara* marble for the floors, and surrounds a fine large floor mosaic of the state seal of Maryland.

GEOLOGICAL DESCRIPTION
Fine-grained Carboniferous black limestone with flecks and veins of white calcite. Crinoids, bivalves and other fossil fragments are abundant, and stylolites are common.

MAJOR USAGE
Paving, wall cladding and other architectural decoration, mainly in interior locations.

Imperial black marble

SOURCE: Thorn Hill, Grainger Co, Tennessee, United States
STATUS: Actively quarried

OxF-DR1811

A rather stagnant ancient sea floor still contained enough living creatures to stir up the sediments and give this stone its typical patchy coloring.

Few if any organisms can survive at the bottom of a deep, rather stagnant, murky sea, but pyrite, a mineral composed of iron sulfide, crystallizes readily in these conditions. It is richly abundant in *imperial black marble*, a limestone that formed in the depths of a sea that covered eastern Tennessee in mid-Cambrian times. The pyrite can sometimes occur in metallic-yellow patches, but mainly as minute crystals that give this stone its brownish black color. Its patchy appearance is due to worms and other organisms burrowing and stirring up the ancient sediments.

This popular black decorative stone is often used to contrast with the pink and white Tennessee marbles, and because it is a very durable stone that resists abrasion well, it is a good choice for either honed or polished floors. It features in many churches, banks and other public buildings around the United States—the internal flooring in the Clinton Library in Little Rock, Arkansas, for example—and for pillars and other decoration in the Cathedral of St. Peter in Chains in Cincinnati, Ohio. *Imperial black marble* is a very hard but popular medium for sculpture.

GEOLOGICAL DESCRIPTION

Black, fine-grained limestone of mid-Cambrian age, dolomitic in places, containing dispersed pyrite and fossils. Patchy coloration is due to bioturbation.

MAJOR USAGE

Flooring and other architectural applications; sculpture.

Marmo Portoferraio

SOURCE: Perhaps Portoferraio, Isle of Elba, Italy
STATUS: Quarries not known

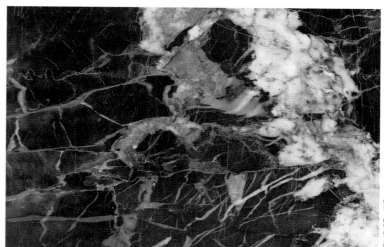

OxF-Corsi 129

This "Porto Ferrajo" marble is a bit of an enigma, for there do not seem to be any records of exactly where it was quarried.

Faustino Corsi had a black marble in his collection with distinctive staggered white veins and he said it came from Porto Ferrajo. Other 19th-century collections have the same stone, but to see it at its best it is necessary to go to the Dominican Church of Santa Maria sopra Minerva in Rome where there are eight large columns and other panels. Other buildings in Italy also have this stone, and it is found in inlaid tables of the 19th century in museums and private collections around the world.

Portoferraio is a town on Elba, an island famed for its iron mines that also had granite, marble and serpentinite quarries. However, no reference has been found to a black marble from Elba. The curved, overlapping white markings are what geologists call "tension cracks" or "en echelon veins." They are fractures formed when tectonic movements sheared and stretched the rock until it ruptured. The cavities were later infilled with white calcite. *Marmo Portoferraio* sometimes has very fine golden veins suggestive of *Portoro* or the black and yellow marble of Carrara; neither locality is too far from the Isle of Elba.

GEOLOGICAL DESCRIPTION

Fine-grained somewhat recrystallized black limestone with tension cracks filled with granular or fibrous white calcite, and with minor yellow siderite-filled stylolites and veins.

MAJOR USAGE

Columns and wall panels; inlays in furniture.

Grand antique, petit antique

SOURCE: Hautes-Pyrénées, France
STATUS: No longer quarried

grand antique Oxf–Corsi 125

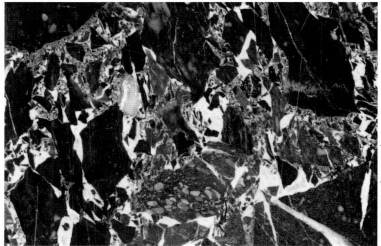

petit antique Oxf–Corsi 126

Grand antique is the famous old black and white breccia from the French Pyrenees, but *petit antique* can look very similar.

In French, this stone is known as *grand antique* or *grand deuil*; to the Italian scalpellini, it was *bianco e nero antico* or *marmo di Aquitania*. At its best, it is a striking combination of large and small angular fragments of pitch black limestone, cemented by pure white calcite, but fragments can be a uniform gray or dark brown, and then it is less distinctive. *Grand antique* comes from the Lez valley near Aubert, a village close to St. Girons in Midi-Pyrenees. *Petit antique* has smaller fragments of limestone that are both black and gray. It is also called *noir pompéen* or *Hèchettes*, and was quarried in the neighboring villages of Hèche and Hèchettes in Haute-Pyrénées.

It is well known that *grand antique* was quarried by the Romans from the third century CE and was very popular in the Byzantine era. It was particularly used for pillars and can be seen decorating that masterpiece of Byzantine architecture, Hagia Sophia, in Istanbul. It is likely that *petit antique* was also worked in ancient times, and the Roman name *marmor Celticum* was applicable to both. When the quarries closed later in the Byzantine era, the stones continued to be recycled by the Roman scalpellini,

and can be seen in many of the medieval and baroque churches of Rome. They were also employed in the pietre dure workshops.

Petit antique was quarried again in the time of the "Sun King," Louis XIV, and used for the bathroom walls in the Palace of Versailles and for decoration in the Church of La Madeleine in Paris. During the 18th century, the quarries at Aubert also reopened. In Les Invalides in Paris, the pillars around the altar in the chapel are twisted columns of *grand antique*, and the tomb of Joseph Napoleon Bonaparte is one of a number carved from this stone. Both marbles continued to be extracted well into the 20th century and as well as being widely used in France, they have been exported all over the world.

GEOLOGICAL DESCRIPTION

Lower Cretaceous tectonic breccias of black limestone clasts in a white calcite matrix. *Petit antique* has gray limestone clasts too, and is more heavily crushed.

MAJOR USAGE

Columns, wall claddings and other architectural decoration; chimneypieces, tabletops and pietre dure work.

ABOVE *Grand antique* borders this late 16th-century Italian pietre dure tabletop.

LEFT The plinth of the statue of St. Peter in Westminster Cathedral, London, is *grand antique* marble.

When marble becomes too costly to buy, then in time-honored tradition, it is faked. There are two ways to replicate decorative stones. Faux marble is a surface finish made to look like natural stone. Scagliola is made by coloring and mixing plasters to resemble marble, and can be used in thin layers or carved to make three-dimensional objects.

Throughout the history of interior decoration there have been people with far greater aspirations than the financial means to achieve them. If precious marbles could not be afforded, then well-executed copies would suffice admirably. Fake marble is by no means uncommon even in the most prestigious buildings. It has other advantages. Sometimes the kind of marble most appropriate to the building or a restoration project is simply no longer available, and a replica is needed. Real marble pillars may be too heavy for a structure, and hollow columns coated with plaster to resemble natural stone can provide a much lighter alternative.

Creating something that looks so realistic that it can be passed off as the real thing takes time, skill and experience. It requires an artistic eye, technical knowledge of the ingredients used and a good understanding of the structures and patterns that give each natural marble its individual appearance. Such skilled artisanry does not come cheaply.

PAINTS AND GLAZES

The finest marbles have a subtle translucency to them, and to capture this quality in faux marble, color is applied within a series of glazes. Any well-prepared surface—paper, wood, stone, plaster or metal—can be marbled, and as the ancient Romans had discovered long ago, even a plain white marble could be embellished to resemble the more luxurious colored stones. The faux marbler's tool kit includes brushes, goose feathers, combs, scrumpled bags, sponges and the all-important paints and glazes. Basecoats are applied and blended, and then patterning is added. Drawing a flat-toothed comb through the colored glaze gives the impression of laminations. Veins are painted in with brushes or goose feathers. Mottled stones such as porphyries are simulated by spattering colored paints. At each step, artificial looking patterns and textures are gently blended away. The buildup of layers of glaze gives the impression of translucency seen in real marble.

WORKING IN THREE DIMENSIONS

The replication of marble runs deeper in scagliola, a technique that was perfected in baroque Italy and practiced all over Europe in the 18th and 19th centuries. During the 19th and early 20th centuries, scagliola was widely used in public buildings and wealthier homes of the United States. Because the marble patterning traverses the whole depth of the simulated stone, scagliola is less easily scratched or damaged than faux marble. Scagliola paste is a mixture of plaster or gypsum, pigment and glue; ground marble may also be added. Different colored pastes are combined to show the various colorings of natural stone. Colored veins are traditionally added by drawing silk threads laden with pigment through the paste. The pastes can be set in molds or spread in thin sheets and applied while they are still malleable to floors, walls and columns. Once they have set completely, they can be cut and polished in much the same way as real stone.

Scagliola has been used for inlays that resemble Florentine pietre dure work in all their beauty and complexity. These must be hand-tinted using methods that are still practiced today. The scagliola technique is of special interest to conservators, for it is found in many buildings that are now undergoing restoration. For those with vision, it can be used to create futuristic marblelike designs impossible to create using real stone.

RIGHT Recent scagliola columns and walls by expert Richard Ferroze in the Brompton Oratory in London.

LEFT Scagliola pillars and floors at Syon House in London.
RIGHT Artist creating a faux marble floor.

Portoro

SOURCE: La Spezia region, Liguria, Italy
STATUS: Some quarrying still takes place

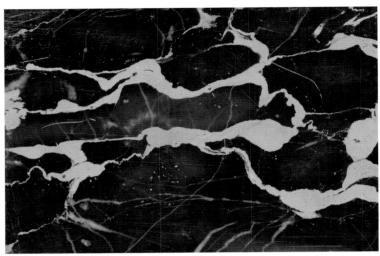

Oxf-Corsi 133

Gold veining in a black marble gives an appearance of opulence, and this classic Italian marble has been much prized by marble lovers since baroque times.

The word *portoro* comes from Porto d'Oro, an old name for the area of La Spezia, Liguria, famed for its beautiful black and gold marble. In the past the term was used for any similar colored marbles but nowadays it is used exclusively for the Ligurian stones. The quarries are at Portovenere, Lerici and on the Island of Palmaria. Quarrying began on a significant scale toward the end of the 16th century. The high cost and some difficulty working the stone reduced its popularity in Italy, so it was mainly exported to France and England. During the 18th and 19th centuries and art nouveau period of the 20th century, it was widely used for chimneypieces, and for tabletops and inlaying in other furniture. Quarrying continues on a smaller scale today.

Portoro is used extensively in the interior of the Church of La Madeleine in Paris, completed in 1842. The traditional store façade of the "House of Gentlemen" in Kohlmarkt, Vienna, is an eye-catching use of this stone.

GEOLOGICAL DESCRIPTION

A fine-grained black calcitic marble of Triassic age, colored by finely disseminated organic matter. It is crossed by sinuous parallel fracture zones, slender veins and stylolites. These contain granular calcite, yellow to brown where ferruginous clay is also present; elsewhere, white.

MAJOR USAGE

Wall cladding, sculpture, chimneypieces, tabletops and inlays.

LEFT A triptych of *portoro* paneling fronts this altar in the Chapel of the Holy Souls in Westminster Cathedral.

Giallo e nero di Carrara

SOURCE: Carrara, Tuscany, Italy
STATUS: No longer quarried

Oxf-Corsi 131

It is surprising that such a distinctive and strikingly beautiful stone should have twice been the subject of mistaken identity.

Corsi, in his published catalog, believed it was the marble with veins similar to gold which, according to the ancient author Pliny, came from Rhodes. But Pliny's stone was a kind of *bigio morato* with yellow veining, quite unlike Corsi's sample. This error was being perpetuated in publications as late as the 1960s, and many samples of yellow and black marble in old collections are incorrectly labeled *marmor Rhodium*.

Others have assumed that it is *portoro* from Portovenere (see opposite) but are puzzled as to how the mask of Pope Paul III in St. Peter's Basilica in the Vatican, carved from this stone by Guglielmo Della Porta (ca. 1515–77), could predate the opening of the *portoro* quarries. Corsi's sample was identified as coming from Carrara by marble expert William Brindley in the early 20th century (a view supported by a small hand-painted illustration of a *Carrara* stone in Adam Wirsing's treatise on marbles of 1775). Small amounts of *portor* came from the Monte Arme and other Tuscan quarries, but probably only until the early 19th century; later stones were very inferior.

GEOLOGICAL DESCRIPTION

Fine-grained weakly metamorphosed limestone of Triassic or early Jurassic age, with orange-yellow and white calcite veins. The orange color is due to iron oxides disseminated in the calcite.

MAJOR USAGE

Decorative panels and slabs; memorials; Florentine pietre dure furniture and Roman inlaid tabletops of the 17th, 18th and early 19th centuries.

Noir St. Laurent

SOURCE: Laurens, near Béziers, Herault, France
STATUS: Actively quarried

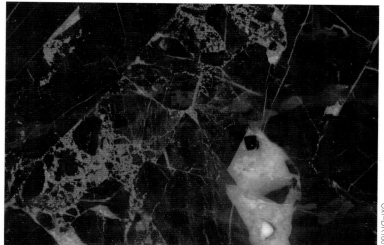

Oxf-DR1801

Noir St. Laurent is a warm black stone with very delicate veining. It's the kind of marble often seen decorating high-end hotels.

Noir St. Laurent, a Devonian limestone, is currently quarried in Laurens, near Béziers in France. It is black with veins that are mainly white, but can also be yellow and occasionally a bright orange-red. It often contains fragments of mollusk shells. This attractive stone has been worked since the 1950s, perhaps earlier. Good examples can be seen in the hall of the Crédit Agricole Bank, at Montparnasse, in Paris, France, and in the interiors of various hotels including the Conrad Hilton in Hong Kong and the Ritz Carlton in Seoul.

A very similar stone from Morocco is traded as *port laurent*, a strategic play on the names of two better known stones. Both *noir St. Laurent* and *port laurent* look black at first, but when they are placed next to the black and yellow limestones from Italy, they seem to have a distinctly brown tint.

GEOLOGICAL DESCRIPTION

Brownish-black ferruginous limestone of Devonian age, containing fragments of mollusk shells and other fossils. It is crossed by white, yellow or orange angular calcite-filled veins and cream-colored stylolites.

MAJOR USAGE

Tiles, countertops, cladding and other mainly interior architectural elements.

King gold

SOURCE: Baluchistan, Pakistan
STATUS: Actively quarried

Courtesy of Monica Price

LEFT Black and yellow *king gold* marble is made into many small decorative pieces, such as this obelisk and tealight holder.

There must be millions of people with a little piece of *king gold* marble in their homes, perhaps a trinket or a vase.

Pakistan has been particularly successful at producing small marble ornaments that sell well in department stores, everything from tealight holders to bookends, vases to paperweights, and the ubiquitous polished eggs. A range of these are made with *king gold*, a stone that is also traded as *black and gold*.

It comes from Baluchistan, Pakistan. Although it is usually classed as a black marble, it is in fact a ferruginous limestone, and the groundmass is distinctly brown. The golden color is present in large patches, veins and stylolites.

Pakistan has large reserves of decorative stones, and is meeting the challenge of working these on a sound commercial basis. Traditional methods of cutting stone using explosives are very wasteful, but the installation of modern diamond wire saws,

though making huge improvements to productivity, requires considerable financial investment. *King gold* is fabricated for architectural applications, and it will be interesting to see how sales of this product grow.

GEOLOGICAL DESCRIPTION

Ferruginous limestone; the golden color is present in large patches, veins and stylolites. White calcite veins are commonly present.

MAJOR USAGE

Tiles, countertops and architectural elements; vases, candle holders and other small decorative items.

Other gray and black marbles and limestones

Gray marbles are very common, coming from many quarries that also produce white marble in Italy, Greece, Turkey and many other countries around the world. A gray and white striped marble from Mount Hymetos in Attica, Greece, has a finer grain and softer bluish gray coloration than *Proconnesian marble*. *Chillagoe marble* from Queensland and *Wombeyan marble* from New South Walesare two of the better known decorative stones from Australia. Large deposits of *Chillagoe gray* are worked for architectural applications but also made into tourist souvenirs.

The black stones are normally limestones and rarely completely lack fossils. *Irish black* marble can easily be confused with *Poolvash* marble from the Isle of Man, which was used in London, Liverpool and other cities particularly in the 18th century. *Negro*

Monterrey, also called *Mexico black*, is a very fine limestone from Monterrey, Mexico. In past times, a brittle black marble was obtained in Carrara, Italy, from the Colonnata quarry.

White-veined black limestone from the Pas de Calais in France was known as *grand antique de nord*. A stone that closely resembles *negro Marquina* is called *taurus black* and is quarried at Kayseri, Develi, and other locations in Turkey. Iran also has good black limestones with white veins, referenced by code numbers. Black marbles with yellow and white veins known as *portoro leonardo* come from Namibia and the Dominican Republic, and a smoky-brown stone with white, orange and red veins called *mystique dark* comes from China. Gold veins can occur sporadically in white-veined black stones.

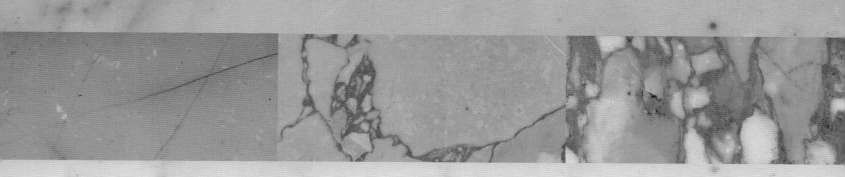

Yellow and brown marbles and limestones

Although most of the stones in this section are classified as "marbles" in the stone trade, nearly all of them are limestones that take a good polish. Cream and beige limestones are extremely common all over the world, so only a small selection can be included here. Their understated color makes them very popular for flooring and interior cladding of buildings. By contrast, richly colored yellow stones are more ostentatious but much less common. The finest ones come from Siena in Italy and Chemtou in Tunisia, and their golden coloring has often been used to embellish churches and palaces. Landscape and ruin marbles are the most curious group of stones in this section. They have formed from the muddy sediments at the bottom of ancient seas. More recent weathering allowed iron and manganese oxides to appear in patterns uncannily resembling ruined buildings, bushes and trees (see pages 100–1).

Giallo antico

SOURCE: Chemtou, Jendouba, Tunisia
STATUS: Sporadically quarried

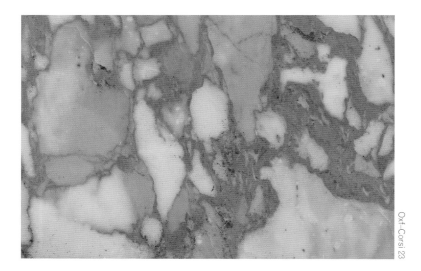

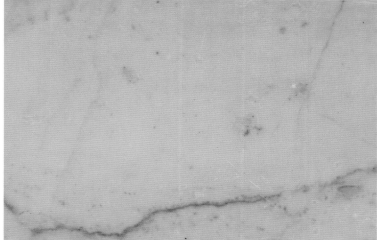

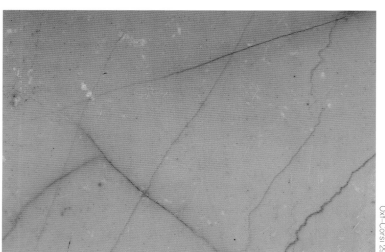

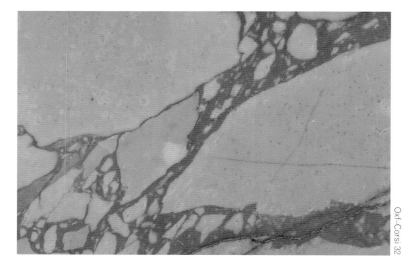

"Gold," "saffron" and "ivory" are all accurate descriptions of this gloriously colored marble. It was one of the most highly prized of all marbles in ancient times, and the quarries were held as Imperial property.

The stone now known as *giallo antico* was quarried from the second century BCE to third century CE, near the ancient Roman city of Simitthus, a place now called Chemtou in Tunisia. Pliny called it *marmor numidicum*, commenting that the revenues of Numidia (as the region was then called) used to lie in the trading of wild beasts and yellow marble. The quarries were worked by a large unskilled labor force of convicts and slaves.

Little *giallo antico* is ever seen in archaeological sites in Tunisia. It was extracted specifically for shipping to Ostia and Rome, and from there it was sent out to ornament building projects in many places around the Mediterranean. By contrast, an attractive yellow marble from Algeria, which has also been referred to as *giallo antico* (see page 113), was only used near the quarries.

Giallo antico from Chemtou could be worked into very large columns, and some of the best examples can be seen in the Pantheon in Rome. Seven of the eight columns in the Arch of Constantine are made of this stone; the eighth was removed and is now in the Basilica of St. John in Lateran. *Giallo antico* was also used for paving and wall cladding, veneers and sculptures.

Some examples of *giallo antico* are monochrome, the color varying from almost white through clear yellow to dark orange-brown. Others are clearly brecciated, with large and small angular fragments cemented by an orange-brown or red matrix. The whole stone may be suffused a warm salmon-pink. *Giallo antico*

has a subtle translucency, and takes a beautiful polish.

The ancient quarries were accidentally rediscovered when the railroad between Algeria and Tunis was constructed in 1876. They were reopened, and were worked sporadically up to recent times. The staircase of the National Gallery in London was decorated with this stone, and has recently been restored with new stone from the same quarries. It has been argued that the production of *giallo antico* declined in the third century CE, as reserves of the best colored stone were depleted. Certainly the color of the stone obtained in recent times has rarely matched that which was quarried in antiquity.

ABOVE Massive paired monolithic *giallo antico* columns in the Pantheon in Rome. Built as a Roman temple and later consecrated as a Catholic church, the only natural light enters through the center of the dome, illuminating the walls and floors of porphyry, granite and yellow marble.

GEOLOGICAL DESCRIPTION

A brecciated fine-grained calcareous limestone of Jurassic age.

MAJOR USAGE

Pillars, paving and other architectural elements; sculpture.

Giallo di Siena

SOURCE: Siena, Tuscany, Italy
STATUS: Actively quarried

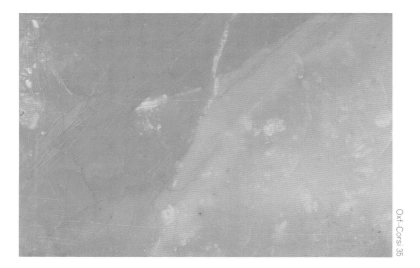

Oxf-Corsi 35

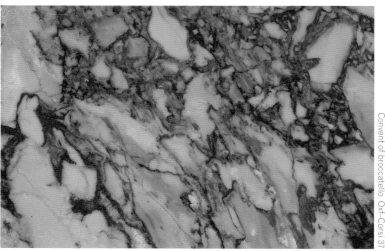

Convent of broccatello Oxf-Corsi 37

ABOVE Marbles from Siena are used in pavements of the city's cathedral. The section shown here portrays the Massacre of the Innocents.

The famous egg-yolk yellow marble of Siena had been used extensively all across Italy and farther afield since at least the 16th century. At its finest, it rivals the famous *giallo antico* of Tunisia for translucency and richness of color.

The best stone has come from Montarrenti in the Montagnola Senese Mountains, near the town of Sovicille. Monochrome yellow stone has always been the most highly prized of the Siena marbles and can be dark or pale yellow. *Convent Siena*, also known as *broccatello di Siena*, is very beautiful too. It is a breccia of yellow fragments that are tinted violet in places, in a rich, deep violet matrix. The name comes from the Convent of Montarrenti, which used to own the lands on which this stone was quarried.

A much rarer Siena marble with yellow marble fragments in a chocolate-brown matrix was used in furniture and inlay work of the early 19th century. The ancient *breccia dorata* (see opposite) was also obtained from Montagnola Senese.

"The quarries do not seem to have been properly opened up," wrote one English stone merchant in 1887, "they are so many scratches on the side of the mountains, and very few large blocks are produced." From this primitive record, quarrying methods modernized in the 20th century, and Siena marble was exported all over the world. There are 24 columns of Siena marble in the Court Chamber of the U.S. Supreme Court in Washington, D.C. It is also used extensively in the rich marble decoration of the Birmingham Oratory in England, built in the early 1900s.

Breccia dorata

SOURCE: Montagnola Senese, Siena, Italy
STATUS: Used in antiquity; not quarried today

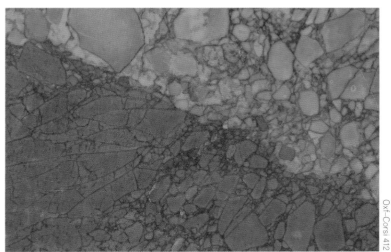

Oxf-Corsi 412

The beautiful golden breccia of antiquity, called *breccia dorata*, puzzled archaeologists for many years. Where did it come from?

Archaeologists excavated *breccia dorata* in Rome and Ostia, but were puzzled by its origins. The puzzle was solved in 1995 by stone experts Matthias Bruno and Lorenzo Lazzarini. They had seen this stone in a plaque ornamenting the confessional in the Basilica of Santa Maria Maggiore and noticed that some fragments in the stone were yellow and others were gray. As both colors were to be seen in varieties of marble from the quarries of Montagnola Senese, they decided to compare the stones using a petrological microscope. The structures and mineral compositions matched well.

In a typical *breccia dorata* the fragments are mainly yellow but some shade to white or gray. They are cemented by small amounts of orange, red or violet matrix. Other varieties have gray or pink fragments. When Bruno and Lazzarini went to the quarries of the famous *giallo di Siena* in search of *breccia dorata*, they were successful, finding beds of the breccia in the Tegoia and Molli quarries, and in outcrops close to the quarry road.

GEOLOGICAL DESCRIPTION

Breccia of weakly metamorphosed fine-grained limestone fragments of lower Jurassic age. The yellow color is due to finely disseminated goethite. The matrix is rich in goethite or hematite. Stylolites are common, and white calcite-filled fractures may be present.

MAJOR USAGE

Small plaques and columns; inlays in tabletops, slabs in decorative stone collections.

GEOLOGICAL DESCRIPTION

Giallo di Siena is a fine-grained calcareous limestone of Jurassic age, weakly metamorphosed in Eocene times. It is colored by finely disseminated goethite and contains abundant stylolites and some white calcite-filled veins. *Convent Siena* has angular fragments of *giallo di Siena* clasts in a hematite-rich calcareous matrix.

MAJOR USAGE

Interior use, including columns, flooring, wall cladding, staircases and ballustrades, and other architectural features; fireplaces, furniture, inlay and small decorative items.

YELLOW AND BROWN MARBLES AND LIMESTONES

Giallo di Verona

SOURCE: Verona, Trento and Vicenza, Italy
STATUS: Some varieties actively quarried

Oxf-Corsi 42

It may be the poor relative of the famous marbles from Siena and Tunisia, but *giallo di Verona* is still one of the richest colored of the yellow decorative stones.

The yellow limestones quarried in the province of Verona and neighboring regions of Trento and Vicenza are collectively known as *giallo di Verona* and locally as *nembri*. They range from pale cream through to dark ocherous-yellow. Traditionally the best golden-yellow stone has come from Mori, Bretonico and Torri del Benaco on the coast of Lake Garda.

Typical *giallo di Verona* features are a nodular structure, plenty of brown stylolites and variable quantities of fossil fragments. It lacks the translucency of the fine yellow marbles from Siena and Tunisia; nevertheless it has been popular since medieval times and is used extensively in the buildings of Italy. Fine pillars can be seen in the Cathedral of Verona, constructed in the 14th century. In the early 1900s, considerable quantities were exported overseas. Large columns can be seen in Westminster Cathedral, London. The stone also decorates the walls of the Hearing Room in the Wisconsin State Capitol, and was used for the altar rails of the Basilica of St. John the Baptist in Newfoundland, Canada.

Giallo reale is the trade name for a popular variety of *giallo di Verona* quarried in Selva di Progno and Roverè, northeast of Verona. It is yellow, mottled with pink. The creamy-white *bianco perlino*, quarried in Asiago, Vicenza, is very subtly colored.

GEOLOGICAL DESCRIPTION

Late Jurassic or early Cretaceous nodular marly limestone with ammonites, bivalves and other fossils. It often shows evidence of extensive burrowing. Brown goethite-rich stylolites are abundant.

ABOVE *Giallo di Verona* pillars flank the main altar of Westminster Cathedral in London. *Verde antico* and *breccia di Seravezza* feature in the panels below.

MAJOR USAGE

Interior paving, staircases, pillars, balustrades, wall cladding; also used in furniture.

Breccia nuvolata

SOURCE: Harmanköy, Bythinia, Turkey
STATUS: Used in antiquity and reused in later times

Oxf–Corsi 137

The distinctive parallel waves of yellow spreading across this ancient marble reminded the Italian stonecutters of "nuvoli"—clouds—hence the name.

Breccia nuvolata was used by the ancient Romans from the second century CE, mainly for cladding the walls of prestigious buildings. It has been found in excavations in Italy, Tunisia, Algeria and Libya. Leptis Magna, near Al-Khums in Libya, is a beautifully preserved ancient Roman city, and the walls of the Serapeum (Temple of Serapis) are clad with *breccia nuvolata*.

As this stone was so often used in north Africa, it was thought to have been quarried there. But the stone has certain features that are very similar to *breccia corallina* and detailed scientific analyses confirmed the two stones originated from the same geological deposit. In 1997, a search for the ancient quarries uncovered them near the village of Harmanköy in Bythinia (not far from Gölpazari's well-preserved *breccia corallina* quarries). Modern quarrying had destroyed the ancient workings near Harmanköy, but *breccia nuvolata* could still be collected.

Fragments of *breccia nuvolata* are creamy-white stained with waves of yellow and pink. The dark coral-pink matrix is not seen if a sample is cut from one large fragment of limestone (see above).

GEOLOGICAL DESCRIPTION

Breccia of Upper Cretaceous limestone clasts in a dark pink or red hematitic matrix. The yellow banding is where iron has been released and redeposited in yellow goethite-rich bands by percolating groundwater.

MAJOR USAGE

Wall cladding; reused in inlaid tabletops and stone collections.

Crema Valencia

SOURCE: Barxeta, Valencia, Spain
STATUS: Actively quarried

Oxf–DR1370

Sunny yellow, marked with orange-red wiggly lines, this popular Spanish marble comes from Valencia, a part of Spain most people associate with sunshine and vacations.

Although referred to as a marble, *crema Valencia* is a yellow limestone crossed by a lattice of sinuously curving stylolites that look like orange-red veins. It contains fossils, but they are rarely very conspicuous.

Crema Valencia is quarried in the Sierra del Buscarró close to the village of Barxeta in Valencia, Spain. Quarrying for marble in this region goes back to Roman times, and the stone has been used extensively in the churches of Valencia and elsewhere in Spain. It is sometimes found in 19th-century fireplaces and furniture, but most of its use outside Spain dates to the latter half of the 20th century.

Occasionally, the stone is pink rather than yellow when it may be traded as *rosa Valencia* or *rosa Buscarro*. Yellow limestones from Var, France, can resemble the usual yellow varieties of *crema Valencia*.

GEOLOGICAL DESCRIPTION

Cretaceous yellow limestone crossed by red hematite-bearing stylolites.

MAJOR USAGE

Interior flooring, wall cladding, bathroom surfaces and other architectural elements.

Giallo tigrato

SOURCE: Monte Calvo, Lazio, Italy
STATUS: Exact site of quarries unknown

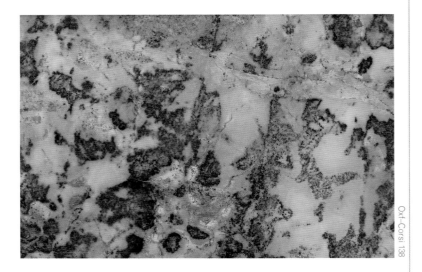

More like a leopard's spots than a tiger's stripes, the dark mottling of this yellow stone nevertheless gives this stone the name *giallo tigrato*.

Some examples of this stone are yellow, patchily speckled with dark brown iron oxide. Others are yellow and creamy white, the yellow patches rimmed with dark mottling, just like the markings of a leopard. Before 1824, *giallo tigrato* was only known from two small plaques in the Church of Sant'Andrea della Valle and a sepulcher in the Church of Santa Maria Maggiore, both in Rome. Then in 1824, an excavation led by the Roman archaeologist Francesco Caprenesi at Monte Calvo, on the road from Rome to Rieti, revealed several more columns.

These were recycled by the scalpellini (stonecutters) of Rome to make items such as a fine two-handled vase now in the Vatican Museum, tablets for inlaid tabletops and the various samples now found in collections of historic marbles such as Corsi's at the Natural History Museum in Oxford, England. Corsi caused some confusion by incorrectly naming the stone *marmor Corinthium*, because he believed it matched the description of a marble of that name made by medieval scholar Isidor of Seville. The stone is certainly not from Corinth, and the source is now believed to be Monte Calvo in Italy.

GEOLOGICAL DESCRIPTION

Ferruginous limestone or limestone breccia with abundant dendritic growths of goethite and manganese oxides.

MAJOR USAGE

Used in antiquity for columns; vases and inlay work using recycled stone. Corsi mentions its suitability for animal carvings.

Breccia corallina giallastra

SOURCE: Not known
STATUS: Used in antiquity

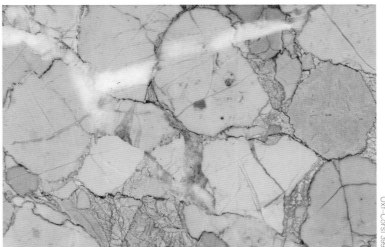

Although it shares the same name as the famous *breccia corallina* of Bythinia in Turkey, this stone's origins are rather more mysterious.

Nineteenth-century collector Faustino Corsi considered this distinctive stone to be a *breccia traccagnina*, one of the "harlequin breccias" found in the ruins of Rome, for which the quarry location is not known. Raniero Gnoli's 1971 treatise on the marbles of Rome called it *breccia corallina giallastra* and this is the name by which it is now more widely known.

Existing fragments are pale gray, buff and ivory colors, and are cemented by white calcite. Red or brown stylolites form the margins of the fragments, giving them a distinctly wiggly appearance. The whole stone is crossed by veins of white calcite.

Breccia corallina giallastra may be found in archaeological excavations, and it has been recycled by the scalpellini of Rome. Rare larger examples of this stone are two pillars in the 18th-century monument to Mariano Benedetti in the Church of Santa Maria Maggiore in Rome. More often it is encountered in inlaid marble tabletops and in collections of ancient marble slabs.

GEOLOGICAL DESCRIPTION

Breccia of limestone clasts with stylolitic boundaries in a hematitic matrix. Abundant fractures are filled with white calcite.

MAJOR USAGE

Mainly in inlaid tabletops and in collections of ancient marbles.

Vratza

SOURCE: Vratza, Bulgaria
STATUS: Actively quarried

Vienna's cube-shaped Leopold Museum is an excellent place to admire paintings by acclaimed Austrian artist Egon Schiele. It is also a great place to see a lot of the Bulgarian *Vratza* limestone, as it is built entirely of this stone.

Vratza is particularly robust and frost-resistant. This is one reason why it is a familiar sight in many countries of central and northern Europe, where it has been used both as a constructional and facing stone since the late 19th century. With its muted color and indistinct patterning, it does little to attract attention. Since the 1990s, the stone industry in Bulgaria has burgeoned and *Vratza* is now exported all over the world. Many good examples of this stone can be seen in Sofia, Bulgaria. They include the National Bank, the National Palace of Culture and the U.S. Embassy. In Neasden, London, large quantities of Vratza were used in the construction of the Shri Swaminarayan Mandir Hindu Temple. The stone was transported first to India for carving and then shipped to England for assembly.

Vratza is quarried near the villages of Gorna Kremena and Varbeshnitsa, a few miles from the town of Vratza (Vratsa) in Bulgaria. It is cream or beige, with scattered slightly darker patches. In German-speaking countries, *Vratza* is often called *Donaukalk*, named after the River Danube. A more fossiliferous variety is traded as *Donau Muschelkalk*.

GEOLOGICAL DESCRIPTION
Cretaceous siliceous limestone.

MAJOR USAGE
Interior and exterior flooring, wall cladding; sculpture, memorials.

Jerusalem stone

SOURCE: Palestine and Israel
STATUS: Actively quarried

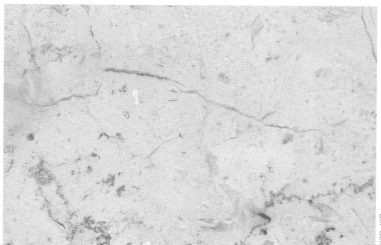

The whole city of Jerusalem appears gold when its buildings, constructed of local limestones, are bathed in morning or evening sunlight.

The name *Jerusalem stone* is given to various limestones quarried in Israel and Palestine, from Mitzpe Ramon in the south, through the Hebron Valley, Bethlehem, Jerusalem and farther north to the Galilee area. The best place to see these stones is in Jerusalem. Between 1917 and 1948, when the city was under British rule, all façades of new buildings had to be built of local limestones. These are mostly yellow or light brown, but sometimes pink or gray. In low sunlight the stone appears golden, which is why Jerusalem is often described as "the golden city."

Much *Jerusalem stone* is exported to the United States under various trade names, and its association with the Jewish faith has resulted in its use in many synagogues and memorials. Huge quantities of stone in a variety of different finishes were used to decorate the Commodore Uriah P. Levy Center and Chapel in the U.S. Naval Academy at Annapolis, Maryland, completed in 2005. The Holocaust Memorial in Miami, Florida, and the auditorium of the Holocaust Museum in Washington, D.C., also feature *Jerusalem stone*. Its attractive coloring and durable nature have made it appealing for both public buildings and private houses.

GEOLOGICAL DESCRIPTION
Calcareous or dolomitic Mesozoic limestones; fossiliferous in places, with abundant red or brown stylolites, and calcite-filled fractures.

MAJOR USAGE
Wall cladding, flooring; memorial stones; sculpture.

Crema marfil

SOURCE: Sierra del Reclot, Alicante Province, Spain
STATUS: Actively quarried

Oxf-DR1788

Modern minimalist architects delight in creating interior spaces that look light, cool and uncluttered. *Crema marfil*—meaning "ivory cream" in Spanish—is an ideal choice for such designs.

Of the many cream- and beige-colored stones available on the commercial market, *crema marfil* has become one of the most popular. It takes a good polish, so it is marketed as a marble, although it is a pale-colored limestone.

Crema marfil has been extracted since 1950 from the huge Monte Coto quarry that lies between Pinoso and La Algueña, in the Sierra del Reclot. Huge quantities are produced each year and exported for building projects worldwide. It can be seen in such random places as the Meadowhall shopping mall in Sheffield, England, and in Lanzarote Airport's passenger terminal in the Canary Islands.

GEOLOGICAL DESCRIPTION

Fine-grained compact Eocene limestone, creamy-white with darker-colored veins and stylolites. Large foraminifera known as nummulites and alveolines are often visible.

MAJOR USAGE

Flooring, cladding, fireplaces and other interior furnishings.

Palombino antico

SOURCE: Various sources
STATUS: Used in antiquity

Oxf-Corsi 13

The ring-necked dove is called "palombo" in Italy, and anyone who has seen the color of its plumage will understand how the pale buff-colored *palombino* marble got its name.

Creamy-white and buff-colored limestones are very common, and it is likely that stones referred to as *palombino* have come from a number of different places. In Italy, both Tolfa and Subiaco in Lazio are sources of limestones known as *palombino marble*.

The astute 19th-century collector Faustino Corsi believed the *palombini* referred to by Romans came from Turkey or Egypt. For the former, he cites the Roman author Pliny's description of a marble found on the banks of a river rising in Phrygia that had the color and texture of ivory, and was only available in small pieces. He points out that there are no large items made of *palombino antico* in Rome. He thought Egypt was the source of the sample shown here because an Egyptian idol made of this stone could be seen in the Vatican Museum. Similar limestones from the Eastern Desert were certainly used by the ancient Egyptians.

Palombino antico is used a great deal in the mosaics and marble paving of ancient Rome. It is fine-grained and compact, and it can be cut into small geometric shapes. It has also been used for figures depicted in inlay work, such as wall panels found in the ruins of Pompeii. Sculptures and vases are occasionally carved from *palombino*.

GEOLOGICAL DESCRIPTION

Fine-grained compact calcareous or dolomitic limestones.

MAJOR USAGE

Interior paving, mosaics, vases and sculptures.

Alberese

SOURCE: Val d'Arno, Tuscany, Italy
STATUS: Still collected on an informal basis

Oxf-Corsi 524

Nature has painted the most exquisitely delicate trees and shrubs on this creamy-white limestone, turning a mundane building stone into a thing of special beauty.

The "trees" are growths of tiny crystals composed of black and brown oxides, and are referred to as "dendrites." The name Alberese comes from the Italian "albero," meaning "tree," because this geological formation often contains dendrites. These are quite common in fine-grained muddy limestones and marls, and form where iron and manganese oxides are deposited by groundwater percolating through cracks and joints in the rock.

The Alberese limestone has been used extensively for building and decoration in the area of Tuscany around Florence and Prato since at least medieval times. The finest slabs would be carefully polished and incorporated in inlaid tabletops and other decorative items, and are often found in marble collections. Faustino Corsi, the 19th-century collector, described the sample of Alberese shown here as "canary yellow ground with tall trees resembling the fir," and said it came from Ponte a Rignano in the valley of the River Arno, a location about 6 miles (10 km) from Florence.

GEOLOGICAL DESCRIPTION

Marly limestone from the Upper Cretaceous Alberese Formation, with dendritic growths of goethite and manganese oxides.

MAJOR USAGE

Inlay work, marble collections.

Cotham marble

SOURCE: Cotham, Bristol, England
STATUS: Small quantities collected from working quarries and coastal exposures

Oxf-Geol.

A leafy suburb of Bristol, England, Cotham is home to a burgeoning student population, but some 203 million years ago it was a shallow salty lagoon, home to colonies of algae.

For centuries the curious *Cotham marble* was regarded as the epitome of a "landscape marble." Rounded cushion-shaped masses of the marble are found in a bed of rock that outcrops from south Wales through Bristol and Taunton, down to the Dorset coast of England. The landscape pattern forms a band an inch or so deep, with a darker "hedge" and "trees," against a pale background, all covered by a finely banded brown "mantle." The pattern may be repeated two or three times vertically, especially in samples from the Bristol area. The first description of *Cotham marble* was by Edward Owen in 1754, and the stone was used in the ornamentation of the exterior of Cotham House in the early 19th century. Other uses were mainly for interior decoration, but marble collector John Watson was to write in 1916 that the stone was so rare, most examples were reserved for museums.

Polished slabs were also much sought after by geologists, who conjectured how the stone had formed. It was not until the early 1960s that the mystery was solved, and now *Cotham marble* is recognized as ancient stromatolites (see page 100), formed by microorganisms living in an ancient tropical intertidal lagoon. Small quantities of this fascinating stone are still cut and polished to make paperweights and obelisks.

GEOLOGICAL DESCRIPTION

Upper Triassic calcareous mudstone with stromatolites.

MAJOR USAGE

Decorative slabs and paperweights.

"It seems that this stone may have been made to indulge nature's sense of humor," wrote Faustino Corsi, the famous 19th-century collector, when he introduced the different varieties of landscape marble in his collection catalog. The fantastic patterns resembling hedges, trees, castles and cloudy skies have long been a subject of curiosity and amusement, but just how did they form?

HEDGES AND TREES

The tree- and hedgelike markings seen in *Cotham marble* owe their origins to cyanobacteria (formerly called blue-green algae). These microscopic organisms have inhabited our planet since Precambrian times, and helped generate the oxygen in the atmosphere that supports life on Earth today. Cyanobacteria are found in many different environments on land and under the sea. They thrive in inhospitable salty tidal lagoons, and if the temperature is warm and the water movement is gentle, they form dome-shaped mounds known as stromatolites. They do this by generating mats of sticky mucus-covered filaments that trap fine particles of mud. The cyanobacteria then move up to colonize the new surface

and generate more filaments, which in turn trap more mud particles. This cycle of events gives stromatolites their characteristic layered appearance. Some cyanobacteria also draw calcium carbonate from seawater as they photosynthesize, and this helps to cement the sediments in the stromatolite.

Cotham marble is a stromatolitic limestone formed in the muddy intertidal zone of the ancient Rhaetic sea, some 203 million years ago. The hedge- and treelike patterns are the structures of different kinds of cyanobacteria colonies, growing upward through trapped mud to reach the light and air. The thin layers of "mantle" that cover the "trees" are mats of bacterial filaments and trapped mud grains.

The delicate black and brown tree markings in Alberese limestone have a very different and entirely inorganic origin. When water containing dissolved iron and manganese percolates through a porous fine-grained rock, it deposits minute crystals of brown iron oxides and black manganese oxides in treelike patterns known as dendrites. Sometimes the dendrites form on broken surfaces, at other times they follow natural joints where the rock tends to split, and in other cases

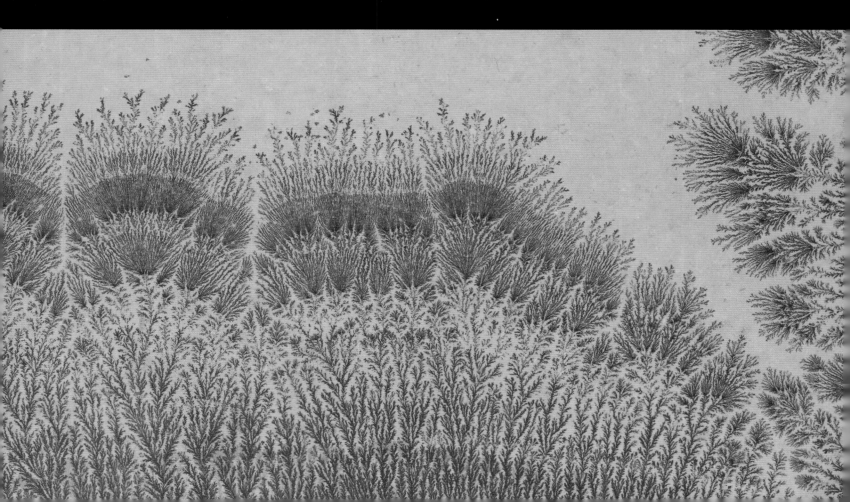

RIGHT The shapes of "buildings" in *pietra paesina* are defined by microscopic fractures running through the rock.

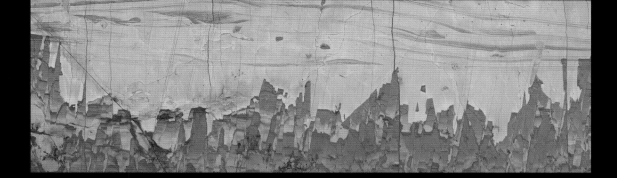

RIGHT The shapes of "buildings" in *pietra paesina* are defined by microscopic fractures running through the rock.

they permeate randomly through the stone. Dendrites are a very common form of natural crystal growth: frost on a window pane, the "moss" in a moss agate, the intergrowth of metals in many alloys, or the delicate tree patterns seen in Alberese and other fine-grained limestones, are all examples of dendritic growth.

CASTLES AND TOWERS

Like the "trees" in Alberese limestone, the castles and towers in *pietra paesina* formed much more recently than the rock itself (see page 102). In fact they are only seen in boulders of stone that have been weathered by rainwater. The boulders are a marly limestone containing finely disseminated iron minerals. As rainwater seeps through cracks, it is sucked into the porous rock and converts the iron minerals to brown iron oxide in much the same way that rust forms. The iron oxide diffuses outward in waves giving alternate dark and light bands. Scientists refer to these bands as "Liesegang rings," and are still trying to find out why they form in this way.

Pietra paesina and other ruin marbles have another special feature. They are crossed by a network of very slender fractures that have been "healed" subsequently by microscopic calcite crystals. The fluids depositing the Leisegang rings of brown iron oxide cannot penetrate the healed fractures, and so the fractures control how far the bands of brown iron-staining will spread—in other words, the sizes of the "towers," "castles" and other ruins. Some of the most beautiful landscape marbles combine "ruined buildings" and delicate dendritic "trees."

ABOVE Dendritic iron and manganese oxides form treelike growths in the Alberese limestone.

BELOW "Shrubs" in *Cotham marble* were formed by the activity of ancient cyanobacteria. Superb dendrites are found in lithographic limestone (opposite) from the famous Solnhofen quarries in Bavaria, Germany.

Pietra paesina

SOURCE: Val d'Arno, Tuscany, Italy
STATUS: Commercially available

Oxf-Min1473

It takes little imagination to see castles, ruined cities and rocky mountains in the famous ruin marble of Florence—undoubtedly the best known of all the landscape marbles.

As early as the 16th century, philosophers were intrigued by stones that showed the shapes of buildings and rocky landscapes marked out in shades of dark brown on a buff, gray or green limestone backdrop. They called the stone *pietra paesina*, which roughly translates as "landscape stone." *Pietra paesina* comes from various locations where the Alberese limestone outcrops in Tuscany, Liguria and Lazio, Italy. It occurs most famously as scattered boulders at Rignano sull'Arno and elsewhere along the valley of the Arno River outside Florence. *Pietra paesina* from here was one of the stones highly favored by the Florentine ruling family the Medicis, and was sawn into thin slices for use as small panels in the decoration of churches and palaces. In the pietre dure workshops in Florence, it was incorporated into furniture designs and used as a ready-prepared mountainous landscape upon which artists would paint figures.

Ruin marbles that resemble *pietra paesina* are found in various other places around the world, notably Klosterneuburg in Austria, Horná Breznika in Slovakia, Brewster County in Texas and Baluchistan in Pakistan. Only *pietra paesina* and the Pakistani *teakwood marble* deposits (see page 104) have been worked on any substantial commercial basis. *Pietra paesina* continues to be manufactured into high-end gifts of all kinds.

GEOLOGICAL DESCRIPTION
Calcareous siltstone of Cretaceous age with ferruginous staining constrained by internal fractures.

MAJOR USAGE
Furniture, pietre dure and other inlay work, ornamental items.

ABOVE Hand-colored plate from Adam Ludwig Wirsing's book on marble, *Marmora et adfines aliquos lapides colorbus ...* (1775) gives a fanciful interpretation of *pietra paesina*.

Teakwood

SOURCE: Baluchistan, Pakistan
STATUS: Actively quarried

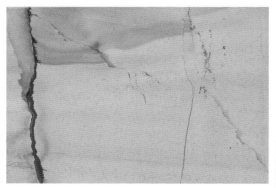

OXF-DR1706

Imagine a parquet flooring made with blocks of stone that look like wood. This is one of the more striking ways that *teakwood marble* can be used.

In recent years, a stone which at first glance looks like the famous *pietra paesina* has been quarried in the Pakistani province of Baluchistan. It is known as *teakwood*, or *Burma teak*, because the patterning resembles wood grain. *Teakwood* is used to make a wide variety of ornamental items—bookends, candle holders, plates and bowls, vases, eggs and obelisks—all widely available in stores around the world. Because quite large slabs of this stone can be cut, it is also made into sinks, countertops, wall claddings and floor tiles.

The patterning of *teakwood* is formed by the same processes that occur in the formation of *pietra paesina*—water penetrating the stone releases iron oxide that is constrained within a network of slender calcite-filled fractures. The patterning is more curvaceous and less sharply defined than in *paesina*.

GEOLOGICAL DESCRIPTION

Calcareous siltstone with fracture-controlled ferruginous staining. It is traversed by wider fractures infilled with white calcite.

MAJOR USAGE

Decorative items and interior architectural applications.

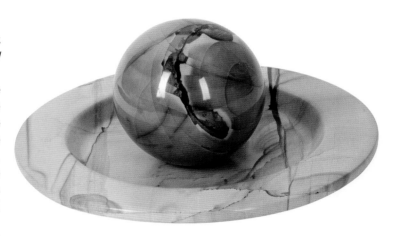

ABOVE Two *teakwood* ornaments showing the versatility of this stone.

Other yellow and brown marbles and limestones

Good yellow marbles and limestones are not common. *Amarillo Macael*, often called *amarillo Triana*, comes from Macael and other places in the Sierra de los Filabres in Almería, Spain. It is a yellow to yellowish brown marble with abundant dendrites developed along a close network of fractures. *Jaune de Var* is a fine French limestone once used in architecture and for furniture and chimney pieces. It is crossed by red stylolites, and can resemble the best quality *crema Valencia* in appearance. Some varieties are richly fossiliferous. It is not currently quarried.

Of the many cream and beige limestones, those of Trani and Bursa deserve special mention. *Trani marble* is a very well-known Italian limestone with several different color and pattern variations, all a cream or beige color. It comes from outside the coastal town Trani in Puglia, Italy, and is used for sculpture and furniture, memorials and many architectural applications. *Bursa marble* comes from various places in the province of Bursa in Turkey and is beige, mottled with transparent calcite. It can be quite fossiliferous.

Darker brown has never been a popular color for decorative stones, but a few do have a special appeal. *Rosewood marble* is a rich brown-banded algal limestone, the pattern resembling wood grain. It used to be obtained from Derbyshire in England, and was used in Derbyshire inlay work. *Emperador* from Alicante in Spain is a dolomitic limestone rich in clay minerals that has a breccialike structure and a rich brown color.

Pink marbles and limestones

Marbles and limestones in shades of pink combine a warmth of coloring with a light, fresh appearance. They are highly sought after for contemporary styles of architecture but still work well with traditional building materials such as brick and stone. Many of the pink limestones of the Mediterranean region date back to the days when dinosaurs roamed the Earth. They formed at the bottom of the ancient Tethys Ocean that covered a huge swath of what is now Europe, north Africa and the Middle East. The famous pink marbles of Georgia and Tennessee are more than twice as old, ancient sediments altered or metamorphosed during the formation of the Appalachian mountain chain. All the pink marbles and limestones shown here are colored by iron oxide minerals. A minute amount of red hematite gives a clear pink color; a little goethite mixed with it makes the stone salmon-pink or orange.

Marmo del Duomo

SOURCE: Candoglia, Piedmont, Italy
STATUS: Actively quarried

If you want to see the beautiful peachy-white *Candoglio marble*, there is just one place to go: Milan's splendidly ornate Duomo.

Duke Gian Galeazzo Visconti wanted an edifice that would display all the wealth and prestige of the dukedom of Milan. In 1387, he gave the Veneranda factory of the Duomo the sole rights to quarry *Candoglia marble* to build a huge, spectacular new Gothic cathedral. This warm pinkish white marble had been quarried in Roman times but nothing compared to the scale of operations over the following centuries. The marble was transported on huge barges from the quarries at Candoglia, near Mergozzo in Piedmont, across Lake Maggiore, down the Ticino River, along the Naviglio Grande and into Milan. Here it was cut and sculpted by a huge team of marble masons and sculptors at the Veneranda works. The façade was finally completed at the behest of Napoleon Bonaparte when he became king of Italy in 1805.

The Duomo has about 3,400 statues and 135 spires and pinnacles. It is a hugely complicated structure to maintain and preserve, and the Candoglia quarries are still reserved primarily to supply marble for restoration work. The Madre quarry is one of two working quarries, and is a huge underground cavern. The introduction of diamond wire saws has improved production so much that some marble is now available commercially.

GEOLOGICAL DESCRIPTION
Coarse-grained pink, white or gray calcitic marble.

MAJOR USAGE
Until recently, reserved almost exclusively for the construction and repair of the Duomo in Milan.

Rosa Portogallo

SOURCE: Évora, Portugal
STATUS: Actively quarried

Visit the small town of Borba in Portugal's Évora district and you can't help but notice the ubiquitous use of marble in buildings, sidewalks and curbstones. The reason lies farther along the road from Estremoz to Vila Vicosa: it is riddled with marble quarries—the source of some of Portugal's best known decorative stones.

The Évora marbles are translucent with a granular texture and can vary widely in color. Pure white, cream, pale orange and pink are the most popular. Marbles at the pink end of this spectrum come mainly from Borba and Estremoz. They are marketed under such names as *rosa Portogallo*, *rosa Portuguese*, *Estremoz rosa* and *rosa Borba*. In the United States they are often called *rosa aurora*—the same as a pink marble from Mexico. They are notoriously variable in appearance, typically crossed by red or grayish green veins. The best quality stone has the most uniform background color and least conspicuous veining.

Rosa Portogallo has been used widely in Portugal and Spain, but is now exported overseas, and new underground workings are being opened to satisfy the demand. The Palace of Vila Vicosa is built of marble from Borba, and fine pillars can be seen in the Monastery of Jeronimos in Lisbon. *Rosa Portogallo* has been used for furniture and inlay work and is a popular marble for sculpture.

GEOLOGICAL DESCRIPTION
Cambrian limestone metamorphosed in the Devonian period to form a medium-grained calcitic marble tinted by disseminated iron oxides, mainly hematite. Serpentine fills green veins.

MAJOR USAGE
Internal architectural decoration, sculpture.

Etowah marble

SOURCE: Tate, Pickens County, Georgia, United States
STATUS: Intermittently quarried as required

Just next to the quarry for the pale gray *Cherokee marble* in Tate, Georgia, there is another quarry that produces the glowing pink *Etowah marble*.

Etowah varies from pale to dark pink with streaks of dark gray, and at first it was used mainly for wall panels, fireplaces, counters and tabletops. In the 1880s the Georgia marbles came to the attention of the wider American building trade, and the Georgia Marble Company was set up in 1884 to develop the business. An important early project was the supply of *Etowah marble* for interior wall claddings in the new State Capitol in Atlanta, Georgia, completed in 1889. Members of the Tate family were local landowners and founders of the company, and in 1905 Colonel Sam Tate became the president and general manager. In the 1920s, he had a lavish new mansion built of pink marble within sight of the quarries. Tate House was appropriately dubbed the "pink palace," and is now preserved on the National Register of Historic Places.

The marble was later used to decorate subway stations in New York, and in 1823, huge quantities were required to face the Federal Reserve Bank in Cleveland, Ohio. Another 1920s building, the Joslyn Museum in Omaha, Nebraska, is clad with *Etowah marble*, and it is used extensively in the Anderson Hospital in Houston, Texas (1964). The stone is still available, marketed as *Etowah fleuri*.

GEOLOGICAL DESCRIPTION
Limestone metamorphosed during Cambrian times to form a medium-grained calcitic marble colored by disseminated hematite.

MAJOR USAGE
Wall claddings and floorings; sculpture.

Tennessee pink marble

SOURCE: Friendsville, Blount County, Tennessee, United States
STATUS: Actively quarried

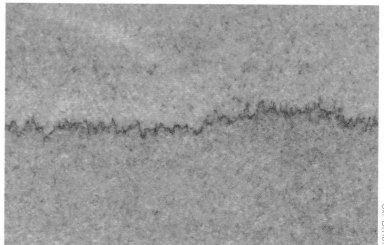

Long ago these limestones were fossil reef deposits crushed during the formation of the Appalachian Mountains, the grains welded together to form a durable and very decorative stone.

Tennessee marbles range from black and chocolate brown to buff and gray, but those of a mottled pink color are most popular. Named varieties include *Tennessee rose*, coarser-grained *Holston pink*, dark pink *Tennessee cedar* and white-veined *Tennessee fleuri*. Gray stylolites, dubbed "crows' feet," zigzag across the stone and are a particularly decorative feature. Fossils are also usually easy to see.

Quarrying began in Rogersville in 1838, and with contracts for the new U.S. State Capitol in Washington, D.C., the industry burgeoned. From 1862, excavations moved to Knoxville and Friendsville. The Great Depression and changes in fashion meant many lean years in the mid-1900s, but the industry is thriving again. Tennessee marble has been supplied for the new visitor center at the U.S. State Capitol, the east extension of the National Gallery of Art and the renovation of the National Archives (both in Washington), and for New York's Grand Central Station.

GEOLOGICAL DESCRIPTION
Ordovician medium- to coarse-grained limestones, mottled pink and white, and containing abundant bryozoa, crinoid ossicles, mollusk shells and other fossil debris. Long parallel gray stylolites feature prominently.

MAJOR USAGE
Interior and exterior paving; wall cladding, staircases, bathrooms and kitchens; fountains, memorials, furniture and sculpture.

Stone in a New World

"In the great pits, yawning wider and deeper every year, men and engines, in sunshine and in storm, delve all the seasons through. When the landscape is bright under the summer sun they may be seen, like ants toiling in their cells, hundreds of feet below the surface. Now and then an ant grows into a burly, grimy man, climbing the giddy stairs; or a small watercarrier, bearing, with careful steps, his heavy bucket to the thirsty workmen ...."

When Roland Robinson wrote this evocative description of the marble quarries of Vermont in 1890, the American stone industry was burgeoning. These were rough and dangerous places to work, supplying construction and ornamental stones for public buildings and prestigious private residences.

"In winter, when the barbaric towers of marble piled along the quarry's brink look dingy under their whiter copings of snow, such volumes of smoke and steam rise out of the caverns that more is heard than seen of the workers and their work. It is a devil's caldron, bubbling with spit of engines, clink of drills, and murmur of smothered voices."

America looked to the best of classical European architecture for inspiration, and imported large quantities of marble from Italy for polished columns and richly decorative interiors. But by this time, the Americans had also learned just how valuable their native stones were.

A GROWING DEMAND

Building stone houses was hardly a high priority for the first European settlers in the New World. With ample wood for building, stone was only needed for hearths, gravestones, lintels and millstones; quarrying took place in quiet times in the agricultural year. The growing prosperity that followed the War of Independence brought an increased desire for stone-built homes and businesses. Commercial quarries supplied granites, gneisses, marbles and serpentinites from many places along the length of the Appalachians. Further deposits would be found in the Rocky Mountains and farther west into California. New railroads replaced oxen and wagons, transporting stone from quarries to towns and cities. Immigrants from Tuscany brought new expertise, and the use of steam-power for cutting and processing stone helped quarry owners meet the growing demand.

BUILDING CONFIDENCE

But there was a problem. It was widely believed that U.S. marbles could not match the quality of the famous Italian marbles. By the end of the 19th century, it was apparent that those of Europe were superb for interior decoration, but often broke up in the harsher outdoor weather. By contrast many of their U.S. counterparts endured repeated cycles of soaking, freezing and thawing, with little ill effect. This engendered new confidence in the U.S. stones and ensured their use for the Lincoln Memorial completed in 1922 and the Jefferson Memorial 21 years later.

ROCK BOTTOM TO REVIVAL

The 1930s to 1970s were dreadful ones for the stone trade. The Great Depression was followed by World War II and then a new fashion for concrete and glass. From this rather shaky past, the major U.S. marble and granite companies are now facing a promising future. Since the 1980s there has been a huge revival in the use of natural stone in contemporary architecture and a growing movement to preserve heritage buildings using new stone from old quarries.

Granite Quarries, Barre, Vt.

ABOVE Spoil tips and wooden derricks used to lift giant blocks from the quarry depths at the Barre Granite Quarry, Vermont, at the turn of the last century. Today the quarry is around 600 feet (180 m) deep (right).

RIGHT The Grand Central terminal in New York, built between 1903 and 1913, is paved with the hardwearing *Tennessee pink marble*. Additional stone has been supplied in recent years for restoration work in the staion concourse.

Norwegian rose

SOURCE: Fauske, Nordland, Norway
STATUS: Actively quarried

A beautiful pink and white marble is sourced from around Fauske in northern Norway. It is known by its English name *Norwegian rose* even in Norway, but is also traded as *rosa Norvegia*.

Although *Norwegian rose* was first discovered in the 18th century, quarries were not opened until the 1880s. The ancient Fauske marble deposit is rather variable. The popular lighter form of *Norwegian rose* is a sheared and contorted pink and white marble conglomerate with some streaks of green. A darker variety shows a dark violet-gray matrix. Other marbles coming from the Fauske quarries are monochrome white (*white Salten* or *Furuli white*), cloudy gray (*Hermelin* or *antique foncé*) and pale green (*Arctic green*).

Through the 20th century, *Norwegian rose* was widely exported to Denmark, Sweden, England and other countries, often sold under the names *Furuli rose* or *brèche rosé*. Fine large columns of this stone can be seen in Westminster Cathedral, London, and a large quantity clads the walls and floors in the City Hall in Oslo. Today, *Norwegian rose* is quarried at Løvgavlen quarry, northwest of Fauske, and it was recently used to pave the floor of the Gardemoen airport in Oslo.

GEOLOGICAL DESCRIPTION

Precambrian or Cambrian conglomerate of medium- or fine-grained calcitic (pink) and dolomitic (white) marble clasts in a pink, violet or gray matrix. The stone is highly deformed, and some banding rich in green diopside may be prevalent.

MAJOR USAGE

Interior wall cladding, countertops, and bathroom surfaces.

Cork red marble

SOURCE: County Cork, Ireland
STATUS: No longer available

Many of the finest examples of the distinctly mottled *Cork red* are to be seen in churches and cathedrals of Ireland and England.

Cork red marble is a limestone conglomerate, and the small white spots are often ring-shaped segments of sea lily stems. These attractive stones were quarried at various locations in County Cork, notably at Midleton, Baneshane and Little Island, east of Cork city. The best dark pink stone was called *Victoria red*.

Commercial working had commenced by 1850, especially in churches and cathedrals, for example St. Fin Barre's Cathedral in Cork and Westminster Cathedral in London. Here, stone used to decorate the Chapel of St. Patrick came from Baneshane quarry in 1910. The work continued in 1920 when all the *Cork red* quarries had probably closed, but stockpiles of Baneshane stone were available. In the 1950s, more *Cork red* from Baneshane was needed for the cladding of the nave. With the help of the Geological Survey of Ireland, the flooded and overgrown quarry was drained and reopened, and the building work was completed. Sadly, this did not signal the revival of the marble industry in Cork and the quarry was soon abandoned again.

Other examples of a non-ecclesiastical nature include beautiful pillars in the museum of Trinity College Dublin (1857) and the Oxford University Museum of Natural History (1860).

GEOLOGICAL DESCRIPTION

Carboniferous conglomerate of white limestone pebbles, crinoid ossicles and other fossil fragments in a pink, red or brown clay-rich matrix.

MAJOR USAGE

Architectural columns and claddings, ecclesiastical fittings.

Breccia corallina

SOURCE: Vezirhan, Bilecik, Turkey
STATUS: Actively quarried

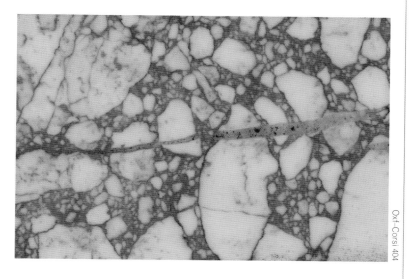

Dark coral-pink cement binds ivory-white limestone fragments together, giving this famous old breccia its traditional name.

Breccia corallina has been found in excavations of ancient Roman settlements all around the Mediterranean and large quantities have been reused by later generations. The old quarries are around the modern village of Vezirhan in the province of Bilecik, close to a tributary of the River Sakarya. In ancient times, this was the kingdom of Bythinia, and the river was called Sagarius. It provided easy transport of the stone by barge for much of the journey to the sea, and gave the stone its ancient name, *marmor Sagarium*. Some of the Roman workings have been obliterated by modern quarrying, but others still exist and preserve evidence of ancient toolmarks in the quarry faces. The same geological deposit is quarried today under the trade name *rosalia* but the modern stone is beige colored, with only slender veins of orange-red.

Breccia corallina di Cori from the town of that name in Lazio, Italy, can easily be confused with the ancient *breccia corallina*. This stone was probably first used for decorative purposes in the 16th or 17th century and was quarried at least until the mid-1800s.

GEOLOGICAL DESCRIPTION

Large and small creamy-white limestone clasts of Cretaceous age, in an orange, salmon-pink or brown hematitic matrix. Fractures are filled with sparry white calcite. Yellow iron staining may suffuse the whole rock.

MAJOR USAGE

Pillars, paving and other architectural elements; bathtubs, fountain basins and sculptures.

Broccatellone

SOURCE: Bilecik, Turkey
STATUS: Quarried in antiquity

It is easy to see why the Roman scalpellini (stonecutters) of the 16th and 17th centuries thought this stone was a variety of Spanish *broccatello*, but looks can be very deceptive.

Broccatellone is a breccia of limestone clasts in a pink cement. The main colors are dark pink, light pink, yellow and white, and samples that combine yellow and pink can, at first glance, easily be muddled with Spanish *broccatello*. But large fragments of bivalve shells, abundant in the Spanish stone, are not seen in this one.

The ancient Romans cut slabs and pillars from *broccatellone*, and the stone was reused in Rennaissance and baroque architecture. A good place to see this stone is the Church of Santa Maria in Aracoeli in Rome, where columns surround the monument to St. Helena.

The correct source of this stone became evident when some curious columns were found near the Temple of Hadrian at Ephesus in Turkey. They were cut from a stone that was part *broccatellone* and part *breccia corallina*, showing that although these stones look very different, they rest one on the other in the ground. It is still not known exactly where in Bilecik Province *broccatellone* was quarried.

GEOLOGICAL DESCRIPTION

A breccia of large and small limestone and limestone breccia clasts in a finely granular pink matrix. Samples show varying amounts of tectonic alteration; clast boundaries typically have dark suturing. Cavities and abundant slender fractures are infilled with white or colorless calcite.

MAJOR USAGE

Pillars, slabs for wall cladding.

Cottanello

SOURCE: Cottanello, Lazio, Italy

STATUS: No longer quarried

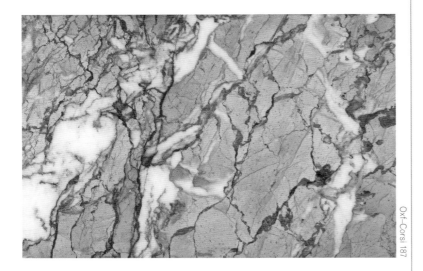

Oxf–Corsi 187

In the early 1500s the Vatican basilica of St. Peter's was being built, and sculptor-architect Gian Lorenzo Bernini needed a new decorative stone to construct the huge supporting pillars.

He didn't have to look farther than the little hilltop town of Cottanello, about 28 miles (45 km) north of Rome. It lies on a fault line that runs through central Italy. Some five million years earlier, stresses had built up along the fault until finally it ruptured, causing an earthquake that shattered the local rosy pink *scaglia* limestone. Over time, the fragments were cemented together with pure white calcite, creating an elegant pink and white breccia. A quarry was opened that supplied 44 huge pillars to ornament the new basilica, superb columns for the elliptical Church of Sant'Andrea al Quirinale, and plenty of stone for the decoration of other buildings.

Brecciated limestones like *Cottanello* occur at other places where fault movements have disturbed the pink *scaglia* limestone. *Cottanello antico* resembles the baroque stone but exactly where it was quarried is not known. Floor tiles and slabs were found in archaeological excavations in Rome, Ostia, Herculaneum and Pompeii, and it is often featured in tabletops and collections of ancient marbles. Another similar stone was obtained from nearby Cesi, in the province of Terni, at least until the mid-19th century.

GEOLOGICAL DESCRIPTION

A breccia of late Cretaceous or Paleogene pink to red marly limestone fragments cemented by dense white calcite. Veins and stylolites of red clay, and microfossils are common.

MAJOR USAGE

Floor tiles, columns and architectural decoration; inlay work.

Marmo carnagione

SOURCE: Umbria and Marche, Italy

STATUS: Some minor quarrying

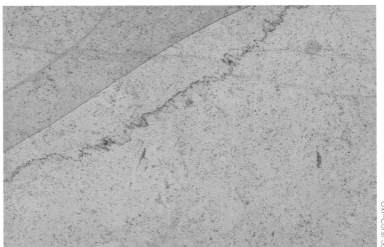

Oxf–Corsi 56

The tiny speckles in these stones are beautifully preserved microscopic fossils—remains of tiny plankton that lived more than 60 million years ago.

Back then, Italy was covered by the ancient Tethys Ocean. There was a deep basin in the area of Umbria and Marche, and the bottom was covered with calcareous mud and the remains of tiny plankton and other organisms that had thrived in the deep water above. As more sediments accumulated, the mud cemented to form a hard pink to dull red limestone that geologists call the "scaglia rossa." This rather porous stone takes a good polish, and in historic furniture and marble collections it is called *marmo carnagione*, alluding to its typical flesh-pink coloring.

It is likely that this stone was quarried in many places in the Umbria and Marche regions of central Italy, in the regions of Perugia, Gubbio, Fossombrone and Monte Subasio. Stone from Subasio is called *pietra rosa di Assisi*, because it was widely used in that city, for example, decorating the Basilica of St. Clare.

The name *marmo carnagione* has also been used for the pink varieties of *giallo antico* from Chemtou, Tunisia (see page 90), a desirable color that occurs naturally but is also obtained artificially by heating the yellow stone.

GEOLOGICAL DESCRIPTION

Pink marly limestone of late Cretaceous to Eocene age, containing abundant microfossils and stylolites. Wider fractures are filled with white calcite. Coloration may be controlled by slender fractures giving the appearance of a pink *paesina* (see page 102).

MAJOR USAGE

Architecture, furniture, inlay work, polished stone collections.

Breccia degli Appennini

SOURCE: Apennine Mountains, Italy
STATUS: No longer quarried

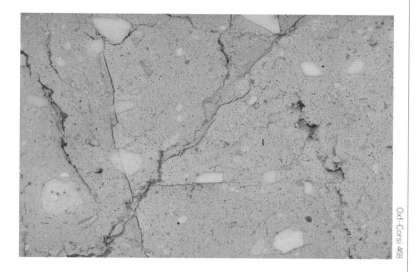

Oxf–Corsi 468

The tiny white fragments of limestone in this Italian breccia make it a very distinctive stone, but exactly where it comes from remains a mystery.

Breccia degli Appennini is a variety of *marmo carnagione* (see opposite) containing small fragments of cream-colored limestone. Like *marmo carnagione*, it is speckled by the remains of planktonic foraminifera—the tiny creatures that lived in the ocean. It was formed by a mudslide down a slope to the bottom of the ancient Tethys Ocean. Historic sources such as Corsi's catalog say it came from the Apennines. Although the exact location of the quarries is not known, it is likely that it comes from the Marche region, where debris flows like this are not uncommon. It was quarried in the 18th and 19th centuries, perhaps earlier.

Pink marly limestones of Eocene age quarried at Riziani (*rosa Riziani*) and Arta (*Rozalito*) in Thesprotia, Greece, can closely resemble *marmo carnagione* and *breccia degli Appennini*.

GEOLOGICAL DESCRIPTION

A debris flow deposit of late Cretaceous to Eocene age. Creamy-white fragments of limestone are supported by a pink marly limestone matrix containing abundant microfossils and stylolites.

MAJOR USAGE

Found mainly in inlay work and in collections of polished stones dating from the 18th and 19th centuries.

Rose de Numidie

SOURCE: Sidi Benyebka, near Oran, Algeria
STATUS: No longer quarried

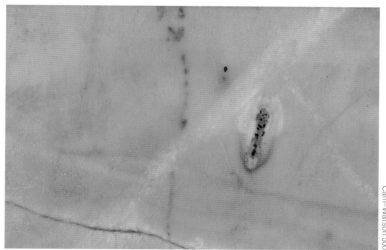

Cam–Watson 500

"As regards quantity, beauty and variety, the world contains nothing comparable to the treasures of Numidian marble in this mountain," reported the British Consul to Algeria in the 1880s.

Sir Lambert Playfair first visited the summit of Gebel Arousse near the village of Kleber (now Sidi Benyebka) in 1880, and he was overwhelmed by the beauty of the marbles he found there. The colors ranged from creamy-white to dark red, with every shade between. In many respects the pink and yellow stones resembled *giallo antico* from Chemtou in Tunisia (see page 90), having a similar translucency and fine grain. He believed the Kleber quarries were of Roman age, although it is not thought these stones were transported to Rome in ancient times or used at any great distance from the quarries. Playfair's report came to the notice of the marble trade, and in the latter years of the 19th century and the first part of the 20th, the marbles of Oran were worked on a commercial basis to decorate churches and public buildings in Europe and the United States.

The pink marble, known as *rose de Numidie*, was a popular color. It lines the walls of the Blessed Sacrament Chapel in Westminster Cathedral, London, and also the dining room of Marble House, the Vanderbilts' summer home in Newport, Rhode Island. Quarry working had become sporadic in the 1920s and ceased by 1950.

GEOLOGICAL DESCRIPTION

Fine-grained pink and yellow dolomitic limestone or low-grade marble, with brown ferruginous infills to slender fractures.

MAJOR USAGE

Interior wall cladding and flooring.

Nembro rosato

SOURCE: Province of Verona, Veneto, Italy
STATUS: Actively quarried

Oxf–Corsi 50

The nodules in this attractive Veronese marble look like puffy clouds, and the colors are much more subtle than its illustrious salmon-pink neighbor *rosso Verona*.

Both *nembro rosato* and the well-known salmon-pink *rosso Verona* (see opposite) come from the same quarries in Caprino Veronese, Sant' Ambrogio di Valpolicella, and other locations in Valpolicella and the shores of Lake Garda. At its most beautiful, *nembro* is colored with waves of clear pink and bright yellow, although some prefer a light buff-pink variety of this stone, similar to pale *rosso Verona*. The puffy nodular structure is characteristic, and *nembro* has sometimes been called *mandola* or *mandorla* from the Italian word for "almond" when the shape of the nodules take this form.

Nembro rosato is one of the Jurassic and Cretaceous limestones used locally as a building stone but also exported worldwide as a polished decorative stone. Both *nembro* and *rosso Verona* have been extracted since ancient times and are commonly used together. These days, they are often laid in patterned paving, and look good in the home as well as in offices, hotels and public buildings.

GEOLOGICAL DESCRIPTION

Nodular, burrowed, fine-grained limestones of late Jurassic age, rich in fossil fragments and with abundant stylolites.

MAJOR USAGE

Paving, staircases, wall cladding, fireplaces, bathroom surfaces and other architectural uses; mosaics and inlays.

Rosa perlino

SOURCE: Provinces of Verona and Vicenza, Italy
STATUS: Actively quarried

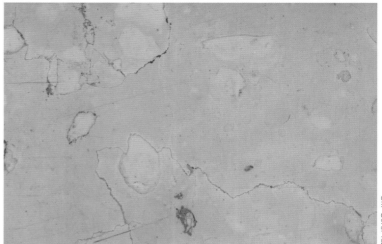

Oxf–Corsi 182

Various pink limestones from the provinces of Verona and Vicenza can be hard to tell apart. Pretty in pink, but they lack the distinctive nodular structures of *nembro rosato* and *rosso Verona*.

Rosa corallo used to come from Valpolicella, outside Verona, but is now rare. The beds rest on those of *rosso Verona*, and were deposited in calm, deep seas at the end of the Jurassic period. It often has paler streaks bleached by fluids passing along slender fractures crossing the stone. These are not seen in *rosa perlino*—a limestone of much the same age quarried farther east, near Valstagna and Asiago in Vicenza. It is often traded as *perlino rosata* and *rosa Asiago*. The stones of the Lessinia hills near the towns of Prun, Fane and Torbe can also be clear pink. They are from the Cretaceous to Eocene Scaglia Rossa formation that forms 73 distinct beds divided by thin, marly layers. Some are used for construction, while others, like the pink *pietra della Lessinia rosa*, take an excellent polish.

All these limestones have a long history of quarrying. The specimen shown here is from Corsi's early 19th-century collection and could be any of them, although it most closely resembles the *rosa perlino* quarried today.

GEOLOGICAL DESCRIPTION

Late Jurassic to Eocene pink fine-grained limestones, rich in microfossils, with little or no nodular structure. They have abundant darker pink stylolites and may be crossed by calcite-filled veins. Their age may be indicated by identification of the microfossils.

MAJOR USAGE

Mainly interior uses, for paving, staircases and other architectural features; also used for mosaics.

Rosso Verona

SOURCE: Province of Verona, Veneto, Italy
STATUS: Actively quarried

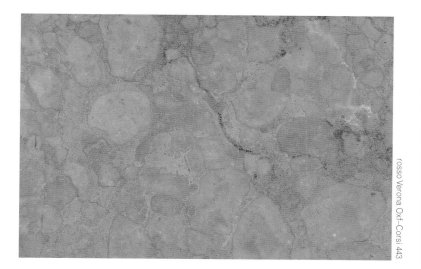

rosso Verona Oxf–Corsi 443

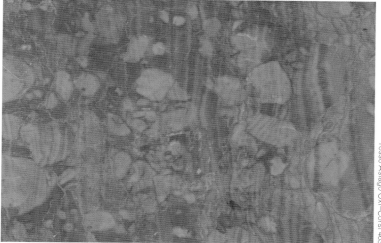

rosso Asiago Oxf–Corsi 463

With its rich salmon-pink color, lumpy nodular texture and a good scattering of ammonites and other fossils, this is without doubt the most famous and easily recognized of Verona's marbles.

Rosso Verona is a hugely popular marble, exported all around the world. Its warm coloring contrasts well with whites and creams, and it is both durable and readily available. The ancient Romans used it for building in the city of Verona, and when the famous Arena was damaged by an earthquake in the 12th century, much of the stone was recycled for other Veronese buildings. It has been used on a huge scale for buildings, monuments and sarcophagi in the cities of north and eastern Italy. In Venice's Basilica of San Marco, it forms a geometric pattern with white Istrian marble in the upper story of the Ducal Palace. The 13th-century baptistry in Parma is paved and richly ornamented with it.

The stone forms an extensive deposit in the hills north of Verona, but the principal area of quarrying is the Val d'Adige, between Sant'Ambrogio di Valpolicella and Dolcè. Geologists regard this stone as a classic example of Rosso Ammonitico, the red nodular ammonite-rich limestones deposited on the shallow Tethys Ocean floor over 100 million years ago. *Rosso Asiago* is a stone very similar in structure, but is a darker orange-red color.

GEOLOGICAL DESCRIPTION

Salmon-pink to red nodular marly limestone; a typical Rosso Ammonitico deposit of Middle to Upper Jurassic age. It contains abundant fossils and stylolites.

MAJOR USAGE

Architectural purposes including flooring, wall cladding and decoration; also chimneypieces and furniture; sculpture.

ABOVE Both dark pink *rosso Verona* and lighter pink *nembro rosato* are used in these panels under an arch in Westminster Cathedral, London.

Breccia pernice

SOURCE: Fumane, Veneto, Italy
STATUS: Actively quarried

An amazing jumble of fossil shells and fragments of different colored limestones, *breccia pernice* has become one of the most popular of Verona's decorative stones.

"Pernice" means partridge in Italian and this stone used to be known as *occhio di pernice*. It can contain many brachiopod shells that would have given the impression of round eyes. In the past it was quarried in Val Pernise and other locations between Grezzana and Lugo in Valpantena, but today it comes from Monte Pastello near the town of Fumane.

Breccia pernice is a chaotic jumble of pink, beige, cream and red limestone fragments, mixed with large and small mollusk shells, very variable in appearance. Pink calcareous limestone cements the fragments together, and cavities are infilled with white calcite. It has many uses from paving and wall cladding, staircases and fireplaces, to funerary urns and sculptures. Interior walls of the Trump Tower in New York are clad with this stone, and it is also used extensively in the Piccadilly Centre in Sydney, Australia. *Breccia pernice* is a popular choice for bathrooms in many prestigious hotels.

GEOLOGICAL DESCRIPTION

Jurassic breccia of mixed limestones and shell fragments in a pink limestone matrix, extensively fractured, with cracks and cavities infilled with white calcite.

MAJOR USAGE

Mainly interior uses, for floors tiles and wall claddings, bathroom and kitchen surfaces; funerary urns.

Encarnado

SOURCE: Montelavar, Lisbon, Portugal
STATUS: Actively quarried

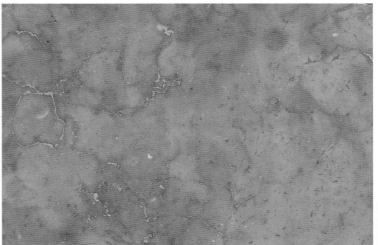

Local pink nodular limestones have been used for at least six centuries in the buildings of the Lisbon area. Since the 19th century, they have found new markets in other countries.

Encarnado is the name given to the cloudy pink or orange-pink nodular limestones quarried a short distance northwest of Lisbon. They were used for many centuries in Portugal, especially in the churches and public buildings in and around Lisbon, but only found a wider market in the 19th century. *Encarnado da Pedra Furada*, from the Pedra Furada quarries near Montelavar, was exported in large quantities to other countries during the 19th and early 20th centuries. In Portugal it is also known as *Vidraço da Pedra Furada*, and in Britain it has been called *Emperor's red*. *Encarnado de Negrais* and the similar but yellow *amarelo Negrais* are quarried farther east, near the town of Negrais.

Examples of *encarnado* in England can be seen in the floors of both Bristol and Truro cathedrals and in the decoration of Drapers Hall in London.

GEOLOGICAL DESCRIPTION

Cretaceous pink nodular limestone with abundant fragments of fossils, and stylolites.

MAJOR USAGE

Interior and exterior paving, wall cladding, architectural features.

Adneter marmor

SOURCE: Adnet, Salzburg, Austria
STATUS: Very limited quarrying

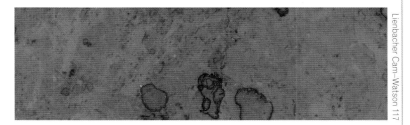

Lienbacher Cam-Watson 117

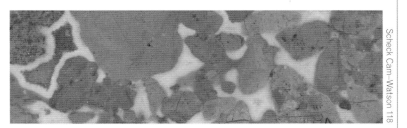

Scheck Cam-Watson 118

Visitors to the historic cities of Salzburg and Vienna will see again and again an attractive orange-brown nodular limestone decorating stores, subway stations, churches and museums.

This is the famous *Adneter marmor (Adnet marble)*, quarried since medieval times around the village of Adnet, near Hallein in Austria. Typically, it looks very much like a brownish red *rosso Verona*, and this is no coincidence for it also comes from the Jurassic Rosso Ammonitico formation. The Adnet area was a coral reef over 100 million years ago, and corals, ammonites, sponges and other fossils are often beautifully preserved. A variety known as *Lienbacher* has considerable amounts of black manganese oxides, while the stone that the quarryworkers called *scheck* is a conglomerate of nodular Adnet marble cemented with white calcite crystals. Both are shown here.

Adneter marmor has been used extensively across Europe, particularly in Austria and Bavaria. It is also used a great deal in Budapest, Hungary, although from a very early date, similar nodular red limestones were quarried for decorative use in the Gerecse Mountains near Tatábanya. Today, little stone is extracted, but Adnet has a museum devoted to its famous old industry, and it is possible to visit some of the many quarries in the area.

GEOLOGICAL DESCRIPTION

Early to mid-Jurassic pale buff, orange-red or brown limestones, typically nodular and with abundant fossils. Brecciated varieties are cemented with white calcite. Black manganese oxides may form coatings.

MAJOR USAGE

Paving, wall cladding and staircases, as well as sculptures.

Rosso Montecitorio

SOURCE: Monte Kumeta, Sicily, Italy
STATUS: Actively quarried

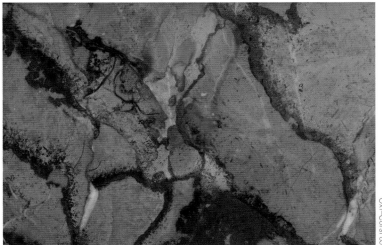

Oxf-Corsi 85

Historic samples of this marble have been the subject of a classic case of mistaken identity. The 19th-century stonecutters in Rome thought it was *portasanta,* but they were quite wrong.

It is not just Corsi's sample that was misidentified, but other similar slabs in historic collections. Careful examination shows that this stone matches closely the kind of marble quarried on the sides of Monte Kumeta in Palermo, Sicily, and traded today as *rosso Kumeta* or *rosso Montecitorio*. Since the scalpellini obtained all their *portasanta* from the ruins of Rome, it can be safely presumed that this stone had the same origins, transported from Sicily long ago by the ancient Romans.

The name *rosso Montecitorio* was given when considerable quantities were used in the interior decoration of the Palazzo Montecitorio, the seat of the Italian Chamber of Deputies. But the stone was popular long before this. It was admired for its bright coloring and was widely employed from the 17th century onward in many of the palaces and churches of Sicily.

GEOLOGICAL DESCRIPTION

Pink nodular limestone rich in microfossils, from the Rosso Ammonitico of mid-Jurassic age. Black manganese oxides were deposited when little new sediment fell to the seafloor and the soft surface had started to cement to form a "hard ground." Ammonites and other fossils are common. The stone is crossed by white calcite-filled fractures.

MAJOR USAGE

Wall cladding, paving, pillars and other architectural features; inlays in furniture.

Rojo Alicante

SOURCE: Monóvar and La Romana, Alicante, Spain
STATUS: Actively quarried

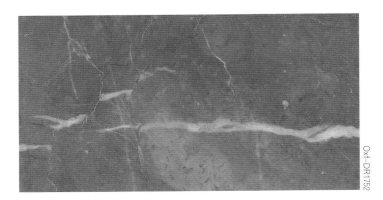

One of the classic Spanish decorative limestones, *rojo Alicante* is more a dark salmon-pink color than red, and always crossed by veins filled with white calcite.

A closer look shows that it is packed full of the fragments of fossil shells, but it is very fine-grained and takes an excellent polish. *Rojo Alicante* is a popular choice of stone for floors and walls when a warm color is wanted, contrasting well with its creamy-white compatriot, *crema marfil* (see page 98).

Until the 20th century, quarrying was largely carried out by local farmworkers as a way to supplement their incomes. Still, the red marbles of the Aspe and La Romana came to be used in many of the more prestigious buildings of Spain. The development of the modern marble industry in Alicante had its origins in the reconstruction that followed the Spanish Civil War, and with improved transportation and increased mechanization, it is has become a major export industry. Today, *rojo Alicante* comes

LEFT Plaza de la Seo Zaragoza, Spain.

from quarries on Monte Cavarrasa near Monóvar and the small town of La Romana.

GEOLOGICAL DESCRIPTION

Jurassic red very fine-grained limestone, rich in bivalve and other shell fragments, with slender veins of colorless calcite and wider veins of white calcite. There are abundant stylolites.

MAJOR USAGE

Flooring, wall cladding, bathrooms, countertops and other architectural applications; furniture, inlay work.

Other pink marbles and limestones

Rosa Egeo has several other names including *Lafkos pink*, *Pilion pink* and *alexandra pink*. It is a fine-grained white marble with delicate waves of pink and comes from the Lafkos area of Thessaly, Greece. Pink marbles also come from nearby Pteleos and from Levadia in central Greece. *Rosa Patamuté* from Curaçá, Bahia, Brazil, is an attractive rich rose-pink marble with waves of brown mica. *Rosa aurora* from Torreón in northern Mexico is yellow-flushed pink.

The popular *rosa tea*, also called *Hazar pembe*, is a bright pink, fossiliferous limestone with eye-catching red stylolites. It comes from Çermik near Diyarbakir, Turkey. Attractive pink limestones come from around Bajestan and Gonabad in Iran. *Rosato di Brignoles* from Var, France, is a pale pink limestone with red stylolites and white veins. It was used for furniture and fireplaces

until the quarries closed in the 1950s. The limestones from Cimay near Sainte Anne d'Evenos include the orange-pink *Marseilles pink* or *rosé phocéen*. *Rosé vif du Pyrenees* is a famous old pink limestone breccia, extracted in the Ariege area and extensively used in France. *Rojo coralito*, currently quarried in Abanilla, Murcia, Spain, is rich coral-pink, tending to buff around white veins of calcite.

There are pink forms of some of the limestones described elsewhere in this book, for example the beige *Trani*, and the fossiliferous *Botticino* and *Chiampo* can all be tinted pink. However *rosa marfilia*, a pink limestone with abundant red stylolites, comes from China and is not a variety of the well-known Spanish *crema marfil*.

Red and violet marbles and limestones

Red and violet are traditionally the colors associated with royalty and nobility, and the richest red marbles and limestones have always commanded a high price. In Emperor Diocletian's Edict of Maximum Prices of 310 CE, the beautiful red *rosso antico* came second only to the precious *imperial porphyry* of Egypt. During the 17th century, King Louis XIV of France sought fine marbles to embellish his palace at Versailles. Red marbles such as the beautiful scarlet *rouge Languedoc* and cherry-red *griotte* from the Pyrenees, and the finest *rouge royal* and *Rance* from Belgium, feature prominently in this palace. In the 1800s, the sixth Duke of Devonshire delighted in acquiring columns and urns of *pavonazzetto* and *fior di pesco* to decorate Chatsworth House, and he opened mines for the vivid *duke's red marble* on his own estates. Today, bright red stones are not particularly fashionable, but those in attractive tints of violet continue to find a ready market.

Cipollino rosso, rosso brecciato

SOURCE: Kiyikislacik, Muğla, Turkey
STATUS: Monochrome stone is still quarried in this area

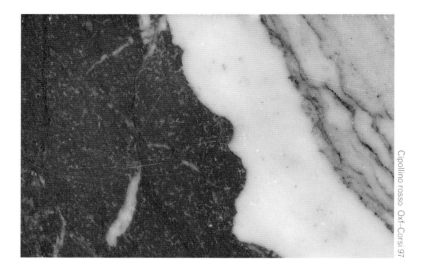

Cipollino rosso Oxf-Corsi 97

rosso brecciato Oxf-Corsi 389

Today, just as in ancient times, some of the brightest red marble on the market comes from the Turkish province of Muğla.

The ancient town of Iasos, in Caria, lies around what is now the village of Kiyikislacik, just across the water from Güllück, in the province of Muğla. As far back as Hellenistic times, marble was quarried from Iasos, but it was the Romans who extracted considerable quantities of the stone. They called it *marmor Carium* or *marmor Iassense*. Three distinct varieties were obtained. The most common, with swirling bands of red, gray and white, came to be known as *cipollino rosso*, and in the 19th century was also called *africanone*. It was brought from Caria to Rome and employed extensively around the Roman Empire in the fourth and fifth centuries CE. There are many pillars of this stone as well as panels in walls and floors. It was particularly popular in Byzantine times and can be seen in the Hagia Sophia and Kariye Camii museums in Istanbul.

Less abundant is a fine red and white breccia, known as *cipollino rosso brecciato* or simply as *rosso brecciato*, for it has none of the curved onionlike layering that gives the cipollini their name. Some gray or violet fragments may also be present in this stone. The rarest variety is the monochrome red stone, called *rosso antico* by the stonecutters of Rome, but not to be confused with the better known *rosso antico* from Cape Matapan (see page 122). They look so similar that isotope and trace chemical element analyses are usually needed to distinguish them from each other—and from an even rarer red marble from Aphrodisias, Turkey, that was also used in ancient times.

Today, red marble is still quarried in Muğla, near Kalınağıl Köyü, and is traded as *rosso laguna* or *Ege bordo*. "Ege" is from the Turkish for the Aegean, and "bordo"—from Bordeaux—alludes to the wine-red coloring. This is one of the brightest red marbles on the market today.

GEOLOGICAL DESCRIPTION

Cipollino rosso is a fine- to medium-grained folded impure calcitic marble, with some bands rich in red hematite and gray graphite. *Rosso brecciato* is a breccio-conglomerate of fine- to medium-grained white calcitic marble clasts, in a red hematite-rich marble matrix. The *rosso antico* variety is composed only of fine-grained hematite-rich marble.

MAJOR USAGE

Pillars, panels and slabs for walls and floors; *cipollino rosso* is often cut "open-book" style, as in the picture (right).

RIGHT The walls of the Byzantine Kariye Camii in Istanbul are clad with the most beautiful array of colored marbles including superb panels of *cipollino rosso*. Originally built as a Christian church in 534 CE, it became a mosque when the Turks invaded Istanbul in 1511, and is now a museum.

Rosso antico

SOURCE: Máni Peninsula, Peloponnese region, Greece
STATUS: Sporadic quarrying has taken place

Oxf-Corsi 62

In the writings of the ancients it is not always clear whether they were praising the beautiful *rosso antico* or the precious *imperial porphyry*.

Rosso antico was first used around 1700 BCE, but it was not exploited on any great scale until the days of the Roman Empire, and especially in the second century CE when Hadrian was emperor. It was called *marmor Taenarium* after Cape Taenaro on the Máni Peninsula. The purple-red color was largely reserved for the use of emperors and the higher classes of society, and of all the decorative stones used at this time, only the purple Egyptian *imperial porphyry* (see page 202) was more highly treasured. Panels of *rosso antico* were used in paving and it was employed in sculpture. The Ny Carlsberg Glyptotek in Copenhagen has a delightful hippopotamus that was carved from *rosso antico* in the second century CE.

For many centuries the ancient quarries were lost. Stonework carried out in the Renaissance and baroque eras reused stone salvaged from ancient ruins. *Rosso antico* was rediscovered at Skutari on the Máni Peninsula in 1830, and ancient quarries have been located farther inland, at Profitis Elias and Paganea. The stone was little used until later in the century when the London stone merchants Farmer and Brindley advertised its sale, and for a few years became proprietors of the quarries. It was William Brindley who supplied *rosso antico* for a low screen and steps between the sanctuary and the nave in Westminster Cathedral, London, one of the best examples of its use in 20th-century architecture. Sporadic quarrying took place later in the 20th century.

Cipollino rosso from Asin Kurin (see page 120) may resemble white-banded *rosso antico*, although the cipollino bands tend to be more convoluted. Monochrome red stone from that locality is

ABOVE Very large masses of precious *rosso antico* were used for the steps to the high altar in the Church of Santa Prassede in Rome.

particularly hard to distinguish, but is rather rare. Heavy wear in paving substantially dulls the intensity of the red color.

GEOLOGICAL DESCRIPTION

Fine-grained impure calcitic marble of Upper Cretaceous to Eocene age, colored by hematite and traces of manganese. Fine black veining is usually present. In the ground, the red marble is interspersed with bands of white marble, so generally only small blocks of monochrome red stone can be cut.

MAJOR USAGE

Sculptures, reliefs and vases using both monochrome red and red and white banded marble; smaller architectural elements; opus sectile pavements; mosaics.

RIGHT *Rosso antico* interbedded with white marble on a rocky outcrop along the Aegean coast, just north of the village of Paganea on Cape Matapan.

Duke's red

SOURCE: Derbyshire, England
STATUS: No longer available

Oxf-Corsi 65

One of the brightest red of all marbles is the historic *duke's red marble*, worked on the orders of the marble-loving sixth Duke of Devonshire.

Duke's red was named after William Cavendish, sixth Duke of Devonshire, a great enthusiast for colored marble. He used a variety of different stones for plinths in his sculpture gallery and other decorations in his country house, Chatsworth in Derbyshire. It is recorded that in 1823, he had shafts sunk for the "newly discovered red marble" at nearby Newhaven. The block shown here comes from these shafts and is one of the earliest examples of the stone. It was given to Faustino Corsi by the Duke after his visit to the great marble collector in Rome around 1823 or 1824. *Duke's red* was subsequently obtained mainly from the Alport mines near Youlgreave, and all remaining stocks are now stored at Chatsworth.

It was never available in large pieces, and its use was restricted mainly to the decoration of pulpits and other furnishings in local churches, various decorative items commissioned by the dukes of Devonshire and local inlay work. Vases, tables, jewelry and other items made of *duke's red* and other colored stones inlaid in the local *Ashford black marble* were sold mainly as souvenirs for visitors and are highly collectable today.

GEOLOGICAL DESCRIPTION

Weakly metamorphosed limestone of Carboniferous age, composed of colorless fine-grained calcite colored by red hematitic and occasional yellow goethitic threadlike inclusions.

MAJOR USAGE

Inlay work.

Griotte

SOURCE: The Pyrenees, France
STATUS: No longer quarried

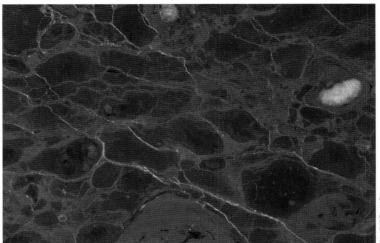

Oxf-Corsi 457

The rich red coloring and round nodular texture of this marble are more than a little reminiscent of the delicious "griotte" (morello) cherry.

One of the most distinctive marbles of the French Pyrenees is *griotte*, rather aptly taking its name from the French word for the morello cherry. It has been misleadingly traded as *griotte d'Italie*, but the principal sources were in the vicinity of Caunes-Minervois and Félines-Minervois, to the northeast of Carcassonne. These quarries have been worked extensively since the 17th century, supplying marble for the decoration of the palaces and churches patronized by King Louis XIV, such as the Palace of Versailles. The quarries were still active in the 20th century. *Griotte* has been extracted at various other places including Sost near Mauléon-Barousse, the Coumiac quarry in Cessenon-sur-Orb, and in Spain, near Lezo and Renteria. These stones were exported to many other countries including the United States.

Some nodules in *griotte* show relics of the shells of goniatites, mollusks related to ammonites. If they are part-filled with white calcite, the nodules seem to have white "eyes" and the stone is called *oeil de perdrix* (partridge eye).

GEOLOGICAL DESCRIPTION

Late Devonian or early Carboniferous hematitic nodular limestone rich in goniatites. Stylolites are common, and other fossils such as corals and trilobites may be present. Often seen white calcite-filled fractures are considered to lower its commercial value.

MAJOR USAGE

Interior use for decorative panels, and most especially fireplaces, tabletops and other furniture.

Rouge Languedoc, incarnat

SOURCE: Montagne Noire, Languedoc, France
STATUS: Actively quarried

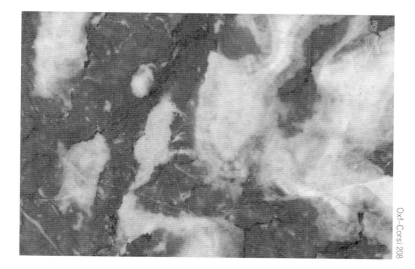

Oxf-Corsi 208

The Petit Trianon at the Palace of Versailles is one of the best places to see the beautiful marble known as *rouge Languedoc* or, simply, *Languedoc*.

Rouge Languedoc, the *rosso di Francia* of the Italians, has been extracted since Roman times from localities on the southern side of the Montagne Noire in Languedoc. The oldest quarries are near Caunes-Minervois. The Carrière du Roy (the King's quarry) was worked particularly during the reign of Louis XIV to supply stone for the furbishment of the Palace of Versailles, the Palace of St. Cloud and other royal buildings and monuments. Later, the stone was extensively used in prestigious building projects in France and across Europe and the United States. The Notre Dame du Cros quarry continued to work up to the end of the 20th century. The other main source of *Languedoc* is St. Nazaire-de-Ladareze in the Department of Hérault, where it is traded under the name *rouge incarnat*. Quarries here are still working. *Languedoc* was obtained farther south, at Villefranche-de-Conflent, and traded as *incarnat de Villefranche*, but the quarries have been closed for many years now. Other historic quarries were in l'Hôpital, Portes and Alais (now Alès).

Languedoc varies from orange-scarlet to bright red, with scattered white crinoid ossicles and shell fragments. It is crossed by interconnected pods filled with gray or white calcite crystals that sometimes show distinct layers. Opinions differ about whether these "stromatactis" cavities result from bacterial activity, fossil sponges, rare conditions of sedimentation or a combination of these factors. *Bleu turquin* is a variety composed predominantly of gray and white stromatactis cavities with fewer areas of orange-red limestone. *Cevenol*, from St. Nazaire-de-Ladareze, is similar but darker gray.

ABOVE *Rouge Languedoc* was used extensively for the external decoration of the Petit Trianon, a small château built in the grounds of the Palace of Versailles in the 1760s.

GEOLOGICAL DESCRIPTION

Mid-Devonian red crinoidal limestone with stromatactis cavities infilled with layers of elongate gray and white calcite crystals.

MAJOR USAGE

Architectural uses including wall cladding, chimneypieces and paving; furniture, and inlay work.

Brèche sanguine

SOURCE: Sidi Benyebka, near Oran, Algeria
STATUS: No longer quarried

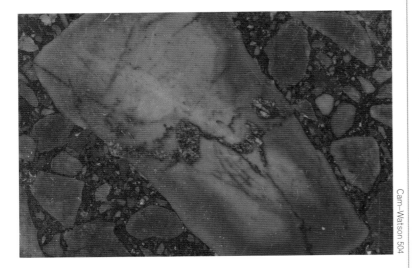

Cam-Watson 504

When diplomat Sir Lambert Playfair saw the colored marbles of Algeria in 1880, he was amazed they were so underexploited.

The Roman quarries had been rediscovered near Sidi Benyebka (Kleber) along a plateau at the summit of Gebel Arousse by Emile Delmonte, an Italian resident of Algeria. He purchased the rights to quarry the stone, and he must have been delighted at the enthusiastic response of the British Consul General in Algeria. To the east of Gebel Arousse, the stone was creamy-white. Progressing westward, it was flesh-colored, then yellow, then red. Movements of the ground at the far west of the plateau resulted in the breaking up and recementing of the stone, forming some beautiful breccias including the luxurious *brèche sanguine*. This stone has pebble or boulder sized clasts of limestone, and the whole stone is suffused deep red with hematite.

Following Playfair's visit and the publicity he generated, *brèche sanguine*, the orange-red *grand brèche de Kleber*, red *rouge damask* and pink *rose de Numidie* were all exported to Europe and the United States, extraction becoming sporadic and ceasing completely by 1950. Fine large panels of *brèche sanguine* can be seen high in the nave of Westminster Cathedral, London.

GEOLOGICAL DESCRIPTION

Breccia of large clasts of fine-grained dolomitic limestone or low-grade marble, with many veins of white calcite. The whole stone is heavily suffused red with disseminated hematite and has abundant stylolites.

MAJOR USAGE

Architectural, interior flooring, wall cladding and other features.

Breccia rossa Appenninica

SOURCE: Biassa-Pegazzano, Liguria, Italy
STATUS: No longer quarried

Oxf-Corsi 485

From time to time, an expedition to solve one marble mystery inadvertently solves quite another.

In the 1990s, Matthias Bruno and Lorenzo Lazzarini were in Liguria searching for the 'lost' quarries of *breccia dorato*. Instead, they found an abandoned quarry that yielded a brownish red stone with more than a passing similarity to the so-called *breccia rossa Appenninica*.

Breccia rossa Appenninica is a limestone conglomerate or nodular limestone that formed while the sediment was still rather soft. The rounded clasts range from creamy-white to pink and brown, sometimes pressed together in a dark brownish red matrix. The name of the stone suggested it was quarried in the Apennines, but some authorities believed that it came from the Apuan Alps. Neither are correct, for the quarry was on the road between Biassa and Pegazzano, in the suburbs of La Spezia, Liguria. *Breccia rossa Appenninica* has been found as pieces of paving stone and small columns in Roman excavations in Rome, Pompeii and Herculaneum, often in designs that use other valuable marbles of the time. Evidence of ancient working in the Ligurian quarry had been erased by modern working that was probably resumed in the 17th century.

GEOLOGICAL DESCRIPTION

Nodular limestone or limestone conglomerate composed of light and dark clasts in a ferruginous matrix. Stylolites are present.

MAJOR USAGE

Paving stones, small columns; reused in inlaid furniture and decorative wall panels, and found in historical collections of ancient stone.

Belgian red marbles

SOURCE: Namur, Belgium

STATUS: Rarely quarried now

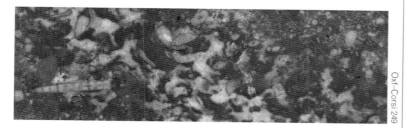

Oxf-Corsi 249

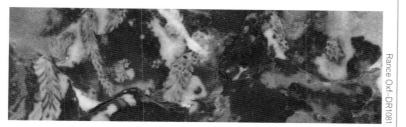

Rance Oxf-DR1081

The subdued and dignified Belgian red marbles can be seen in most Belgian churches and they have been exported globally.

There are many names given to the Belgian red marbles. *Rouge royale* is a widely used general term, and recognizes the patronage of this stone by King Louis XIV of France. The brightest red varieties, termed *rouge griotte*, lack the cherry-like nodular texture of the classic French *griotte* (see page 124). *Rance* and *royal St. Remy* are named after two of the best-known quarry locations. The stone from Rance is rich in corals and was used in the decoration of Versailles, but the quarries closed in the early 1950s. Other quarries are scattered across a roughly elliptical region of Namur, around Neuville, Frasnes and Philippeville, and to the east, Vodolée. Quarrying reached a peak in the 17th and 18th centuries, and continues to a very limited extent to this day.

Most of the Belgian red marbles are a rather brownish red but other features can vary considerably. They can be richly fossiliferous, have large patches of gray and white calcite or simply are mottled with these colors. Like the *Languedoc* marble (see page 125) the formation of these stones has been the subject of considerable geological research.

GEOLOGICAL DESCRIPTION

Fine-grained Devonian limestone containing brachiopods, nautiloids, echinoderm debris and other fossils. Stromatactis cavities are infilled with gray and white calcite crystals. Stylolites are common and calcite-filled fractures may be present.

MAJOR USAGE

Flooring, wall cladding and other architectural features; furniture; urns, vases and sculpture.

Breccia pavonazza

SOURCE: Source unknown

STATUS: Location of quarries is unknown

Oxf-Corsi 945

Mysterious and beautiful—this is one of the many gorgeous breccias used by the scalpellini, but exactly where it was quarried remains a mystery.

Pavonazza, sometimes in the past spelled *paonazzo,* comes from "pavone," the Italian name for a peacock, and is commonly used in the names and descriptions of marbles to indicate a violet color. Anyone who examines a peacock's feathers will only see rare iridescent reflections of violet. Still, the tradition holds, and this stone is so called because of its color.

It is a breccia of mixed limestone fragments in a granular dark red groundmass that is sometimes fragmented and cemented by pure white calcite. The marble collector Francesco Belli called this stone *breccia pavonazza bruna*, and H. W. Pullen, in his little book on Roman marbles, named it an appetizing *breccia pavonazza cioccolato*. It has also been termed *breccia pavonazza bruna del Suffragio* because it is used in panels above the skirtings in one of the chapels of the 17th-century Church of Santa Maria del Suffragio in Rome. It is one of the many beautiful breccias used by the scalpellini of Rome and found as decorative panels and in inlaid furniture, but the location of the quarry is not known.

GEOLOGICAL DESCRIPTION

Breccia of very mixed gray, white, brownish red and occasional pink limestone fragments in a brownish red granular matrix. Cavities in the matrix are filled with white calcite.

MAJOR USAGE

Decorative wall and floor panels; inlaid furniture made in Rome.

Fior di pesco

SOURCE: Eretria, Euboea, Greece
STATUS: Recently quarried

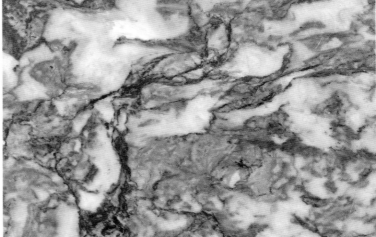

Both its names, *fior di pesco* and *fior di persico*, refer to peach blossom, but not to the vivid pink flowers of modern hybrids.

The color of this marble is its most distinctive feature. It is white and brownish red, and where the darker color suffuses into the white, it imparts a delicate shade of pink. In its entirety it is reminiscent of the pinkish white wild peach blossom with its deep pink center. Sometimes the stone is mainly brownish red with just a few white veins; at other times it is clearly a breccia of white marble clasts in a brownish red matrix, and yet again it may be so deformed that the color is rather randomly streaked through the white.

Fior di pesco was worked in ancient times and first brought to Rome, around the beginning of the first century CE. It has been found in many archaeological excavations, especially in Italy and North Africa. In ancient times it was known as *marmor Chalcidicum* after Chalcis, the principal town on Euboea. This stone was highly sought after in Rome during the 17th and 18th centuries, and was used, for example, in the Corsini Chapel of the Basilica of St. John Lateran. The sixth Duke of Devonshire greatly admired it, and had a fine tazza brought from Italy to decorate the painted hall of Chatsworth House in Derbyshire, England. Darker-colored stone quarried in recent years has been traded as *Eretria* or *Eretria red*.

GEOLOGICAL DESCRIPTION
Carboniferous limestone, metamorphosed into a fine-grained calcitic marble or marble breccia, heavily crushed and sheared.

MAJOR USAGE
Pillars; panels in walls and floors; vases; inlaid tables.

ABOVE The sixth Duke of Devonshire was passionately fond of colored marble and had this huge *fior di pesco* tazza sent to him from Rome to display in his country residence, Chatsworth House, in Derbyshire. The pedestal can be seen to be a composite of smaller pieces of stone.

Breccia di Settebasi, semesanto

SOURCE: Island of Skyros, Greece

STATUS: Only white marble quarried now

semesanto Oxf–Corsi 409

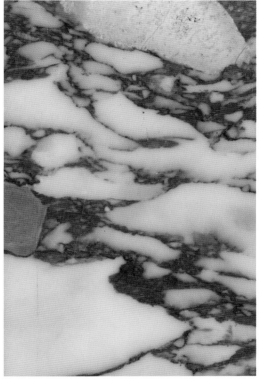

Breccia di Settebasi Oxf–Corsi 405

It took some time for marble experts to realize that both these red and white marbles came from the same Greek island.

The villa of the fourth century CE urban prefect Septimius Bassus was referred to as the "Villa dei Sette Bassi" as early as medieval times. It lies in Osteria del Curato on the outskirts of Rome, and it is where a substantial amount of a red and white marble was found. The scalpellini called it *breccia di Settebassi* or *Settebasi*. It is a strikingly colored marble, a mixture of elongate white and pink marble fragments in a bright red or deep purplish red cement. Another very distinctive breccia in the same colors has fragments consistently the size of sunflower seed kernels. It was named *semesanto*, after colorful sugar confections made by pharmacists to conceal medicines that were given to children. These marbles were first brought to Rome around the time when Augustus was emperor. While *breccia di Settebasi* was widely dispersed around the ancient Roman Empire, the distribution of *semesanto* was much more restricted.

Faustino Corsi had examples of both stones in his collection, and he also records how the ancient authors had referred to *marmor Scyrium*, a breccia coming from the Greek island of Skyros, but as they did not describe the stone clearly, he had no idea that his samples of *breccia di Settebasi* and *semesanto* were in fact Skyros marble. It was not until later in the 19th century that the mystery was solved by the rediscovery of the ancient quarries on the island. They are located at Tris Boukes, Kourisies and Renes on the southern coast of Skyros, and Aghios Panteleimon to the northwest. More recently, ancient quarries have been found on the adjacent islands of Rinia and Valaxa.

Quarries were reopened in 1899, working both the red and white *breccia di Settebasi* (*breccia di Sciro*) and a plain white marble. *Semesanto* has been found at Kourisies but was already virtually worked out. Marble has continued to be extracted from the south of the island of Skyros until quite recently and has been exported all over the world.

GEOLOGICAL DESCRIPTION

Triassic or early Jurassic breccias of predominantly white, some pink and occasional red fine-grained calcitic marble clasts. In *breccia di Settebasi*, they are sheared and aligned in a red hematic calcite matrix. Some yellow iron-staining is often present.

MAJOR USAGE

Paving and wall cladding; plinths, pillars and architectural features; tables and inlaid furniture.

Marmo pavonazzetto

SOURCE: İscehisar, Afyon, Turkey
STATUS: No longer quarried

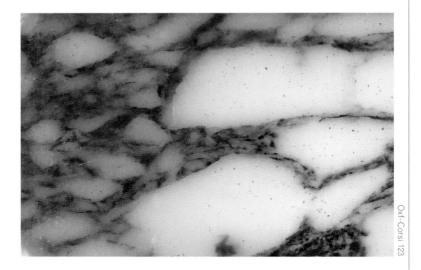

There may be several breccias of white marble fragments in a red matrix, but *marmo pavonazzetto* has certain distinctive features.

First, it is a breccia of large and small marble fragments that are pure white and have a particularly sugary texture. Then the matrix is red or dark violet tending to black. Third, the boundaries between the marble clasts and the surrounding matrix are quite diffuse, unlike the sharp boundaries seen in, say, *breccia di Seravezza* (opposite) or the white *Carrara breccia* (see page 65).

This stone has acquired various names. Strabo, writing early in the first century CE, tells us that it was quarried in the village of Docimia, close to the small city of Synnada, in the ancient kingdom of Phrygia. Consequently it was known in ancient times as *marmor Docimenium, marmor Synnadicum* or *marmor Phrygium*. It was quarried from the first century BCE to around the sixth century CE, and used not only for walls, paving and columns, but also for sculpture. The scalpellini's name *marmo pavonazzetto* comes from the Italian "pavone," meaning peacock (see page 127). In English-speaking countries it is also referred to as *Docimion* or *Phrygian marble*. Both this breccia and a pure white marble were quarried at Docimia, the modern town of İscehisar. White marble is still quarried in this area, and marketed as *Afyon white*.

GEOLOGICAL DESCRIPTION
Breccia of medium-grained white calcitic marble clasts in a deep violet hematite-rich calcite matrix.

MAJOR USAGE
Floor, paving, columns, sculptures; furniture panels and inlays.

Breccia bruna del Testaccio

SOURCE: Probably Greece or Turkey
STATUS: Source not known

Exactly where the rare and beautiful *breccia bruna del Testaccio* was quarried is a mystery, for its quarry has yet to be discovered.

This is an intensely dark purple-red marble that every so often has bands of pink and white marble fragments running through it. It can be seen in small pieces either decorating buildings or found in inlaid tables and historic collections of marble samples. Evidently it was used in antiquity, for various fragments were found during the 19th century in the Testaccio district of Rome, now better known for its restaurants and lively nightlife. This source has earned the marble its name *breccia bruna del Testaccio*.

Faustino Corsi thought his samples of this stone came from the Apuan Alps. The great marble expert William Brindley was the first to suggest they may be from Greece, and modern stone experts have agreed, suggesting either Greece or Turkey. But this debate has now gone full circle, for recent research has shown that the violet color in *breccia bruna del Testaccio* is due to a manganese mineral called piedmontite, and as piedmontite is known to color rocks in the Monte Corchia region of the Apuan Alps, this is once again considered to be a possible source.

GEOLOGICAL DESCRIPTION
Calcitic marble colored by piedmontite, containing bands of pink and white angular or rounded marble clasts and a few quartz fragments. Cavities and veins within the breccia bands are filled with white calcite.

MAJOR USAGE
Small panels in buildings and furniture; historic collections.

Breccia di Seravezza

SOURCE: Apuan Alps, Tuscany, Italy

STATUS: Only small amounts still being quarried

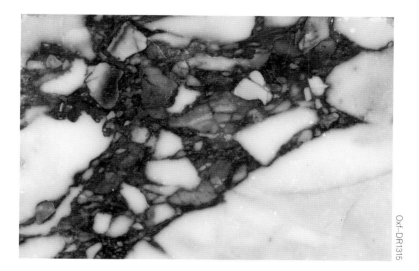

Oxf-DR1315

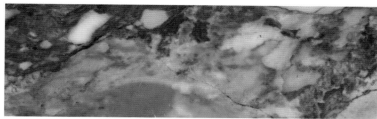

Oxf-Corsi 479

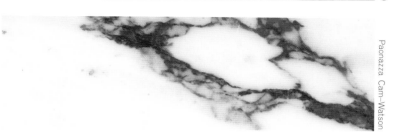

Paonazza Cam-Watson

There are many varied names for the breccias from Seravezza, and very little agreement about which stones they apply to!

It was under the patronage of Cosimo di Medici in the 16th century that the Seravezza quarries first flourished, yielding a variety of brecciated stones that some authors have called *mischio di Seravezza*, and today are loosely termed *breccia di Seravezza*. The name has been extended to encompass the diverse breccias found in the environs of Seravezza and Stazzema. They may have been extracted in much earlier times and evidence is growing of a very limited use by the ancient Romans. Large-scale production continued through the 19th century with exports to many countries. Since the 1970s, it has dwindled and they are of limited availability today.

These stones can be very variable in appearance, not only from one variety to another, but even within a single large slab of stone. The clasts may be monochrome white or they can be a mixture of white, pink, yellow and red. The cement can be deep violet, yellow, red or streaky green. Clasts can vary enormously in size. It is generally agreed that *paonazza* has white fragments with more or less violet matrix. *Skyros d'Italia* has white and pink fragments in a violet matrix resembling the true *Skyros breccia* but with less alignment of its clasts. There is remarkably little agreement about what should be called *breccia Medicea*, *breccia violetta*, *breccia arlecchina* and various other varieties.

GEOLOGICAL DESCRIPTION

Breccias of single or mixed marble fragments in a calcareous matrix, rich in either iron oxides (red, yellow) or in chlorite and other iron silicates (green). More rarely, the violet manganese mineral piedmontite may be the coloring agent.

MAJOR USAGE

Walls and flooring, fireplaces, balustrades and banister rails.

ABOVE Fine oval panels of *breccia di Seravezza* framed by *Belgian black*, white *Carrara* statuary and green *verde antico*, clad the base of the columns that support the canopy over the high altar in Westminster Cathedral, London.

Fior di pesco Apuano

SOURCE: Apuan Alps, Italy
STATUS: Actively quarried

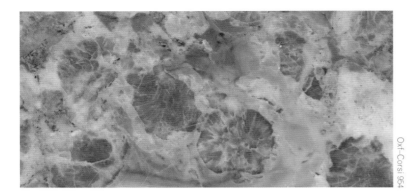

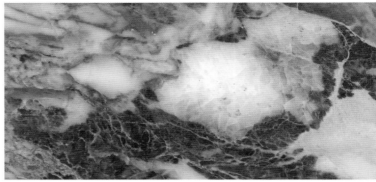

The characteristic markings of this marble resemble drops of violet-pink ink spreading on the surface of water.

One of the prettiest of the colored marbles from the Apuan Alps is known as *fior di pesco*, the "peach blossom" marble. In France it is *fleur de pêcher*, and these days it is called *fior di pesco Apuano* to distinguish it from its Greek namesake (see page 128) and from a gray stone called *fior di pesco Carnico* from Udine. It is a breccia of large irregular marble clasts heavily spotted with purple-red and violet-pink, in a streaky green marble matrix, the whole stone having undergone considerable deformation in the ground. It is the distinctive appearance of the round spots of pink that distinguish this stone from other breccias of the Apuan Alps loosely referred to as *breccie di Seravezza*.

Fior di pesco Apuano has been quarried since the 17th century. At first it came from Stazzema and Seravezza, then in the 20th century from the regions of Versilia and Garfagnana, and most recently from quarries in Renana, Forno and elsewhere in Massa. Little is quarried today and the stone has become quite rare. *Fior di pesco Apuano* was obtained mainly in rather small pieces and was a popular choice for using in furniture, particularly tabletops; in the 17th century it was highly sought after for ecclesiastical decoration.

GEOLOGICAL DESCRIPTION

Deformed breccia of white, violet and pink marble clasts in a chlorite-rich calcitic marble matrix.

MAJOR USAGE

Interior walls, usually as small panels; furniture.

Other red and violet marbles and limestones

Rosso rubino is a red marble with a wavy, streaky appearance. It is quarried in Lucca, Tuscany, Italy. Another good red marble from Lucca is *rosso Collemandina*, quarried at Villa Collemandina. It is crossed with slender straight white veins. Marbles with a nodular structure like that of *rosso Verona* (see page 115) but a much darker color include *rosso Asiago* and *porfirico magnaboschi* from Vincenza, and the stones known as *porfirico ramello rosso* and *porfirico ramello bruno* from Udine. *Diaspro tenero di Sicilia* (see page 150) can be plain red.

In the past, France has supplied a number of good red and violet marbles. *Rouge de France* is a red limestone with white or pink veins and pale stylolites, and comes from Gres-en-Bouère in Pays de la Loire. *Rouge de Vitrolles* is also called *rouge jaspé antique* and *rouge Etrusque*, and comes from Vitrolles, Bouches du Rhône. It is a curious orange-red limestone with elongate pale bands running through it and has been used in Marseilles Cathedral and the New York Public Library. *Escalettes* has strings of buff-colored clasts in a brownish red matrix and comes from Uchentein in Ariège; it has been used a lot in furniture. *Rouge antique de France* from Villerambert in Languedoc has the color of *Languedoc* marble and contains small white crinoid fragments. It was much used for clocks and other decorative pieces in the 19th century. *Cipollino mandolato* (see page 134) can be red.

In the past, a limestone of similar color to *Belgian red* was quarried at Knoxville, Tennessee, and marketed as *royal rouge*. The overall effect of *Tennessee cedar* available today is a brownish red and white mottled coloring (see page 164).

Multicolored marbles and limestones

When marbles and limestones display a mix of different colors, with no single color predominating, they tend to be either breccias that have angular fragments of different stones cemented together, or conglomerates, where the fragments are rounded. Multicolored stones used to be more fashionable than they are today. Antique tables and chests are topped with beautiful breccias from the Pyrenees, while churches and mosques are decorated with multicolored marbles from countries all around the Mediterranean. Names such as *Africano, portasanta, breccia d'Aleppo* and *breccia frutticolosa* were coined by the Italian scalpellini who recycled these stones long after the quarries were closed and forgotten. In the late 19th century, commercial objectives fueled the desire to rediscover the ancient quarries, but in recent times, it is the more altruistic desire to better understand our cultural history that motivates archaeologists and geologists to become quarry hunters.

Cipollino mandolato, Campan

SOURCE: Campan Valley, Hautes-Pyrénées, France

STATUS: Quarries recently closed

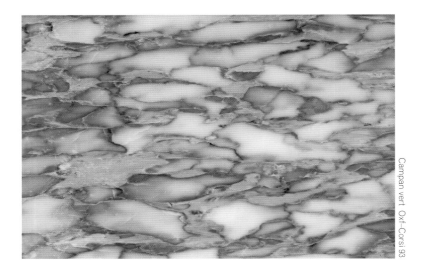

Campan vert Oxf–Corsi 93

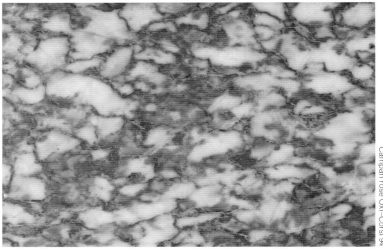

Campan rosé Oxf–Corsi 94

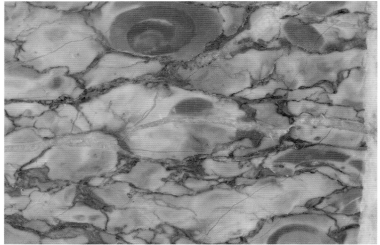

Cam–Percy 26

These famous marbles may have all sorts of color combinations, but their nodular structure makes them instantly recognizable.

The Italian stonecutters' name *cipollino verde mandolato* is still used by archaeologists for the green, pink and red marbles with almond-shaped nodules obtained from the French Pyrenees. From the first century BCE, the Romans quarried them from various locations, notably Pont de la Taule and the best known source, the Campan Valley. Although quarrying was halted in medieval times, it recommenced in the Campan Valley in the 17th century.

The green marble is known in French as *Campan vert* or *griotte vert*. *Campan mélangé* has alternate bands of green and pink, and is sometimes called *ribbon Campan*. Predominantly pink varieties include *Campan rosé* and *Campan Isabelle*. The red *Campan rouge* grades into the famous *griotte* marble (see page 124). The centers of nodules are often white.

These marbles were among those reserved for exclusive use of the French king Louis XIV. They were employed extensively in the interior decoration of the Palace of Versailles and other buildings constructed under royal patronage, and were also used in the decoration of furniture. They continued to be used through the 18th and 19th centuries. The green variety in particular was very fashionable as an interior cladding for buildings constructed at the end of the 19th and early 20th centuries. Excellent examples of its use can be seen across the English Channel in Westminster Cathedral and the cathedrals at Peterborough and Bristol. The quarries finally closed toward the end of the 20th century.

Vert d'Estours is a very similar stone to *Campan vert,* and quarries were opened in the Estour Valley at the end of the 19th century. It was used particularly for decorating furniture. The quarries probably closed around the time of World War I.

GEOLOGICAL DESCRIPTION

A lightly metamorphosed early Devonian nodular limestone, composed of compressed fine-grained granular calcite nodules in a green, pink or red calcitic matrix. The green coloring is predominantly chlorite; red and pink are where hematite is present. The rock may be folded and cut by white calcite-filled fractures.

MAJOR USAGE

Used for pillars and extensively for interior wall cladding, paving, chimneypieces, tabletops and other furniture decoration. *Campan mélangé* is often cut in an "open book" style so that one side of the panel is a mirror image of the other.

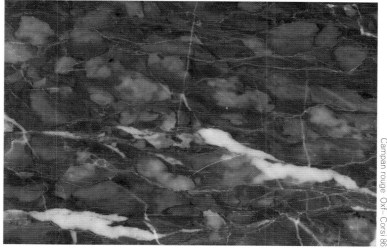

RIGHT AND ABOVE *Campan marble* is used extensively in the Palace of Versailles. *Campan mélangé* is seen below the balustrades of the Queen's Staircase, while large panels of *Campan mélangé* and *Campan vert* decorate walls in the Salon de la Paix.

Africano

SOURCE: Teos (Sığacık), İzmir, Turkey
STATUS: Quarried in antiquity

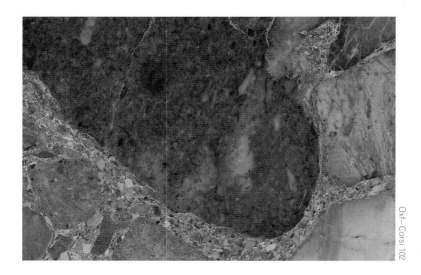

Oxf– Corsi 102

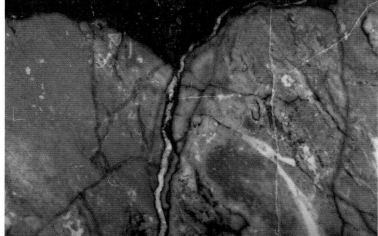

Oxf– Corsi 115

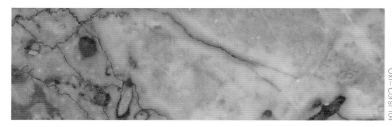

Oxf– Corsi 104

Oxf– Corsi 116

Why *africano*? Nobody is quite sure, and confusion regarding the naming of this ancient stone remains to this day.

Africano is a limestone breccia or conglomerate with a distinctive palette of colors—red, pink, gray, green, white and particularly black. Most clasts are mottled, banded or rimmed with different colors, and they range from large cobbles to small grit-sized grains. The matrix is usually black but can also be brown or grayish green.

Pliny recounts how the consul Lucius Licinius Lucullus (ca. 118–56 BCE) introduced a stone to Rome that was in general black, and was known as *marmor luculleum*. He said it came from an island that Faustino Corsi at first believed to be Chios, consequently confusing the stone with *portasanta* (see page 140). By 1845, Corsi had reinterpreted Pliny's locality as Melos, one of the islands in the delta of the Nile. It is perhaps this that led to the Roman stonecutters using the modern name *africano*; or it may just have been that the color black, characteristic of this stone, had African connotations. Archaeologists still correlate the Roman *marmor luculleum* with *africano*. Large quantities were quarried in the first and second centuries CE, and used particularly in Italy and northern Africa. Two tiers of *africano* pillars were used, for example, in the Basilica Aemilia in the Forum of Rome. *Africano* was extensively recycled long after the quarries had closed and their location had been forgotten. Huge columns can be seen flanking the great door of the façade of the Vatican Basilica.

Neither of Corsi's localities is correct, although his errors were perpetuated in subsequent literature. There is a curious lake called Kara Göl in a quarry of gray-white marble near the ruins of the ancient city of Teos, close to Sığacık in western Turkey.

Closer examination by archaeologist Michael Ballance in 1966 revealed that it was the flooded *africano* quarry. A second quarry was later discovered about 10 miles (15 km) away, at Beylerköy.

GEOLOGICAL DESCRIPTION

Cretaceous tectonic breccia or conglomerate of mixed limestone clasts; green chlorite results from slight metamorphism of the stone. Fossils such as crinoid ossicles and bivalve fragments occur in the matrix and in some limestone fragments. Fractures infilled with white calcite or quartz run through individual clasts or through the stone as a whole.

MAJOR USAGE

Pillars, wall cladding, inlay work.

LEFT In a juxtaposition of ancient and modern stones, this rhombic panel of *africano* is surrounded by *rouge Languedoc*. It is in Westminster Cathedral, London.

BELOW *Africano* from Teos and *cipollino verde* from Euboea are among the marbles used for this Roman store countertop at Herculaneum.

Brèche Bénou

SOURCE: Plateau de Bénou, Bilhères, Pyrénées-Atlantique
STATUS: Some quarrying still takes place

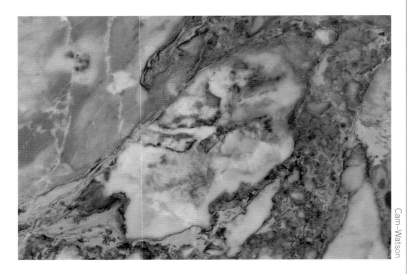

Cam–Watson

A classy marble, *brèche Bénou* has green, cream, yellow and violet all blended elegantly together.

The mountain road from Escot to Bielle in the western Pyrenees runs along the foot of the Col de Marie Blanque, and passes the Plateau de Bénou before it enters the village of Bilhères. It is here that this beautiful marble has been quarried since the 18th century and perhaps earlier. It was very popular in the early decades of the 20th century and has been quarried sporadically up to the present day.

There are two varieties: the more richly colored classic stone is a breccia with large fragments of a deformed white marble lightly to heavily suffused with yellow and violet, in a streaky green matrix. *Bénou jaune* is a cloudy mixture mainly of yellow and creamy-white with scattered whiteish veins, and has little or no green coloration.

Brèche Bénou is most often used for chimneypieces, tabletops and chest-tops and in other furniture, but it is also seen as panels and pillars in architectural decoration. The fireplace in the Founder's Room of the art deco Joslyn Museum in Omaha, Nebraska, is made of *Bénou jaune*, and there are pillars of the classic *Bénou* in the Wisconsin State Capital. *Brèche Bénou* is sometimes traded under the name *brèche de Vendome*.

GEOLOGICAL DESCRIPTION

A breccia of distorted impure marble clasts in a green chlorite-rich matrix. Fractures are filled with white calcite.

MAJOR USAGE

Fireplaces and furniture; wall panels and other interior architectural features.

Breccia aurora

SOURCE: Paitone and Gavardo, Lombardy, Italy
STATUS: Actively quarried

Cam–Watson 326

The "dawn breccia," *breccia aurora* is one of relatively few multicolored limestone or marble breccias still quarried today.

There are not many stones in this section of the book that are still quarried, but *breccia aurora* is a worthy exception. It is quite variable in appearance, but heavily veined with white calcite and is often fossiliferous. Stone extracted in the past was light beige, richly veined with red and green as shown above, although it is not so intensely colored as *Sarrancolin* (see opposite). The stone sold today is predominantly creamy-beige with a little subtle color veining and may be mottled with smaller dark brown fragments.

Breccia aurora is quarried at Paitone, Gavardo and nearby villages in Brescia. These quarries also yield the famous *Botticino marble* (see page 169) that has been worked in this area since Roman times, but references to *breccia aurora* do not go back as far. It has been quarried since the end of the 19th century, and fine columns were installed in the entrance to the Victoria and Albert Museum in London, built in 1901. It has also been used on the walls in Milan's central railroad station.

GEOLOGICAL DESCRIPTION

Early Jurassic limestone breccia containing scattered fossils, with some olive-green and red veining and abundant white calcite-filled fractures.

MAJOR USAGE

Paving, wall cladding and other architectural applications; tabletops and other furniture.

Sarrancolin

SOURCE: Sarrancolin area, Hautes-Pyrénées, France
STATUS: Actively quarried

A night out at the famous Garnier Opera House in Paris is a perfect opportunity to admire this luxurious marble.

Quarries near the villages of Sarrancolin, Ilhet and Beyrede-Jumet have all produced *Sarrancolin*, one of the most beautiful of the French marbles. It is a medley of cream, yellow, buff, pink, gray and greenish fragments, brought to life by a few deep blood-red vein and cavity fills, and traversed by slender white calcite veins.

The stone was extracted for local use by the ancient Romans, and the quarries were operating in the 16th century. During the 17th century they supplied marble for the Palace of Versailles and other building projects of King Louis XIV. In the 19th century the stone was again used for prestigious projects, most notably 30 pillars in the Grand Opera House in Paris, built in 1887. These two famous applications of the stone are commemorated in its modern trade names, *Sarrancolin opera fantastico* and *Sarrancolin Versaille*. *Sarrancolin* can also be seen in the Louvre, the Sénat and other public buildings in Paris.

GEOLOGICAL DESCRIPTION

Weakly metamorphosed Devonian limestone breccia, with several generations of fracturing and vein infilling.

MAJOR USAGE

Interior architectural uses such as flooring, wall cladding, mantelpieces; furniture.

RIGHT *Sarrancolin* column in the Sénat, Paris (above right), and in this 19th-century fireplace (detail).

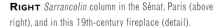

Portasanta

SOURCE: Island of Chios, Greece
STATUS: No longer quarried

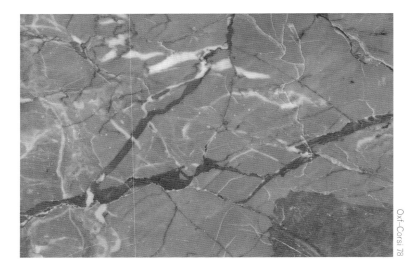

Oxf–Corsi 78

reticulated portasanta Oxf–Corsi 80

Many thousands of visitors each year are photographed in front of the Holy Door of St. Peter's, framed by *portasanta* marble.

Portasanta is named after the Holy Door leading into St. Peter's Basilica in the Vatican, where it forms the door jambs. It is also used for the jambs of doors of other basilicas in Rome. These are some of many reuses of stone that was extensively quarried by the ancient Romans from the first century BCE, and worked long before this by the Greeks. By all accounts it was one of the most important colored marbles to be used in ancient times, mentioned by Pliny, Strabo and Theophrastus.

There are several very different varieties of *portasanta* but certain features are typical. They are fine-grained and compact stones, predominantly dull red, salmon-pink and gray in color. Other colors such as orange, brown and yellow also occur, but never green. *Portasanta* has white calcite-filled fractures that may run abundantly through the rock. Some varieties show a distinctive reticulated appearance.

The quarries closed in Byzantine times and were lost for many centuries. Opinions varied about the original source of *portasanta* until the late 19th century, when English stone merchant William Brindley visited the Aegean island of Chios and saw the *portasanta* quarries for himself. They are located a short distance northwest of Chora. Since then, there has been sporadic quarrying on the island, most recently for a brown limestone known as *Chios brown*.

Another excellent place to see *portasanta* is the Church of Sant'Agnese Fuori le Mura in Rome, which has four exceptional columns of the stone. It was also used for the fountain basins in the Piazza Navona.

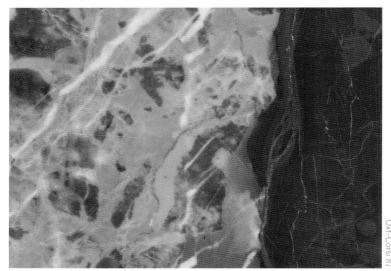

Oxf–Corsi 87

GEOLOGICAL DESCRIPTION

Fine-grained limestones and low-grade marbles of Triassic age, generally brecciated with clasts from fractions of an inch to around a foot in size. Stylolites and white calcite-filled fractures are common. Crinoids, bivalves and other fossils are preserved in the limestones. Reticulated *portasanta* is partially recrystallized limestone with iron oxides concentrated in abundant stylolites.

MAJOR USAGE

Columns, sculpture and architectural elements; basins and tabletops; 18th- and 19th-century furniture and inlay work.

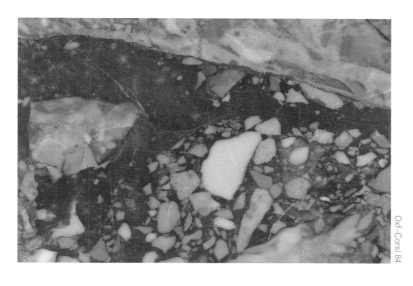

Oxf-Corsi 84

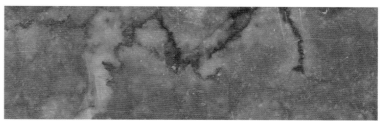

Oxf-Corsi 906

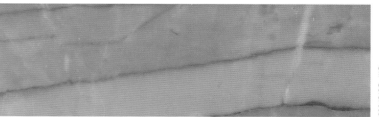

Oxf-Corsi 908

ABOVE *Portasanta* surrounds the Holy Door of St. Peter's Basilica in the Vatican. It is from this architectural feature that the marble gets its name.

LEFT The basins of the famous Piazza Navona Fountains in Rome are made of *portasanta*.

There is nothing more frustrating than forgetting an important piece of information. By the time Faustino Corsi (see page 12) started his collection in the early 1800s, everyone had forgotten where most of the ancient stones had been quarried. Corsi did some detective work, and tried to determine where the quarries must have been, based on the writings of ancient authors, the verbal traditions of the scalpellini and the accounts of contemporary scientists and travelers. This was pioneering research, but only the first step. Others went further, and journals of the 1830s and 1840s announced, for example, the rediscovery of the *rosso antico* quarries in Greece, and those of *imperial porphyry* in Egypt. Quarry-hunting took on a new intensity in the late 19th century, and the motivation was very simple: commercial gain.

THE QUARRY HUNTER

The greatest quarry hunter was William Brindley of the London firm of Messrs. Farmer and Brindley, sculptors and stone merchants. Brindley was considered the decorative stone expert of his time. He was a competent sculptor but also an astute businessman who recognized that the growing taste for natural stone in architecture and the fashion for all things classical could best be exploited by making the stones that had been used in classical times available on the current market. He was a great researcher and insatiable traveler. Having read Corsi's books and followed up the classical literature, he would go to places where he thought ancient quarries should be located, talk to local people and follow their leads. When he found a possible quarry he would search for evidence to confirm the antiquity of the site, such as pick or wedge marks, and waste tips with discarded blocks or pillars. If the rock found in the ground matched one of the classic ancient stones, Brindley had indeed struck gold. He would report his findings to the Royal Institute of British Architects, negotiate with local officials for the necessary licenses and in due course reopen the ancient quarries to commercial working; alas, by doing this, he invariably destroyed part or all of the ancient site. Between 1880 and 1910 he had brought back into production the quarries of *rosso antico*,

cipollino verde, *verde antico* and several other marbles, supplying stone for inumerable neoclassical buildings that embellish our architectural heritage today.

MODERN RESEARCHERS

Modern quarry hunters have an entirely different motivation. In the 1960s, the English archaeologist John Ward Perkins set out in search of ancient quarries, to understand the extraordinarily complex nature of the Roman stone trade, and the processes by which stone was cut, processed and transported. Since then, innumerable ancient quarries have been rediscovered, and inscriptions on discarded blocks in quarries have revealed a wealth of information about where and when the stone was used. Regularly, the Association for the Study of Marble and Stone in Antiquity (ASMOSIA) brings scientists together to discuss the latest quarry finds and the huge amount of research into the identification, history and use of ancient stones. In the last couple of decades we have discovered where *breccia d'Aleppo*, *breccia rossa Appeninica*, *breccia frutticolosa* and many others were quarried ... but as fast as ancient quarries are identified, so scientific methods have enabled yet more mystery stones to be distinguished.

ABOVE The ancient quarry of *rosso antico* was rediscovered on the Mani Peninsula in Greece by a French scientific expedition in the 1830s. This is the main face of the quarry at Profitis Elias.

LEFT This panel of *cipollino verde* in Westminster Cathedral is made from the stone obtained after William Brindley had reopened the ancient quarries on Euboea. It is cut in the "open book" style.

LEFT Huge great monolith columns of *cipollino verde* still lie strewn across the ancient quarries near Karystos on the island of Euboea in Greece. Damaged or rejected columns, sarcophagi and other worked pieces are unmistakable signs that quarrying took place in ancient times. More subtle clues include the tool marks left by ancient quarrying methods.

Breccia di Aleppo

SOURCE: Chios, Greece
STATUS: Quarried in antiquity

Oxf-Corsi 394

The only connection *breccia di Aleppo* has with the city of Aleppo in Syria is its name. Where it was actually quarried is a very recent discovery.

Introduced by the ancient Romans for paving, wall panels, and pillars around the first century CE, *breccia di Aleppo* was recycled for interior decoration particularly during baroque times. Although it was never quarried in very large quantities, it is a classic among ancient Roman marbles, always found in collections of ancient stones and among samples in inlaid tabletops made by the Roman scalpellini in the 18th and 19th centuries.

The name has long been a cause of confusion. While some authors believed it was quarried in Aleppo, Syria, others thought it had been muddled with the French *brèche d'Alet* (see page 145), another colorful stone but of very different appearance. At all accounts, the actual place it was quarried remained lost in history until 2001, when Lorenzo Lazzarini rediscovered the quarries at Kariès, several miles north of the town of Chios, on the Greek island of the same name.

Breccia di Aleppo is a limestone breccia, and some clasts are fossiliferous. Generally, they are different shades of gray, but scattered through the stone are smaller fragments that are brilliant yellow. In a much rarer variety, they are coral-pink instead. The matrix is orange or red.

GEOLOGICAL DESCRIPTION
Mid-Triassic breccia of mixed limestone clasts in a red hematitic matrix. Some clasts are fossiliferous.

MAJOR USAGE
Pavings, pillars, tabletops; panels inlaid in furniture.

Brèche Nouvelle

SOURCE: La Palme and Cap Romarin, Languedoc-Roussillon, France
STATUS: Actively quarried

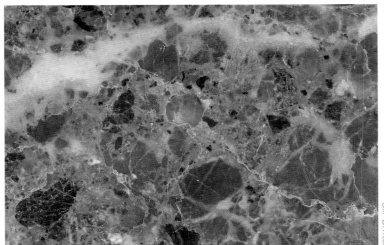

Oxf-DR1680

Not as "nouvelle" as its name would suggest, *brèche Nouvelle* has been quarried since the 19th century.

Brèche Nouvelle is named after the fishing village of Port-la-Nouvelle, a popular vacation destination on the Aude coast. It has also been called *brèche Cap Romarin* from the name of the cape to the south. Quarries opened between La Palme and Port-la-Nouvelle in 1889 and are still working.

It is typically composed of grayish brown mottled limestone fragments in a mixture of white and orange-red matrix. At its most superb, the clasts are very dark brown and the cement is almost entirely an intense red. The whole stone is heavily fractured, the cracks filled with white calcite. Stylolites as sinuous lines crossing the stone are very characteristic. *Saint-Jean Fleuri* comes from the same quarry and resembles *brèche Nouvelle* but has a white calcite cement with just traces of orange iron oxides.

Although it has many architectural uses, it is also used for chest-tops and tabletops.

GEOLOGICAL DESCRIPTION
Jurassic breccia with a ferruginous cement and abundant pale-colored stylolites. White calcite fills veins and cavities in the rock.

MAJOR USAGE
Floors, walls and other architectural elements; furniture.

Brèche d'Alet

SOURCE: Near Aix-aux-Provence, France
STATUS: No longer quarried

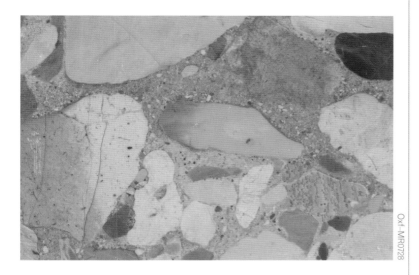

Oxf-MR0728

The name of this stone may sound similar to that of the historic *breccia di Aleppo*, and it is every bit as beautiful, but it looks completely different.

Brèche d'Alet is also called *brèche d'Alep* or *brèche du Tholonet*. It was quarried east of Aix-aux-Provence at a place called Roques-Hautes, between Le Tholonet and St. Antonin-sur-Bayon. The clasts tend to be rather rounded and are predominantly ocherous-yellow and red, with minor dark gray and brown fragments. The matrix is a gritty mixture of red and yellow. This stone should not be confused with the ancient *breccia di Aleppo* (see opposite).

The quarries were most active during the 17th, 18th and 19th centuries and supplied stone for interior decoration and especially for mantelpieces and furniture. The stone was used in hotels and public buildings in Provence, Paris and elsewhere in France, and was exported overseas. Quarrying ceased just before World War II.

In Paris, *brèche d'Alet* can be seen in the Ecole des Beaux-Arts and the Church of the Madeleine. There are several columns in the Louvre, and it was one of the many decorative stones used in the Garnier Opera House. It was combined with Tivoli travertine in the floor of the Dwight Eisenhower Library built in 1962 in Abilene, Kansas.

GEOLOGICAL DESCRIPTION
Late Cretaceous conglomerate of mixed limestone clasts in a gritty calcareous sandstone (calcarenite) cement.

MAJOR USAGE
Furniture, mantelpieces, pillars and plinths; also used for flooring and wall cladding.

Brèche Médous

SOURCE: Médous, Hautes-Pyrénées, France
STATUS: No longer quarried

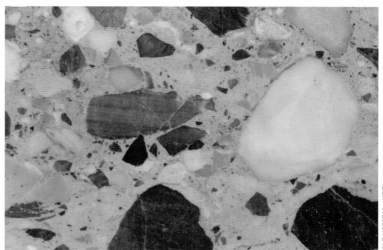

Cam-Watson 246

If you took a black and white photograph of the pretty yellow *brèche Médous*, it would come out looking just like *brèche Médous gris*.

There are two distinct varieties of *brèche Médous*, obtained from neighboring quarries. *Brèche Médous jaune* has fragments of limestone, predominantly black and yellow, but also gray, white and brown, in an orange-brown matrix. In *brèche Médous gris*, the fragments are black, white and predominantly gray, and the matrix is also gray. The quarries were in Médous (also spelled Médoux by various authors) near Bagnères-de-Bigorre. They were probably active in the 17th century and worked up until the 1960s, but are now no longer visible.

Brèche Médous has also been called *brèche Grammont* and *brèche universelle* (not to be confused with the Egyptian stone of a similar name, described on page 194). One authority says it is a rather friable stone and that it was hard to obtain in large blocks. It seems to have been very popular for use in mantelpieces and it can be seen in larger hotels of the area. In Paris, it was used for wall claddings in the Church of the Madeleine.

GEOLOGICAL DESCRIPTION
Paleocene breccio-conglomerate of mixed marble, limestone and dolomite clasts in a gray or yellowish ferruginous matrix.

MAJOR USAGE
Paving, claddings and mantelpieces; architectural elements.

Sabalgarh marble

SOURCE: Sabalgarh, Madhya Pradesh, India
STATUS: Probably still quarried

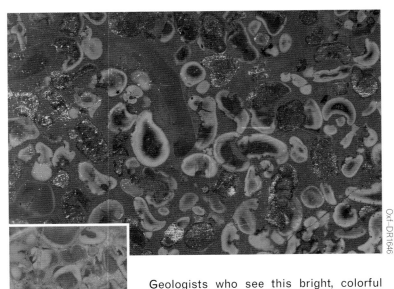

Oxf-DR1646

Geologists who see this bright, colorful stone are invariably puzzled as to how it formed. It is certainly not a typical breccia or conglomerate.

Sabalgarh marble, also called *Ujuba*, is an extraordinary-looking stone with bright red, green and orange "nodules" in a granular buff or brown matrix. The sample in the Watson Collection at Cambridge University was a gift from the President of Gwalior (since then the state of Gwalior has been subsumed into Madhyar Pradesh) and comes from the Gora quarry at Sabalgarh. The Oxford collection sample was a gift from the Geological Survey of India, part of a collection of classic marbles from India, and is said to come from near Jowarhirgarh Fort in Gwalior. Both samples date from the first decades of the 20th century.

How this stone formed is a matter of conjecture, but it has the appearance of a heavily altered fossiliferous limestone. John Watson (who formed the Cambridge collection) believed it was of Silurian age, and reported in 1916 that it was extensively employed in ornamenting the Mogul buildings of Agra. Small amounts of stone have been seen on the market in recent years, suggesting it may still be quarried on a small scale.

GEOLOGICAL DESCRIPTION

Silurian limestone of color-banded calcitic nodules in a granular buff dolomitic matrix, perhaps a heavily altered fossil limestone.

MAJOR USAGE

Architectural elements.

Breccia frutticolosa

SOURCE: Bourdeau, Savoie, France
STATUS: No longer quarried

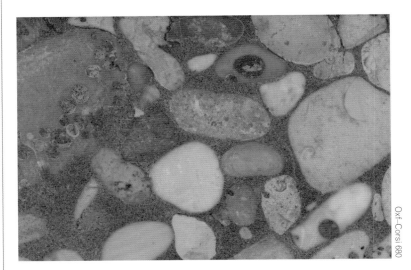

Oxf-Corsi 680

A passing resemblance to a dried fruit pudding has earned this stone the scalpellini's name *breccia frutticolosa*.

Breccia frutticolosa is a conglomerate of limestone pebbles colored various shades of cream, buff and brown, in a gray matrix. The holes in the pebbles were made by marine bivalves that were able to bore into sediments, and they make it a rather distinctive and easily recognized stone. Bivalves and sharks' teeth have been found that show it is of Miocene age.

Small quantities of *breccia frutticolosa* have been found in the ruins of Rome, showing that it was quarried in Roman times. Where the quarry had been was a mystery that was only solved in the 1990s. *Breccia frutticolosa* was found to match a conglomerate that had been quarried close by the village of Bourdeau, on the western bank of Lake du Bourget, northwest of Chambéry.

Although more recent stone extraction had obliterated any evidence of Roman quarrying, its use in late Roman times was confirmed when the fourth-century baptistry of Notre Dame Cathedral in Grenoble was discovered, where this stone had been employed with other local breccias and more exotic marbles for the pavement. Now, *breccia frutticolosa* is also called *conglomérat de Bourdeau*.

GEOLOGICAL DESCRIPTION

Miocene conglomerate of limestone pebbles bored by bivalves. The matrix is a calcareous sandstone rich in grains of dark silicate minerals.

MAJOR USAGE

Pillars, paving and plinths; Roman inlay work; collections of ancient marbles.

Breccia della Villa Casali

SOURCE: Not known
STATUS: Quarried in antiquity

Oxf-Corsi 408

Fragments of large seashells are interspersed with rounded pebbles in the red, pink and yellow *breccia della Villa Casali*.

The historic Villa Casali on the Caelian Hill in Rome was demolished in 1885, but it left a rich archaeological legacy. Excavations over the years in the grounds of the villa had revealed a wealth of sculptures, reliefs and other treasures. Among them were two beautiful columns of this distinctive stone that the archaeologist Rodolfo Lanciani named *breccia della Villa Casali*.

Faustino Corsi's sample (shown above) was cut from stone obtained in excavations there a little before his catalog was published in 1825. He calls the stone simply *breccia rossa* and mentions that it was a recent discovery. He believed his sample was unique, but the scalpellini had more available, for they used it sparingly in inlays in tabletops and in sets of marble samples sold to visitors doing the Grand Tour.

The pink, yellow and cream limestone fragments are sometimes beautifully patterned in a similar way to *pietra paesina* (see page 102), or rimmed in a darker or lighter shade. Some are quite angular, others are rounded. They are dispersed in a red granular matrix rich in small gritty fragments of limestone and large white bivalve shells that have a distinctively streaky appearance.

GEOLOGICAL DESCRIPTION
Breccio-conglomerate of mixed limestone clasts, bivalve shells (probably oysters) and limestone grit in a red hematitic matrix.

MAJOR USAGE
Pillars, inlaid furniture.

Occhio di pernice

SOURCE: Not known
STATUS: No longer available

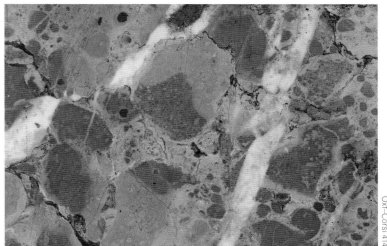

Oxf-Corsi 414

Whenever the word "occhio"—meaning eye—is used in the name of a marble, the pattern is sure to have a lot of circles.

This stone is no exception. The Roman scalpellini called it *occhio di pernice*, meaning "partridge eye." Anyone who has seen the red-legged partridge and noticed the bird's distinctive red eye-ring will see the connection. *Occhio di pernice* is a breccia of beige limestone fragments mottled and spotted with red and violet. Zigzagging stylolites follow the boundaries of the clasts, and the whole stone is crossed by thick white calcite-filled veins.

Like *breccia frutticolosa* and *breccia della Villa Casali, occhio di pernice* was used routinely by the scalpellini of Rome in the 18th and 19th centuries to make panels for inlaid tables and cut blocks for marble collections to sell to the ladies and gentlemen undertaking the Grand Tour. It is a curious stone, probably formed in a mudslide at the bottom of the sea millions of years ago. Nobody knows where it was quarried, and it is presumed that it was quarried in Roman or Byzantine times.

GEOLOGICAL DESCRIPTION
Breccia of limestone clasts and intraclasts (pieces of preexisting rock insides clasts) patchily oxidized to red hematite. It has abundant stylolites that follow clast boundaries, and it is crossed by white calcite veins.

MAJOR USAGE
Inlaid furniture and historic decorative stone collections.

Breccia traccagnina

SOURCE: Not known

STATUS: Quarried in antiquity

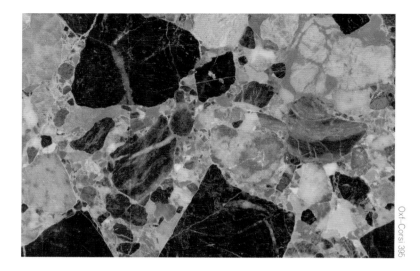

Oxf-Corsi 395

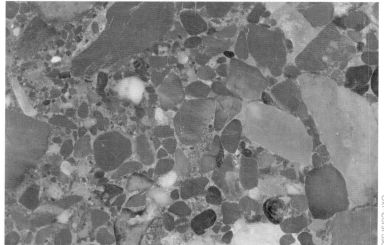

Oxf-Corsi 396

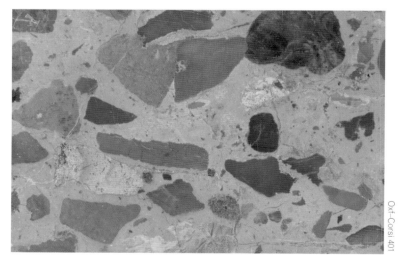

Oxf-Corsi 401

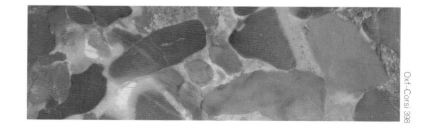

Oxf-Corsi 398

Harlequin breccias are cheerful stones in a brilliant mixture of different colors, quarried so long ago that nobody knows where they are from.

Breccia traccagnina was also called *breccia arlecchina*, the "harlequin breccia," and is a rather appropriate catch-all term used by the Italian stonecutters for multicolored limestone breccias and conglomerates of unknown provenance. The marble collector Francesco Belli simply called it *breccia polycroma*. There is some doubt as to whether these stones were used in ancient times, but Faustino Corsi believed this was the case and included them in his book *Delle pietre antiche*, about ancient stones. He pointed out that they are very beautiful and could command a high price. They are used in small pieces for pillars, plinths for statues and inlays in walls and furniture.

It is likely that some of the stones were of Italian origin and the original deposits were long ago worked out. Others may have provenances farther afield; for example, one of Corsi's *breccia traccagnina* samples obtained from the Italian stonecutters, is a red, brown and white conglomerate that is strikingly similar to a stone from Bulgaria recently marketed as *Balkan red*. Another is almost certainly from Arrábida in Portugal (see opposite).

GEOLOGICAL DESCRIPTION

Breccias of various colored limestone clasts in a calcareous matrix.

MAJOR USAGE

Pillars, inlays, sculptures.

Breccia capitolina

SOURCE: Possibly Anatolia, Turkey

STATUS: Quarried in antiquity

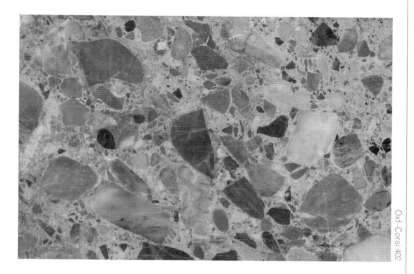

Oxf-Corsi 402

Of all the stones called *breccia traccagnina*, this one is surely the most pleasingly colored, and it is very old, too.

Corsi regarded this stone as a *breccia traccagnina*, but it was labeled *breccia policroma capitolina* by another famous marble collector, Francesco Belli, because there is a fine medium-sized pillar on display in the Room of the Dying Gladiator in the Capitoline Museums. It is also found in collections of ancient marbles and in Roman inlaid tabletops and other furniture.

It is a limestone breccia of red, white and black fragments in an ocherous-yellow matrix. Samples of *brèche Médous* from France (see page 145) can appear similar, but lack the red clasts.

GEOLOGICAL DESCRIPTION

Breccio-conglomerate of red, gray, white and brown limestone clasts in a ferruginous yellow calcareous matrix.

MAJOR USAGE

Pillars, panels and other inlays.

Brecha da Arrábida

SOURCE: Siera di Arrábida, Setúbal, Portugal

STATUS: No longer quarried

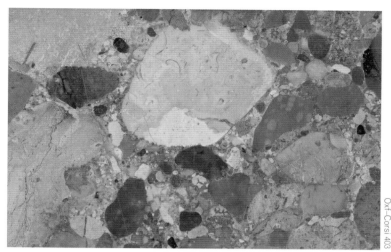

Oxf-Corsi 403

How did Corsi's sample of this marble arrive in Rome? Was it brought there in ancient times?

Brecha da Arrábida is a mottled multicolored conglomerate cemented by a particularly gritty matrix. It used to come from the Arrábida Mountains southwest of Setúbal in Portugal. The area around Setúbal was occupied by the ancient Romans, and it is possible that they brought the stone to Rome. In Corsi's collection, it is among the ancient stones called *breccia traccagnina* that were most probably obtained by the scalpellini from the ruins of ancient Rome.

Ornamental uses in churches and other buildings in Portugal date back to at least as early as the 17th century, and Dubarry de Lassale refers to its use in the 18th century.

In the 1970s the Parque Natural da Arrábida was established to preserve the rich biological and geological heritage of the area. The quarrying business was not considered compatible with the new conservation objectives, and as a result the stone is no longer quarried.

GEOLOGICAL DESCRIPTION

Upper Jurassic conglomerate of very poorly sorted limestone fragments in a very gritty yellowish iron-rich matrix.

MAJOR USAGE

Architectural applications, furniture.

Diaspro tenero di Sicilia

SOURCE: Sicily, Italy
STATUS: Actively quarried

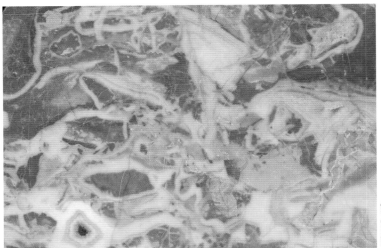

OxF-DR1364

Compared with the vibrant true jaspers of Sicily, the soft jaspers appear decidedly muted, but they have some wonderfully striking patterns.

The most historic of the various marbles that come from Sicily is called *libeccio antico* or *diaspro tenero* ("soft jasper"). This is a calcareous rock, whereas the true jaspers for which Sicily is also famous (see page 246) are much harder, siliceous rocks. Although the soft jaspers are more muted than the true jaspers, they are still richly colored stones, predominantly brick-red, ocherous-yellow, cream and olive-green. Lesser amounts of violet, pink and gray may also be present.

The *diaspri teneri* are bedded infills in ancient cavities and caves in the local buff-colored limestone, and like the true jaspers, are colored by iron oxides. Slumping and fracturing, and subsequent recementing with pink limestone or cream-colored calcite, results in a wide variety of textures. Shell fragments can be common; for example, *lumachella tigrato di Sicilia* is packed full of "shipworm," wood-boring bivalves that colonized driftwood.

The quarries are near Custonaci in the province of Trapani, western Sicily. The stone may have been used in ancient times, but it was exploited most extensively in Byzantine and later architecture. It can be seen in churches and cathedrals across Italy and has been exported to many other countries. There are many examples of Sicilian soft jasper in pavements, wall panels and sculptures all around the interior of St. Peter's Basilica in the

LEFT A star shape comprised of *diaspro tenero* with a pale *giallo antico* in white marble from the Apuan Alps. It is part of the marble paving in Chatsworth House, Derbyshire, England.

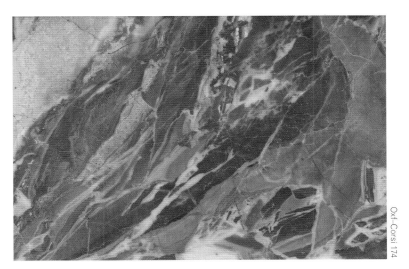

Oxf–Corsi 174

Pietra topografica Oxf–Corsi 537

Oxf–Corsi 206

tigrato Oxf–Corsi 536

Oxf–Corsi 166

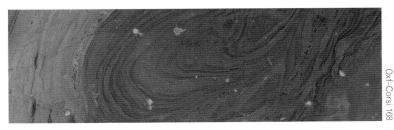

Oxf–Corsi 168

Vatican. Most of the quarries are now worked out, but some stone is still extracted and traded under the names *breccia pontifica* (or *pontificia*) and *libeccio di Trapani*.

A distinctive variety found in old collections was referred to by Corsi as *pietra topografica*. This is more appropriate than ever he could have realized, for the criss-cross of red lines is strikingly reminiscent of a modern cityscape viewed from the air. The pattern is caused by fluids penetrating the rock through hairline fractures in a similar way to *pietra paesina* (see page 102).

GEOLOGICAL DESCRIPTION

Limestone infills in caves of late Triassic to early Jurassic age. The wide variety of textures results from fracturing, slumping and bioturbation of the infills, and subsequent recementing by pink limestone of late Jurassic to Cretaceous age, or by cream-colored calcite.

MAJOR USAGE

Flooring and wall cladding; in furniture and inlay work; sculpture.

Breccia Dalmazio, rozalit

SOURCE: Dalmatian coast of Croatia
STATUS: Recently quarried

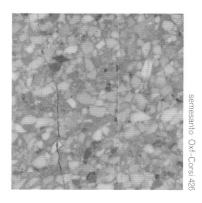

semesanto Oxf-Corsi 426

rozalit Oxf-DR1798

The larger clast version, which has also been called *pomarolo*, has been extracted commercially until very recently and traded as *rozalit*.

GEOLOGICAL DESCRIPTION
A conglomerate of brown, buff and cream limestone clasts in a fine-grained orange-pink limestone matrix.

MAJOR USAGE
Architectural elements and inlay work.

The fragments in this Croatian marble may be large pebbles or grains of grit but the color scheme is always the same.

Although this breccia is found under many names and is very variable in fragment size, the colors of cream, buff and brown fragments in a distinctly orange-pink cement are very distinctive. It has been quarried on the Dalmatian coast of Croatia since the 12th century, and particularly from the Island of Rab, formerly called Arbe. It has been widely used in this region, and there are four fine pillars and a baptismal font to be seen in the Church of St. Philip in Split (Spoleto). Other names given to this stone are *breccia d'Arbe*, *mandolato di Arbe* and *breccia di San Ipolito*.

The small clast form, with fragments uniformly no more than ⅙ inch (4 mm) across, has exactly the same color scheme as its larger clast relative. It may be referred to as *semesanto* in the literature but should not be confused with the ancient marble of that name from Skyros (see page 129). Corsi called it *breccia a semesanto di Dalmazia*. It is used in the decoration of the Archbishop's throne in Westminster Cathedral, London.

LEFT The four roundels in the decoration in the Archbishop's throne at Westminster Cathedral, London, are made of *breccia a semesanto di Dalmazia*.

Other multicolored marbles and limestones

(see page 129)

The country that surpasses all others in the variety of its multicolored marbles and limestones is France, and many more could be added to those already described. *Brèche Vimines* from Vimines, south of Chambery, has been used since ancient times. The matrix is a grainy bright orange, and each cream or yellow clast has a distinctive orange "halo." *Brèche de Salernes* also has a bright orange matrix and the clasts range from dark brown to red and yellow. It comes from Salernes in Var. French breccias are well illustrated and described in the beautiful books of Jacques Dubarry de Lassale.

There are other breccias that were often used by the Italian scalpellini. *Breccia di Sicilia* is a conglomerate of brown limestone pebbles in a creamy-white limestone matrix that when viewed under a microscope, is seen to be teaming with tiny fossil plankton. *Breccia d'Arzo* comes from Monte San Giorgio in Ticino, Switzerland, close to the border with Italy and bears a striking resemblance to the pink, scarlet and gray clast varieties of *diaspro tenero di Sicilia*. It is quarried and marketed today as *macchiavecchia*.

From the other side of the globe, *Dreamtime* is a conglomerate from Chillagoe in Australia. The white pebbles are delicately rimmed with salmon-pink and sometimes marked with pitch black, and the gray matrix is formed from large calcite crystals.

Lumachelle and other fossiliferous limestones

The stones in this section come in many different colors, but they all share one important feature—they derive their beauty from the presence of fossils. The remains of seashells, sponges, corals and skeletons of other creatures that lived in lakes or seas millions of years ago can turn a drab limestone into a fascinating ornamental stone. Limestones packed full of seashells are traditionally known by the Italian name "lumachella." Perhaps the most famous lumachella is the *Austrian fire marble* from Carinthia, which contains seashells that can flash bright spectral colors as the stone is turned in the light. Such optical effects are rare, and in most fossiliferous limestones the visual appeal lies in the natural forms of living organisms. The coiled shell of an ammonite, spiral of a gastropod and radiating septa of a coral are just a few of the exquisite natural patterns preserved in these rocks.

Lumachella nera

SOURCE: Not known
STATUS: Not used in recent times

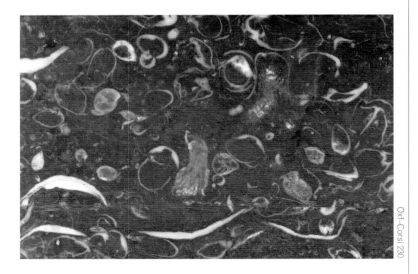

Oxf-Corsi 230

A dark gray stone with thin-shelled white fossils, *lumachella nera* was considered very rare indeed when Corsi made his collection in the early 1800s.

Lumachella nera is crammed full of interesting fossils, a mixture of brachiopods, solitary corals and crinoid debris. Identification of these ancient creatures reveals that it is late Jurassic in age. There is just one place in Rome that shows this stone particularly well and that is in the Church of Sant'Agostino, where veneered panels form a horizontal band around the walls of the Chapel of San Tommaso da Villanova. This was installed around 1660. The same stone is often found in tabletops inlaid with ancient marbles and the collections of ancient stones sold to 18th- and 19th-century tourists visiting Rome. Whether the stone had been used in ancient times is open to debate. The marble expert Raniero Gnoli suggested it may have been introduced in the 17th century.

It is not known where this stone was quarried, but stones of similar general appearance (although not necessarily the same age) come from many different places. Closer examination shows that this stone contains very thin-shelled brachiopods, giving it a particularly delicate appearance compared with many other black fossil limestones.

GEOLOGICAL DESCRIPTION

Brachiopods, solitary corals, crinoid ossicles and other fossil debris in a black carbonaceous limestone of late Jurassic age.

MAJOR USAGE

Rare wall panels; mainly found in inlaid tabletops and collections of ancient marbles.

Vytina black

SOURCE: Vytina, Arcadia, Greece
STATUS: Actively quarried

Oxf-Corsi 920

The stunning statue of Matidia, her white arms outstretched, and body draped in *Vytina marble*, shows that this stone was appreciated in Roman times.

This black fossil limestone was discovered in Roman excavations, and a particularly fine example is the statue of Matidia (Aura) carved in the second century CE. She has white marble for her head, arms and feet, and this black limestone and a gray marble for her clothing. This amazing statue, 8½ feet (2.6 m) high, was found in excavations at Sessa Aurunca and can now be seen in the Ducal Castle there.

For a long time there was confusion about where this stone came from. Faustino Corsi called it *nero lumachellato* or *nero del Campidoglio* and said it was from Egypt because several items in the Egyptian room of the Campidoglio Museum (Capitoline Museums) were made of it. In 1971, marble expert Raniero Gnoli referred to it as *bigio morato,* saying it was also misnamed *bianco e nero d'Egitto*. Now it is recognized as the black marble of Vytina (or Vitina).

Vytina black has large white shells of bivalves and a peppering of other fossils in a deep black groundmass. It has been quarried on a commercial basis extensively in the 20th century from just southeast of the village of Vytina in the middle of the Peloponnese. Other trade names include *black of Vytina* and *black of Arcadia*.

GEOLOGICAL DESCRIPTION

Black fine-grained limestone of Cretaceous age with white fragments of rudist bivalve shells.

MAJOR USAGE

Floor and wall claddings and other architectural elements.

Occhio di pavone bianco

SOURCE: Unknown
STATUS: Used in antiquity

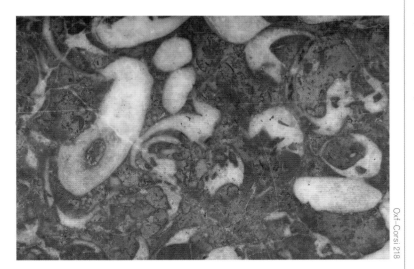

Oxf-Corsi 218

In other sections of this book, "pavone" alludes to the color violet. In this section it is the pattern of the stone and not its color that brings the peacock to mind.

The Italian scalpellini compared the fossils in this "white peacock's eye marble" to the eyes on a peacock's tail. In fact the white markings are bivalve shells, heavily recrystallized, giving them a sugary texture. It is quite easy to confuse the different stones known in the past as *occhio di pavone*. This is the stone called *occhio di pavone bigio* in Borghini's book on ancient marbles and *occhio di pavone bianco* in Corsi's catalog. It is not the stone of that name found in recent years on the island of Chios in Greece that is very dark gray and contains brachiopods, corals, foraminifera and algae. This one contains bivalves known as rudists. Other rudist limestones called *occhio di pavone* come from Turkey and are shades of pink, red and violet (see page 162). Exactly where this stone comes from remains a mystery.

It was certainly a rare stone, and Corsi tells us it was occasionally found in archaeological excavations. Like the other ancient lumachelle, it was employed in the souvenirs made by the scalpellini of Rome for the gentry doing the Grand Tour, items that today turn up in museum collections and auction sales.

GEOLOGICAL DESCRIPTION

Gray limestone of late Jurassic or Cretaceous age containing recrystallized rudist bivalve shells.

MAJOR USAGE

Inlaid tabletops and historic collections of decorative stones.

Kilkenny fossil marble

SOURCE: County Kilkenny, Ireland
STATUS: Minor quarrying, mainly for restoration work

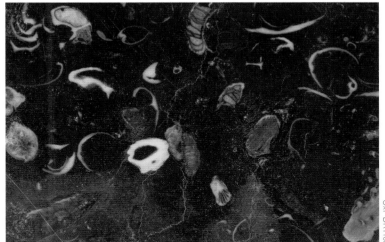

Oxf-DR1163

One of the blackest of all fossil limestones comes from Kilkenny in Ireland, but until it is polished it still looks gray.

This limestone of Carboniferous age polishes to a jet black finish. It contains scattered white fossils, and is known as *Kilkenny fossil marble*. While some examples show mainly brachiopods, others are rich in corals. The sample shown above has both, along with a few round crinoid ossicles.

Kilkenny fossil marble was extracted from the same quarries as the famous *Irish black marble* (see page 77), but in particular from Black quarry at Archer's Grove, on the outskirts of the city of Kilkenny. This old quarry was already working by the mid-17th century, supplying stone mainly for house building, and by the mid-18th century the stone was being transported to the mill at Maddockstown for polishing. The quarry continued working up until 1920, when the economic depression forced its closure. Other quarries around Kilkenny have been worked in recent times and this stone is sometimes available on the commercial market.

Kilkenny fossil marble is used for sidewalks along the streets of Amsterdam, and the white fossils show particularly when they are dampened with rain. It was one of the stones preferred for sculpture by English sculptor Dame Barbara Hepworth.

GEOLOGICAL DESCRIPTION

Black bituminous fine-grained limestones of Carboniferous age containing scattered spiriferids and other brachiopods, corals (e.g., *Lithostrotion*) and crinoid debris. It has many pale stylolites.

MAJOR USAGE

Floors, wall cladding, stairways and chimneypieces; sculpture.

Morocco fossil black

SOURCE: Tazzarine, Anti Atlas, Morocco
STATUS: Actively quarried

With its torpedo-shaped fossils, this big, bold fossil limestone is used for a whole range of home and fashion items from jewelry to bathtubs.

Morocco is the source of an amazing black limestone full of torpedo-shaped fossils that used to be called *Orthoceras*, but turn out to include a number of different "orthocone nautiloids." These are straight-shelled relatives of *Nautilus*, a cephalopod with a coiled shell that was alive when the stone formed, and still lives in modern oceans. It in turn is related to squid, octopus and cuttlefish, and to extinct ammonites. Orthocone nautiloids can be 6 feet (2 m) or more in length but most are less than 12 inches (30 cm). Buyers should beware, because "giant" fossils may be fabricated from sections of several different individuals. Exactly why so many of these cephalopods are found together is a matter of conjecture and some suggest they died after a mass spawning session.

The first examples of Moroccan *Orthoceras* limestone to come onto the market in the 1980s were small rounded blocks with two or three of the fossils carved out in relief. These are still very widely available at fossil fairs and stores. Dinner plates, tabletops and even sinks soon followed. Today, large slabs of polished stone are also available, traded as *Morocco fossil black* and aimed at an architectural market.

GEOLOGICAL DESCRIPTION

Silurian black limestone with abundant shells of orthocone nautiloids including *Michelinoceras* and *Arionoceras*.

MAJOR USAGE

Floor and wall claddings; tabletops, countertops, sinks and bathtubs; jewelry and gift items.

Morocco fossil brown

SOURCE: Near Tazzarine, Anti Atlas, Morocco
STATUS: Actively quarried

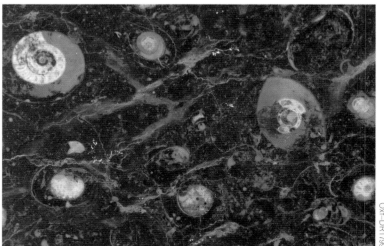

There are more varieties of fossils in the brown fossil limestone from Morocco, and this stone is just as versatile as its black neighbor.

One of the features of the black *Orthoceras* limestone from Morocco (see left) is how few other kinds of fossil are found in it. Brown fossil limestones come from the same area and have a more diverse fauna. The most eye-catching fossils are the straight "orthocone nautiloids" and coiled ammonides, but crinoid ossicles can be abundant. When they were alive, both creatures used the chambers in their shells to control their buoyancy. After they died and fell to the bottom of the sea, the chambers filled up with mud, which is often preserved in a different color from all the surrounding sediments because it is less contaminated by organic material. Although referred to as brown, the groundmass of this limestone can be red, brown or gray.

The range of uses of Moroccan brown is much the same as for the black stone. When slabbed and polished for architectural use it is traded as *Morocco fossil brown* or *pietra di Erfoud*. The town of Erfoud, to the south of the Anti Atlas Mountains, is where many of these stones are processed after quarrying.

GEOLOGICAL DESCRIPTION

Silurian brown limestone with abundant shells of orthocone nautiloids and ammonides, and abundant crinoid ossicles.

MAJOR USAGE

Floor and wall claddings and other internal architectural uses; tabletops, countertops, sinks; jewelry and gift items.

Lumachella d'Egitto

SOURCE: Henchir Kasbat, Tunisia

STATUS: Quarried in antiquity

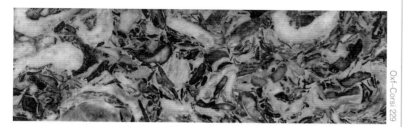

Oxf-Corsi 229

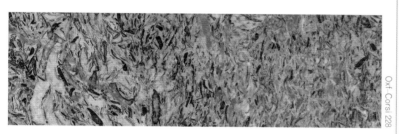

Oxf-Corsi 228

There was very little of this beautiful shelly limestone to be found in the ruins of Rome and the stonecutters prized it very highly indeed.

Despite its name, this lumachella, much used in ancient times, is not from Egypt. The scalpellini of Rome also called it *lumachella orientale*, the eastern lumachella, suggesting a source east of Rome. This is in fact the case, for it has been found as loose boulders of local rock near Henchir Kasbat, the ancient city of Thuburbo Maius, in Tunisia.

It is a shelly limestone composed of fragments of mainly gray and white bivalve shells, sometimes finely crushed. The groundmass is either pale gray, brownish yellow or more rarely a coral-pink color. Samples found in the ruins of Rome were used mainly for small slabs in paving. Today, it can be seen forming the breastplate of the third century CE bust of Gordianus II in the Room of the Emperors in the Capitoline Museums. In the 16th and 17th centuries it was highly prized by the scalpellini of Rome. A larger block discovered in 1830 in vineyards in the Testaccio district of Rome was, Corsi tells us, sawn to make 12 tabletops. Perhaps this, too, supplied the stone the stonecutters used in collections of ancient marbles and in tabletop inlays.

GEOLOGICAL DESCRIPTION

Mesozoic limestone of crushed bivalve (e.g., *Ostrea*) fragments and other fossil debris in a fine-grained calcareous matrix that may be heavily iron-stained.

MAJOR USAGE

Small slabs in paving, small columns; reused in tabletops and other decoration.

Lumachella d'Abruzzo

SOURCE: Scontrone, Abruzzo, Italy

STATUS: No longer quarried

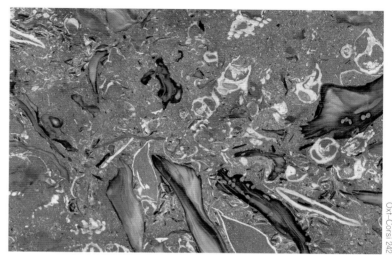

Oxf-Corsi 242

Turtles, crocodiles and prehistoric hoofed animals are among the fossils found in the *lumachella d'Abruzzo* from Scontrone.

The *lumachella d'Abruzzo* is a striking stone packed full of elongate gastropods and large fossil oysters. The oysters clearly show the layered structure of their shells. In some examples of this stone, the fossils are mixed with limestone pebbles showing that they were deposited very close to the shore. This limestone is of Miocene age and it comes from Scontrone, a small town situated in the Abruzzo National Park. In the 1990s Scontrone became famous for the amazing vertebrate fossils found in the lumachella, including mammals, turtles and crocodiles. The beds of this rock are now a protected site.

Lumachella d'Abruzzo was never used in ancient times. When it was first quarried is indicated by the presence of two fine columns decorating the Caetani Chapel in the Church of Santa Pudenziana in Rome, which was completed early in the 17th century. Another column from that time is in the Borghese Gallery. It is sometimes overlooked or confused with the better known *astracane di Verona* and *lumachella d'Egitto*, but closer examination shows the Abruzzo stone has a coarser-grained matrix.

GEOLOGICAL DESCRIPTION

Miocene limestone of oyster (*Ostrea*), gastropod, foraminifera and other fossils in a sandy or pebbly matrix.

MAJOR USAGE

Decorative panels and furniture inlays; samples found in historic marble collections.

Pakistan fossil stone

SOURCE: Baluchistan, Pakistan

STATUS: Actively quarried

Courtesy of Monica Price

Just a small vase or polished sphere is needed to see the array of marine fossils preserved in *Pakistan fossil stone*.

Pakistan fossil stone is one of the fossil limestones most likely to turn up in homes, for it is often made into nightlight holders, vases, obelisks, decorative polished spheres and eggs, and many other small decorative items. It is a very beautiful stone, creamy-yellow in color and full of fossils. All sorts of different organisms can be identified including bivalves, corals, bryozoa and sea urchin spines, but the most distinctive are the long spiral shells of gastropods.

Pakistan fossil stone comes from Baluchistan in Pakistan, where the decorative stone industry is still under development. Explosives are still commonly used, and this means that it is much harder to get large slabs of sound stone and wastage rates are very high. Small-scale enterprises are better able to supply smaller blocks of stone for handicraft industries rather than produce slabs of sizes suitable for architectural applications.

GEOLOGICAL DESCRIPTION

Late Cretaceous or Cenozoic fine-grained limestone rich in bivalves, large naticid and high-spired cerathiid gastropods, bryozoa, corals, echinoid spines and other fossil debris, probably from a lagoon deposit.

MAJOR USAGE

Vases, candle holders and small decorative items; funerary urns.

LEFT The large fossil seen at the top of this fossil limestone vase is a part of a naticid gastropod, a kind of predatory marine snail that drilled holes through the shells of other mollusks to eat the contents.

Lumachellone antica

SOURCE: Not known

STATUS: Used in antiquity

Oxf-Corsi 231

A large slab of this lumachella must have been a very impressive sight because the gastropods are always very large.

When Faustino Corsi wrote his catalog in 1825, this stone had just been discovered for the first time in excavations on the estate of Tormarancio. It was so rare that Corsi's sample is of two thin pieces spliced together on a backing slab of *Carrara marble*. The stone was called *lumachellone antico* by the scalpellini. It had been found from time to time in archaeological excavations in Rome, where it was used mainly for doorsteps and paving. In 1864, a fine panel was installed on the wall of a confessional in the Church of Santa Maria Maggiore in Rome.

It has been suggested that the fossils bear more than a passing resemblance to giant *Actaeonella* gastropods that are found in Upper Cretaceous rocks in Austria. This genus of gastropod is most often found in sediments deposited in the ancient Tethys Ocean, but the Austrian deposit is particularly well known.

GEOLOGICAL DESCRIPTION

Limestone, probably of Cretaceous age, with very large actaeonellid gastropods in a gray- to buff-colored calcareous cement rich in very small shell fragments. It is crossed by white calcite-filled fractures.

MAJOR USAGE

Door steps and paving, reused in wall panels, tabletop inlays and collections of ancient marbles.

LUMACHELLE AND OTHER FOSSILIFEROUS LIMESTONES

Sussex marble

SOURCE: Southeast England
STATUS: No longer quarried

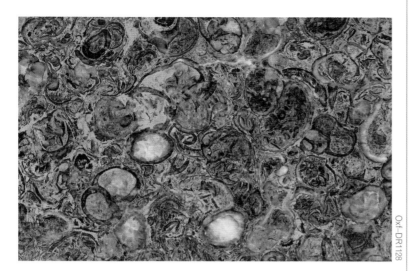

Oxf-DR1128

It is the fossil shells of millions of tiny pond snails that make *Sussex marble* such an attractive stone.

Petworth marble is very definitely a limestone, packed with the shells of a little round gastropod called *Viviparus fluviorum*, better known as the pond snail. It is one of several freshwater limestones collectively known as *Sussex marble*. They were quarried at Bethersden in Kent; Kirdford, Northchapel, Petworth and Laughton in Sussex; at Charlwood, Outwood and Ewhurst in Surrey, and other locations in the Weald of southeast England. Like *Petworth marble*, the other stones were named after the place they were quarried.

The first quarries of *Petworth marble* opened in the 13th century (maybe earlier), and the stone was in considerable demand for the decoration of churches and manufacture of baptismal fonts. It was also used in private homes, and extensively in the restoration of Petworth House (1905–1906), where it forms columns and chimneypieces. There is also a column in Oxford University's Museum of Natural History. When John Watson was writing his decorative stone catalog in 1916, he noted that *Sussex marble* was less sought after than the growing number of other British and foreign stones. All quarrying has now long ceased.

GEOLOGICAL DESCRIPTION

Fine-grained compact freshwater limestone of early Cretaceous age containing abundant gastropods (*Viviparus fluviorum*) larger than those in *Purbeck marble* (see right).

MAJOR USAGE

Pillars, flooring, walls; baptismal fonts and ecclesiastical items; gravestones; chimneypieces and furniture.

Purbeck marble

SOURCE: Isle of Purbeck, Dorset, England
STATUS: Some quarrying takes place

Oxf-DR 1020

Purbeck marble is about 140 million years old, and it has been used as a decorative stone for a very long time as well.

This eye-catching limestone was quarried near Swanage on the Isle of Purbeck, and from early in its history it was referred to as a "marble." The characteristic gastropods are small freshwater snails, and shells of a freshwater mussel are sometimes also present. *Purbeck marble* is usually blue or greenish gray but can be yellowish too. It was first used in Roman times around 43 CE for wall claddings, paving and decorative items such as mortars. Many samples have been found in the Roman villa at Fishbourne, as well as in Colchester and other Roman sites in England.

In medieval times, the demand for *Purbeck marble* grew considerably with the building of the great English cathedrals. It was employed for the pillars in the 12th-century Galilee Chapel of Durham Cathedral and for the shafts that cloak the piers in the 13th-century Salisbury Cathedral. Later, *Purbeck marble* fell out of fashion, although there has been a steady revival since the 1900s. New supplies have been needed for restoration projects, and small quarries have been reopened to supply the stone. Since *Purbeck marble* has become available again, it has been used for contemporary designs as well, including furniture and paving.

GEOLOGICAL DESCRIPTION

Fine-grained compact freshwater limestone of early Cretaceous age containing abundant gastropods (*Viviparus cariniferus*) and mussels (*Unio*).

MAJOR USAGE

Interior paving, columns, steps and wall claddings; tables and other furniture.

Astracane dorato

SOURCE: Henchir Kasbat, Tunisia
STATUS: Quarried in antiquity

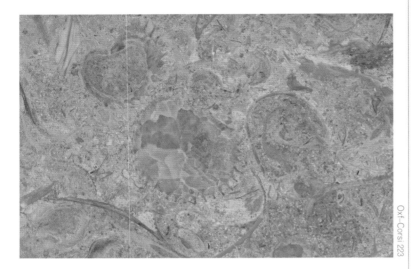

Oxf-Corsi 223

The name *astracane* or *castracane* has been in common use for many centuries, but where did it come from?

This is the beautiful golden *astracane marble* of the ancients. The derivation of the name *astracane* or *castracane* has been a subject of considerable debate. In 1807, the French geologist Alexandre Brongniart confirmed that the stone did not come from the Russian city of Astrakhan on the shores of the Caspian Sea. In 1811 John Pinkerton suggested it was a misspelling of Castracani, a town in Syria, but this was also disproved. Cyprien-Prosper Brard, writing in 1821, supported the views of M. Léman and others, that the city of Agra in Italy was very probably the provenance of this marble, but he was confusing it with the beautiful *Jaisalmer marble* (see right) that was extensively used in Agra. Today it is generally agreed that the round shells in *astracane* were reminiscent of the curls in "astrakhan," a soft, curly lamb's fleece obtained from the Middle East.

While the debate about the origin of *astracane* rolled on, the source of *astracane dorato* is now known to be, like *lumachella d'Egitto*, Henchir Kasbat, the ancient Thuburbo Maius in Tunisia. It is extremely rare and was highly prized by the scalpellini of baroque and more recent times.

GEOLOGICAL DESCRIPTION

Limestone probably of Eocene age, with abundant shells of *Venericardia* (cockles) and other bivalves and gastropods in a fine-grained golden-yellow calcareous matrix.

MAJOR USAGE

Small pieces used in paving and inlays.

Jaisalmer marble

SOURCE: Jaisalmer, Rajputana, India
STATUS: Actively quarried

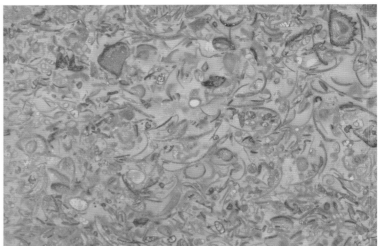

Oxf-DR1653

This is the famous golden *astracane marble* from India, a truly exquisite stone, famed outside the subcontinent as well.

So much has been written about a beautiful golden-yellow lumachella from India, the *astracane* of Cyprien-Prosper Brard and other authors, that it seems appropriate to include this stone here. It is a rich, golden color with a compact structure, and contains abundant small bivalves and gastropods. It comes from near Jaisalmer in Rajasthan, and is known as *Jaisalmer marble*. The arid desert around Jaisalmer is one of India's main limestone-producing regions and the city used to be a halting point along a trade route linking India to Central Asia, Africa and Europe. The decorative limestone today sold as *Jaisalmer yellow* has a consistently attractive yellow color. Within the deposit of this stone there are beds particularly rich in the shells of mollusks, and it is from these that the beautiful fossiliferous *Jaisalmer marble* is cut.

Fossiliferous *Jaisalmer marble* and the plain *Jaisalmer yellow* are the typical Indian "yellow marbles" used in decorative inlay work in India. They were extensively used in the ornamentation of the Taj Mahal, built in the 17th century. A yellow and brown variety considered to have spiritual properties and named *Arbur stone* comes from the town of Habur.

GEOLOGICAL DESCRIPTION

Yellow fossiliferous limestone of Jurassic or Cretaceous age, composed almost entirely of small, thin-shelled bivalves and high-spired gastropods.

MAJOR USAGE

Mainly used in inlay work, tabletops and other decoration; *Jaisalmer yellow* is used for various architectural applications.

Astracane di Verona

SOURCE: Province of Verona, Italy

STATUS: No longer quarried

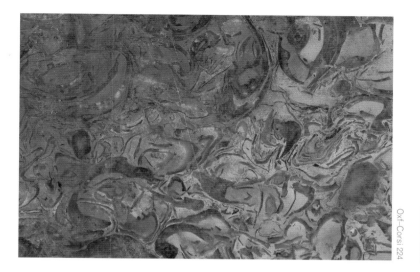

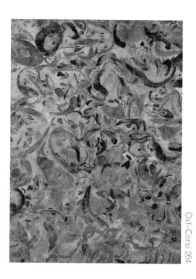

Once upon a time, the mountains outside the Italian city of Verona yielded a beautiful shelly marble that was much admired in baroque times.

When Faustino Corsi described the lumachelle in his collection, he included two stones, the darker labeled *astracane maschio* (the masculine astracane) and the lighter *astracane femina* (the feminine astracane). This 19th-century collector believed they came from the ruins of Rome, but there is now general agreement that these stones were not used in ancient times, and instead were brought to Rome in the 17th and 18th centuries. He had several other lumachelle in his collection that came from contemporary sources in the province of Verona, but it seems he did not recognize their remarkable similarity.

The shell fragments are buff or gray, and consist mainly of bivalves. The matrix is a straw-yellow to light brown color, sometimes with patches of pink—colors often seen together in the Veronese limestones. Agostino Del Riccio, in his history of stones published in 1597, says this stone came from the mountains around Verona. More specifically, in 1889 William Jervis described a lumachella with small shells of dark gray, in a paste of the most delicate tawny-yellow that takes a good polish, resists abrasion and is an excellent decorative stone. He said it came from near Grezzana in the Val Pantena. It must surely be the same stone.

Today these stones are referred to as *astracane di Verona* or *lumachella di Verona*. They can be seen in the Church of Sant'Andrea della Valle in Rome, where they are used for the communion rail balustrade. They are also used for the holy water stoup and other decoration in the richly ornamented baroque Church of San Pietro in Valle in the Marche town of Fano.

ABOVE The balustrade in the Church of Sant'Andrea della Valle in Rome shows different varieties of *astracane di Verona*.

GEOLOGICAL DESCRIPTION

Mesozoic fossiliferous limestone rich in bivalves, in a fine-grained matrix.

MAJOR USAGE

Balustrades, pillars and paving; tabletop inlays; furniture.

Occhio di pavone

SOURCE: Kutluca, İzmit, Turkey
STATUS: No longer quarried

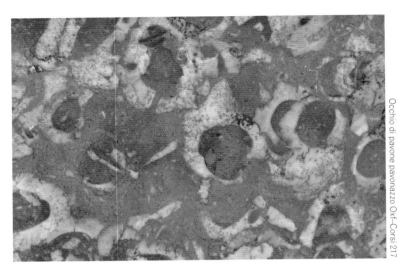

Occhio di pavone pavonazzo Oxf-Corsi 217

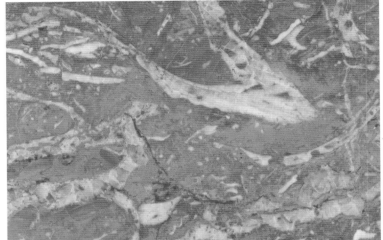

Occhio di pavone rosso Oxf-Corsi 220

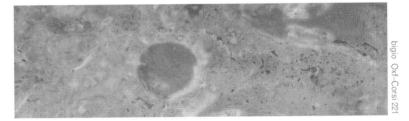

bigio Oxf-Corsi 221

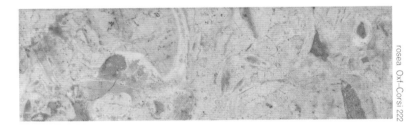

rosea Oxf-Corsi 222

It was a chance visit to a marble store in Turkey that led to the extraordinary rediscovery of the quarries of the famous peacock's eye marble.

These are the famous *occhio di pavone* marbles used in ancient times, all with distinctive round markings like the eyes in a peacock's tail. They vary in color from the purplish red *occhio di pavone pavonazzo*, the more common red *occhio di pavone rosso*, pink *rosea* and pale buff *bigio*. The "eyes" are the shells of curiously shaped bivalves known as rudists that lived during late Jurassic and Cretaceous times in warm shallow seas and evolved very strangely shaped shells that can make them easy to identify. Faustino Corsi noted how they always seemed to show the same pattern, no matter which direction they were cut. Rudists would congregate to form shallow reeflike structures, and it is these that are preserved in this limestone.

When Lorenzo Lazzarini was in Turkey in the 1990s trying to find the ancient *occhio di pavone* quarries, he showed a sample to a marble store owner who recognized it as a stone he called *Gebze elma çiçei* (apple blossom of Gebze) that his family had quarried some 30 years previously. They went to the quarries at Tasagili southwest of Kutluca. Despite the fact that modern working had erased nearly all traces of the ancient site, there were still broken fragments of amphorae and other artifacts that attested to a great deal of quarrying activity in Byzantine times.

Occhio di pavone was much used especially in the eastern part of the Roman Empire, and was introduced to Rome in the second or third century CE. Lazzarini concluded that this marble must be the *marmor triponticum* of Diocletian's Edict of Maximum Prices of the fourth century CE, since it lay midway between the three seas—the Pontus Euxenis (Black Sea), Propontis (sea of Mamora) and Lake Sophon (Lake Sapanca)—which flooded a much greater area in antiquity than it does today. It was not a costly stone and was easily transported via the coastal port of Nicomedia, the modern Izmit. Later generations reused this stone, so it is found in many churches and mosques. Two fine columns support an arch in the Vatican library.

GEOLOGICAL DESCRIPTION

Late Cretaceous rudist limestone, colored by trace hematite and also containing foraminifera and other fossils.

MAJOR USAGE

Slabs for floors, walls and other architectural decoration; baths, sarcophagi, vases; inlays in furniture.

LUMACHELLE AND OTHER FOSSILIFEROUS LIMESTONES

Lumachella rosea

SOURCE: Kairouan, Tunisia

STATUS: Quarried in antiquity

Oxf–Corsi 232

The fossils in this limestone are not mollusk shells, but the shells of nummulites, simple single-celled organisms that lived in the sea.

The delicate pink limestone known as *lumachella rosea* contains many small, creamy-white fossils that Faustino Corsi likened to pumpkin seeds. They are in fact the shells of nummulites, button-shaped foraminifera that were very common in the seas that covered much of the Mediterranean area in Tertiary times. Fragments of bivalves, corals and other fossils can also be seen in this stone.

Lumachella rosea was quarried a short distance from the historic Tunisian city of Kairouan, which is now a UNESCO World Heritage Site. This stone was used by the ancient Romans rather rarely in Rome, but many columns have been found in Tunisia and elsewhere in north Africa. It was reused by the scalpellini, and is commonly seen in the collections of marble samples and tabletops inlaid with mixed marbles that were sold to visitors doing the Grand Tour in the 18th and 19th centuries. The columns in the Palazzo Sciarra in Rome are particularly noteworthy. There are also two superb vases made of *lumachella rosea* in Chatsworth House, Derbyshire, which were brought back from Rome in the first half of the 19th century.

GEOLOGICAL DESCRIPTION
Eocene fossiliferous limestone containing abundant nummulites, with fragments of sponges, mollusks and other fossil debris. It has stylolites and a few white calcite-filled fractures.

MAJOR USAGE
Columns, vases, decorative panels.

Austrian fire marble

SOURCE: Bad Bleiberg, Carinthia, Austria

STATUS: Small pieces sometimes sold

Oxf–Min 1478

The nacre of some seashells shows a subtle play of colors, the "mother of pearl" effect. Those in *Austrian fire marble* are positively vibrant in color.

There are many beautiful fossil limestones, but this stone is exceptional and, not surprisingly, it is only ever found in small pieces. *Fire marble* is a fossiliferous limestone containing fragments of ammonites, gastropods, bivalves and occasional corals in a brown matrix that can be seen under a microscope to be a mixture of metallic pale yellow pyrite and colorless calcite. But the beauty of this stone lies in the fragments of ammonite that retain a composition of aragonite and show a stunning iridescence, glinting bright reds and green as the stone is turned in the light. *Fire marble* came from St. Oswald tunnel near Bleiberg in Carinthia, and was first described in 1785. It has traditionally been used for decorating snuff boxes and other small decorative items, but was also inlaid in furniture. Today, small pieces can sometimes be purchased secondhand at mineral fairs.

A similar iridescence is seen in Cretaceous ammonites from southern Alberta in Canada that have been preserved as aragonite under a layer of volcanic bentonite clay. The vividly colored iridescent layer is as little as 1/300 inch (0.08 mm) thick. This stone is sold as *ammolite*.

GEOLOGICAL DESCRIPTION
Triassic limestone of fossil mollusks—including irridescent *Carnites floridus*—and corals in a matrix of calcite and pyrite.

MAJOR USAGE
Veneers in snuff boxes, inlays in furniture.

Tennessee cedar

SOURCE: Friendsville, Blount County, Tennessee, United States
STATUS: Actively quarried

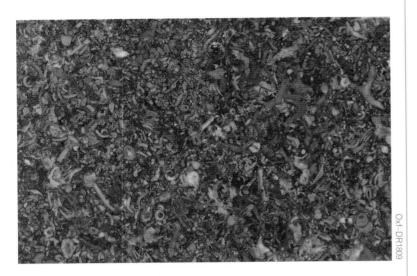

Oxf-DR1809

Tennessee cedar may be some 460 million years old, but it is packed full of the most beautifully preserved fossils.

Fossils feature in most of the Tennessee "marbles," but in none so prominently as the lovely dark *Tennessee cedar*. It contains a mass of small white crinoid ossicles, bryozoan and mollusk shell fragments cemented in a contrasting matrix, often referred to as "chocolate" in color but tending to deep red. Under a microscope it is possible to see that the fine structure of these ancient creatures is beautifully preserved. It was deposited behind bryozoan reefs, in sheltered sea conditions during Ordovician times.

Tennessee cedar, also traded as *Lambert cedar*, is one of the Tennesssee marbles that has been quarried in the Knoxville, Rogersville and Friendsville areas since 1838. At first it was the more popular of the colors available, but fashions changed and the preference has grown for lighter pink shades. *Cedar* is often used for skirtings and decorative details inset in pink Tennessee limestone (see page 107) in walls and floors, for example in the renovations of the Smithsonian Institution and of the National Archives, both in Washington, D.C. Today the stone is in demand for restoration work as well as innumerable new projects.

GEOLOGICAL DESCRIPTION

Mid-Ordovician fossiliferous limestone, containing crinoids, bryozoan and other fossil debris in a matrix colored by hematite. Stylolites are less prominent than in the pink Tennesssee limestones.

MAJOR USAGE

Walls, floors and other architectural features; countertops; furniture and sculpture.

Spanish broccatello

SOURCE: Tortosa, Catalonia, Spain
STATUS: Occasionally quarried

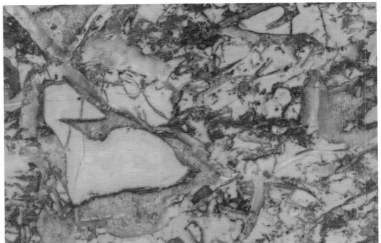

Oxf-Corsi 390

With its rich tints of purple and gold, this marble is aptly named after brocade, a luxurious fabric with silk and gold thread.

Broccatello is the most famous of all Spain's decorative stones, and it is indeed very richly colored. The large creamy-white fragments are rudist bivalve shells, and they are cemented in a fine-grained groundmass that is dark violet, golden-yellow or most commonly a mixture of the two colors. It comes from quarries at Raval de la Llet, southeast of Tortosa. La Cinta quarry supplies the traditional violet and yellow forms of *broccatello*, while farther south, the smaller Els Valencians quarry yields a predominantly yellow stone. The name, alluding to gold-threaded brocade fabric, was probably assigned to this stone in medieval times, but the stone's use goes back much further in time.

The more ancient quarry is La Cinta, and it is possible that *broccatello* was employed as early as the end of the first century BCE for decoration in Spain, but it was not transported to Rome until the third or fourth century CE, when its use grew through the Byzantine period. As well as Spain and Italy, it was employed in Tunisia, Algeria and France, but little if at all farther east in Greece and Turkey. Paving and wall claddings, columns and sarcophagi were all made of this stone. By medieval times, the quarries had closed, but stone was recycled, as can be seen in St. Mark's Basilica in Venice and the Baptistry in Florence.

From the 16th century, *broccatello* reached new heights of popularity. It was extensively used in the palaces, churches and cathedrals of both Spain and Italy. In Spain it was known as *jaspi de la cinta* because it was used in the decoration of the chapel in Tortosa Cathedral that houses the holy cincture said to have been left by the Virgin Mary during an apparition in 1178. In Italy, the Chapel of San Gennaro in the Cathedral at Naples

LUMACHELLE AND OTHER FOSSILIFEROUS LIMESTONES

is heavily ornamented with *Spanish broccatello*. It was exported farther afield too, and used in the decoration of churches in Latin American countries. Considerable amounts of *Spanish broccatello* were used for inlay work at the Opificio delle Pietre Dure in Florence. Such was the demand for the stone that La Cinta quarry was reopened, and the Els Valencians quarry also opened at about this time.

In 1887, marble merchant Arthur Lee commented that *broccatello* was little used. It was still employed in ecclesiastical architecture, and can be seen in the pavements of various English cathedrals. It was also made into domestic items such as clock cases and mantelpieces. The quarries have continued to work, somewhat intermittently, right up to recent times.

GEOLOGICAL DESCRIPTION

Early Cretaceous rudist limestone with a crystalline calcite cement variously tinted by iron oxides. Cavities in bivalves are often filled with coarsely granular calcite.

MAJOR USAGE

Columns, wall cladding, ecclesiastical pavements; sarcophagi; mantelpieces, clock cases; pietre dure work.

RIGHT *Broccatello* was often used in Italian pietre dure work, such as this beautiful old tabletop made in Rome.

Rosone di Trapani

SOURCE: Trapani, Sicily
STATUS: No longer quarried

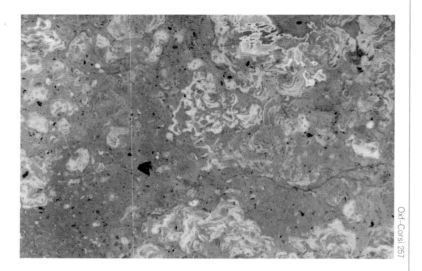

Oxf-Corsi 257

At first glance it may be hard to see any fossils, but a closer look shows the unusual nodular appearance of *rosone di Trapani* disguises a veritable stew of marine life.

The curious *rosone di Trapani* was obtained along the Trapani coastline between the Torre di Ligny and the old tuna fishery of San Giuliano, and also around the Island of Colombaia. To some extent it varied in color and markings depending on where it was collected. It was given this name because the stone that used to be extracted by the beach of Pietro Palazzo had rounded markings that apparently resembled rosebuds. This sample shows lovely delicate tints of pink and yellow, but often the stone is dirty-white or plain gray. It has also been known by many other names including *lumachella di Trapani* and *pietra mischio*.

Under a microscope *rosone di Trapani* is seen to be a crowded mass of algae, foraminifera, seashells, bryozoans and sea urchin spines. It was quarried from the 17th century onward, and mainly used for architectural elements such as windowsills, steps and columns in churches and palaces in Trapani and surrounding areas. It was also brought to Rome and used there for small inlays in furniture. The last quarry of this stone closed in 1950.

GEOLOGICAL DESCRIPTION

Predominantly algal limestone composed of calcareous algae, with foraminifera, mollusks, bryozoans and echinoderms in a fine-grained matrix.

MAJOR USAGE

Steps, sills, columns and other architectural elements; used in inlaid furniture made in Rome in the 18th and 19th centuries.

Rasotica

SOURCE: Brač, Croatia
STATUS: Actively quarried

Oxf-DR1710

Only the better grade of *Rasotica* has the beautifully preserved bivalves that make this such a fascinating rock for geologists.

One of the most popular fossiliferous limestones of recent years is the stone known as *Rasotica* named after Rasotica Bay at the far eastern end of the Croatian island of Brač. It is a brown Cretaceous limestone, about 75 million years old. Two grades are sold. *Rasotica B* contains beautifully preserved large rudist bivalves in a coarse-grained matrix of mud, shell fragments, foraminifera and other fossil debris. The inferior *Rasotica C* has poorly defined bivalves, but derives some patterning from natural black stains.

Rasotica and other limestones quarried on Brač have been supplied for much of the local reconstruction work, but they are also exported all over the world. *Rasotica* makes an interesting and elegant contrast in floor designs with the paler-colored limestones of Croatia.

GEOLOGICAL DESCRIPTION

Coarse-grained Cretaceous limestone containing rudist bivalves, abundant foraminifera and other fossil debris.

MAJOR USAGE

Paving, wall cladding; other interior architectural applications.

Jura marble

SOURCE: Fränkische Jura, Bavaria, Germany
STATUS: Actively quarried

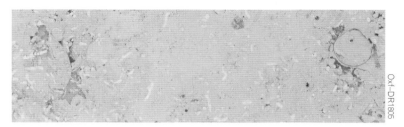

Oxf-DR1805

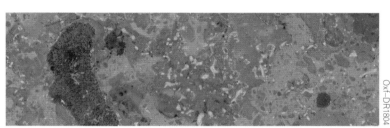

Oxf-DR1804

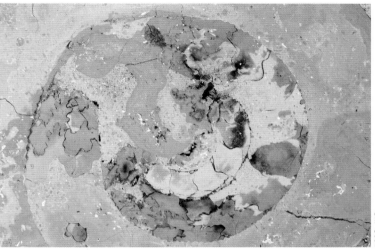

Oxf-Geol.

Jura marble is quarried so close to the famous *Archaeopteryx* quarries at Solnhofen that it is not surprising this stone can be richly fossiliferous too.

Jura limestone is often referred to as *Jura marble* because it takes a very good polish. It is quarried in the Fränkische Jura (Fränkische Alb), from a number of quarries in the Altmühltal Naturpark. The region is famous for its rich Jurassic fossil fauna and, not surprisingly, this limestone contains many well-preserved marine fossils, particularly ammonites. The color varies from cream and beige to gray depending on which level in the quarries the stone is extracted from. It is always flecked with white.

The quarries were opened in the 1830s to supply vast quantities of stone to build the Walhalla, the classical Greek temple on the Rhine at Donaustauf. Since then *Jura marble* has been used for the new Reichstag in Berlin, the Sadlers Wells Theatre in London, the John Wayne Airport in California and innumerable other projects around the world.

GEOLOGICAL DESCRIPTION

Late Jurassic fine-grained limestone with scattered fossils including ammonites, bivalves, echinoid spines and other fossil debris.

MAJOR USAGE

Internal and external architectural cladding, flooring, other fixtures.

RIGHT A close encounter with prehistoric life is guaranteed when *Jura marble* is used to pave a shopping mall, as here in the Clarendon Centre, Oxford, England.

LUMACHELLE AND OTHER FOSSILIFEROUS LIMESTONES

Lumachella di San Vitale

SOURCE: San Vitale and Rovere Veronese, Veneto, Italy
STATUS: Some quarrying still occurs

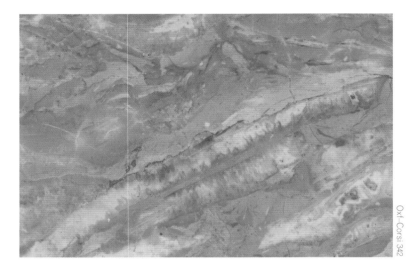

Oxf-Corsi 342

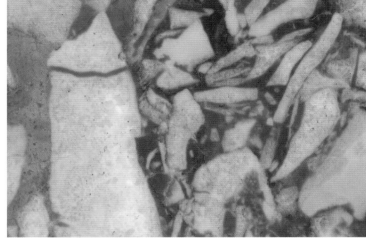

Oxf-Corsi 921

It is very hard to make out what the fossils are in the extraordinary *lumachella di San Vitale*, and they do indeed have more than a passing resemblance to bones.

Early stoneworkers thought the elongated white fragments in this limestone were bones, and coined the name *ossifere* or *bone marble* for it. Others thought they were fossil sponges or corals. Later in the 19th century they were recognized as recrystallized shell fragments of a large bivalve called *Lithiotis problematica*. This mollusk lived in lagoons close to the shore in early Jurassic times, and would congregate to form substantial reefs that could be up to 10 feet (3 m) high and around 30 feet (10 m) across. The space around the bivalves would slowly fill with muddy sediment and other fossil debris, and it is this that now forms the matrix around the shell fragments.

The color of this lumachella can vary enormously. Specimens in the oldest collections often have a clear gray matrix, and the recrystallized *Lithiotis* shell fragments have a sugary texture. Alternatively the cement is the typical buff and pink colors so often seen in the limestones of Verona, and the shell fragments are less altered. More recently, quarried stone usually has a red, yellow or brown matrix.

Lumachella di San Vitale was first discovered near the village of San Vitale in the Valle di Squaranto. Nowadays it is quarried closer to the neighboring town of Roverè Veronese. It is one of many stones from the hills outside Verona that have been used for decorative purposes for hundreds of years. Similar stones come from Cadine, Sardagne and other places near Trento (Trient).

GEOLOGICAL DESCRIPTION

Lower Jurassic limestone containing *Lithiotis problematica*

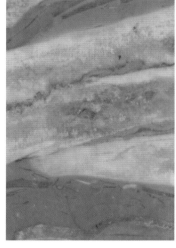

Oxf-DR1723

LEFT A modern vase made out of *lumachella di San Vitale* designed by Raffaello Galiotto for Decormarmi. It is 16 inches (40 cm) high. The shape was inspired by the fossils in the stone, recalling "a material of biological fermentation."

and other fossil debris in a fine-grained cement colored by carbonaceous matter or iron oxides.

MAJOR USAGE

Floors, wall claddings, tabletops, vases, other decorative items.

Chiampo

SOURCE: Chiampo, Vicenza, Italy
STATUS: Actively quarried

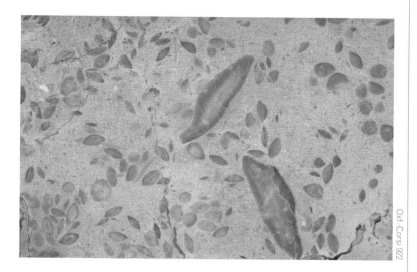

Oxf-Corsi 922

The name "nummulite" comes from the Latin for a small coin, and it very neatly describes the shape of the fossils in *Chiampo*.

The characteristic feature of *Chiampo* is its button-shaped nummulites: calcium carbonate shells of simple, single-celled organisms that are a kind of foraminifera. Normally foraminifera are tiny, less than 1/30 inch (1 mm) across, but the nummulites of Eocene times were much bigger.

Chiampo has been quarried for a very long time on either side of the valley of the River Chiampo near the town of the same name. The stone shown here is from Corsi's collection of 1827. Writing in 1889, William Jervis listed the quarryworker's names for these stones as yellowish *stellar bianco* and pink *stellar rosa*. Today they are termed *Chiampo perlino* and *Chiampo rosato*, and various other varieties of *Chiampo* are recognized as well. The growth of the quarrying industry in Chiampo grew rapidly after the unification of Italy, and was highly successful in the latter half of the 20th century. This limestone was exported all over the world, and is often seen in banks, churches, offices and public buildings. Today the industry has slowed, and many of the quarries have closed.

GEOLOGICAL DESCRIPTION

Mid-Eocene fine-grained nummulitic limestone featuring abundant stylolites.

MAJOR USAGE

Flooring, cladding, countertops, staircases; altars and other ecclesiastical items.

Botticino

SOURCE: Botticino area, Lombardy, Italy
STATUS: Actively quarried

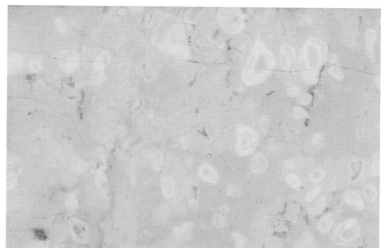

Oxf-Corsi 237

The fossils in *Botticino* give a subtle patterning to this classic marble from the Lombardy region of Italy.

Botticino was used locally by the ancient Romans, the earliest inscribed column dating to the first century BCE. It is seen in many public buildings in Brescia built from medieval times onward, and its popularity has grown in recent years. Today, most of the quarries are owned by the Botticino commune's local council, and the Cooperativa Operai Cavatori del Botticino, set up in 1932, runs quarries and processing plants, and trains workers in all aspects of stone extraction and processing. Large quantities of the stone are exported all over the world. The monument to Victor Emmanuel II in Rome, completed in 1911, is made of *Botticino*, and this stone was extensively used in the palace of the parliament of Vienna. In the United States, it clads many of the interior walls of the public library in Cleveland, Ohio.

GEOLOGICAL DESCRIPTION

A fine-grained compact limestone of Lower Jurassic age, containing foraminifera, algae, corals, echinoderms, sponges and gastropods. It has abundant darker-colored stylolites.

MAJOR USAGE

Flooring, cladding, countertops, staircases; altars and other ecclesiastical fixtures.

LUMACHELLE AND OTHER FOSSILIFEROUS LIMESTONES

Derbyshire fossil limestone

SOURCE: Derbyshire, England

STATUS: Rarely quarried for decorative purposes

Crinoidal Oxf-Corsi 285

Moneyash Oxf-Corsi 284

Coral Oxf-Corsi 288

Some Derbyshire fossil limestones are rich in crinoid debris, others in corals, while brachiopods predominate in yet others.

The Derbyshire fossil limestones most often used for decorative purposes are the first of these. Crinoids are sometimes referred to as sea lilies; misleading in that they are not plants at all, but animals related to starfish and sea urchins. Their "stems" are made up of ossicles that look like English "polo mints," small white disks with a hole in the middle. Limestones rich in crinoid debris are called crinoidal limestones, and some very decorative examples have come from the Peak District of Derbyshire. Buff and gray varieties known as *Hopton Wood stone* have been quarried from Hopton Wood and other locations since the 1750s.

Moneyash marble was quarried at Ricklow Dale near Moneyash, and is buff colored with distinctive violet veins running through it. These are two named examples, but it can be difficult to localize the Derbyshire limestones with certainty as they were quarried in many places for use as a construction stone or aggregate, any of which could have provided stone for polishing. The coral limestones of Derbyshire are less often encountered. They are rich in the colonial coral *Lithostrotion* and other kinds of coral, and they, too, can be found in many locations around the Peak District.

The balustrades of the staircase (left) are just one example of the many uses of Derbyshire fossil limestone at Chatsworth House in Derbyshire, and it is extensively used in Derbyshire's Kedleston Hall, too. These are local uses but the stone was transported considerable distances and used, for example, in the Houses of Parliament and the Bank of England in London. Nowadays little if any Derbyshire limestone is quarried for decorative purposes.

GEOLOGICAL DESCRIPTION

Carboniferous limestone containing abundant crinoid ossicles, corals, bryozoans, algae, brachiopods, foraminifera and other fossil debris. Purple stylolites are colored by hematite.

MAJOR USAGE

Floors, walls, windowsills, stairs, columns, fireplaces, tabletops, inlay work, sculpture.

LEFT The staircase balustrades are among many examples of the use of local fossil limestones for architectural decoration in Chatsworth House in Derbyshire.

Frosterley marble

SOURCE: Frosterley, Durham, England
STATUS: Intermittently quarried

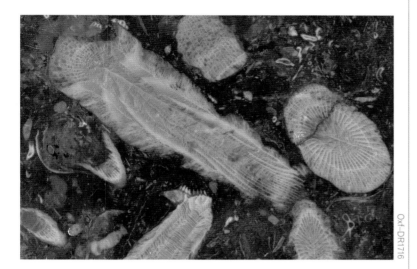

Oxf-DR1716

If you go into the Anglican Cathedral in Mumbai, India, and look at the base of the pulpit, you will see a distinctive black limestone with scattered white corals.

This is *Frosterley marble*, a tough gray Carboniferous limestone that polishes to a fine black finish. It contains a variety of different white corals, of which large specimens of *Dibunophyllum bipartitum* are very noticeable. It has been quarried in a number of places near the English village of Frosterley, on the banks of the River Wear, and was also named *Stanhope black marble* after the nearby village of Stanhope. The quarrymen called it "cockle" and they extracted it from a coral-rich bed no more than 3 feet (1 m) in thickness.

Frosterley marble is most closely associated with English ecclesiastical architecture, and there are fine columns in the 13th-century Nine Altars Chapel of Durham Cathedral, and paving in York Minster laid in the 14th century. Its use declined in the 18th century, but revived again in the 19th century when marble again became very fashionable for public buildings. Pillars can be seen in the Oxford University's Natural History Museum, and the stone was indeed used in Mumbai. Today, one of the quarries, Harehope, is preserved as an environmental education center and visitors can see where the stone was extracted. Another, the Broadwood quarry, is still worked from time to time.

GEOLOGICAL DESCRIPTION

Medium-grained Lower Carboniferous bituminous limestone containing the solitary coral *Dibunophyllum bipartitum* and other corals, shell fragments, crinoids and carbonaceous matter.

MAJOR USAGE

Paving, staircases, pillars; fonts, tombs; fireplaces, furniture.

Madrepore marble

SOURCE: South Devon, England
STATUS: No longer quarried

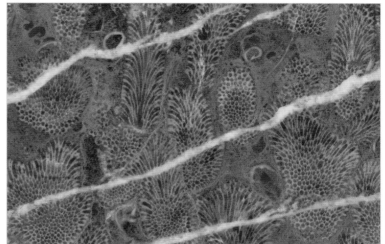

Oxf-Geol D80a

Feathery fossil corals feature prominently in the Devonian rocks of south Devon and were made into pretty souvenirs for tourists.

The Devonian period of geological time is named after the county of Devon in England, and the Devonian rocks of the Torbay area include various colorful fossiliferous limestones once traded as Devon "marbles." Those rich in corals were called *madrepore marble* by the madrepore manufacturers of the seaside towns of Teignmouth, Dawlish, Babbacombe and Torquay. They cut and polished the stone and fashioned it into boxes, paperweights and other small gifts that they sold to tourists.

"Madrepore" is an archaic name for fossil corals, and the most striking *madrepore marble* contains the branching coral *Thamnopora cervicornis* that lived some 370 million years ago. When cut obliquely, it has a distinctly featherlike appearance, which has earned it the name "feather madrepore." This stone was quarried between Newton Abbot and the village of East Ogwell during the 19th and early 20th centuries, perhaps earlier, and used to make mantelpieces, tabletops and vases, as well as souvenirs. Writing in 1916, John Watson said that the stone was by then in little demand. Now the only examples of madrepore marbleware to be bought are lucky finds in antique stores and garage sales.

GEOLOGICAL DESCRIPTION

Devonian compact gray limestone containing *Thamnopora cervicornis* and other corals and stromatoporids.

MAJOR USAGE

Mantelpieces, tabletops, vases; boxes, paperweights and other small gift items.

Stellaria

SOURCE: Italy and elsewhere
STATUS: Occasional quarry finds

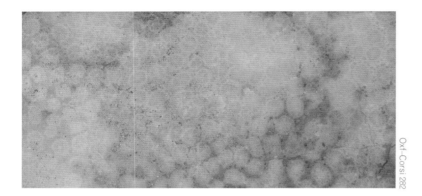

Oxf–Corsi 282

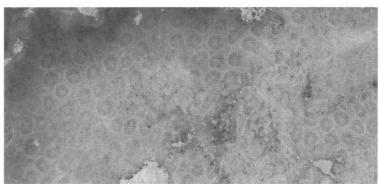

Oxf–Corsi 227

Ask any marble lover to choose their favorite stone in an inlaid table of samples, and it is likely they will choose *stellaria*.

These beautifully marked coral limestones were highly prized because they looked so mysterious, the septa of the corals giving a starlike appearance. It is for this reason they were called *stellaria* and in past times they were often worn as amulets and attributed with healing properties. Today they are just as much a conversation piece as ever they were.

It is likely that decorative stones known as *stellaria* came from many different places, and by no means confined to Italy, although the examples shown here are Italian and most probably from the Mesozoic and Cenozoic rocks of the valleys north of Verona. As they would not necessarily have been of any great lateral extent, they would have been a chance discovery by an eagle-eyed quarryman. Corsi mentions the discovery of just one column fragment of this stone in his treatise on ancient marbles. Both

the scalpellini and the pietre dure workers delighted in employing *stellaria* in inlaid furniture and other decorative work.

Fossil corals can also be preserved in chalcedony (see page 240), for example those of Hillsborough Bay and other locations in Florida. These silicified corals are very much harder than those preserved in calcite, and they may show agate banding.

GEOLOGICAL DESCRIPTION
Mesozoic and Cenozoic coral limestones containing recrystallized colonial scleractinian corals; a little hematite and goethite tint the stone red or yellow.

MAJOR USAGE
Decorative inlays.

Other lumachellas and fossiliferous limestones

Although the crinoidal limestones of Derbyshire, England, have received special mention, the Carboniferous limestone covered large areas of Britain and similar stones can be found in Bristol, Dent in Yorkshire, and locations in Ireland. A fine dark gray limestone packed with bivalves used to come from Latschach in Carinthia, Austria.

A very attractive red limestone with large bivalves comes from Spain and is traded as *rojo Daniel*. Creamy-colored lumachelle

are included in the Aurisina family of decorative stones quarried at Aurisina near Trieste, Italy. A good highly fossiliferous limestone comes from Colombia.

Greenport in Columbia County, New York, supplied a pinkish-gray fossil limestone that was used for decorative purposes in the late 19th century. The *Petoskey stone* of Petoskey in Michigan is another excellent example of coral limestone, and it cut and polished for a variety of decorative purposes.

Green marbles, "ophicalcites" and serpentinites

Onions and serpents feature prominently in the names in this section. The striped cipollini of Greece and Italy are impure marbles with flaky green crystals of chlorite forming sinuous bands of color that look just like the layers of an onion. The serpentinites, rocks composed mainly of serpentine minerals, often have colors and patterns that resemble snakeskin. An old fashioned name "ophicalcite" is sometimes used for rocks that are neither marble nor serpentinite but somewhere in between. They may be composed of green serpentinite fragments cemented by white calcite or dolomite, or simply impure marbles containing serpentine minerals. Serpentinites are rarely very durable outside, but they are popular for interior decoration, especially when patterned with white marble. The name "serpentine" is familiar to many visitors to Cornwall, England, where local stone is turned by artisans into ornaments and jewelry, a craft that flourishes in Scotland and Ireland too.

Cipollino verde

SOURCE: Euboea, Greece
STATUS: Intermittently quarried

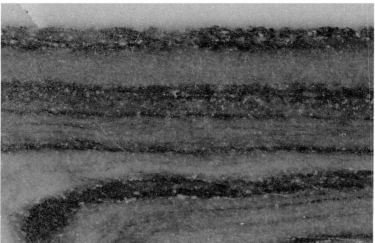

Oxf-Corsi DR1423

Italian stonecutters called this stone *cipollino* because the undulating bands of color reminded them of an onion—"cipolla," in Italian.

The Romans were the first to exploit *cipollino verde* on a large scale. They thought the patterning looked like waves from the sea, and they called it *marmor Carystium* after Karystos, a town at the southern end of the Greek island of Euboea. They opened many quarries in the southwest of the island and one, on the slopes of Mount Okhi northeast of Karystos, still has several rough-hewn pillars lying about.

The first records of the use of *marmor Carystium* in Rome date to the second century BCE when huge columns were used in a temple that Agrippa dedicated to Neptune, god of the sea. In the Forum of Rome, 10 huge, 55-foot (17 m) high columns front the temple of Antoninus and Faustina, built in 141 CE. To early Christians the pattern of *cipollino* was reminiscent of the wood of the Holy Cross, ensuring the stone's popularity into Byzantine times. By the time the quarries ceased working in the seventh century, huge quantities of stone had been transported across the Roman Empire, affording ample spolia for subsequent generations to reuse.

The reopening of the Greek *cipollino* quarries at the end of the 19th century may have a French connection. Architect Charles Garnier's quest for *cipollino* to use in the new Paris Opera House was unsuccessful and he resorted to using Italian *cipollino* for the building, which opened in 1878. But this may have prompted the famous marble merchant William Brindley to seek out and reopen the original quarries on Euboea. By 1881, Brindley was advertising

LEFT *Cipollino* column in the grounds of Hadrian's Villa at Tivoli, outside Rome.

as sole agent for Greek *cipollino*, and in 1907 he reported that over 100 large columns had been exported to Britain, Germany and the United States. Some of these can be seen in Westminster Cathedral, London, where there are also good examples of the use of *cipollino* in opened-out slabs, showing the banding in mirror image. The 1911 *cipollino* façade of the Loos Haus on Michaelerplatz, in Vienna, designed by Adolf Loos, is another striking example of this stone. Early in the 20th century, ownership of the quarries at Styra had transferred to the Anglo-Greek Marmor Company. The quarries have continued to work intermittently up to the present day, most recently trading the stone as *Styra green*.

GEOLOGICAL DESCRIPTION

A sheared and folded impure calcitic marble, the diffuse green bands are rich in silicate minerals, predominantly chlorite. *Cipollino verde* was deposited as a limestone in Permian times and metamorphosed during the late Cretaceous and Tertiary periods.

MAJOR USAGE

Cipollino from Euboea makes excellent load-bearing columns. The stone has also been used extensively for cladding, paving, bathtubs and opus sectile. The appearance of the stone depends on how it is cut. When sawn perpendicular to the bedding, the stone has characteristic banding, but sawn parallel to the bedding, it can appear a cloudy green.

BELOW AND INSET
Cipollino verde forms the façade of the Loos Haus built in 1911 in Vienna.

Cipollino Apuano

SOURCE: Apuan Alps, Tuscany, Italy
STATUS: Rarely quarried today

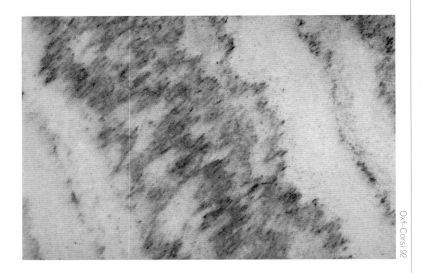

Oxf-Corsi 92

The Apuan Alps of Italy have yielded such a wide variety of different marbles, it is not surprising that *cipollino* marbles have been found there too.

The green *cipollini* of the Apuan Alps are similar to Greek *cipollino* (see pages 174–5) but the bands tend to be more closely spaced. In small fragments, you can only tell them apart by scientific analysis of the chemical and mineral composition of the rock. *Cipollino Apuano* comes from Alta Versilia, in the area of Arni, Monte Corchia, Isola Santa and north toward Careggine. The ancient Romans quarried it at Monte Corchia, and samples found in historic marble collections and inlaid tabletops of the early 19th century are most likely to be stone obtained from archaeological sites.

Modern quarrying did not begin until about 1855. It reached a peak in the first part of the 20th century with 20 active quarries, but after World War II the industry declined and the stone is rarely quarried today. Modern trade names include *cipollino Versilia* and *cremo Tirreno*.

GEOLOGICAL DESCRIPTION

Strongly sheared and folded impure calcitic marbles, the green bands are rich in silicate minerals, predominantly chlorite. They were deposited as limestones and clays in the Jurassic period and metamorphosed during the formation of the Alps in Tertiary times.

MAJOR USAGE

Architectural cladding, paving and other fittings; ornaments, tabletops and other decorative objects.

Connemara marble

SOURCE: Connemara, County Galway, Ireland
STATUS: Actively quarried

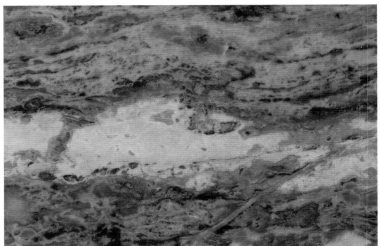

Oxf-DR1172

One of the most vibrantly colored of all serpentine marbles, this stone is also fittingly known as *Irish green*, sitting as it does amid the most wild and romantic Gaelic scenery.

Connemara marble ranges from pale yellow to dark green, banded and veined with gray and white. It was first quarried early in the 19th century from an opening on the side of a hill just north of Clifden in Connemara. This rugged site has been worked under a number of different proprietors right up to the present day. A more turbulent looking variety comes from Barnanoraun quarry, 6 miles (10 km) east of Clifden. This too has been worked since the early 19th century. A third quarry of green marble is at Lissoughter Hill, near Recess. It was worked in the 19th century but only rarely used today. Fine pillars can be seen in Trinity College Dublin (1857) and in the Oxford University Museum of Natural History (1860) where a bust of the Irish architect of both buildings, Benjamin Woodward, is mounted in *Connemara marble*.

This marble is still marketed across the world for cladding and other architectural uses, but a thriving industry revolves around the local tourist trade. A visitor center at the processing works in Moycullen has guided tours and sells a wide range of souvenirs.

GEOLOGICAL DESCRIPTION

Impure limestone metamorphosed during Precambrian times to form a marble with bands of serpentine minerals.

MAJOR USAGE

Interior architecture, monuments, ecclesiastical items, sculpture and small gifts.

Verde ranocchia

SOURCE: Eastern Desert, Egypt
STATUS: No longer quarried

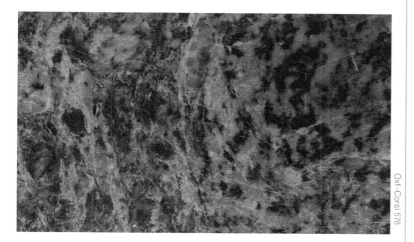

Oxf-Corsi 578

Oxf-Corsi 567

The Italian word "ranocchia" means frog and the name *verde ranocchia* given by Italian stonecutters rather graphically describes the green mottled appearance of this stone.

This is most probably the same stone that Pliny, writing in the first century CE, called *lapis batrachitis* (frog stone). He said it came from Coptis, an ancient city on the banks of Nile not far from where the quarries have since been rediscovered. *Verde ranocchia* is a fine-grained serpentinite of a distinctly yellowish green color, with a network of yellowish talc-rich veins. A beautiful sculpture of a dog, carved in Imperial Roman times, is in the Palazzo dei Conservatori, in the Capitoline Museums of Rome. The variety *serpentina moschinata* has distinctive dark mosslike or insectlike spots. Both these varieties were quarried by the ancient Romans at Wadi Umm Esh (near Wadi Atalla) in Egypt's Eastern Desert, but evidence of these workings was largely destroyed when quarrying resumed in the 1900s. All quarrying has now ceased.

GEOLOGICAL DESCRIPTION

Serpentinite of Precambrian age with fine talcose veins, often spotted with disseminated black metal oxides.

MAJOR USAGE

Used in ancient times as wall cladding, in paving and for sculpture. It was reused by Roman stonecutters for inlay work.

Verde Impruneta

SOURCE: Impruneta, Tuscany, Italy
STATUS: No longer quarried

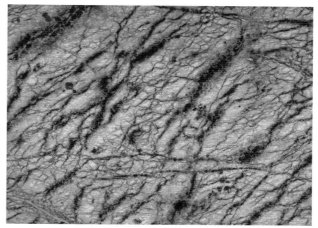

Oxf-DR1224

With such a distinctive snakeskin appearance, this rock from Impruneta shows admirably why the rock called serpentine was given this name by early geologists.

Strikingly marked, this stone comes from the pretty Tuscan village of Impruneta, south of Florence. All serpentine marbles with a reticulate pattern of veins were called *verde ranocchia* by the Italian stonecutters, and this name has often been applied to *verde Impruneta*. It is a very pale green serpentinite with a network of black veins, rich in metal oxides.

Verde Impruneta is seen in many collections of stone and in inlaid tabletops of the 18th and 19th centuries, but was probably little worked after the middle of that century.

GEOLOGICAL DESCRIPTION

Talc-rich serpentinite with reticulated veins that are rich in black metal oxides.

MAJOR USAGE

Paving, inlay work.

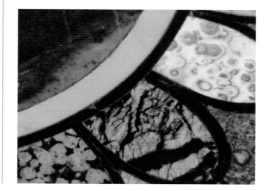

LEFT *Verde Impruneta* in an inlaid tabletop made in Rome in the late 1820s and now in Farnborough Hall, Warwickshire.

Verde di Prato

SOURCE: Prato, Tuscany, Italy
STATUS: No longer quarried

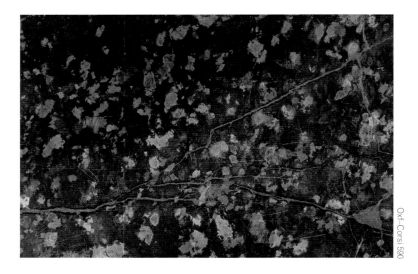

Some of the most famous buildings in Florence are ornamented with this green stone from Prato, with its glinting spots of altered enstatite.

The green serpentinite known as *verde di Prato* has been used with striking effect in the Romanesque baroque architecture of northern Tuscany. A superb example is in Prato itself, where it is banded with pale-colored Alberese limestone in the façades and interior decoration of the Cathedral of San Stefano. In Florence it is combined with white marbles to decorate the Cathedral of Santa Maria del Fiore, and the San Giovanni Baptistry. It was first used in the 12th century and the oldest quarries were at Pian di Gello on the eastern side of Monte Piccioli, one of the three peaks of Monte Ferrato, just north of Prato. As demand for the stone grew, a second quarry was opened at nearby Figline. During the 16th century the stones of the ancient world and pietre dure (hard stones) became more fashionable for polychrome marble decoration, so use of the Prato serpentinite declined.

The Figline quarry was reopened around 1860 to supply stone for the repair of older buildings, for *verde di Prato* had not fared well in places exposed to the elements. The fashion for neo-Gothic architecture, which sought to emulate the beautiful stonework of medieval times, also stimulated new markets for the stone. It was sometimes used for sculpture; for example, *Mother and Child* (1931), one of the early works of Henry Moore, is carved in *verde di Prato*. Quarrying dwindled and ceased in the 1950s.

Much *verde di Prato* is rather distinctive in appearance. The serpentine groundmass can be various shades of green, and scattered through it are lustrous greenish brown crystals that lend it a rather distinctive appearance. They are relics of enstatite crystals that formed in the original igneous rock.

GEOLOGICAL DESCRIPTION

Serpentinite formed by metamorphism of enstatite-bearing peridotite. It may have slender reticulated veins of talc, calcite and hydromagnesite.

MAJOR USAGE

Architecture of medieval and Renaissance buildings; sculpture, furniture and decorative inlay work of the 19th century.

BELOW *Verde di Prato* and creamy white Alberese limestone are used together for the exterior decoration of the San Giovanni Baptistry in Florence.

Rosso Levanto

SOURCE: Levanto, Liguria, Italy
STATUS: Commercially available

Cam–Watson 790

Normally considered to be a green stone, serpentinite can turn red when water percolates through the rock. Of all the red serpentinites, the best known is *rosso Levanto*.

Serpentinite rocks tend to be rich in an iron oxide mineral called magnetite, making them appear a darker green. If percolating water alters the magnetite to hematite, the stone turns red. Although red serpentinites occur quite commonly, none has been worked on such a large scale as *rosso di Levanto*. It was first quarried in the 16th century near Levanto on the Ligurian coast and quarrying continues today farther north, near Bonassola. Mixed red and green colors are not uncommon, and an entirely green variety, marketed as *verde Levanto*, resembles some other serpentine marble breccias from the Italian Alps.

Confusingly the trade name *rosso Levanto* is also used for brecciated red serpentinite from Turkey, as is *rosso Lepanto*.

GEOLOGICAL DESCRIPTION
Breccia of serpentinite clasts colored red by disseminated hematite, with scattered green bastite crystals. The matrix is a mixture of hydromagnesite, calcite and talc.

MAJOR USAGE
Interior flooring, wall cladding and other architectural features. It is particularly attractive when used in inlay work or mosaic with white marble and green serpentinite.

Breccia Quintilina

SOURCE: Levanto area, Liguria, Italy
STATUS: No longer available

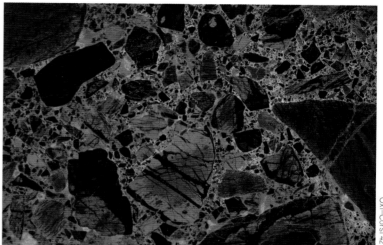

Oxf-Corsi 421

Marble collector Faustino Corsi called this stone the most beautiful breccia that might ever be seen, and it is certainly a remarkably attractive and richly colored stone.

Corsi called it *breccia della Villa Adriana* because small fragments had been found in the excavations of Hadrian's Villa at Tivoli. He later used the name by which it is known today, *breccia Quintilina*, after the villa of Quintilius Varrus, also at Tivoli. A cache of small unworked blocks had been found in the ruins of the villa in 1565 and from that date onward, the stone appears in some of the finest works of the Roman scalpellini. It richly ornaments an inlaid table made in Rome in the last quarter of the 16th century that was sold at auction in London in 2005, and there are four tablets in the wall of the Church of Sant'Andrea della Valle in Rome. Corsi says he sometimes found fragments of the stone in the vicinity of the villa but by the 19th century it must have been very rare indeed.

Breccia Quintilina is composed of brown serpentinite fragments, subtly shading to all other colors, and cemented by white calcite. It is thought to have come from near Levanto in Liguria.

GEOLOGICAL DESCRIPTION
Breccia of altered serpentinite clasts in a calcite matrix.

MAJOR USAGE
Used for inlay work and found in collections of ancient marbles.

Cornish serpentine

SOURCE: Lizard Peninsula, Cornwall, England
STATUS: Currently available

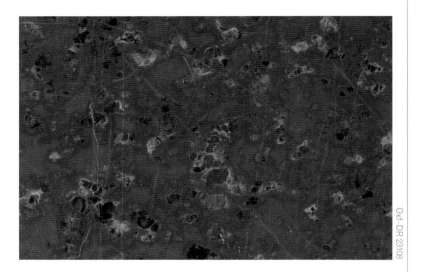

Oxf-DR 23108

When Queen Victoria and Prince Albert visited Cornwall in 1846, they started a new fashion for Cornwall's best known decorative stone. A little royal patronage can be very useful ...

The flat and windswept Lizard Peninsula produces a remarkable variety of different serpentine rocks. Some are mottled dark green or brown, others veined pale green, nearly white, and yet others are red and black. Just a few of these stones lend themselves to turning on lathes, and small decorative items were being produced as early as the 1820s. On their visit to Cornwall, Queen Victoria and Prince Albert purchased several ornaments for their new home, Osborne House. This, together with a stand at the Great Exhibition in London of 1851, brought Cornish serpentine to the notice of the British gentry. Processing mills in Penzance and Poltesco supplied large quantities of carved and polished stone for churches, public buildings and stately homes.

However, competition from Italian serpentine industries, and the fact that this stone did not weather well when used for exterior cladding, forced both mills to close by the end of the 19th century. Cottage industries remained, producing gifts made of serpentine for tourists (see pages 182–3), and business flourished up to the 1940s. Today, just a few craftspeople turn the stone.

GEOLOGICAL DESCRIPTION
Serpentinized gabbros and peridotites, red varieties colored by disseminated hematite. Veins are talc and hydromagnesite.

MAJOR USAGE
Sculpture and souvenirs, but once used for fireplaces and other architectural fittings, large urns, clock surrounds and other fine ornaments, and for fonts, altars and other ecclesiastical objects.

Mona marble

SOURCE: Rhoscolyn, Isle of Anglesey, Wales
STATUS: No longer quarried

Oxf-pillar

The Romans called the Isle of Anglesey "Mona" but it seems they did not unearth the striking green stone of the same name.

Serpentine-bearing rock outcrops exist in various places on the island but it was quarried only at Rhoscolyn on Holy Island, off the coast of Anglesey. Writing in the 18th century the writer Thomas Pennant records that he "saw the noted quarry of marble, common to the place, some parts of Italy, and to Corsica ... its colours are green, black, white, and dull purple, irregularly disposed ... it is apt to be intersected by small cracks or by asbestos veins, and is, therefore, incapable of taking a high polish." Blagrove, who wrote a classic reference on marbles in the 19th century, simply but positively described it as "very beautiful."

Mona marble was used in fine furniture designed by cabinetmaker George Bullock (ca. 1782–1818), who sculptured in marble before turning his hand to furniture making. Among his commissions was the supply of furniture to Napoleon (a great lover of marble) during his exile on the Atlantic island of St. Helena. *Mona marble* was used in various churches and cathedrals in England and can be seen in the chancels of both Worcester and Truro cathedrals. Near the quarries, the historic church of St. Cybi in Holyhead, Anglesey, has steps of *Mona marble* in a chapel that was added in 1897. Use of the marble declined and the quarries have not been worked since the early 1900s.

GEOLOGICAL DESCRIPTION
Green serpentinite or grayish green ophicalcite of Precambrian age—sometimes veined with gray or white calcite.

MAJOR USAGE
Used in architectural items and in furniture.

Tinos green

SOURCE: Near Marlas and Panormos, Isle of Tinos, Cyclades, Greece

STATUS: Actively quarried

Oxf-DR1428

The ancient *Tinos green*—quarried from the Cyclades island of Tinos—is set apart from other serpentine marbles by the pale bluish green veins that consistently run through it.

For some reason, Tinos is often overlooked as a source of stone in antiquity, and it rarely features in collections of ancient marbles. *Tinos green* was certainly used in ancient times, but the quarries were abandoned for many centuries. They were reopened in the 19th century, and worked by the Anglo-Greek Marmor Marble Company. Sound blocks up to 20 feet (6 m) in length could be obtained that were strong in texture and would take a good polish. Much of the stone was exported to England and the United States. Huge columns of *Tinos green* ornament the music hall of the Carnegie Museum of Art in Pittsburgh. The marble is also used in St. Paul's Cathedral and Westminster Cathedral, London. The quarries are still working today.

Tinos is a source of white marble *(Tinos marble)* as well as this green stone, and stone carving was once a major source of employment on the island. Evidence of this industry can be seen at the marble Church of the Panagia, built on the site where a miraculous icon of the Virgin Mary was found. Today, sculpture is taught and local carvings are available as souvenirs for visitors.

GEOLOGICAL DESCRIPTION
Dark green serpentinite or ophicalcite, heavily veined with calcite, remarkably consistent in appearance.

MAJOR USAGE
Sculpture, tiles, cladding and other architectural elements.

Vermont verde antique

SOURCE: Vermont, United States

STATUS: Actively quarried

Oxf-DR1639

Verde antique, a curious mixture of Italian and French, was no doubt intended to bring to mind the ancient *verde antico* of Greece, but now this famous old American stone has its own long and illustrious history.

Serpentinites and ophicalcites have been worked in many U.S. states, including Maryland, Connecticut, California and New Mexico, but most notably in Vermont. *Vermont verde antique* is quarried on the eastern side of the Green Mountains.

The first workings were in Cavendish, and opened in 1835. Later the marble was quarried in Roxbury, and since the early 1900s at Rochester. More recently it is being extracted at Cavendish again, and is traded as *Cavendish green*.

Verde antique can be seen in the National Gallery of Art West Building, Washington, D.C.; Cornell University's Mann Library; and, appropriately, in the Vermont Marble Museum in Proctor, Vermont.

GEOLOGICAL DESCRIPTION
Dark green serpentinite of Ordovician age, richly veined with white dolomite. Although very similar in appearance to some serpentinites from the European Alps, the European ones are generally veined with calcite rather than dolomite.

MAJOR USAGE
Slabbed for use as facing stones, floor tiles and kitchen countertops; sculpture; ornamental items.

Souvenirs in stone

RIGHT The cliffs of Kynance Cove on the Lizard Peninsula in Cornwall, which attract thousands of tourists each year, are composed of serpentinite rock.

Gifts and souvenirs made of serpentine marble have long lured tourists in Cornwall, Ireland and Scotland—Celtic lands that all have wild and stunningly beautiful coastal scenery.

The 1950s saw a boon in the number of resorts and hotels on the Lizard Peninsula in Cornwall, England, and this was good news for the serpentine workers who would eke an income by producing vases and barometers, trinket pots and ashtrays to sell to visitors during the short summer season. Model lighthouses, small and large, and with varying amounts of detail, were a favorite among vacationers seeking a memento of the rugged peninsula with its own lighthouse. At the gaudier end of the market, lead (and later, plastic) seagulls astride crudely varnished chunks of serpentine were in particular demand. Some marked "Exmouth" or "Ilfracombe" show that sales were not just restricted to the workshops on the Lizard and nearby Penzance.

Gifts and souvenirs made of serpentine marble were a traditional souvenir in Ireland, too. One observer of *Connemara* marble in 1886 commented on the great variety, "both in beauty and colour, as exhibited in the ornaments manufactured by the McDonnells of Clifden—self taught artists—who manufacture brooches and other articles of vertu by hand." Today, there is a visitor center at the marble works at Moycullen that sells everything from wishing stones and lucky charms to beautiful Celtic jewelry. The peripatetic pope John Paul II visited Ireland in 1981, and was presented with a Celtic cross and candlesticks made of *Connemara* marble, a gift from the youth of Ireland.

Another tradition of making souvenirs from local serpentine marble is found on the Scottish island of Iona. St. Columba landed here when he sailed from Ireland, and the monastery he founded has grown to be an ancient abbey and place of pilgrimage. Commercial exploitation of the island's serpentine marble, briefly in the 1790s, and again in the early 20th century, met with little success, although it can be seen in some churches and cathedrals. By contrast, the trade in souvenirs for pilgrims provided an ongoing source of income for islanders since at least the 18th century, when children used to sell pieces of serpentine marble to visitors. Today, fine jewelry and small carvings are made by islanders from marble found as pebbles on the beach.

On the Lizard, the souvenir trade has moved on. There are still a handful of serpentine workers trading, now at a time when there is greater respect for traditional crafts. Stone suitable for cutting has become rather scarce, and has to be extracted with minimal impact on the landscape. Working together, they dig a temporary pit, extract the stone, then restore the site again. There are no cheap souvenirs made from serpentine; rather, individually crafted objects, some turned on electric lathes and others hand-sculpted are made from this beautiful stone.

ABOVE Beach pebbles of Iona marble were cut to make souvenirs for pilgrims.

RIGHT Various different colors of serpentine have been used to make these ornaments.

LEFT Ian Casley is one of the few remaining craftspeople still turning serpentine to make gifts and souvenirs for visitors to the Lizard, Cornwall.

Verde Genova

SOURCE: Pietralavezzara, Genova, Italy
STATUS: No longer quarried

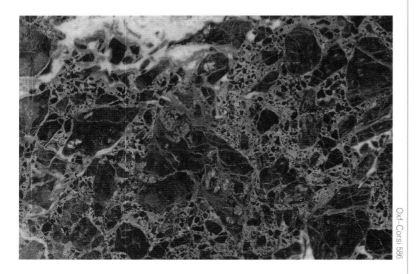

Oxf-Corsi 586

Also known as *Polcevera di Genova*, this stone was already regarded as "a well known and much esteemed calcareous serpentine [from] the famous quarries of Polcevera" in the 1860s, at a time when there were numerous serpentine deposits in Italy, but few of them quarried.

The quarries of this stone were opened at Pietralavezzara, near Campomorone, toward the end of the 16th century, and some 200 years later, the stone was being used for decorating churches, palaces and public buildings all across Europe. Just two of the many examples are the skirtings and architraves in the National Gallery in London and the marble ornamentation in the entrance hall of the Fitzwilliam Museum, Cambridge. *Polcevera* was still being quarried in the 1950s.

Typical *Polcevera* is a dark green brecciated stone with white veins, but a red brecciated variety, *rosso di Polcevera* (*rosso di Genova*), is also known. French stoneworkers have made particular use of green serpentine marbles from the Genoa area, introducing their own names. They called dark green serpentinites with few white veins *vert de mer,* and, confusingly, they gave the name *vert d'Egypt* to another variety with more, and wider, calcite veins.

GEOLOGICAL DESCRIPTION

Brecciated green serpentinite or ophicalcite, veined with white calcite. In the variety *rosso di Polcevera*, black magnetite has altered to red hematite.

MAJOR USAGE

Generally suitable for internal use only; applications include floorings, wall claddings and other architectural features.

Vert Maurin

SOURCE: Maurin, Alpes-de-Haute-Provence, France
STATUS: No longer quarried

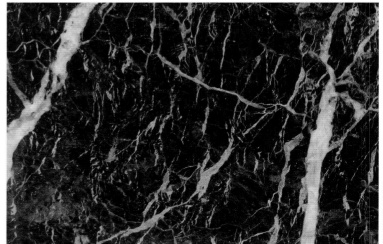

Cam-Watson 782

One of the darkest serpentines used for decorative purposes, this fine, beautiful marble used to be quarried in Alpes-de-Haute-Provence.

First quarried in 1851 near the hamlet of Maurin in Alpes-de-Haute-Provence, *vert Maurin* was used mostly in France for plinths, clock cases and other decorative items as well as for architectural purposes. When Napoleon Bonaparte was reinterred in the chapel of Les Invalides in Paris in 1861, *vert Maurin* was used in the decoration of his tomb.

It is a breccia of nearly black angular fragments in a pale green to white matrix. Possibly less durable than the Italian serpentine marbles, it is nonetheless an eye-catching stone. The quarries ceased working for ornamental stone in 1950.

GEOLOGICAL DESCRIPTION

Breccia of serpentinite clasts cemented by calcite and calcite-serpentine mixtures. The very dark color is due to disseminated metal oxides in the serpentinite.

MAJOR USAGE

Decorative items, architecture.

Val d'Aosta marbles

SOURCE: Val d'Aosta, Italy

STATUS: Limited quarrying still takes place

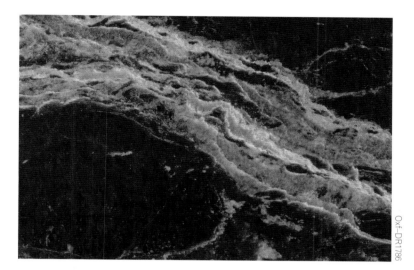

Oxf-DR1786

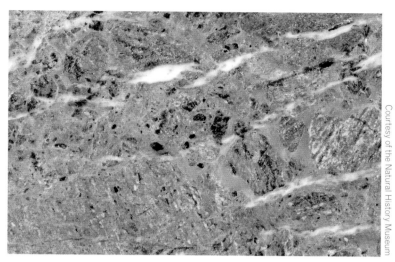

Courtesy of the Natural History Museum

The green serpentine marbles of the Val d'Aosta are relative newcomers compared with those of the Genoa region, but they are among the most familiar of 20th-century serpentine marbles.

There was minimal quarrying in the Val d'Aosta before the 1920s, but the industry took off after World War II and reached a peak of production in the 1960s. A small number of quarries are still producing marble that is exported all over the world.

There are several named varieties of stone but there is rather limited consistency within the trade in correlating names with visual characteristics. Only some of the best known are listed here. *Verde Issorie* is generally a light grayish green stone with scattered small fragments of dark serpentinite and abundant fractured veins of white calcite. *Verde Aver* is similar, but lacks the dark serpentinite fragments. By contrast, *verde Patrizia (verde Patricia)* has abundant large rounded, or angular, dark serpentinite clasts in a light green and white matrix, again traversed by fractured white calcite veins. *Verde St. Denis* has rounded fragments of dark green serpentinite in a pale green to white groundmass, and *verde Gressoney* obtained from underground workings in Gressoney St. Jean is a particularly fine breccia of dark serpentinite in a very pale green groundmass.

GEOLOGICAL DESCRIPTION

Ophicalcites composed of serpentinite clasts in a light green serpentine and calcite matrix, the whole rock traversed by white calcite veins.

MAJOR USAGE

Mainly for internal use, floorings, wall claddings and other architectural features.

RIGHT *Verde Patrizia* was used to face the fronts of Cartier stores in the early 1900s.

Verde antico

SOURCE: Lárisa, Thessaly, Greece
STATUS: No longer quarried

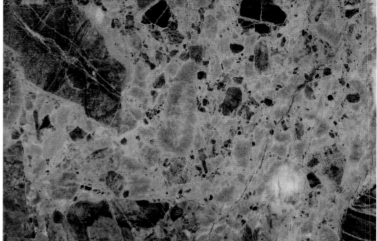

Impressive columns of *verde antico*—four dozen of them—ornament Hagia Sophia, the greatest architectural masterpiece of the Byzantine Empire. However, a visit to Istanbul is not necessary to see this stone, for it has been used in buildings all around the world.

The name *verde antico* was given to this stone by the stonecutters of medieval Italy. The ancient Romans called it *marmor Atracium* or *marmor Thessalonicum*, because it was quarried near the city of Atrax in Thessaly, Greece. First records of its use date back to the first century CE, and it reached a height of popularity in the fifth and sixth centuries. Nine of the Byzantine emperors chose this stone for their coffins.

No place has shown its use to greater effect than Hagia Sophia. Built as an Eastern Orthodox church in Constantinople (Istanbul) during the sixth century under the supervision of Emperor Justinian, Hagia Sophia was richly ornamented with marble. Each of the 48 columns is over 56 feet (17 m) tall, and Paul the Silentiary Court Poet of the time described them as

> ... that which the land of Atrax yields, not from some upland glen, but from the level plain: in parts vivid green not unlike emerald, in others of a darker green, almost blue. It has spots resembling snow next to flashes of black so that in the one stone various beauties mingle.

By the time the Turks invaded Constantinople in 1453 and converted the church into a mosque, all knowledge of where the stone had been quarried had been lost.

The great English marble seeker William Brindley visited Constantinople in 1886. He noted the extensive use of *verde antico* and started to hunt for the quarries. After a difficult search, he found eight old quarries near Omorphochori (Chasambali), north of Lárisa. Commercial quarrying resumed and the first new columns were transported to England for use in Westminster Cathedral in 1898. In subsequent years the stone grew in popularity, and quarrying continued right up to 1985. Since then, little stone has been extracted because of competition with the new Indian serpentinites.

Two distinctive varieties of *verde antico* have been recognized. One is a particularly bright green with many larger fragments, and the other is a paler grayish green, with white marble clasts attractively haloed in darker green serpentine. Both are shown here. Serpentine breccia from the Aosta Valley in northern Italy occasionally has white marble fragments and is then very similar in appearance.

GEOLOGICAL DESCRIPTION

A late Jurassic sedimentary breccio-conglomerate of serpentinite, schist and marble fragments in a serpentine and calcite matrix.

MAJOR USAGE

Columns, paving, wall cladding and other architectural features; furniture, inlay work.

ABOVE Hagia Sophia, built in Byzantine times, has 48 huge columns of *verde antico*.

RIGHT An ancient *verde antico* quarry near Larissa, photographed in 2002.

Serpentines from India

SOURCE: Rajasthan, India
STATUS: Actively quarried

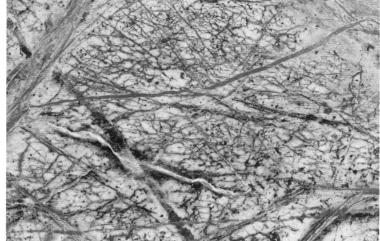

The green "marbles" of India may be newcomers to the world market, but they have had a massive impact—few other green serpentine marble producers can compete on such a scale.

The Indian serpentine marbles have dominated the trade in polished serpentine marble since the 1990s, and massive quantities have been quarried and exported all around the world. They are mainly used for architectural applications, but are also utilized for smaller decorative crafts such as mosaic work, and for making kitchenware.

Indian serpentinites vary considerably in shade of green—and the extent to which they are brecciated and veined. Veining may be white but is most often gray or green tending to black. These stones come from the state of Rajasthan, from the area of Keshariyaji (Rikhabdev) near Udaipur. They are traded under a wide variety of names, including *Indian green, emerald green, forest green, verde Udaipur, Rajasthan sea green* and, confusingly, *Guatemala green*. Guatemala itself has supplied a variety of serpentinites in recent years, including lighter green *verde quetzal*, and darker green-gray *verde tikal*.

GEOLOGICAL DESCRIPTION
Serpentinites and serpentinite breccias.

MAJOR USAGE
Architectural applications, decorative items and mosaics.

Other green marbles, "ophicalcites" and serpentinites

In the past, *cipollino* marbles have come from Corsica, Elba and Valais in Switzerland, as well as West Rutland in Vermont.

The Alps are a rich source of serpentine marbles. *Verde di Susa* from Bussoleno, *verde di Cesana* from Cesana Torinese and *verde di Varallo* from Cillimo are the better known of those used locally in Piedmont and exported to other countries in the past two centuries. There are many recorded serpentinite occurrences in the United States. A breccia of very dark green or red serpentine in white calcite, used to make small candleholders and vases sold in stores in recent years, comes from Pakistan. *Verdite*, a serpentinous rock from South Africa that can be various shades of green, is usually employed in sculpture.

Other kinds of serpentinite and ophicalcite currently available include *Tauerngrün* from Austria, *verde decalio* from China, *empress green* and *emerald green* from Taiwan and *verde serrano* from Cuba. These are slabbed and polished for architectural use and many of these other marbles can be viewed on trade Internet sites.

GREEN MARBLES, "OPHICALCITES" AND SERPENTINITES

Other metamorphic rocks

When the temperature goes up or the pressure increases (and both often happen at the same time), a rock can change in various ways. Even quite a low grade of metamorphism is sufficient to weld mineral grains together, producing a stone that is much more cohesive and better able to take a good polish than its unmetamorphosed "protolith" (original stone). Quartzites and metaconglomerates can make very practical decorative rocks, but their protoliths—sandstones, gravels and siliceous conglomerates—are rarely cohesive enough to be used in this way. A second change may be the minerals present in the stone, sometimes generating colorful new species, such as epidote, actinolite and garnet. Under much more extreme conditions, gneisses, granulites and migmatites can form, and are often beautifully banded. Just a little more heat and the migmatite melts completely and becomes a granite, an igneous rock again.

Cumbrian slate

SOURCE: Cumbria, England
STATUS: Actively quarried, and mined

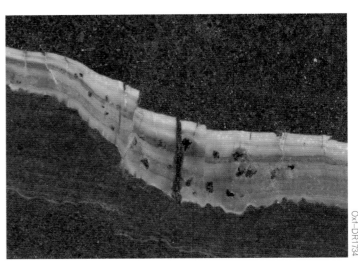

OXf-DR1734

A rock that splits easily to make roofing tiles can make a surprisingly good decorative stone too.

There is a growing awareness that some kinds of slate make excellent decorative stones, combining good color with fascinating patterns, impressive durability and the ability to take a certain amount of polish. Among the best are the Cumbrian slates that come mainly from Elterwater, Honister Crag, Kirkstone Pass, Broughton Moor and Kirkby Moor. Generally the slates are named according to their source and color, for example *Kirkstone green*.

Cumbrian slate was worked back in medieval times, probably earlier. It was used for sills, cold pantry slabs, hearths and roofs. The slates are metamorphosed tuffs, originally deposited as volcanic ash on land or in shallow lakes. They sometimes show graded bedding where coarser-grained ash settled first and successively finer grains followed after. The coarser-grained layers appear darker than the finer ones. Slump structures and small faults (as above) contribute to the visual appeal of this stone. Cumbrian slate can be various shades of gray or green. It remains a versatile decorative stone, polished, honed or riven (split).

GEOLOGICAL DESCRIPTION

Late Ordovician slates formed by metamorphism of tuffs of the Borrowdale Volcanic Group. White quartz veins, graded bedding, slump structures and small faults may be present.

MAJOR USAGE

Staircases, walls, paving; kitchen countertops; fireplaces; gravestones; lamps, clocks, tablemats.

LEFT Modern letter carving by John Neilson in Cumbrian slate.

Bekhen-stone

SOURCE: Eastern Desert, Egypt
STATUS: Quarried in antiquity

Oxf-Corsi 676

Around 1150 BCE, King Rameses IV sent out an expedition to obtain the precious *bekhen-stone*, and a map was drawn to show where it was found.

The ancient Egyptians considered this stone very precious. It was reserved for carving deities and Pharaohs. Even one of the places it was extracted, Wadi Hammamat in the Eastern Desert, was regarded as sacred ground, dedicated to the god Min. One of the earliest geological maps, known as the Turin Papyrus, was drawn ca. 1150 BCE to guide King Rameses IV's quarrying expedition across the desert to obtain supplies of *bekhen-stone* and other precious rocks and minerals. When the ancient Romans brought Egypt into their Empire, they, too, extracted *bekhen-stone* and there are innumerable artifacts—statues, sarcophagi and stelae—that were made from it. They called it *lapis basanites*. The scalpellini's name was *basalto verde antico*, although it should not be confused with the igneous rock called basalt. *Bekhen-stone* was originally a siltstone or a greywacke. Greywackes are sedimentary rocks composed of clay, sand and silt that was deposited by submarine turbidity currents that churned all the debris together. Low levels of metamorphism have converted it into a hard, dense, dark greenish gray rock.

GEOLOGICAL DESCRIPTION

Late Precambrian metagreywacke or metasiltstone composed of mixed terrigenous material. The greenish color is chlorite formed by the low-grade metamorphism.

MAJOR USAGE

Sarcophagi, stelae, baths, sculptures.

Pietra Braschia

SOURCE: Probably the Western Alps
STATUS: Used in antiquity

Oxf-Corsi 574

A large block of this green rock spotted with large garnets was discovered when Pius VI was pope, and given his family name of Braschi.

Giovanni Angelo Braschi was elected pope in 1775 and took the name Pius VI. While affairs of the Church occupied much of his time, he still found many opportunities to patronize the arts, and will be remembered as the last of the popes to retain this tradition. Among his many achievements, he established the Vatican Museum, bringing into reality a concept first suggested by his predecessor, Pope Clement XIV. Today the Pio-Clementine Museum is visited by thousands of people each year.

Among the many treasures he had made for his new museum were two fine large vases made of this stone cut from a large block discovered, so Faustini Corsi said, at Smyrna (Izmir in Turkey). At first the scalpellini called the stone *pietra granata* (garnet stone) but later they named it after the pope, *pietra Braschia*.

Pietra Braschia had been used in late Roman times for inlays, cinerary urns and other small items. The precise source is not known but it resembles metamorphosed peridotites found in the Western Alps. There was sufficient quantity of this stone that it is sometimes seen in the tabletops of marble samples sold to tourists in the 19th century.

GEOLOGICAL DESCRIPTION

A metamorphosed garnet peridotite, the green matrix containing olivine and the red garnets having rims of dark pyroxene.

MAJOR USAGE

Inlays, vases and cinerary urns; inlays in furniture.

Russian aventurine

SOURCE: Russia

STATUS: Probably no longer quarried

Oxf-Corsi 722

The sparkling, shimmering red aventurine of Russia is named after a lucky accident in a glass-making workshop.

Aventurine is a quartzite or quartz schist that sparkles when it is turned in the light. This may be because it has scaly crystals of mica, hematite or another mineral trapped among the grains of quartz, or alternatively the gaps around quartz grains may be filled with iron oxides and give a similar spangled effect.

The red aventurine from Siberia is the "classic" aventurine of mineral textbooks. Much of the color is a very thin coating of iron oxide on the grains of quartz, but it also contains crystals of mica, which adds to the sparkle. Only small areas of a rock would show this quality well, and they could be used selectively in jewelry. For larger items such as the giant vases, bowls and other ornaments sometimes given as official gifts by the czars, there would be very little if any shimmer. Russian aventurine was found in beds in a quartz schist north of the city of Zlatoust in Chelybinsk Oblast' and at Kossulina, southwest of Ekaterinburg, and cut in Ekaterinburg. Other deposits of red and white aventurine were found in the Altai Mountains and processed at the famous Korivan works.

In the 18th and 19th centuries Shoksha, near Lake Onega in Karelia, supplied much of the red quartzite for which Russia is famous, and this, too, was turned into vases and bowls, although it was not noted as having the shimmer of an aventurine. This stone was sometimes misleadingly referred to as "Russian porphyry." It is very widely used in Russia, and was used for the tomb of Napoleon in Paris.

Aventurine should never be confused with aventurine glass or goldstone, the manmade glass containing tiny flecks of copper after which it is named. The name aventurine comes from the Latin for "by chance" because it is said that the glass was first made by a lucky accident when copper filings fell into the molten glass.

GEOLOGICAL DESCRIPTION

Precambrian quartzites or quartz schists colored by iron oxides, and containing muscovite mica.

MAJOR USAGE

Bowls, vases and other decorative items; jewelry; carved plaques; various architectural applications.

LEFT The tomb of Napoleon in Les Invalides in Paris is carved from Shoksha quartzite from northwestern Russia.

Indian aventurine

SOURCE: Karnataka, India
STATUS: Actively quarried

Oxf-Mini 3411

Emeralds and aventurine have one important thing in common: they are both colored bright green by tiny amounts of chromium.

Fuchsite is a variety of muscovite mica that is colored bright green by traces of chromium. It very rarely forms a rock that is hard and compact enough to use for decorative purposes, but it can occur as minute scaly crystals disseminated through a quartzite. These rocks, known as green aventurine, glitter as they catch the light. They are very popular indeed as decorative stones. When the fuchsite is sufficiently fine-grained, the stone can lose its spangle and resemble jade. Such stone is referred to as *Indian jade*.

Bellary in Karnataka is cited in all the historic literature as the principal source of green aventurine, but by the 20th century there were active quarries in Belavadi. Karnataka continues to supply much of the green aventurine that is sold today. The finest quality tends to occur in rather small pieces, and it is used mainly for jewelry and small decorative items. Less gaudy stone, often white or gray streaked with green, is slabbed or cut into tiles and polished for interior decoration. Whether polished or honed, it makes a very hard, durable surface.

GEOLOGICAL DESCRIPTION

Metaquartzite with disseminated crystals of chromium-bearing muscovite (fuchsite).

MAJOR USAGE

Floor tiles and wall claddings; jewelry and small decorative items; sculpture.

Azul Macaubas

SOURCE: Vaca Morta quarry, Macaubas, Bahia, Brazil
STATUS: Actively quarried

Oxf-DR1782

Geologists tend to look at this classy and expensive decorative stone with disbelief. Just what gives it its unusual blue color? Is it natural?

Blue decorative stones are relatively uncommon and usually derive their colorings from lazurite, sodalite or a blue feldspar. None of these minerals occur in quartzites, which is why this stone can confuse even experienced geologists.

Dumortierite is an uncommon borosilicate mineral that can be polished to make a beautiful blue or mauve decorative stone. Lazulite is a rare blue phosphate mineral. In the Vaca Morta quarry on the Sierra del Macaubas, an otherwise nondescript white quartzite is streaked with grains of dumortierite and lazulite, resulting in one of the most beautiful of blue stones used for architectural purposes. In the trade, it is known variously as *azul do Macaubas*, *azul Macaubas* or *blue Macaubas*. Quartzites are metamorphosed sandstones, and this stone can often show relics of the original cross-bedding of the sand, adding to the attractive appearance. It may have dots or veins of other colors: yellow, gray or pink. *Azul Macaubas* is most definitely a luxury stone, not cheap to buy, but guaranteed to be a talking point in any home.

GEOLOGICAL DESCRIPTION

Mid-Proterozoic quartzite colored by disseminated dumortierite and lazulite, commonly showing relic cross-bedding.

MAJOR USAGE

Kitchen and bathroom surfaces; floors, walls; furniture, fountains and memorials.

Breccia verde d'Egitto

SOURCE: Wadi Hammamat, Eastern Desert, Egypt
STATUS: Some small-scale quarrying

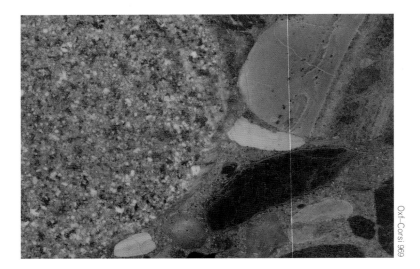

Oxf-Corsi 969

Oxf-Corsi 679

"Sixty stones" may be an exaggeration, but there are a remarkable number of different rock types in this metaconglomerate.

The ancient Romans called this stone *hexecontalithos*, meaning "60 stones" and by Byzantine times it was *hecatontalithos*. Later generations called it *breccia universale*. All these names allude to the enormous variety of different stones that make up the different pebbly clasts. They range from volcanic tuffs and lavas to granites and marine sediments. Anyone who is curious at the significance of the number 60 should read James Harrell's excellent account. Now it is known as *breccia verde d'Egitto* or *breccia verde antico*.

Two quarries have now been discovered at Wadi Hammamat in the Eastern Desert of Egypt, with stone from the western quarry containing more pink granitic clasts. The quarries preserve a large number of tool marks, wedge holes, inscriptions, old slipways and other evidence of the ancient workings, as well as the remains of the houses that accommodated the workers nearby. The quarries were worked by the Romans during the first three centuries CE, perhaps longer, but they were not the first to exploit this stone. The sarcophagi of kings Rameses VI, Nectanebo I and Nectanebo II are all made of the green Egyptian breccia. In fact rare fragments date back to the time of Rameses II (1290–1224 BCE). Small number of artifacts were made of this stone, including the superb 14-foot (4.3 m) high columns now flanking the doorway of the Yeni Camii in Istanbul, Turkey. *Breccia verde d'Egitto* appears among the stones recycled by later generations in Rome and elsewhere.

One of the quarries was worked in 1988 and perhaps more recently, too, for the stone, traded as *breccia Fawakhir* after the nearby Wadi Fawakhir, is currently commercially available.

GEOLOGICAL DESCRIPTION

Metaconglomerate of pebble- to cobble-sized clasts composed predominantly of rhyolitic to andesitic tuffs and lavas; granites and other granitic rocks; and greywackes and other sedimentary rocks; small amounts of vein quartz and serpentinite. The green coloration is due to the presence of epidote and chlorite formed during low-grade metamorphism.

MAJOR USAGE

Mainly used for columns, but also for sarcophagi and a few other items; reused in architectural decoration.

LEFT *Breccia verde d'Egitto* was reused for these two 14-foot (4.3 m) high columns in the Yeni Camii (New Mosque) in Istanbul.

Breccia verde di Sparta

SOURCE: Krokeai, Laconia, Greece
STATUS: No longer available

Oxf-Corsi 968

At first glance, this dark conglomerate is easily mistaken for the famous *breccia verde d'Egitto,* but the porphyry pebbles suggest a rather different origin.

The region around Krokeai (Krokees) in Laconia is better known for its famous *porfido verde antico* (see page 206), but it also has a deposit of a lightly-metamorphosed conglomerate that, like the porphyry, is predominantly green in color. It is known as *breccia del Taigeto* after Mount Taygetus, where it was obtained, or *breccia verde di Sparta*, after the ancient Greek city that was sited nearby. It contains a mixture of well-rounded pebbles of porphyritic rocks in a matrix of silicified volcanic ash.

There was probably no formal quarrying of this breccia. It seems likely that broken pieces were gathered from the ground in much the same way that the porphyry was obtained. This stone can easily be confused with the beautiful *breccia verde d'Egitto* from Egypt (see opposite), but it is far less colorful and variable in composition, and in particular lacks the pink granite clasts so often seen in the Egyptian stone. Occasional pieces are encountered in excavations of Roman age, but it was used more often in later times. It can be seen, for example, in the Byzantine decoration of Hagia Sophia in Istanbul.

GEOLOGICAL DESCRIPTION

Metaconglomerate or meta-agglomerate of fairly well-rounded pebbles, predominantly of andesite porphyry with volcanic ash and lava fragments. The green is due to the presence of epidote.

MAJOR USAGE

Small decorative panels and inlays; features in historic collections of decorative stones.

Verde marinace

SOURCE: Oliveira dos Brejinhos, Bahia, Brazil
STATUS: Actively quarried

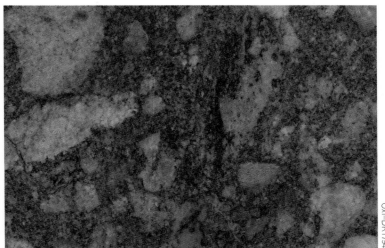

Oxf-DR1794

"A green metaconglomerate with pebbles of pink granite" could be the famous *breccia d'Egitto* but it could also be this modern introduction from Brazil.

Verde marinace may be classified in the trade as a granite but it is actually a metamorphosed conglomerate. The pink pebbles are gneiss rather than granite, and although there are pebbles of other rocks, it does not contain the amazing variety seen in the Egyptian stone (see opposite). It is colored by crystals of pistachio-green epidote and slender fibers of an amphibole called actinolite disseminated in the matrix.

The quarries are in the area of Canabrava, near Oliveira dos Brejinhos in the state of Bahia. *Verde marinace* is also marketed as *calypso green*, and *nero marinace* is a variety with a particularly dark green matrix. These stones are usually referred to as *conglomerado marinace* in Brazil. *Verde marinace* is a relatively recent addition to the trade, but it is one of the most successful of all the metaconglomerates, particularly sought after for countertops and tabletops because it is so eye-catching.

GEOLOGICAL DESCRIPTION

Precambrian conglomerate composed mainly of mixed granitic gneiss clasts that range from grit- to cobble-sized. The matrix was an arkose (feldspar-rich sandstone) or greywacke. The rock has subsequently been weakly metamorphosed, converting the matrix to compact coarse-grained quartz, colored green by disseminated epidote and actinolite.

MAJOR USAGE

Kitchen countertops, tables and furniture; flooring, wall cladding and other architectural features.

OTHER METAMORPHIC ROCKS

Smaragdite di Corsica

SOURCE: Mont San Pedrone, Corsica, France
STATUS: Small amounts still available

Oxf-Corsi 700

The beautiful green mountains of Corsica are the source of *smaragdite*, one of the most beautiful and distinctive of all the green decorative stones.

Smaragdite is an old name for emerald, but it has also come to be used for the bright green crystals in this Corsican rock, and indeed for the rock itself. The rare and distinctive *smaragdite di Corsica* is a vividly colored *gabbro eufotide* (see right), technically a metagabbro. It comes from a heavily folded metagabbro deposit, the best quality stone being obtained around Carcheto, Piobetta and Pietricaggio, on the eastern flank of Mont San Pedrone. It is also known as *verdi di Corsica, plasma di smeraldo* or *vert d'Orezza*, after the nearby valley of Orezza.

Smaragdite di Corsica was highly sought after for veneers and decorative panels in buildings, monuments and furniture, and particularly in pietre dure work. It can be seen in the decoration of the tombs of the Medici family in Florence, and in Rome there is a beautiful urn under an altar in the Church of Sant'Antonio dei Portoghesi. Quarries have been working in recent years supplying stone for kitchen countertops and other purposes.

GEOLOGICAL DESCRIPTION

A coarse-grained metagabbro. The green crystals are diopside (pyroxene) and actinolite-tremolite (amphibole) colored by small amounts of chromium. The gray crystals were originally plagioclase, now metamorphosed to form a mixture of rarer silicate minerals lawsonite and pumellyite.

MAJOR USAGE

Slabs and veneers in building decoration, furniture and pietre dure work; jewelry.

Gabbro eufotide

SOURCE: Tuscany and Liguria, Italy
STATUS: Probably no longer quarried

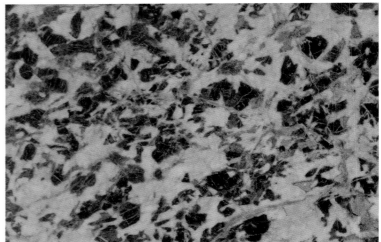

Oxf-Corsi 1000

Eufotide is an old-fashioned geological name, but it is still commonly used for these green and gray mottled rocks.

Eufotide (*euphotide*) is a traditional name, still used by some geologists, for gabbros that have been metamorphosed but retain their original texture; a kind of metagabbro in modern terminology. Archaeologists are sometimes very specific and use it only for a metagabbro from Wadi Maghrabiya in Egypt, but the name was employed very much more widely in the older literature.

Gabbro eufotide (or just *eufotide*) is a mottled mixture of dark green altered pyroxene and gray plagioclase feldspar. It is sometimes called *granito verde* or *granitone* in historic literature, both potentially misleading names. It has been quarried in various locations in Genova, the Isle of Elba, and the area of Monteferrato in Tuscany. It is not easy to distinguish stone from the different localities. *Gabbro eufotide* was employed in pietre dure work and used for decorative panels in floors and walls. The stone shown above forms the main decorative panels of the throne in the Basilica of St. John Lateran in Rome, and for this reason it is sometimes called *granito verde della sedia di San Giovanni*. Any quarrying today is most probably for the conservation of older buildings.

GEOLOGICAL DESCRIPTION

A medium- to coarse-grained metagabbro, composed principally of altered green pyroxene crystals and gray or white plagioclase feldspar. Such altered intrusions are usually found associated with serpentinites.

MAJOR USAGE

Decorative panels in floors, walls and furniture.

Kashmir white

SOURCE: Madurai district, Tamil Nadu, India
STATUS: Actively quarried

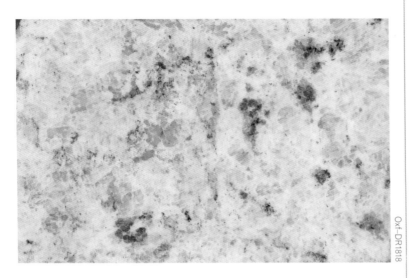

Oxf-DR1818

Stones such as *Kashmir white* combine the light airy appearance associated with marble, with all the durability of granite.

Kashmir white is termed a leucocratic granulite, a pale-colored kind of rock similar to a gneiss that formed at very high temperatures and pressures. It does have a little extra color in the form of small pink crystals of almandine garnet and a very little dark brown biotite mica. A combination of a light, attractive color and an extremely hard and durable structure has helped to ensure that this stone has stayed in fashion for some years now.

Kashmir white is quarried in various places around the town of Melur, in the Madurai district of Tamil Nadu. The town has grown up around the quarrying industry, which is now the main source of employment in the area. Riding on the success of *Kashmir white,* similar stones from other countries are traded under the name "Kashmir"; for example *Kashmir Bahia* is a leucocratic gneiss from Jequié in Bahia, while *Kashmir nuovo* is another granulite and comes from Vittoria, in Minas Gerais, Brazil. Both stones are virtually white with small almandine and biotite crystals.

GEOLOGICAL DESCRIPTION

A leucocratic granulite of Proterozoic age composed of coarse quartz, pale orange feldspar and small pink almandine garnets, some rimmed by brown biotite. It has undergone several metamorphic events between 1.4 billion and 500 million years ago.

MAJOR USAGE

Flooring, wall cladding and other architectural features; countertops in bathrooms; sinks and washbasins.

Kinawa

SOURCE: Itapecerica, Minas Gerais, Brazil
STATUS: Actively quarried

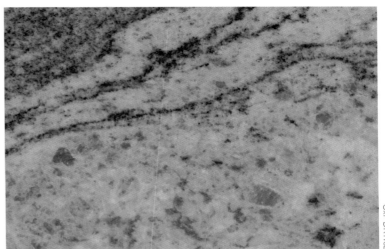

Oxf-DR1732

Kinawa is a typical migmatite, a gneiss with its wavy bands of gray and pink, containing bits that have partially melted.

The *Kinawa* quarry is in the town of Itapecerica, southwest of Belo Horizonte, and it opened around 1986 or 1987. It produces a stone, traded as *Kinawa* or *rosa raissa*. *Kinawa* is a typical example of a very high-grade metamorphic rock known as a migmatite. It looks in part like a pink and gray banded gneiss. The pink parts of the stone have the crystalline texture of a granite, formed where the heat of metamorphism has completely melted the rock.

Itapecerica lies on the São Francisco craton and *Kinawa* is a very ancient rock. The original rock, referred to as the protolith, was deposited about 3 billion to 3.38 billion years ago, and it was metamorphosed between 2.72 and 2.75 billion years ago.

Kinawa is one of many very popular gneisses and migmatites used for decorative purposes and is very well suited to floors, walls, countertops and all the other usual architectural applications. The name *Kinawa* has also been used for similar migmatites from India, and a stone that resembles *Kinawa* but is from Ghana is traded as *Kinawatiger*.

GEOLOGICAL DESCRIPTION

Precambrian migmatite with dark foliated bands rich in brown biotite and paler granite bands. The pink is potassium feldspar and gray is quartz.

MAJOR USAGE

Architectural applications including floor and wall claddings.

Stone in the street

Geological field trips do not necessarily involve getting caked in mud in a remote quarry, or treading perilously across a rocky beach to examine a cliff face. They can be infinitely more civilized affairs when they explore the building and decorative stones used in our towns and cities, the façades of stores, the stones used for monuments and urban sculptures, even the wonderful variety of stones used for monuments in cemeteries.

Urban field trips have a double fascination, for not only do they offer wonderful opportunities to see a wide variety of rock types from all around the world, but also to explore the social histories of different decorative stones. When were they used? By whom? Where did the stone come from? Is there a special reason why it was chosen?

Rough building stones allow glimpses of the texture and composition of a rock but when it is polished, it can be even easier to see what minerals and fossils it contains. Structures such as faults and folds or subtle traces of past life such as burrows and tracks may be beautifully preserved. Granites can have "xenoliths," lumps of country rock trapped in them, while sedimentary rocks may show graded or current bedding, a relic of their watery origins. Each stone is a snapshot of geological history and has its own story waiting to be discovered.

GUIDED TOURS

There is no better way to discover the stories of stones in the street than to join a guided tour led by someone who knows where to find the most interesting rocks and can explain how they formed and what they show. An increasing number of community organizations run urban "field days," while universities, museums and geological surveys can tap in on the expertise of their academic staff who often relish sharing their passion for geology with much wider audiences. There are many clubs, and societies, too, aimed at the amateur geologist.

But it is by no means essential to join an organized group to discover more about stones in the street. All sorts of geological "field" guides are available as books or leaflets, or on the Internet. Some feature buildings, monuments or streets, for example Eric Robinson's *Holiday Geology Guide: Trafalgar Square*. Others such as Patrick Wyse Jackson's *Building Stones of Dublin*, and Robert Seeman and Herbert Summerberger's *Wiener Steinwanderwege* describe stones to be seen in a particular town or city. Sherry McCann-Murray's *A Geologic Walking Tour of Building Stones of Downtown Baltimore, Maryland*, the Australian Museums Online's *Building Stones of Sydney* and A.G. Bulakh's *Building Stones of St. Petersburg* are online guides that will add a new dimension to vacation travel. The best field equipment for an urban field trip are a magnifying glass, notebook and pen for recording names and sketching structures; a camera can be very useful too. The urban geologist should leave their geological hammer at home!

Comfortable shoes are essential, and a raincoat seems to be required surprisingly often. But even this is not such a bad thing, for an unpolished wet rock surface can show colors, structures and patterns much more clearly than a dry one.

RIGHT To the right of Stephansplatz in Vienna is the new Haas Haus, clad with glass, the Swiss quartzite *verde spluga* and gneiss *verde Andeer*.

FAR LEFT A Sunday morning guided walk around London provides a chance to examine the rapakivi granite *Baltic brown* from Finland.

LEFT Seats carved by Philip Bews, using Portland stone quarried on England's Dorset coast, can be seen on Birley Street in Blackpool, England.

Verde tropicale

SOURCE: Candeias-Campo Belo area, Minas Gerais, Brazil
STATUS: Actively quarried

Oxf-DR1796

It is ironic that modern kitchens can get such a stunning contemporary look by featuring rocks so ancient they are literally billions of years old.

The mountainous area to the south of the Brazilian state of Minas Gerais lies on the Säo Francisco craton, a very ancient and stable piece of the Earth's crust. Around the towns of Candeias and Campo Belo, most of the rocks are gneisses and migmatites, and they are about three billion years old. They are quarried as ornamental stones, and are traded under a variety of names including *verde tropicale*, *verde San Francisco*, *verde San Francisco tropicale*, *verde Candeias* and *verde Maritaca*.

A characteristic feature of these stones is their distinctly green tint, caused by small amounts of chlorite and epidote coloring the plagioclase feldspar. They are attractively swirled and banded with dark brown biotite. *Verde tropicale* often has streaks of red feldspar too. These ancient stones are very tough, well-suited to a variety of interior and exterior applications, but they are particularly popular as kitchen countertops. The sample shown

ABOVE A typically modern application for the wavy, green decorative stone *verde tropicale*.

above is one of those traded as *verde San Francisco tropicale* and has a clear olive-green coloration.

GEOLOGICAL DESCRIPTION
Precambrian tonalite gneiss. The dark bands are composed of biotite and minor iron and titanium minerals; the lighter bands are predominantly plagioclase feldspar, and can show a slight schiller. Gentle folding gives the wavy form.

MAJOR USAGE
Kitchen countertops and bathroom surfaces; walls, floors, staircases and other architectural features.

Other metamorphic stones

While the Mediterranean countries and Middle East have been a rich source of marbles and serpentinites, the greater wealth of other metamorphic rocks comes from the Americas, Asia and Africa. Brazil, in particular, supplies an extraordinary range of quartzites, gneisses and migmatites.

Among the most popular are *giallo Veneziano*, a coarse-grained yellowish brown gneiss from Nova Venécia in Espirito Santo, and the fine-grained yellowish *Juparano classico* quarried near Rio de Janeiro. The name *Juparana* is used for various gneissic rocks from India and Africa too. Beautiful predominantly white gneisses and migmatites come from various locations in Espirito Santo,

Brazil. India produces various varieties of the the swirling pink and gray *paradiso* migmatite. The dark pink and gray gneiss quarried at Morton in Minnesota is traded as *rainbow*. The family firm that quarries this stone has been trading for more than a century.

It is easy to think of slate as a dull gray stone, but the palette of colors for the many slates from India is remarkably diverse, and some take an excellent polish. Among the more attractive quartzites are the pink *quartzite rosa* from Lencois and green *esmeralda Bahia* from Fazenda Oliviera, both in Bahia, Brazil. *Black mosaic* is a stunning metaconglomerate from Brazil, composed of different colored gray pebbles in a pitch-black matrix.

"Porphyries" and volcanic rocks

The word "porphyry" comes from the Latin word "porpora" meaning purple, and was first used to describe the famous Egyptian *imperial porphyry*. This hard volcanic rock is a deep purple-red with a peppering of tiny white crystals of feldspar, and has been prized by kings, popes and emperors since ancient times. Geologists now use the term "porphyritic" to describe any igneous rock that has larger crystals embedded in a fine-grained groundmass, so colors and compositions can vary considerably. The larger crystals are referred to as "phenocrysts." Because many of the decorative stones traditionally called porphyry are of volcanic origin, all the "porphyries" are included in this section with the decorative volcanic rocks. Glassy pitch-black obsidian, gray and green banded tuffs, and dark-colored basalts are all the products of dramatic volcanic eruptions.

Imperial porphyry

SOURCE: Gebel Dokhan, Eastern Desert, Egypt
STATUS: Some new stone now available

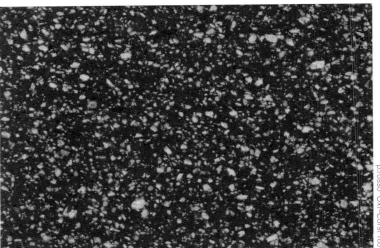

p.rosso Oxf-Corsi 783

It is amazing to think that virtually every piece of this stone seen anywhere in the world today was quarried by convicts and slaves in the dry heat of the Egyptian desert thousands of years ago.

This is the *lapis porphyrites* of the ancient Romans, a purple-red to black igneous rock peppered with small white crystals of feldspar. They quarried it at Gebel Dokhan in the Eastern Desert, the place that came to be known as Mons Porphyrites. The quarries were opened early in the first century CE and worked until the fifth century, but most actively in the times of Nero, Trajan and Hadrian. There are records of thousands of slaves and convicts being employed in the working of this stone, with many early Christians condemned to this fate. The quarries were Imperial property, and just as the color purple was highly prized and reserved for use of the emperor, so too, the stone became the emperor's exclusive property.

Not all porphyry from Gebel Dokhan is purple. The Romans called

FAR LEFT "The Four Tetrarchs," sculpted around 300 CE can be seen on the façade of St. Mark's Basilica in Venice. They are thought to represent the emperors Diocletian and Maximillian, and their heirs.

LEFT *Imperial porphyry* is used in the floors of churches across Europe. This one is in Monreale Cathedral in Sicily.

p.bastardone Oxf–Corsi 785

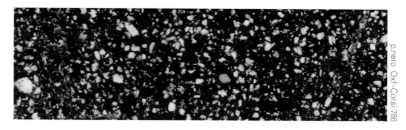

p.verde (hieracitis) Oxf–Corsi 787

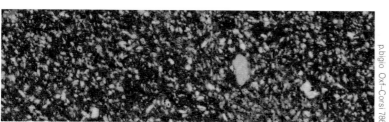

p.bigio Oxf–Corsi 786

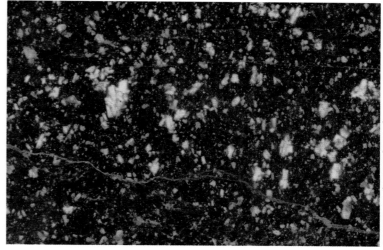

p.nero Oxf–Corsi 788

a greenish variety *lapis hieracitis* or simply *hieracitis*, meaning "hawk." The scalpellini called the same stone *porfido verde Egiziano*. Black porphyry was named *lapis porphyrites niger* by the Romans and *porfido nero* by the stonecutters. It has similar small white phenocrysts to *imperial porphyry*, easily distinguishing it from the black porphyry of Wadi Umm Towat (see page 210).

After the Gebel Dokhan quarries were abandoned, *imperial porphyry* was extensively recycled by the scalpellini of Rome, who called it *porfido rosso antico* or *porfido rosso Egiziano*. They sliced it thinly and used it for the famous Cosmati pavements of the churches of Rome and other European cities, and as inlays in altars and furniture. It remained popular for sarcophagi and monuments, and continued to have a particular allure for imperial and royal families. In time, the precise location of the quarries was forgotten. The quarries were rediscovered in 1823 by the English archaeologist John Gardner Wilkinson, and it was in his footsteps that the intrepid marble hunter William Brindley traveled by camel in 1887. At first disheartened at finding little more than discarded pillars and boulders, he then spotted a stain of purple on the mountain opposite and set off to explore:

> On arriving ... my delight knew no bounds, the ground being strewn with pieces of the most sumptuous porphyry,

while a little farther on was the actual pitched way or slide, some 15 foot wide, down which the blocks came.

A little farther, and he had reached the ancient quarries, and not wishing to miss out on an opportunity for trade, he negotiated a concession to quarry the stone. But the logistics and cost of supplying water and transporting the stone were beyond his means, and no further stone was extracted. Since then, only very rare blocks of stone have been quarried, mainly for special sculptures and monuments. The original Roman quarries are protected sites, but some *imperial porphyry* has recently been extracted nearby, and is available on the commercial market.

GEOLOGICAL DESCRIPTION

Porphyritic andesite-dacite of Precambrian age. The groundmass is colored by hematite and the manganese-bearing silicate mineral piemontite. The pink or white phenocrysts are plagioclase feldspar, and any small black crystals are biotite or hornblende.

MAJOR USAGE

Extracted in very large blocks and made into columns, walls and floors; baths, vases, sepulchers and urns. Reused in Cosmati pavements and inlaid furniture.

Porfido Trentino

SOURCE: Trentino-Alto Adige, Italy
STATUS: Actively quarried

Explosive volcanic eruptions of superheated lava and gas in Permian times formed the huge porphyry deposit of Trentino.

Explosive volcanic eruptions rained ash and fragments of glassy lava for vast distances across what is now southern Tyrol. These pyroclastic sediments welded together to form the tough mottled rock known as *porfido Trentino*. It has been quarried at many locations around Bolzano (Bozen) and Trento (Trient). The color can be very variable, typically violet, brown, beige, pink and gray; more rarely yellow. It is always mottled with crystals of gray quartz, pink or white feldspar and black biotite.

This stone naturally splits into beds about an inch thick. By the ninth century, it was being employed for making paving stones and cobbles, and then for roofing slates. As it is hard and compact, it takes a fair polish, and was used for funeral monuments and inlays in furniture. After World War I, quarrying became a major industry, and now *porfido Trentino* is exported worldwide. When used for paving and furniture, a mixture of the different colored varieties is very attractive. It is also honed or polished for countertops and wall claddings. Varieties are named after the place they are quarried; for example *porfido di Albiano* comes from the village of Albiano north of Trento.

GEOLOGICAL DESCRIPTION
Porphyritic rhyolite or dacite with phenocrysts of quartz, feldspar and biotite; an ignimbrite deposit from the Permian Atesino-Cima d'Asta volcanic complex.

MAJOR USAGE
Interior and exterior paving, cobbles and wall cladding.

Elvan

SOURCE: Cornwall, England
STATUS: No longer quarried

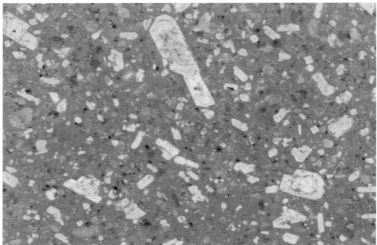

Elvan is an old Cornish miner's term for the hard porphyritic rocks that form dikes in and around the Cornish granite.

Elvan is found as dikes, small igneous intrusions, in many locations around Cornwall, all associated with the great bodies of granite that give this county its characteristic scenery and historic mineral wealth. Most elvans have a pink or gray groundmass with larger phenocrysts of gray quartz, white or pink feldspar and sometimes black tourmaline.

These are hard stones that take a very good polish and they have been widely used for decorative purposes. Polished slabs from the quarry in the Tremore valley, west of Bodmin, were supplied in the 1830s to line the spectacular Porphyry Hall of Place House, Fowey (the seat of the Treffry family that is now open to the public). Queen Victoria and Prince Albert visited the quarry in 1846, and were presented with a slab of Tremore elvan, which they used for sills in ornamental alcoves in Osborne House on the Isle of Wight. This stone and other elvans can be seen in many buildings of the West Country of England. *Cataclews (Catacleuse)* is named after Cataclews Point a few miles from Padstow, where it was quarried. It is one of the so-called "blue elvans," rocks of doleritic composition, used as construction stones. There are several 15th-century sculptures carved of *Cataclews*.

GEOLOGICAL DESCRIPTION
Quartz porphyries of granitic composition formed as dikes in the Cornish granite or its surrounding rocks. Blue elvans are dolerite.

MAJOR USAGE
Tabletops and other furniture; church decorations; gravestones.

Swedish porphyry

SOURCE: Älvdalen, Dalarna, Sweden
STATUS: Actively quarried

The most famous decorative stone of Sweden is a porphyry, and it was a favorite with the Swedish royal family.

Swedish porphyry can be brownish red, purple or nearly black, always speckled with crystals of white feldspar. It is a volcanic rock found in the neighborhood of Älvdalen. The first published reference to the porphyry of Dalarna dates back to 1679. Royal patronage always assists in bringing a stone to public attention, and when King Gustaff III was shown samples of this stone in 1785, he wanted to use it in the Haga Palace, starting a new fashion. Three years later, the Elfdahls Porfyrwerk was established in Älvdalen to produce all manner of items made from porphyry. When the firm fell into financial difficulties in the 1830s, it was purchased by King Karl XIV Johan, and under royal patronage continued to produce fine porphyry vases and other manufactured pieces. These were a favorite gift for visiting royalty, nobility and diplomats.

The most exceptional porphyry vase was given to the King himself in 1825. Known as the Rosendal Vase, it stands in the park outside the Rosendal Palace in Stockholm. With a diameter of over 11 feet (3.5 m), and a height of nearly 9 feet (3 m), it took two years to manufacture. When the King died in 1844, his sarcophagus was made from the same porphyry, although it took four years before ground conditions were suitable to sledge it to the coast at Gävle, to be shipped to Stockholm.

The porphyry mill continued to produce fine porphyry pieces until the works were destroyed by fire in 1867. New mills were established in Västermyckeläng 30 years later, and the porphyry is still made into jewelry and small gift items to this day. The porphyry museum at Älvdalen tells the story of this stone and has many items made of the *Swedish porphyry*.

ABOVE *Swedish prophyry* takes a superb polish as shown by these two vases made about 1830.

GEOLOGICAL DESCRIPTION

Precambrian rhyolitic or trachytic porphyry with phenocrysts of quartz and feldspar.

MAJOR USAGE

Vases and other decorative pieces; jewelry; also used for architectural decoration.

Porfido verde antico

SOURCE: Levetsova, Laconia, Greece
STATUS: No longer quarried

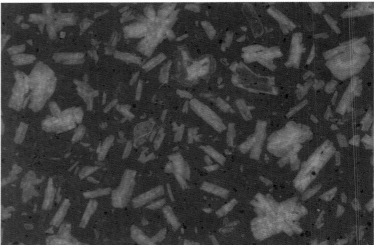

Oxf-Corsi 797

One of the classic colored stones of ancient times, *porfido verde antico* is a famous Greek porphyry that is usually very easy to recognize.

The rich green color misled early geologists to think that it was serpentine, and they called it by the confusing name *porfido serpentino antico*, but it is an igneous rock and does not contain any serpentine minerals. There are a few carvings that date to the Minoan and Mycenaean civilizations, but the later Greeks did not use it. It was the Romans, in the first century CE, who adopted this stone with great relish. Ancient authors have referred to it as *lapis Lacedaemonius*, after the ancient name for Laconia; *lapis Taygetas* from the name of the mountain where it was quarried; *Lapis Croceus* after the nearby town of Croceae (the modern Krokeai or Krokees); or *lapis Spartanus* because Krokeai was close to the city of Sparta.

The groundmass ranges from violet to green or nearly black. The rectangular phenocrysts of plagioclase feldspar can be creamy-white or green, and they are often crossed, or clustered in star shapes. A variety with very small uncrossed phenocrysts was first discovered by Signor Vitelli at Ostia and is known as *porfido Vitelli*. The kind referred to as "agatata" has gas bubbles that have subsequently filled with red and white quartz. *Porfido risata* has small black and white phenocrysts. *Breccia di Sparta* (see page 195), which comes from the same area, has fragments of porphyry.

Faustino Corsi noted that *porfido verde antico* was only ever found in rather small pieces, and his observation was confirmed

LEFT The large rondel in this flooring in Westminster Cathedral, London, is *porfido verde antico* quarried in the early 20th century. Other stones include *Carrara marble*, *verde antico* and *imperial porphyry*.

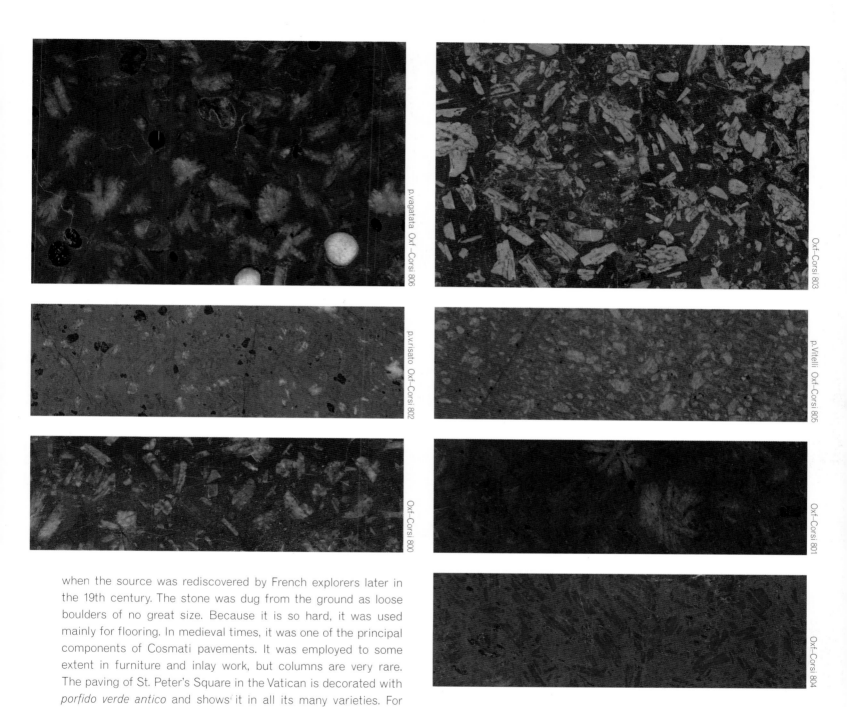

p.vagatata Oxf–Corsi 806

Oxf–Corsi 803

p.vrisato Oxf–Corsi 802

p.Vitelli Oxf–Corsi 805

Oxf–Corsi 800

Oxf–Corsi 801

Oxf–Corsi 804

when the source was rediscovered by French explorers later in the 19th century. The stone was dug from the ground as loose boulders of no great size. Because it is so hard, it was used mainly for flooring. In medieval times, it was one of the principal components of Cosmati pavements. It was employed to some extent in furniture and inlay work, but columns are very rare. The paving of St. Peter's Square in the Vatican is decorated with *porfido verde antico* and shows it in all its many varieties. For a short time at least, the stone was extracted in the early 20th century, but large-scale quarrying has never taken place.

GEOLOGICAL DESCRIPTION

Altered porphyritic andesite or dolerite of Permian to Carboniferous age, colored green by silicate minerals epidote and chlorite. Phenocrysts are light-colored plagioclase feldspar and black pyroxenes. Quartz-filled amygdules may be present.

MAJOR USAGE

Veneers and flooring, especially Cosmati pavements and similar modern ecclesiastical floorings; furniture and pietre dure work.

Enter any cathedral and the lofty painted vaults and colorful stained glass windows will purposefully draw your eye heavenward. But stop. Look down. The paving under your feet may be a work of art too.

In the later Middle Ages, a number of Roman families with architectural and decorative workshops in Via Lata and the Trevi district of Rome perfected a new kind of opus sectile (cut stone) mosaic work. They would cut pieces of colored stone and glass into regular shapes—triangles, circles, parallelograms and rectangles—and arrange them in intricate interweaving geometric patterns of extraordinary complexity. The different elements of the work—squares, circles, borders—would be framed with white marble. Some of the family members signed their work with the name Cosma, and collectively they are known as the Cosmati. The style of pavement they created has come to be known as Cosmati or Cosmatesque ornamentation.

The older family members had learnt the craft of opus sectile work in Constantinople. Some were sculptors, others architects. All were master stonecutters. Their originality lay in the way they brought together elements of the Byzantine and Islamic traditions, merging them with their own native Roman heritage.

PATTERNS IN STONE

Byzantine fashions favored intertwining patterns, and the filling of larger geometric shapes with an arrangement of smaller ones. The preference for angular designs, very small pieces of stone and the occasional use of glass stem from the Islamic tradition, as did the absence of any representations of people, plants or animals in the designs. Many of the patterns, and the way in which sections of the design were framed with white marble, had their origins in the opus sectile work of the Roman villas. All the stone was recycled, either from earlier church flooring or from the ruins of Rome. They preferred to use purple *imperial porphyry* from Egypt, green *porfido verde* from Greece, yellow *giallo antico* from Tunisia and white *Carrara marble*. Each piece was carefully bedded in mortar, making a hard-wearing but richly ornamental surface.

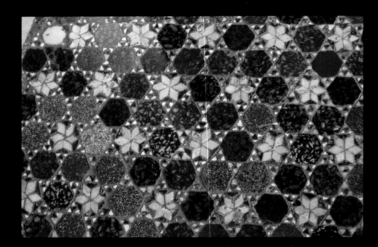

ABOVE Patterns within patterns are a recurring theme in Cosmati pavements. This panel is in the bookshop of the Church of Santa Maria Maggiore in Rome. The yellow inlays are *giallo antico*, and the smallest pieces in the design are less than ¼ inch (1 cm) across.

RIGHT This broken sample of Cosmati work shows how thin veneers of *porfido verde antico* and *imperial porphyry* have been inlaid into chiseled-out sections of white marble.

ABOVE Remarkable geometrical accuracy was needed to create the Cosmati pavements. The main aisle in the Church of Santa Prassede in Rome has a chain of guilloches, interlinking circles, enclosing roundels of different porphyries and marbles

ABOVE The middle of the 13th-century Great Pavement in Westminster Abbey, London, was laid in the form of a quincunx, a classic pattern of Cosmati pavements in which five interlacing circles fill a square.

Through the 12th and 13th centuries, successive generations of Cosmati designed and created the most exquisitely intricate pavements in the churches of Rome. They decorated altars and monuments, door frames, cathedras and pulpits. Their work became so famous that patrons of churches in other cities would pay to have new paving installed. A Cosmati worker by the name of Petrus Oderisius came to England in the second half of the 13th century, commissioned by King Henry III to lay the

superb sanctuary pavement of Westminster Abbey in London. The genuine Cosmati tradition ended at the beginning of the 14th century, but it has influenced generations of architects, artists and craftspeople. Geometric designs made of richly colored marbles and granites continue to be used to pave places of worship right up to the present day.

Analysis of the pavements has been approached with remarkable relish by modern mathematicians who use Cosmati pavements to illustrate complex concepts of geometry and symmetry. But for most of us, it is sufficient to enter a church in Rome and marvel at the sheer beauty of the designs that encrust the floors and walls—testimony to the extraordinary imagination and craftsmanship of those medieval stoneworkers.

Porfido serpentino nero

SOURCE: Wadi Umm Towat, Eastern Desert, Egypt
STATUS: Quarried in antiquity

Oxf–Corsi 809

Imagine the famous *porfido serpentino verde (see page 206)* photographed in black and white, and you have the perfect image of this stone.

Dark gray or black porphyritic stones with large gray or white plagioclase phenocrysts can look remarkably like a black and white version of the famous *porfido verde antico* (see page 206). A deposit of this stone used to be quarried in Wadi Umm Towat, quite close to Gebel Dokhan, the source of the famous purple *imperial porphyry*. It was first extracted early in the first century CE and was used for small pillars, basins and inlaid walls and paving. It came to be known by the scalpellini as *porfido serpentino nero*.

Similar black and white porphyries come from many other places around the world, and it would be easy to confuse the Egyptian stone with some of the modern varieties. These include a particularly striking stone with large pure white feldspar phenocrysts that comes from California. It has been called *Chinese writing rock*, a name it shares with similar modern stones. It is made into jewelry and small gift items.

GEOLOGICAL DESCRIPTION
Precambrian trachyandesite porphyry with large plagioclase phenocrysts.

MAJOR USAGE
Basins, small pillars, panels in floors and walls.

Granito bigio

SOURCE: Frejus and Boulouris, Esterel, France
STATUS: No longer quarried for decorative use

p.morviglione Oxf–Corsi 816

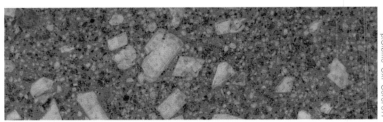

p.Sibilio Oxf–Corsi 817

p.pediculare Oxf–Corsi 826

Bugs and diseases have inspired the traditional names for the gray porphyries of the Esterel coast.

Granito bigio is the famous blue porphyry of the Esterel mountains. Despite its traditional name, it is a volcanic rock and does not have plutonic origins. It comes from ancient quarries near the coastal towns of Frejus and Boulouris, where the famous porphyries of Esterel outcrop along the coast and give a wild and beautiful rocky scenery. Most traces of ancient quarrying in this area were destroyed in modern times when large quantities of the stone were extracted for aggregate. The groundmass of this stone is clear bluish gray, and phenocrysts are different shades of gray, white and black.

The stonecutters of Rome called this stone *granito a morviglione* because the mottled appearance reminded them of

a smallpox rash. Another variety called *granito bigio pediculare* has many small dark markings that looked like a swarm of "pidocchi"—creeping insects such as lice or ants. For a long time it was thought that this second stone came from Egypt, but it was found in a quarry near Boulouris in the 1990s.

The etymology of the varieties of *granito bigio* may be unappealing but these stones had great attraction. They were widely used in ancient times in the south of France, and were first brought to Rome about the second or third century CE, when Severus was Emperor. They were mainly employed for pillars, and examples can be seen in the Baths of Caracalla in Rome and the Basilica of St. Peter in the Vatican. In time-honored tradition, they were reworked by the stonecutters of medieval and baroque times. *Porfido bigio di Sibilio* has large white crystals of feldspar, and

ABOVE Where the Esterel Massif meets the Mediterranean coast, the scenery is of wild rocky porphyry cliffs, often weathered to a rich red color. It is here that the ancient stone known as *granito bigio* was quarried in ancient times.

was named after the early 19th-century marbleworker Francesco Sibilio, who had a particularly fine column of this stone.

GEOLOGICAL DESCRIPTION
Porphyritic dacite of Permian age, with phenocrysts of white feldspar and dark green to black hornblende and green chlorite.

MAJOR USAGE
Pillars and plinths.

Peperino

SOURCE: Province of Roma, Lazio, Italy
STATUS: Actively quarried

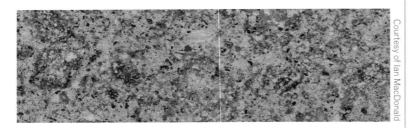

Courtesy of Ian MacDonald

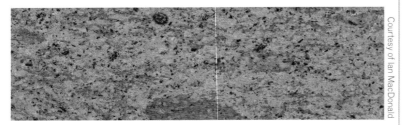

Courtesy of Ian MacDonald

The "peppercorns" in *peperino* are black volcanic glass, some of the volcanic debris that makes up Rome's original building stone.

The first building stones to be used in the city of Rome were made up of volcanic ash and other debris ejected in Pleistocene times from the volcanoes of Lazio. Generally they have no special ornamental merit, but the stone called *peperino* is an exception. It is a jumbled accumulation of ash, lava, country rock and fragments of black volcanic glass—the latter resembling peppercorns that give this stone its well-known name. In ancient times a gray *peperino* was quarried near Albano Laziale and Marino, and was referred to as *lapis Albanus*. A harder buff-colored stone was extracted near the ancient city of Gabii, about 12 miles (19 km) east of Rome, and was called *lapis Gabinus*. After the great fire that destroyed much of Rome in 64 CE, Emperor Nero ordered that these stones be used for the structural support of buildings because they were relatively fireproof.

Peperino has been polished for use in marble sample tables and other inlaid furniture but it does not take polish readily, and is principally employed either sawn or honed as a construction and paving stone. Today, gray and pink varieties of *peperino* are quarried in various places around Rome, notably in the region of Viterbo. The two colors can be used in combination to create attractive patterns.

GEOLOGICAL DESCRIPTION

Trachytic tuff of Pleistocene age.

MAJOR USAGE

Interior and exterior paving and staircases; inlaid tables and other furniture; fireplaces, fountains.

Lava di Borghetto

SOURCE: Borghetto, Civita Castellana, Lazio, Italy
STATUS: No longer quarried for decorative use

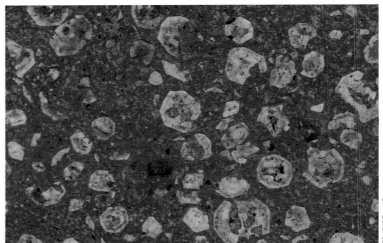

Oxf-Corsi 667

Volcanic lava is usually too dull to use for decorative purposes, but the rounded white crystals of leucite give this stone a rather attractive appearance.

The streets of Rome are paved with *selce*, the basaltic lava from the ancient volcanoes around the city. This stone was quarried in many places, including a lava plain that lies between the towns of Borghetto and Civita Castellina, north of Rome. The lava of Borghetto was used for the construction of the Flaminian Way, the Roman road running north from Rome. It was also considered particularly good for making millstones. Most basalt is a dark brown or gray stone, of no particular decorative value, but the stone quarried at Borghetto is rich in phenocrysts of a mineral called leucite. These rounded eight-sided white crystals give the lava an altogether more interesting appearance and earned it the colloquial name *selce occhialina*, or simply *occhialina*: "little eyes."

The unusual and attractive appearance of the lava of Borghetto did not escape the notice of the Roman stonecutters, nor the fact that it was a compact stone that could take a good polish. During the 18th and 19th centuries they used it for decorative purposes, incorporating it in inlaid tables and other items of furniture.

GEOLOGICAL DESCRIPTION

Leucite trachyte or basalt deposited by the Cimini volcano during Pleistocene times.

MAJOR USAGE

Small panels in building decorations and inlaid furniture.

Obsidian

SOURCE: Many locations

STATUS: Commercially available

When volcanic lava cools too quickly for crystals to form, it turns into a viciously sharp natural glass called obsidian.

Obsidian is translucent, and is normally so dark that it appears black. In thin slices it can be various colors, commonly gray, brown and green. Flow patterns may be seen. Obsidian breaks into viciously sharp shards that have been used for knives, arrowheads and surgical scalpels. The shape of the broken surface is characteristically conchoidal, just like glass.

The ancient peoples of Mexico were among the earliest to exploit the stone they called *itztli*, obtaining it from several places and carving it with great skill. In ancient Rome, carvings made of obsidian were highly prized. The principal sources in Europe were the Italian volcanic islands of Lipari and Vulcano and the lava flows of Iceland, but it is found in many other places. Some of the finest obsidian carvings were made in the Fabergé workshops in the 19th and early 20th centuries. In the United States, a large deposit at Glass Buttes, Oregon, has yielded much stone for lapidarists.

Obsidian typically appears black, but as time progresses, it may start developing white radiating crystals, and stone that shows this striking pattern is known as *snowflake obsidian*. Good snowflake obsidian comes from Delta and Milford areas of Utah. Another variety of obsidian known as *rainbow obsidian* has bands of minute gas bubbles or tiny spherules of crystals that give the stone an iridescent luster. It comes from northern California, Mexico and various other places. *Mahogany obsidian*, with brown bands like wood grain, comes from New Mexico. Obsidian is readily available as a semiprecious gemstone.

GEOLOGICAL DESCRIPTION

Volcanic glass of rhyolitic composition formed by very rapid cooling of magma. It is softer than quartz (see page 237), a little over 5 on Mohs' scale. White crystals in snowflake obsidian are a silica mineral called cristobalite.

MAJOR USAGE

Sculpture and jewelry.

Pietre del Vesuvio

SOURCE: Monte Somma and Vesuvius, Napoli, Italy
STATUS: Not quarried for decorative purposes

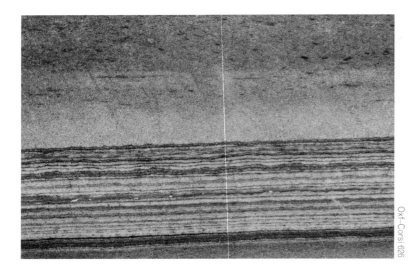

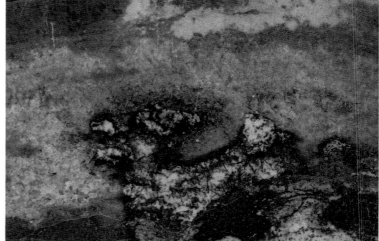

Pietre del Vesuvio is a general term for the volcanic rocks of both Vesuvius and the surrounding older volcano, Monte Somma. The dull-colored volcanic lavas do not lend themselves to decorative uses, but tuffs and ejected blocks of country rock have been polished for small decorative panels and tabletops of marble samples, mainly in the 18th and 19th centuries.

The tuffs are thick ash deposits, a mixture of tiny fragments of pumice, lava and volcanic glass. They often show distinct bedding, like sedimentary rocks deposited in water. They vary in color from creamy-white to blue-gray and some are so fine-grained they can look like a *bardiglio* marble. In composition they are quite different, composed of silicate minerals.

The ejected limestone blocks of Monte Somma are green, white and buff mottled stones derived from the beds of impure limestone through which the great volcano erupted. They were baked up in the volcanic gases, before being thrown out in the eruptions that built the huge ash cone of Monte Somma. Some blocks are full of cavities lined with crystals of rare minerals, and have fascinated mineralogists for many generations. Others are less holey and make attractive polished stones.

GEOLOGICAL DESCRIPTION
Gray bedded tuffs and ejected blocks of contact metamorphosed limestone.

MAJOR USAGE
Small decorative panels; inlays in furniture.

Other "porphyries" and volcanic rocks

There are innumerable porphyry deposits around the world, often of quite a small scale, and sometimes cut and polished for decorative purposes. Porphyries used for architectural purposes have in recent years been quarried in Mexico, Argentina and Iran. More often, these stones are supplied to the lapidary trade and made into jewelry, spheres and eggs, and small carvings. *Chinese writing rock* was mentioned on page 210. Porphyries with radiating flowerlike aggregates of feldspar crystals are sometimes called *chrysanthemum stone or daisy stone*, and good examples come from British Columbia and Ontario. Canada. The red *Shoshka* porphyry of Russia is actually a quartzite (see page 238).

Basalts that polish to a black finish come from India, China, Uruguay and parts of Scandinavia. They are popular as memorial stones. Germany supplies a variety of volcanic rocks that are marketed today, for example, the swirled banded trachytes of Selters and Weidenhahn, a tuff from Ettringer and the basalts of the Eifel volcanic district. The lavas of Etna and the volcanoes of Lazio are quarried and used for a wide variety of purposes but not often polished.

"PORPHYRIES" AND VOLCANIC ROCKS

Granites and other plutonic rocks

Plutonic rocks form when molten rock cools and solidifies inside the crust of the Earth without ever erupting to the surface from a volcano. The crystals of different minerals are jumbled together, giving these stones a mottled appearance, and because the rock cools relatively slowly, the crystals can grow into large sizes. Granites are the best known of the plutonic rocks. They can combine attractive colors with considerable hardness and durability, taking a beautiful polish. Other plutonic rocks that have similar properties, such as syenites, diorites and gabbros, are also termed "granite" in the stone trade. A syenite from Norway called larvikite is one of the most eye-catching of these stones. It contains feldspars that flash with color as the stone is turned in the light. The "granites" are an increasingly popular choice for practical and hard-wearing surfaces in the home. They make superb kitchen countertops, as well as tiles for floors and walls.

Rubislaw granite

SOURCE: Rubislaw, Aberdeen, Scotland
STATUS: No longer quarried

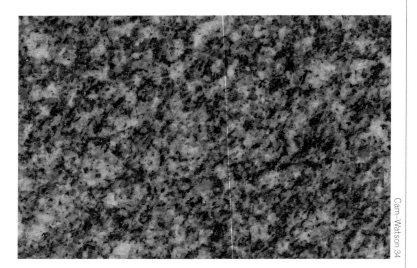

Cam–Watson 34

Stone from quarries in the "granite city" has been supplied to countries as far apart as Japan and the United States.

The city of Aberdeen in Scotland has another name, the "granite city." The imposing Victorian buildings of the city center are built almost exclusively from the local silvery gray granite, much of which was quarried at Rubislaw on the western edge of the city. The quarry was reputed to be the oldest in the county, opening in about 1740. It was during the 19th century that it became a major supplier of granite, not just for the fine new terraces of Aberdeen, but for buildings and sidewalks in London, and in American cities. The business peaked in the early 19th century with more than 20 different quarries producing Aberdeen granite. The quarry at Rubislaw, at some 400 feet (120 m) deep, was at that time the deepest in Europe.

Aberdeen granite is nearly always gray. The stone from the Rubislaw quarry is fine-grained and blue-gray in color. The granite industry in Aberdeen fell into decline in the 1930s and the Rubislaw quarry finally closed in 1971 and is flooded now. Stone for conservation work in the city comes from the city council's stockpiles, salvaged from demolition sites.

GEOLOGICAL DESCRIPTION

Fine-grained granite of Devonian age, comprising crystals of quartz, feldspar, muscovite and biotite. This stone can have a distinct foliation.

MAJOR USAGE

Construction and facing stone for architectural applications.

Barre granite

SOURCE: Websterville and Graniteville, Washington County, Vermont, United States
STATUS: Actively quarried

Cam–Watson 616

Apart from house foundations and fence posts, the early residents of Barre found little use for the granite that outcropped in their community.

It was a returning 1812 War veteran, Robert Parker, who saw the potential for a more commercial enterprise and with his associate, Thomas Courser, opened a quarry on Cobble Hill. In the 1830s they successfully supplied granite for the State Capitol building in Montpelier, Vermont, and new orders started to roll in. Further quarries were opened and thousands of workers arrived from Scotland, Italy, Spain and many other countries, eager to find work in the fledgling granite industry. They included sculptors and letter cutters as well as quarrymen and masons. Transportation remained problematic until the 1900s when a railroad track was laid linking the quarries to the town, on to major cities and ports.

The huge quarry run by the Rock of Ages Company was already a tourist attraction in the 1920s, and today there is a tourist center and museum at the quarry in Graniteville. Barre still has an international population of craftspeople, and although gray granite is no longer fashionable, the demand for fine memorials and gravestones continues to be high. *Barre granite* was used for the memorials of former President Harry S. Truman, Walter Chrysler, John D. Rockefeller Sr. and many other eminent Americans.

GEOLOGICAL DESCRIPTION

Granodiorite of Devonian age composed of white feldspar, gray quartz and black biotite.

MAJOR USAGE

Gravestones and memorials; architectural applications; kitchen countertops and tabletops; sculpture.

Bethel white granite

SOURCE: Bethel, Windsor County, Vermont, United States
STATUS: Actively quarried

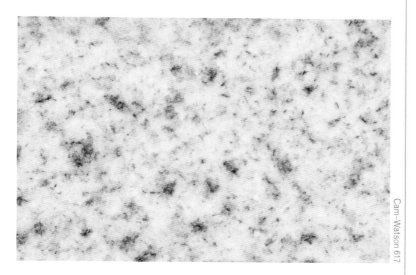

Cam–Watson 617

Light-colored granites combine that fresh look of a marble with the structural durability of a granite. *Bethel white* is one of the lightest-colored "granites" on the commercial market today.

Bethel white granite is quarried at Bethel in Vermont. The first commercial quarry opened there around 1900, and a few years later, a railroad line was installed to transport the stone to the urban centers of the eastern United States. In Washington, D.C., it was used for the frontage of the Union Station in 1907, in the Post Office in 1910 and the Smithsonian Institution in around 1923. The Rock of Ages Company bought the quarry in 1958, but the prevailing fashion for concrete and glass of the 1960s and 1970s saw a significant wind-down in production.

The fortunes of the *Bethel granite* revived in the 1980s when there was renewed demand for it in Europe. It was particularly popular for cladding churches and other religious buildings, and was used for example in the building of the Mormon Bountiful Temple in Salt Lake City, Utah, in the 1990s. Today there is considerable competition from pale-colored "granites" such as *Kashmir white*, but *Bethel white* is holding its own in a very competitive market.

GEOLOGICAL DESCRIPTION

A granitic rock known as a quartz monzonite that has roughly equal quantites of potassium and plagioclase feldspars. It is highly depleted in dark colored minerals.

MAJOR USAGE

Floors, wall claddings and architectural applications; gravestones and memorials; kitchen countertops and tabletops; sculpture.

Cornish granite

SOURCE: Bodmin area, Cornwall, England
STATUS: Actively quarried

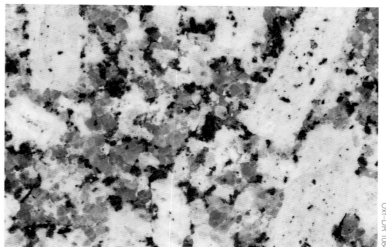

Oxf–DR 1084

The granites that were intruded in Permian times some 280 million years ago have had a huge impact on the landscape and prosperity of southwest England.

Granite that was intruded into the rocks of Cornwall and Devon generated the hot fluids that deposited tin and other metal ores. Deep weathering of granite produced huge commercial quantities of china clay. Much of Cornwall's prosperity has been derived from its granites. There has also been a very long history of using Cornish granite as a robust building and decorative stone.

Cornish granite was first employed as a building stone farther back than records exist, using loose boulders from the ground surface. Since the early 18th century, innumerable quarries have been opened. The best quality stone came from deeper levels, so dimension stone quarries tended to be very deep. Most of the quarries have now closed but the Hantergantick and Delank quarries on Bodmin Moor are still working. The Delank quarry supplied a massive block of granite weighing some 90 tons (100 tonnes), which is being carved by Peter Randall Page for his massive sculpture for the ecological education center in the pioneering Eden Project biospheres in Cornwall.

GEOLOGICAL DESCRIPTION

Late Carboniferous or Permian granite often with large rectangular white alkali feldspar crystals in a matrix of plagioclase, quartz and brown biotite.

MAJOR USAGE

Columns, floors, paving and other architectural elements; memorials and sculptures.

Blanco perla

SOURCE: Valdemanco, Madrid, Spain
STATUS: Actively quarried

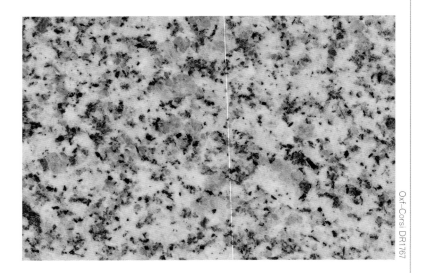

It is hard to select just one of the many varieties of Spanish granite to illustrate. *Blanco perla*, with its elegant light coloring, is certainly one of the most popular.

One hundred years ago, little would have been known about the ornamental granites that come from Spain. They were used in local architecture but rarely seen in other countries. Today they are sold all around the world, evidence of an industry that has grown and modernized at an enormous speed. Indeed Spain now produces more granite than any other European country.

Some of the most attractive of the Spanish granites are pale in color, combining a clean elegant look with natural durability. *Blanco perla* is an excellent example. It is quarried near the town of Valdemanco in the Sierra de la Cabrera, north of Madrid. There is little natural fracturing in the granites of this region, which makes it easier to quarry very large blocks. As a result, the stone can be cut in sizes ranging from huge sheets to conveniently small tiles. It is used mainly for interior and exterior cladding and paving, but is popular for bathroom tiles and kitchen countertops. If this stone looks curiously familiar, it may just be the stone one sees reproduced in fine detail on "granite style" laminate worktops.

GEOLOGICAL DESCRIPTION

A medium-grained granite of Paleozoic age, composed of pale beige orthoclase, white plagioclase feldspar, colorless quartz and black biotite.

MAJOR USAGE

Interior and exterior pavings and wall claddings.

Rosa Baveno

SOURCE: Baveno, Piedmont, Italy
STATUS: Actively quarried

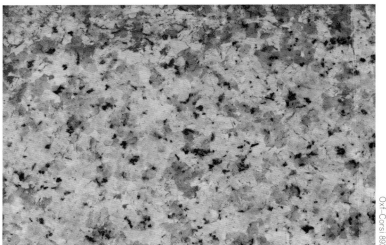

The architectural structures most often made with delicate pink *rosa Baveno* granite are columns. Many thousands can be seen in buildings and monuments all around the world.

Baveno granite comes from the slopes of Monte Mottarone near the vacation resort of Baveno. Mostly it is gray; the popular pink variety comes from a strip just a few hundred yards wide on the eastern flank of the deposit. Quarries were first opened at the beginning of the 16th century, and production increased through the 19th century, reaching a peak in the early 1900s. The granite was transported by barge across Lake Maggiore, to Milan, Novara and the other major cities of Europe. Fine columns can be seen in the cathedrals of Milan and Novara. The Basilica of San Paolo Fuori Le Mura in Rome has 10 monolith columns each 33 feet (10 m) high. *Rosa Baveno* is used for memorials commemorating the loss of U.S. soldiers in Europe, for example, the Montfaucon Monument in the Meuse, France. One of the most delightful examples of *rosa Baveno* in sculpture is sited in Baveno. Carved by local sculptor Raffaele Polli in 1990, it depicts a stonecutter at work, and is dedicated to the "picasass," the stonecutters who worked the *Baveno granite* over the centuries.

GEOLOGICAL DESCRIPTION

Permian granite composed mainly of gray quartz, pink orthoclase and white plagioclase feldspars, and dark biotite. Pegmatite pods contain orthoclase crystals and interesting accessory minerals that are highly sought after by mineral collectors.

MAJOR USAGE

Architectural, especially columns and the bases of monuments.

Granito Sardo

SOURCE: Sardinia, Italy
STATUS: Actively quarried

Oxf–Corsi 856

What have the Statue of Liberty in New York and the wild scenic landscape of northern Sardinia got in common? They both rest on pink Sardinian granite.

Prehistoric monuments made of local granite are scattered across Sardinia, but it was the ancient Romans who first brought this robust stone across to the mainland. The sample shown here is typical of the stone they quarried at Capo Testa on the north coast. It was used for construction, paving and monuments, most famously in the Pantheon in Rome. In medieval times *granito Sardo* was used for the Baptistry of San Giovanni in Florence and for columns in the Duomo of Pisa.

Sardinian granite was extracted only for local use until 1870, when the Società Esportazione Graniti Sardi was founded to develop new export markets, and with considerable success. Large-scale quarrying commenced at La Maddalena to the north of the island, and stone was supplied for projects such as the Milan Stock Exchange, the Palatino Bridge in Rome and the base of the Statue of Liberty in New York Harbor. The great economic depression of the 1930s brought a temporary halt to exports of Sardinian granite. The industry was revived in the 1960s, and now there are more than 125 quarries extracting granite on the island.

GEOLOGICAL DESCRIPTION

Paleozoic granite composed of larger pink orthoclase crystals in a groundmass of white plagioclase feldspar, gray quartz and dark biotite crystals.

MAJOR USAGE

Paving, wall cladding and columns; the stone is also carved for seating, monuments and other smaller decorative uses.

Granito violetto

SOURCE: Çiğri Dağ, near Ezine, Marmara, Turkey
STATUS: Quarried in antiquity

Oxf–Corsi 819

Some of the best clues as to how the ancient Romans cut and shaped enormous tapering stone columns have come from the *granito violetto* quarries in Turkey.

The ancient Romans called this stone *marmor Troadense* because it came from the Troad Peninsula on the Aegean coast of Turkey. It was used in the construction of Alexandria Troas and Neandria, ancient cities on the Troad. The quarries are scattered across a mountain now known as Çiğri Dağ. They are littered with unfinished columns, a treasure trove for archaeologists trying to understand how ancient quarrying was carried out.

Imagine the challenge of cutting an absolutely straight column of stone 30 feet (9 m) or more in length, which must taper slightly from bottom to top. Remarkably, much of the preliminary shaping was carried out as the stone was split from the quarry face. Then, a device was used to mark out bands of the correct diameter at regular intervals down the length of the column, and all superfluous stone could be chiseled away.

From the second century CE, the Romans exported this stone, mainly within eastern parts of the Empire, but then to Rome. It was used, for example, in Hadrian's Villa. Quarrying ceased in the sixth century CE, but the stone was still recycled by the scalpellini, who called it *granito violetto*, because it appears to have a violet tint.

GEOLOGICAL DESCRIPTION

Quartz monzonite with pinkish gray rectangular crystals of potassium feldspar in a dark to pale gray groundmass of plagioclase feldspar and quartz. Black crystals are biotite.

MAJOR USAGE

Mainly used for columns.

Granito rosso antico

SOURCE: Aswan, Nile Valley, Egypt
STATUS: Actively quarried

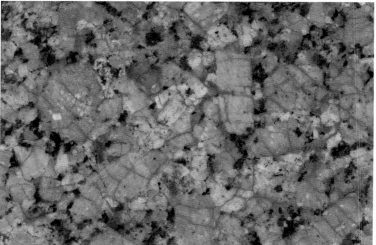

The most famous red granite in the world was first quarried in the third millennium BCE, and is steeped in history.

The red Egyptian granite was extracted at various locations between Aswan and the Shellal district in the Nile Valley of Egypt, and also from islands in the Nile. It was used for interior and exterior claddings and paving but only in the most important buildings. Huge blocks were extracted for obelisks, columns and sarcophagi. Famous obelisks made of *granito rosso antico* are referred to as "Cleopatra's Needle," and can be seen on the Victoria Embankment in London, Place de la Concorde in Paris, and in Central Park, New York. Red Egyptian granite was also sculpted into statues such as the huge figures of King Rameses II in Luxor.

After the Egyptians, this granite was worked by the Greeks who called it *lithos pyrrhopoecilos*, meaning the "red-spotted stone." When the Romans brought Egypt into the Empire, they continued to quarry the granite, particularly for the production of columns, several hundreds of which have been found in Rome, the Middle

LEFT Cleopatra's Needle in Central Park, New York, is an obelisk some 70 feet (21 m) high, carved in about 1450 BCE. It is one of a trio of obelisks originally sited in the ancient city of Heliopolis. The others are now in London and Paris.

INSET The unfinished obelisk in a quarry at Aswan measured nearly 138 feet (42 m) in length, too long to extract without it cracking. It is still attached to the bedrock. Today it is the site of an open-air museum.

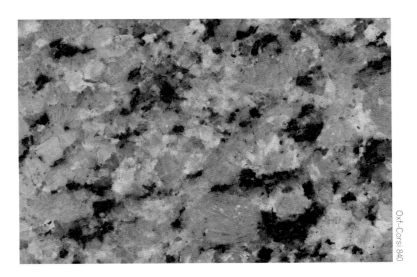

Oxf–Corsi 840

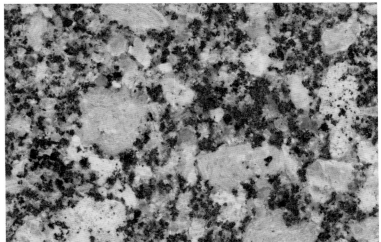

Oxf–Corsi 837

Oxf–Corsi 831

East and Turkey. The Romans called this granite *lapis Thebaicus* after Thebes, the ancient name for Luxor, or *lapis Syenites* after Syene, now called Aswan. This is potentially confusing because the rock that geologists today call "syenite" is misnamed after this stone, which is actually a granite. Other Roman uses of this stone include baths and fountain basins but they rarely used it for statuary.

Most *granito rosso antico* is coarse-grained with pink or red feldspar crystals, but a very fine-grained variety, of rather limited occurrence in veins, was also used to some extent. A gray to black granodiorite and stones of intermediate composition, such as that shown top right, come from the same area.

For many centuries since Byzantine times, quarrying of granite had ceased, and it was not until a hard stone was required for the construction of the first Aswan dam in 1899 that quarries were opened again. The effects of the second huge dam built in the 1960s, the growing urban sprawl from Aswan and consumption of stone by modern quarrying industries are all placing ancient quarries under threat today.

GEOLOGICAL DESCRIPTION
Coarse- or fine-grained granite with pink to red potassium feldspar, gray quartz and black biotite.

MAJOR USAGE
Obelisks, columns, sculpture, baths, fountain basins, pavings, wall cladding.

RIGHT A granite statue of a civil servant called Sekhemka, dating from the fifth dynasty (ca. 2450–2325 BCE). It was found at Saqqarah, Egypt, and is now in the Louvre, Paris.

Shap granite

SOURCE: Wasdale Crag, Cumbria, England
STATUS: Some quarrying still takes place

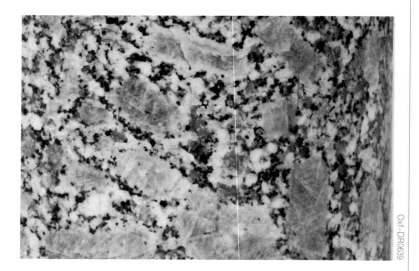

Large crystals of pink feldspar in a mottled backdrop make the light *Shap granite* a beautiful and easily recognized stone.

There are two kinds of *Shap granite*. The darker variety has a brownish tone to the color and is nowhere near as decorative as the beautiful lighter-colored granite with its large pink phenocrysts of feldspar set in a mottled groundmass. The lighter variety (shown above) was used most extensively because it was also available in larger quantities.

The quarries are a few miles from the village of Shap, on the eastern edge of the Lake District National Park in Cumbria. They opened in 1864, and since then *Shap granite* has been used extensively both for construction and as a facing stone. The exterior pillars of the Midland Grand Hotel at St. Pancras Station in London are a superb example of this stone, and it forms shafts and flanking arches in St. Mary's Cathedral, Edinburgh.

Two features often seen in *Shap granite* are small dark-colored patches of mafic rock known as "xenoliths," and crystals of metallic minerals such as yellow chalcopyrite or blue-gray molybdenite. Both add a curiosity value but are undesirable for decorative applications.

GEOLOGICAL DESCRIPTION

Lower Devonian granite with large pink crystals of alkali feldspar in a finer-grained groundmass of plagioclase, quartz and biotite. Xenoliths and metallic crystals of sulfide minerals may also be present.

MAJOR USAGE

Pillars, wall cladding, arches and other architectural features; curbstones; often sold for garden landscape stone.

Rosa Porrino

SOURCE: O Porriño-Vigo region, Galicia, Spain
STATUS: Actively quarried

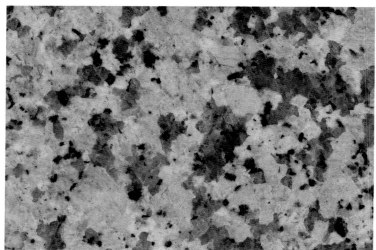

One of the prettiest pink granites is called *rosa Porrino*, but it is a tough stone that can cope well with environmental conditions in major cities.

Rosa Porrino (*rosa Porriño*) takes its name from the industrial town of O Porriño, in Galicia, Spain, and is extracted from around 40 quarries in that vicinity. It has long been used in small pieces for local houses, sidewalks and stone walls, and the council buildings in O Porriño designed by architect Antonio Palacios Ramilo in the early 20th century are constructed from the local granite. The cutting of large blocks for the decorative stone trade began in 1928, but it was in the 1960s, when the stone was taken to Carrara for shaping and polishing, that the demand for this stone saw exponential growth.

Rosa porrino is beautifully colored, the alkali feldspar crystals being a clear delicate pink, but the stone is by no means delicate, and is suitable for both external and internal applications. It is characterized by a very even grain size and pattern, and a lack of inclusions, foliation or other potential forms of internal weakness. It is used in the exterior cladding of Landmark Square in Long Beach, California. In London, the Barclays Bank World Building on Canary Wharf incorporates this granite in its exterior decoration.

GEOLOGICAL DESCRIPTION

A medium-grained granite of Carboniferous age, containing pink alkali feldspars, plagioclase, quartz and black biotite.

MAJOR USAGE

Floors and wall claddings and other internal and external architectural features; store fronts; tables and countertops.

Red Peterhead granite

SOURCE: Peterhead, Aberdeenshire, Scotland
STATUS: No longer quarried

It is surprising how many places there are around the world where *red Peterhead granite* has been used.

The stone shown above is the famous red granite from the Stirling Hill quarries in Peterhead, a coastal town in Aberdeenshire now better known for its fisheries. Quarries in this area were renowned for their colorful granites and also produced a gray granite known as *blue Peterhead*. Both stones were quarried from the 18th century onward and extensively employed not only in the "granite city" of Aberdeen, but in many more distant places. In London, *red Peterhead granite* forms the shaft of the Duke of York's Column on the junction of Regent Street and the Mall, and it forms the fine columns of Fishmongers' Hall at London Bridge. In the United States, there are 18 columns of *Peterhead granite* flanking the nave of the Basilica of Saint Vincent, in Latrobe, Pennsylvania.

Right through the 19th and early 20th centuries the quarries around Peterhead were a major employer, although the Stirling Hill quarry had an alternative regular workforce, the convicts of the Peterhead Prison. The quarrying business declined after the recession of the 1930s and now all the quarries are closed.

GEOLOGICAL DESCRIPTION
Medium-grained Devonian granite containing pink feldspar, gray quartz and black hornblende.

MAJOR USAGE
Columns, facing stones, architectural elements; monuments.

Balmoral granite

SOURCE: Turku district, Länsi-Suomen Lääni, Finland
STATUS: Actively quarried

This stone may have a traditional Scottish name, but it comes from a large granite intrusion in southern Finland.

A little care needs to be taken, for the royal Castle of Balmoral does indeed rest on granite, but the stone that bears this name on the market today comes from Finland. Exactly why it acquired its Scottish name has been a matter of some conjecture. It may be a throwback from the time when granites from Scandinavia were shipped to Aberdeen to be cut and polished before being re-exported all over the world.

There are two varieties of *Balmoral granite*, one with larger crystals than the other. Both are quarried in southwest Finland, in the area around Taivassalo and Vehmaa, northwest of the city of Turku. They are richly colored red stones that have been used extensively for the facings of stores, offices and public buildings in Japan, Australia, the United States, Great Britain and many other countries. In the past, red granite from Sweden has also been traded as *Balmoral granite*.

GEOLOGICAL DESCRIPTION
Medium- to coarse-grained granites of Precambrian age, composed of brownish-red potassium feldspar, gray quartz, and brownish gray plagioclase feldspar. The black mafic minerals are biotite and hornblende.

MAJOR USAGE
Interior and exterior floors and wall claddings; store fronts; kitchen countertops; gravestones and monuments.

Dakota mahogany

SOURCE: Milbank, Grant County, South Dakota, United States

STATUS: Actively quarried

Oxf-DR1790

Memorial stones have always been the principal use for beautiful *Dakota mahogany* granite, but this stone is now proving itself to be far more versatile.

Dakota mahogany is a richly colored stone with medium-sized crystals of dark salmon-pink feldspar, blue-gray quartz, and a spattering of dark brown biotite and hornblende. It comes from Milbank, in Grant County, South Dakota.

It may have formed from a 2.7 billion-year-old granite intrusion, but the working of the stone has a much more recent history. It was first discovered underlying rather poor quality farmland in 1917 by Alex Dewar. He recognized the potential of what turned out to be a very large and homogenous granite intrusion, and was one of the founders that set up the Dakota Granite Company in 1925 to extract and market the stone. At first it was used mainly for memorial stone, but in 1998, the company brought in new modern equipment to fabricate kitchen countertops and floor tiles. Since then, sales have burgeoned, and this attractive stone is now shipped all over the world.

GEOLOGICAL DESCRIPTION

Precambrian granite composed of salmon-pink or red alkali feldspars, gray plagioclase feldspars, bluish gray quartz and dark brown biotite and hornblende.

MAJOR USAGE

Gravestones and monuments; floor tiles, wall claddings and other architectural elements; kitchen countertops and tables.

Baltic brown

SOURCE: Etelä-Suomen Lääni, Finland

STATUS: Actively quarried

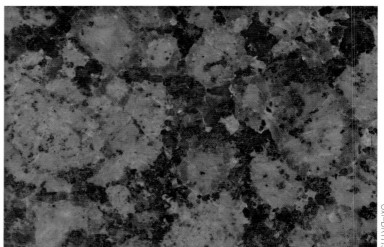

Oxf-DR1773

A classic textured granite from Finland, *Baltic brown* turns up in shopping malls all around the world.

One of the most distinctive of granites seen cladding store fronts, or in the catalogs of kitchen countertops, is called *Baltic brown*. It is quarried at Husu, Pakkola, Lahnajärvi, Hujakkala and other locations east of Ylämaa, in southeast Finland.

The striking feature of *Baltic brown* is its large round pinkish-brown feldspar crystals, each one with a grayish green rim. The original feldspars are orthoclase and the rims are plagioclase feldspar, what is known as Rapakivi texture. This stone is part of the huge Vyborg massif that was emplaced 1,615 to 1,645 million years ago in Precambrian times.

Baltic brown forms fine monolith columns in the St. Isaac's Cathedral in St. Petersburg, and this stone has been widely used elsewhere in Russia. Since the early 20th century, Finland has become a major world supplier of granites. The appearance of *Baltic brown* will vary to some extent depending on where it is quarried, but within a quarry, it is possible to cut very large quantities of this stone of remarkably consistent appearance.

GEOLOGICAL DESCRIPTION

Precambrian rapakivi granite, with large round orthoclase crystals rimmed with green-gray plagioclase, in a groundmass rich in biotite and hornblende.

MAJOR USAGE

Flooring, wall cladding and many other architectural applications; kitchen countertops and tabletops.

Luxullianite

SOURCE: Luxulyan, Cornwall, England
STATUS: No longer available

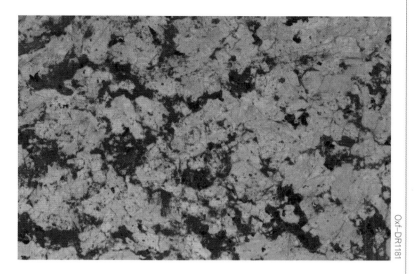

Oxf-DR1181

Both decorative rocks on this page began life as granites, but geological processes have added new and beautiful minerals.

Luxullianite (luxulianite) is named after the Cornish village of Luxulyan, where it was discovered outcropping in a "shabby rock field" on Trevanny Farm. It would perhaps have remained little known except that when the Duke of Wellington died in 1852, a search was made for a suitable stone for his sarcophagus. The Treffry family had already employed luxullianite for decorating walls of the spectacular Porphyry Hall at their residence, Place House at Fowey. No doubt they were instrumental in proposing this stone for the sarcophagus, and it was indeed chosen. A 63-ton (70-tonne) mass was excavated, sawn and polished, a job that took two years to complete. No less arduous was the task of hauling the sarcophagus from the far southwest of England up to London, where it was lodged in the crypt of St. Paul's Cathedral. A few years later, superb luxullianite pillars were incorporated in the building of the (then) new Natural History Museum at Oxford.

Today small amounts of luxullianite are found at the Tregarden quarry in Luxulyan, and at other local quarries, but it is not quarried in its own right.

GEOLOGICAL DESCRIPTION

A granite of Permian age that has been altered by boron-rich fluids in the latest stages of crystallization. It consists predominantly of large, deep pink orthoclase crystals and black schorl. Schorl is the black iron-bearing member of the tourmaline group of minerals. Tourmalines contain boron as well as silicon.

MAJOR USAGE

Columns, tabletops and other decorative items.

Unakite

SOURCE: Various places
STATUS: Actively quarried

Oxf-Min 30095

Polished spheres and small tumblestones in a curious combination of pistachio-green and bright pink are almost certainly the rock called unakite.

This stone is named after the Unaka Mountains in Tennessee, and has been quarried in various places along the Blue Ridge Mountains in Virginia, Tennessee and North Carolina. Unakite was little known as a decorative stone until the latter half of the 20th century but is now widely used for a wide variety of ornaments and jewelry. It has occasionally been used for architectural purposes, and tiles can be seen in the floor of the terrace of the Smithsonian Institution in Washington, D.C.

Unakite is sometimes referred to as "epidotized granite." It occurs where epidote, a silicate mineral with a characteristic yellowish pistachio-green color, has replaced micas and dark mafic minerals in altered granitic deposits. Pink feldspar and colorless quartz resist the chemical changes. Typically unakite forms pods and small dikes in the granitic rock, but some deposits are large enough to work on a commercial scale. Pebbles of unakite may be found in river and beach deposits formed by erosion of altered granites. Similar epidotized rocks are found in many places around the world.

GEOLOGICAL DESCRIPTION

Altered granites or granitic gneisses, the micas and dark colored constituents altered to epidote. It may be found as pebbles in river and beach deposits.

MAJOR USAGE

Polished spheres and eggs, boxes, tealight holders and other ornaments; jewelry.

Larvikite

SOURCE: Larvik, Vestfold, Norway
STATUS: Actively quarried

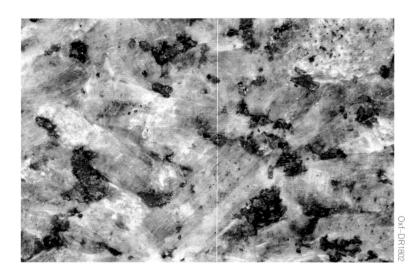

At first glance, larvikite looks dull gray, but it is packed full of feldspar crystals that shimmer silvery blue as they catch the light to reveal an unexpected beauty.

Larvikite is a kind of syenite containing abundant large crystals of an unusual form of anorthoclase that display a beautiful gray-blue schiller when it is turned in the light. It forms a large igneous intrusion in the coastal area of Norway around Larvik, south of Oslo. Larvikite has been used as the local building stone since prehistoric times, but not quarried on any large commercial scale until the late 19th century. Stone expert R.V. Dietrich recounts a tale, perhaps true, that each country participating in an international exhibition in Germany in the 1890s was invited to submit two samples of their best cladding stones for a team of architects to judge. Norway at that time only had one suitable stone, so the planning committee asked the famous Norwegian geologist W.C. Brøgger to recommend a second stone. He suggested the rock he called larvikite, which winked at him in the moonlight as he rode in his buggy beside exposures along the Larvik Fjord. The stone was duly cut, polished and exhibited to prize-winning acclaim.

Since then, larvikite has been exported all over the world, and it has been used so much in England for the cladding of store fronts and public houses ("pubs") that it has earned the nickname "pub-stone." Larvikite is also a practical stone for kitchen counters and other uses in the home. At first glance it might seem that all larvikite looks the same, but there are several different varieties, varying as to how dark they are and the size of the grains.

Modern trade names include *royal blue, blue pearl* and *green pearl*. The memorial to scientist and explorer Thor Heyerdahl in Larvik shows this stone used for sculpture, and regular events are held inside a quarry to give sculptors from around the world an opportunity to carve larvikite.

Nowadays other stones are quarried that also contain feldspar crystals with a distinct schiller. Most notable among these is the stone known as *blue eyes*, which is an anorthosite, a basic plutonic rock composed mainly of coarse-grained labradorite feldspar with a little pyroxene. It comes from Nain on the coast of Labrador in Canada, the original source of labradorite (see page 264). The flashes of blue in this luxurious stone are a much deeper blue than those of larvikite.

GEOLOGICAL DESCRIPTION

Larvikite is a medium- to coarse-grained augite syenite intruded during the Carboniferous period. The iridescent crystals are anorthoclase cryptoperthite ("labradorescent anorthoclase"; see also page 265).

MAJOR USAGE

Store and pub exteriors; flooring and wall cladding, countertops and many other applications; sculpture. Huge blocks of low-grade larvikite have been brought to England for use in coastal defenses, and sea-polished fragments are often found on beaches.

ABOVE The great anthropologist and explorer Thor Heyerdahl was born in Larvik and this memorial to him, sited on the waterfront at Larvik, was carved out of larvikite by Nico Widerberg.

LEFT Larvikite is most often seen in the frontages of stores and public houses.

Marmo Misio

SOURCE: East of Ayvalik, Balikesir, Turkey
STATUS: No longer quarried for decorative use

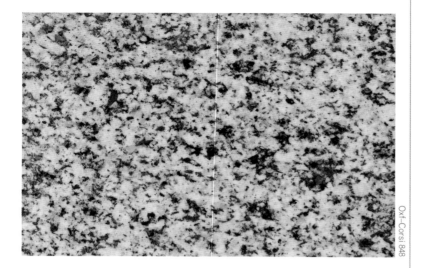

Oxf-Corsi 848

An unassuming gray and white granite, *marmo Misio* is easily overlooked, yet it was employed extensively in ancient times.

This mottled gray and white stone comes from various ancient quarries that exploited the Kozak plutonic intrusion in western Turkey. The greatest concentrations are in the area bounded by the villages of Demircidere, Ukçular and Ayvatlar. In ancient times, it was part of a region known as Mysia that had as its capital the well-known city of Pergamum (the modern Bergama). This is why, when the location of the quarries was discovered in 1988, the stone was named *marmor Misio*.

Many columns of *marmo Misio* have been discovered in archaeological sites in Italy, Greece, Turkey and parts of north Africa. The stone was probably first quarried in the late Hellenistic period (second or first century BCE) and by the first century CE, it was being employed in Rome. The stone continued to be extracted until early Byzantine times.

Despite its name, it is not a marble but a granodiorite or granite. It is easily confused with similar granites from the islands of Elba and Giglio that were also quarried in ancient times, but these do not contain hornblende.

GEOLOGICAL DESCRIPTION

Miocene medium-grained granodiorite or granite, with plagioclase and potassium feldspars, quartz, biotite and hornblende.

MAJOR USAGE

Columns, and to a much lesser extent for paving and sarcophagi.

Granito del foro

SOURCE: Mons Claudianus, Eastern Desert, Egypt
STATUS: Quarried in antiquity

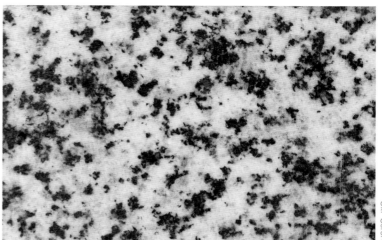

Oxf-Corsi 847

This is the famous "granite" used for the columns of Trajan's Forum in Rome, which is why it was named *granito del foro* by the stonecutters of Rome.

The ancient Romans called this stone *marmor Claudianum* in honor of the Emperor Claudius during whose reign (41 to 54 CE) it was first quarried. It was extracted on Mons Claudianus near Wadi Fatiri el-Bayda. It was used at Hadrian's Villa in Tivoli, and the huge columns of the Forum and the exterior of the Pantheon are particularly noteworthy examples of its many uses in Rome. It was also used for fountain basins such as the two in the Piazza Farnese, originally sited in the baths of Caracalla. Outside Rome and Tivoli, the stone had rather more limited application. By the latter half of the third century, the quarries had fallen into disuse.

Granito del Foro is certainly not a granite. It has been identified variously as a granodiorite, quartz diorite or tonalite, and may be lightly metamorphosed to form a gneiss. The sample shown here is a granodiorite, and when the sample is viewed sideways on, it shows some foliation with the dark crystals in distinct bands. *Granito del Foro* resembles a tonalite gneiss from Wadi Umm Huyut that was also quarried at this time.

GEOLOGICAL DESCRIPTION

Precambrian medium-grained granodiorite composed mainly of white plagioclase feldspar, black hornblende and biotite, and lesser amounts of gray quartz. Minor amphiboles and traces of yellow-green epidote are present.

MAJOR USAGE

Columns, fountain basins, decorative veneers on walls and sometimes floors; reused in inlays and other decorative work.

Orbicular granite

SOURCE: France, Australia and Finland

STATUS: Sporadically quarried in Corsica, actively quarried in Australia and Finland

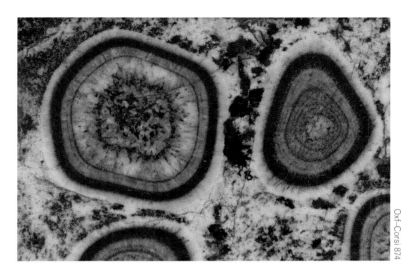

Oxf-Corsi 874

It is a curious quirk of nature that sometimes, when hot molten magma starts to cool, crystals start to grow out from a nucleus in a succession of concentric layers.

Crystals form spherules a few inches in diameter that "float" in a matrix of more conventional structure. Orbicular growth patterns normally only occur in restricted areas of an igneous intrusion, but are found in many places around the world. Just a few deposits are large enough to generate commercial quantities of this highly decorative stone. They tend to be granitic to dioritic in compostion.

The first orbicular "granite" was a large boulder discovered below Olmeto, on the French island of Corsica in 1785. Cyprien-Prosper Brard tells how its appearance was so unusual, it was thought that the boulder had fallen from the heavens. The sample above is from this block. Later the stone was found in *situ* near Santa-Lucia-di-Tallano in the district of Sartene. It was named *Napoleonite* or *Corsite*, and was brought to Paris for cutting and carving into vases and tabletops. It is a diorite, some bands being composed almost entirely of plagioclase and others of black hornblende, yet others a mixture of the two. The deposit was virtually worked out in recent years but some stockpiles exist.

In 1986, an orbicular granite deposit was first worked in Boogardie, near Mount Magnet in Western Australia. The orbicules may be diorite or granite, and the groundmass is granite. In recent years it has been employed as an architectural cladding but now it is more often sold as polished pieces or spheres at mineral fairs. A huge polished sphere turning on water is an ornamental feature in Forrest Place in the center of Perth, Australia.

A third orbicular granite is quarried in Savitaipale, Finland, with large pale-colored orbicules composed of albite, quartz and

ABOVE A polished cube of orbicular granite from Boogardie, Western Australia, is an eye-catching, touchable exhibit in the Oxford University Museum of Natural History.

biotite in a coarse-grained groundmass. The deposit is small and the stone is processed on site.

GEOLOGICAL DESCRIPTION

Granites, granodiorites or diorites with an orbicular structure. The dark minerals are mainly hornblende, biotite, and iron and titanium oxides; white is plagioclase or potassium feldspar depending on the variety. Gray quartz is normally present.

MAJOR USAGE

Architectural claddings, polished spheres, vases, tabletops, boxes and other decorative items.

Granito della colonna

SOURCE: Wadi Umm Shegilat, Eastern Desert, Egypt
STATUS: Used in antiquity

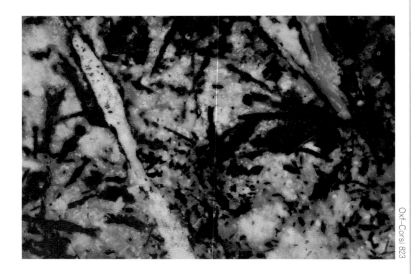

Oxf–Corsi 823

This stone was named by the Italian scalpellini after the column to which, according to an old tradition, Christ was chained during his flagellation.

The column in the San Zenone Chapel, in the Church of Santa Prassede, Rome, was said to have been brought from Jerusalem in 1223. The stone is a distinctive coarse-grained pegmatitic diorite, with elongate large black crystals in a white or pale pink groundmass. It comes from a small quarry (rediscovered in the early 1950s) in Wadi Umm Shegilat near Gebel Abu el-Hasan, in the Eastern Desert of Egypt. An interesting feature is that the stone here, once split from the rock face using iron wedges, was sawn to shape with iron blades charged with abrasive sand. Evidence of sawing of stone by the Romans in a quarry is very unusual.

Granito della colonna was first used in Predynastic Egypt for making vases and small carvings of animals. The Romans exploited it mainly for small columns and *opus sectile* (a mosaic technique made from individually shaped slices of stone) tiles for walls and floors, as seen in Pompeii, Herculaneum and in Hadrian's Villa at Tivoli. Two columns can be seen at the high altar of the Church of San Saba in Rome. It also regularly appears in collections of ancient stones and in inlaid tabletops made from stone samples in the 18th and 19th centuries.

GEOLOGICAL DESCRIPTION
Precambrian very coarse-grained pegmatitic diorite with radiating clusters of large black hornblende crystals in white or pale pink plagioclase feldspar.

MAJOR USAGE
Columns, paving, small table bases; stone samples, inlays.

Granito bianco e nero

SOURCE: Wadi Barud, Eastern Desert, Egypt
STATUS: Used in antiquity

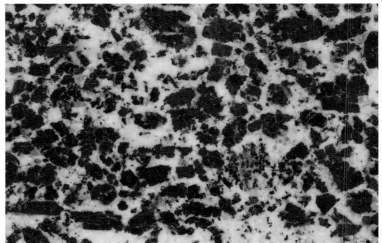

Oxf–Corsi 844

In 1998, researchers found that the quarry of this stone in the Eastern Desert of Egypt also yielded another stone that had been used in Cairo.

In the first century CE, when Augustus was emperor, quarries were opened in Wadi Barud. Near the quarry was a fort that came to be known as Tiberiane. This suggests that the stone extracted from the quarry was what the Roman author Pliny called *marmor Tiberianum*. The scalpellini of medieval and baroque Rome called it *granito bianco e nero*. During Roman times it was employed for small columns and for slabs in opus sectile floors, the quarry continuing to work until later in the second century. When new stone was unavailable, the scalpellini reused older stone, and the finest example is a pillar in the Chapel of San Zenone, in the Church of Santa Prassede. Stone experts James Harrell and Lorenzo Lazzarini now call this distinctive black and white stone (shown above) *granito bianco e nero di Santa Prassede*.

The second variety has the same composition but much smaller crystals, the black hornblende in small clusters. It had been found mainly in medieval buildings in Cairo, so they named it *granito bianco e nero di Cairo*. Fieldwork in the 1990s showed that the original variety formed the lower levels of the quarry and the stone used in Cairo came from the upper levels.

GEOLOGICAL DESCRIPTION
Precambrian quartz diorite with large black crystals of hornblende in a groundmass of white plagioclase feldspar and minor quartz.

MAJOR USAGE
Small columns, paving; reused in decorative panels and inlays in furniture.

Granito verde antico

SOURCE: Wadi umm Wikala, Eastern Desert, Egypt

STATUS: Used in antiquity

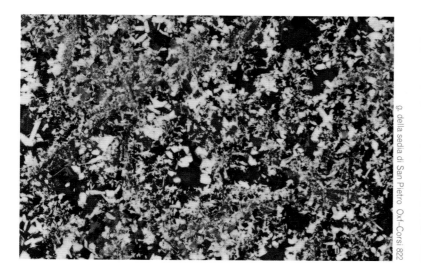

g. della sedia di San Pietro Oxf–Corsi 822

g.della di San Lorenzo Oxf–Corsi 825

g.verde a erbetta Oxf–Corsi 828

Considered a handy charm to ward off the ill effects of snake bites in ancient times, this stone is a spotted green and white gabbro from Egypt.

The gabbros from Wadi umm Wikala include three well-known varieties used in ancient times. The first is called *granito della sedia di San Pietro* because it forms decorative panels in the pedestal of the bronze statue of St. Peter in the Vatican Basilica. It has clots of coarse-grained crystals in a generally medium-grained groundmass. *Granito della sedia di San Lorenzo* is similar but has a uniform medium grain size. The 13th-century cosmati-inspired throne in the church of San Lorenzo in Rome has a fine roundel of this stone. The third variety is named *granito verde a erbetta*, the "grass green granite." This is, of course, a slight exaggeration, but the stone still has a distinctly green tint.

All these varieties come from Wadi umm Wikala close to where it joins Wadi Semna in the Eastern Desert. Artifacts in the Archaeological Museum in Cairo show that this stone was used as early as the Protodynastic period of the late fourth millennium BCE. During Hellenistic times it was worn as amulets, which among other powers were reputed to ward off the effects of snake bites, probably because the pattern resembled snakeskin. The superstition persisted in Roman times when the stone was known as *lapis ophytes* ("*ophytes*" meaning snake). Quarrying inscriptions show that the stone was worked during the time of Emperor Augustus at the end of the first century BCE, continuing into the following century. It has been found in the ruins of Pompeii, Herculaneum and also in Hadrian's Villa at Tivoli. All the varieties of this stone were loosely referred to as *granito verde antico* by the

scalpellini of Rome who recycled it in the decoration of churches and in furniture inlays.

GEOLOGICAL DESCRIPTION

Weakly altered gabbro of Precambrian age, sometimes classified as a metagabbro, with crystals of white plagioclase, dark green augite and some iron oxides that have oxidized, tinting the stone brown.

MAJOR USAGE

Paving and decorative panels; bowls and basins; small columns; amulets; reused for inlays in furniture.

stone in the home

RIGHT Granite countertops create a stunning effect in the modern kitchen, as well as being hygienic for preparation of food and drink. The stone used here is called *paradiso* and comes from India.

Not so long ago, the pictures of kitchens in glossy magazines showed countertops with laminate coatings patterned to look like natural stone. Today's designer multipurpose cooking space must have countertops made of the real thing. The humble domestic kitchen has had an extraordinary effect on international trade relations, for the sale of natural stone countertops in the West has opened the door to millions of dollars worth of trade with the major stone producers in South America, India, China and the Far East. A good choice of stone can look fabulous and because it can enhance property value, it makes a wise investment too.

Of course natural stone is not a newcomer to the domestic scene. Before the days of refrigerators, a cold slab of marble, granite or slate was essential for preserving food in the pantry. Pestles and mortars for grinding spices were—and still are—made of stone. In the days before the in-store bakery, a cool marble pastry board helped ensure the perfect apple pie. Natural stone resists water and is easy to keep clean, and so it was an obvious choice for wash stands. Floors too were often tiled with stone slabs that are easily mopped down. In the dining room or drawing room, a little colorful marble or granite would often be used for the most prominent architectural feature of the whole house, the chimneypiece.

THE LEMON TEST

It is too easy to be wowed by the amazing choice of marbles and granites and choose a stone for kitchen countertops based on appearance alone. How disappointing it must be to find that it is marked by food, or scratches so easily that it starts to lose its polish. Just a single drop of lemon juice or vinegar will etch the surface of countertops containing calcite. This is why the "granites" of the stone trade are specially selected. Porous stones which are stained by oil and grease are unsuitable too. A simple effective test advocated by stone expert Maurizio Bertoli is to apply a small drop of lemon juice to a scrap sample of stone. If it immediately soaks in, forming a dark spot, or if it affects the polish, the stone should not be used. If it takes a couple of minutes to have any effect, it may be possible to use a special coating to protect the stone. If there is no change at all, the stone should work well without an additional coating. Black stone in particular may be coated with colored polish by unscrupulous traders, and if a little nail polish remover takes off a black coating, again the stone should be rejected. But even the stones that pass these tests may be damaged by the daily knocks of the average kitchen work surface. Stones that are honed rather than polished are less likely to be problematic in this way, but the best advice is obtained from a reputable stone merchant.

BATHROOM STONES

Natural stone in the bathroom gives a beautiful finish that is both practical and hygienic. A far wider choice is available, and includes many marbles and limestones. Porous stones are to be avoided as they will encourage mold growth, and there are a few stones that contain small amounts of iron sulfides that may develop rust spots on prolonged exposure to moisture. Once again, the reputable dealer will advise on which stones to use for that gorgeous dream bathroom.

BOTTOM Black "granite" is used for the countertops in this modern kitchen. Similar stones come from various countries but some are more suitable for use in kitchens than others.

BELOW This luxurious bathroom has a bathtub, walls and floors made of travertine, a stone that the ancient Romans used for the same purpose.

Rustenburg

SOURCE: Rustenburg area, North West Province, South Africa
STATUS: Actively quarried

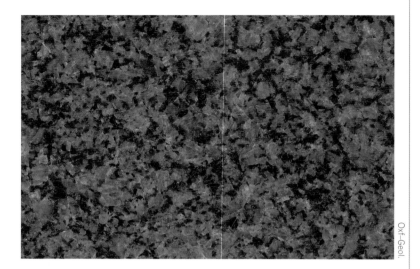

Platinum, chromium and other valuable metals come from the Bushveld rocks around Rustenburg, and so does this dark, robust stone.

Rustenburg is quarried in the area of Bosspruit and Brits near the South African town of Rustenburg. It is also traded as *nero impala*. It was exported to Europe before World War II but postwar times saw a massive growth in its use. A very similar but slightly coarser-grained stone has been traded as *Bon Accord* after the town of that name just north of Pretoria.

These are gabbroic rocks that come from the largest and most economically important igneous intrusion in the world—the Bushveld Igneous Complex. The magma was intruded some two billion years ago, and as it cooled, heavier metals settled out into distinct layers that today form very rich ore bodies. They supply most of the world's chromium, platinum and other precious elements as well as large quantities of vanadium, iron, tin and other metals. The Bushveld Complex is estimated at 70,250 square miles (182,000 km²). The center is buried by volcanic rocks and granites, but Rustenburg and Bon Accord lie on the southwestern fringes, where precious metals and decorative stones are extracted.

GEOLOGICAL DESCRIPTION

Norite composed mainly of colorless plagioclase feldspar and brownish gray orthopyroxene, or gabbro in which clinopyroxene is more abundant; dark coloration is due to the presence of metal oxide inclusions. They are part of the Precambrian Bushveld Igneous Complex.

MAJOR USAGE

Flooring; store fronts; kitchen countertops; monuments.

Granito nero antico

SOURCE: Aswan, Nile Valley, Egypt
STATUS: Commercially available

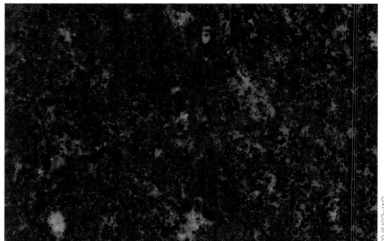

The great lion fountains at the bottom of the steps from the Capitoline Square in Rome were carved in ancient times from the black granodiorite of Aswan.

The quarries near Aswan in the Nile Valley of Egypt are well known for their pink granites (see page 222) but they also yielded smaller amounts of what the stonecutters of Rome called *granito nero* (although it is not a granite, but a granodiorite). It is mottled black or dark gray and white, sometimes with a few scattered larger white or pinkish feldspar crystals. *Granito nero* was first quarried by the ancient Egyptians who used it, for example, in the second millennium BCE for the statues of goddess Sekhmet in Karnak. The Romans called it *lapis Thebaicus* like the pink Egyptian granite, and it was perhaps their *lapis Aethiopicus*.

There is a large basin in the octagonal courtyard of the Vatican Museum made of *granito nero antico,* and the two large lion fountains at the bottom of the steps from the Campidoglio in Rome are also carved of this stone. They were converted into fountains by the sculptor Giacomo della Porta in 1588.

The ancient quarries are located on the edge of the city of Aswan, at Gebel Ibrahim Pasha and Gebel Nagug, and are under considerable threat from the urban sprawl. The stone is available on the commercial market today, sold as *negro Aswan*.

GEOLOGICAL DESCRIPTION

Precambrian medium-grained granodiorite with black hornblende and biotite, gray quartz, white plagioclase and alkali feldspars, and with scattered phenocrysts of pink alkali feldspar.

MAJOR USAGE

Columns, wall and floor veneers; sarcophagi; baths; sculpture.

Nero Zimbabwe

SOURCE: Mashonaland East Province, Zimbabwe
STATUS: Actively quarried

Oxf–DR1739

Zimbabwe produces various decorative stones, but just one is to be seen in catalogs of granites all around the world.

There is just one decorative stone from Zimbabwe that has found a worldwide market and that is a black dolerite known as *nero Zimbabwe*. Dolerite is a hard black igneous rock that forms small igneous intrusions called sills that cut into the ancient continental rocks. These dolerite intrusions, which are about 1,900 million years old, can be seen in the landscape as elongate hills topped with vegetation. The dolerite is quarried mainly in the areas around Mount Darwin, Mutoko and Murehwa northeast of Harare, and more recently in the areas of Shamva, and Mutawatawa.

Nero Zimbabwe is sometimes referred to as *nero assoluto z* or *nero assoluto Zimbabwe* but it is not the blackest of the "granites," more a very dark gray. The color is derived from dusty inclusions of iron oxide in the plagioclase feldspar crystals. It was first made available on a significant commercial scale around 1971, and demand has grown rapidly since the 1990s, although the ability to supply the stone has been tempered by the political and economic instability of the country, and the number of quarries producing this stone has dropped in recent years.

GEOLOGICAL DESCRIPTION

Precambrian dolerite, a medium- to fine-grained rock composed of amphibole, augite and plagioclase feldspar colored by inclusions of magnetite.

MAJOR USAGE

Flooring, wall cladding and other architectural applications; kitchen countertops; also used as a construction stone.

Belfast black

SOURCE: Mpumalanga Province, South Africa
STATUS: Actively quarried

Oxf–DR1784

When the architect of Scotland's new parliament building needed a black stone to complement the gray Scottish granites, he chose *Belfast black*.

Like *Rustenburg*, *Belfast black* is a gabbro-norite from the Bushveld Igneous Complex, but it comes from the eastern fringes of the intrusion. It was first quarried near Belfast, South Africa, and is extracted today at Stoffberg and around Mpumalanga Province, east of Pretoria. It was first exported to Europe in the early 1960s when it was called *nero assoluto* and, until the 1990s, it was the most commonly used black "granite." Today, other black igneous rocks share that name, and *Belfast black* faces strong market competition from stones quarried in India, Brazil, Uruguay and China.

Unpolished *Belfast black* is gray, and this means that when polished stone is engraved, the lettering or patterning stands out very clearly. Not surprisingly, this is a very popular stone for funeral monuments. It is also used for kitchen countertops and many architectural applications. *Belfast black* is used for the curious plaques that are fitted to the gray Aberdeen granite façade of Scotland's new modernist Holyrood parliament building.

GEOLOGICAL DESCRIPTION

A medium-grained gabbro-norite with dark pyroxenes (pigeonite and augite), gray plagioclase crystals, and small grains of opaque iron-titanium oxides that give the pervading black coloration. It comes from the Bushveld Igneous Complex and is of Precambrian age.

MAJOR USAGE

Kitchen countertops; gravestones and monuments; architecture.

Verde Ubatuba

SOURCE: Between Sao Paulo and Rio de Janeiro, Brazil
STATUS: Actively quarried

BELOW The *Ubatuba* plinth of the famous statue of *Christ the Redeemer* overlooking Rio de Janeiro.

Oxf-DR1781

How many of the millions admiring the huge statue *Christ the Redeemer* notice the beautiful dark rock that forms its plinth?

The massive art deco statue *Christ the Redeemer* that towers over the city of Rio de Janeiro in Brazil was completed in 1931 on the top of the Corcovado Mountain. The plinth is made from *verde Ubatuba*, an igneous rock from the coastal town of Ubatuba, between Sao Paulo and Rio de Janeiro. The original quarry is now worked out, but similar stones are quarried between Sao Paulo and Rio de Janeiro, and in the state of Espiritu Santo, and they too are marketed as *verde Ubatuba*, or simply "*Ubatuba*."

Verde Ubatuba has large lustrous brownish green crystals of feldspar, colored by green orthopyroxene minerals. It is an uncommon type of rock known as a charnockite that was intruded very deep in the Earth's crust during Precambrian times. Charnockites are so highly metamorphosed that in effect they have melted completely and become igneous rocks.

The demand for Brazilian granites in the United States has grown enormously, especially for use as kitchen countertops. *Ubatuba* is one of the most popular, being durable and attractive.

GEOLOGICAL DESCRIPTION

Precambrian charnockite composed of large grains of feldspar, with minor quartz and pyroxenes. The green coloration is due to the presence of the pyroxene minerals.

MAJOR USAGE

Interior and exterior; flooring, wall cladding, staircases, kitchens.

Other granites

There are many different granites and plutonic rocks available on the commercial market today, many supplied in recent years by countries such as Brazil, India and China. Many images and some information can be found on the Internet. Only a small number can be described here.

The stone trade gave the name *giallo antico* to a yellowish granite from the state of Espiritu Santo in Brazil. Other pale granites include Deer Island granite from Maine, and *blanco cristal* and many other granites from Spain.

Another commonly encountered Scottish red granite, which is typically suffused pink, comes from Ross of Mull on the Hebridean island of Mull. Sweden has produced a number of red granites including one that was, like the South African stone, named *Bon Accord*. In this case the name was derived from the district of Aberdeen where the stone was taken for cutting and polishing.

Other popular black "granites" include *nero assoluto* (*premium black*) from India, *Swedish black* from Sweden, *Korpi black* from Finland and *Austral black* from Australia. Galaxy black from India is attractively spotted with white. Blue sodalite-bearing syenites, such as the Brazilian *Azul Bahia*, are referred to on page 261.

Quartz and opal

Quartz is a hard and durable mineral that takes an excellent polish. It occurs in many different geological environments, in a remarkable number of different guises. The decorative varieties in this section can be divided into three kinds. First are the "macrocrystalline" varieties that include rock crystal, amethyst and rose quartz. They are typically transparent or translucent and may show clearly defined crystals with flat faces. The second kind are "cryptocrystalline," and include chrysoprase, carnelian, jasper and agate. They are composed of submicroscopic grains and fibers of quartz packed tightly together. Some are translucent, others are opaque, but in all cases individual crystals can only be seen with an electron microscope. In the third kind, quartz has replaced other minerals or fossils. Again the quartz is very fine-grained, but the patterns and texture are those of the original mineral or fossil.

While quartz is composed of silica, opal is a mixture of silica and water. Precious opal, with its glints of rainbow colors, is a stunningly pretty stone.

Rock crystal, smoky quartz

SOURCE: The European Alps, Madagascar and elsewhere

STATUS: Actively quarried

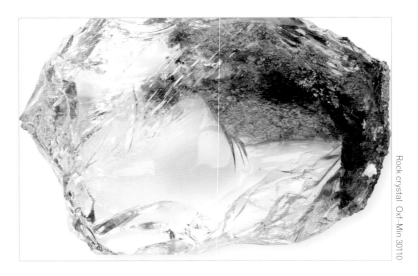

Rock crystal Oxf-Min 30110

Smoky quartz, courtesy of Burhouse Ltd

In the centuries before colorless glass was invented, the ruling classes had vases, bowls and drinking vessels made of rock crystal—as were the classic fortune-tellers' crystal balls.

The ancient Romans carved this colorless variety of quartz with remarkable delicacy, a tradition that was continued particularly in Milan, Turin and Prague during the Renaissance. The rock crystal came from the Alps and, by the 18th century, from Madagascar too. Chinese lapidarists also carved rock crystal; their source was Sakangyi in Myanmar (formerly Burma). Across the Atlantic, carvings of skulls by pre-Columbian Americans—and their fakes—are well documented. In various cultures, clairvoyants have peered into simple polished spheres of rock crystal—"crystal balls" purported to reveal future events.

Flint or lead glass (also called crystal glass) is much cheaper and easier to work, and its invention in the 17th century rendered rock crystal all but obsolete. Just a few master artisans kept the art of carving gem quartz alive, notably those of the Fabergé workshop in St. Petersburg in the late 19th and early 20th centuries.

Some of the most curious and beautiful examples of rock crystal are those that have crystals of other minerals trapped inside. The most commonly seen inclusions are golden hairlike crystals of rutile, slender black schorl crystals, platy orange-red lepidocrocite or mossy growths of green chlorite.

Smoky quartz is transparent and varies from a shade barely darker than rock crystal to dark brown, almost black. It too has been carved, cut and polished since ancient times. Huge pockets of fine quartz crystals were found in the Swiss Alps in the 18th and 19th centuries. In 1719 a crystal cave on the Zinkenstock in Switzerland yielded over 50 tons (56 tonnes) of rock crystal, with a single crystal weighing more than 800 pounds (363 kg). Another massive pocket discovered in 1868 near the Tiefen Glacier in Switzerland produced over 15 tons (17 tonnes) of dark black smoky quartz crystals, two-thirds of which were of gem quality. Much rock crystal now comes from Goiás, Minas Gerais and Bahia in Brazil, and from the Ouachita Mountains in Arkansas. Modern "smoky quartz" is often irradiated rock crystal.

GEOLOGICAL DESCRIPTION

Colorless to brown quartz. Large crystals most often occur in hydrothermal veins and in pegmatites. Waterworn pebbles come from alluvial deposits.

MAJOR USAGE

Bowls, vases and drinking vessels, candlesticks, early chandeliers; carved, engraved, made into crystal balls; used in jewelry.

RIGHT A rock crystal and gold vessel made in the Sarachi workshops in Milan (16th–17th century), now in the Palazzo Pitti, Florence.

QUARTZ AND OPAL

Amethyst, citrine, rose quartz

SOURCE: Russia, Madagascar, Brazil and elsewhere
STATUS: Actively quarried

Amethyst Oxf-Corsi 712

Rose quartz Oxf-Min 27190

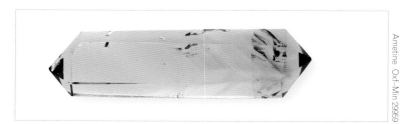

Ametrine Oxf-Min 29959

Some extraordinary powers have been attributed to minerals. The word "amethyst" comes from the ancient Greek for "not drunk," and it was genuinely believed that wearing amethyst would prevent the ill effects of drunkenness.

Of course, amethyst does not ward off drunkenness, but the ancient Greeks and Romans believed the contrary. They carved it into drinking vessels and wore amulets made of it. For centuries, this fine purple gem mineral was considered rare and precious, and reserved for kings, popes and cardinals. It was mined at the famous gem-cutting center of Idar Oberstein in Germany before the 16th century. Meanwhile in Russia, fine deep-colored crystals were obtained near Mursinsk in the Ural Mountains. The 18th century saw the first arrival in Europe of stone from volcanic rocks that run from Rio Grande do Sul in Brazil down to northern Uruguay. This source would eventually flood the market, and it still supplies most amethyst sold today.

Amethyst ranges in color from very dark to very pale purple. Like fluorite (see page 267), individual crystals can often be seen forming a zigzag pattern in a polished slab. The darkest color is toward the tips of the crystals, and amethyst crystals are more steeply pointed than those of fluorite. Quartz has a "conchoidal," or shell-like, fracture and this may also be seen on any broken surface.

Citrine is yellow quartz and comes from the same places as amethyst, but it is quite rare. Most so-called "citrine" on sale is heat-treated amethyst. Natural citrine tends to be a light lemon yellow, but the stone made by heating amethyst is often darker orange-yellow. When a stone is part amethyst and part citrine,

it is known as ametrine. Ametrine occurs naturally but it is also synthesized.

Rose quartz is pale pink, usually rather cloudy, and is found mainly as coarsely crystalline masses that can be very large and are suitable for carving and jewelry. Today, most rose quartz comes from Minas Gerais, Brazil, but past sources have included Madagascar; Rabenstein in Bavaria, Germany; and the southern Black Hills of South Dakota.

GEOLOGICAL DESCRIPTION

Amethyst and citrine occur mainly as linings and infills in gas bubbles, cavities and fractures in volcanic lava, but they also occur in pegmatites. Most rose quartz forms in pegmatites. All varieties are found as waterworn pebbles in alluvial deposits.

MAJOR USAGE

Drinking vessels, vases, jewelry, carvings, as well as other decorative items.

Agate, onyx

SOURCE: Germany, Scotland, Brazil and elsewhere
STATUS: Actively quarried

Scottish Agate Oxf-Min 11832

Blue laceagate Oxf-Min 29975

Found all over the globe, agates are very common indeed. What is more, with so many colors and patterns, no two agates are identical, even when they come from the same part of a lava flow.

The general name for quartz made up of crystals so small they can only be seen with an electron microscope is chalcedony. It is a hard compact stone that takes a good polish. When chalcedony has parallel bands of different colors and transparencies, it is known as agate. Most agates form from silica gel that has infiltrated gas bubbles in volcanic lava. As the gel turns into a crystalline solid from the outside inward, so the impurities are concentrated in concentric colored bands. The center of an agate is usually filled with either rock crystal or amethyst. Agate with straight parallel bands is known as onyx. It forms in cracks and veins in volcanic rocks, but it also can form inside gas bubbles.

Various names are given to agates with particular patterns. Fortification agates have a sharply angular outline to the bands, while island agates have a central area of agate surrounded by colorless quartz crystals. Eyed agates have many small areas of concentric circles, and landscape agates are divided with onyx in the lower part resembling the sea, and concentric banding in the upper part representing the sky. Sagenitic agates contain needlelike crystals of other minerals, or molds where these crystals used to be. Iris agate has an iridescent quality when turned in the light. Other commonly used terms that are largely self-explanatory include flame agates, plume agates and crazy lace agates.

Agate is one of the first stones to have been cut and polished for ornamentation. Today it is used mainly for jewelry, but also for inlays in furniture and boxes and other decorative items. In its rough state it does little to impress. The exterior is usually coated with a green chlorite-like mineral called celadonite, and only if the stone is broken will any banding be visible. But when the agate is sawn and polished, the beautiful semiprecious gem is revealed. Natural colors are mainly pink, violet, red, orange, yellow, brown, black, gray and pale blue. Most agates sold in stores are outrageously unnatural colors such as bright blues or purples. They have been dyed or heat-treated, and were originally rather dull gray or brown agates from the massive lava flows of Brazil and Uruguay. Commercial dying of agates started in the early 19th century at the gem-cutting center of Idar Oberstein in Germany.

The better agates from Idar Oberstein need no enhancement for they are beautiful shades of violet, red, pink and gray. Those from Scotland include some of the best dark salmon-pink stones, and superb landscape agates. They are found on beaches and inland around Perth, Montrose, Dundee and other coastal sites. Blue lace agate is an attractive pale blue onyx that comes from Namibia (*see page 3*) and is often sold as tumble-polished stones. The Laguna agates from Estacion Ojo Laguna in northern Mexico can be exquisite and unusual pastel shades with closely packed bands. These are just a few examples from the many hundreds of places where agate is found around the world.

GEOLOGICAL DESCRIPTION
Banded cryptocrystalline quartz (chalcedony) formed in gas bubbles and other cavities in volcanic lava, deposited as a silica gel by water percolating through the stone. Agate pebbles are found on beaches and in alluvial deposits.

MAJOR USAGE
Decorative items, carvings, inlay work, jewelry.

BELOW Multicolored examples of polished agates from Estacion Ojo Laguna in Mexico, showing their beautiful colored bands. Agates are the banded variety of chalcedony—the name given to cryptocrystalline quartz.

241

Moss agate

SOURCE: India, United States and elsewhere

STATUS: Actively quarried

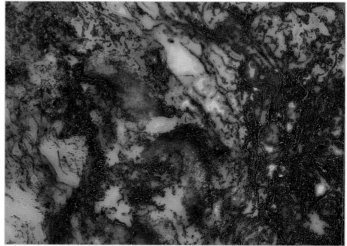

It looks like sprigs of moss are trapped inside this stone, but this is mineral "moss" that has never been alive.

The "moss" in moss agate is actually a branching mass of tiny crystals in transparent or translucent white chalcedony; they are entirely inorganic in origin. Green "moss" is celadonite or chlorite, while orange, yellow, red or brown is iron oxide, and black is manganese oxide.

Large amounts of green moss agate, and other colors, too, have come from the volcanic rocks of the Deccan Plateau in India. Where these rocks have been eroded by rivers and streams, waterworn pebbles are found in the streambeds. The name "mocha stone," also used for moss agate, comes from the seaport of Mocha (Al-Mukha) in Yemen, where it was probably traded. The best known of the American moss agates is Montana agate. It has dark brown to black "moss" in clear or milky chalcedony. Pebbles usually less than 4 inches (10 cm) across have been found in gravel bars and streambeds of the Yellowstone River and its tributaries for well over 60 years. Oregon and Wyoming are among the many other sources worldwide of these fascinating stones.

GEOLOGICAL DESCRIPTION

Chalcedony (very fine-grained quartz) with dendritic inclusions of celadonite, chlorite, hematite, goethite or manganese oxides. Moss agate forms in cavities in volcanic igneous rocks, the colored crystals growing in the gel-like chalcedony before it hardened.

MAJOR USAGE

Inlay work, carving, jewelry. Cabachons (specially cut specimens rounded on top, flat below) of these stones were often used in snuff boxes.

ABOVE Pin bowl in moss agate from India.

Sard, carnelian

SOURCE: Deccan Plateau of India and elsewhere

STATUS: Actively quarried

Sard Oxf-Min 14596

Carnelian Oxf-Min 30619

Some of the oldest carved gemstones ever found are made of the translucent brown and red varieties of chalcedony called, respectively, sard and carnelian.

Chalcedony is the general term for cryptocrystalline quartz with a fibrous structure, but varieties of different colors have more familiar names. Sard is translucent brown and not particularly fashionable. A more attractive form, where the sard is banded with white chalcedony, is known as sardonyx. Carnelian is orange-red and translucent, and is used extensively for carving and jewelry. It also occurs banded with colorless and white chalcedony, forming the brightly colored carnelian agate.

These minerals are found in many places, today coming mainly from the United States, Brazil, Uruguay and Australia. Historically, the most important source was Gujarat, India. Here carnelian and other colored chalcedonies eroded from the Deccan Trap rocks by the Narmada River, accumulated in conglomerates and river gravels farther downstream. For thousands of years, they were mined at Ratanpur and carved in nearby Bharuch and Khambat before being traded across Asia and Europe.

GEOLOGICAL DESCRIPTION

Translucent orange or brown chalcedony (very fine-grained quartz), sometimes agate-banded. Deposited as a gel in cavities in volcanic lavas, or as crusts and coatings in other environments; in beach and alluvial deposits derived from these sources.

MAJOR USAGE

Carvings, cameos, jewelry, mosaics, inlay work.

Prase, bloodstone, plasma

SOURCE: Deccan Plateau of India and elsewhere

STATUS: Commercially available

Prase Oxf-Min 30617

Bloodstone Oxf-Min 30613

At first glance these green chalcedony variants are not the most exciting of decorative stones, but a spattering of bright red spots can make them much more visually arresting.

Prase is slightly translucent and mid-green to leek-green, sometimes mottled with white. Plasma is more opaque and dark green. The names of these two varieties of chalcedony, are frequently confused; suffice it to say that both have been used as decorative stones since Roman times, but nowadays they have little commercial value. Prase has long been obtained from Breitenbrunn in Saxony, and both varieties also come from the Deccan Plateau of India. There are many other sources.

Bloodstone, also known as heliotrope, is much more interesting in appearance. It is darkish green, spattered with bright red dots. It, too, comes from the Deccan Plateau, and masses of 45 pounds (20 kg) or more have been collected from the Kathiawar Peninsula. The Scottish island of Rum is the source of fine bloodstone sometimes incorporated into Scottish agate jewelry.

GEOLOGICAL DESCRIPTION

Green varieties of chalcedony (very fine-grained quartz) colored by inclusions of iron silicate minerals; the red spots in bloodstone are hematite. They form as cavity and vein infills in volcanic rocks or in hydrothermal veins, and are commonly found as waterworn pebbles in alluvial deposits.

MAJOR USAGE

Inlay work, mosaics, carving, jewelry.

QUARTZ AND OPAL

Chrysoprase

SOURCE: Lower Silesia, Poland and elsewhere
STATUS: No longer mined in Poland; actively mined elsewhere

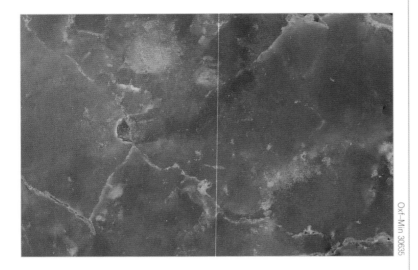

Oxf–Min 30635

With its clear green color and superb translucency, chrysoprase is rather rare and attracts many admirers.

The most precious of all the green chalcedony (very fine-grained quartz) is translucent apple-green chrysoprase. A superb early usage was in the decoration of the 14th-century Wenzel Chapel in Prague. The source was rediscovered in 1740 in Lower Silesia, Poland, the finest stone coming from Gläsendorf (now Szkłary). Frederick the Great, King of Prussia, so admired the stone that he had it used in tabletops and mosaics for his Sanssouci Palace.

From 1878 until about 1911, chrysoprase was mined at Visalia in California. Since the mid-1960s, good quantities have come from Marlborough Creek in Queensland, Australia. Other modern sources include Western Australia and Brazil.

GEOLOGICAL DESCRIPTION
Chrysoprase chalcedony (very fine-grained quartz) colored by nickel silicate inclusions. It forms coatings and infills in veins and cavities associated with nickel-bearing serpentinite deposits.

MAJOR USAGE
Small carvings, jewelry, mosaics, inlay work.

Ribbon jasper

SOURCE: Russia and Germany
STATUS: Rarely available

Oxf–Min 30621

Every museum with a historic mineral collection has samples of the strikingly color-banded Russian ribbon jasper.

The name ribbon, riband, banded or striped jasper is given to any jasper with bands of different colors, but the famous Russian stone is striped medium green and blood-red. Usually cited simply as from Siberia, it is thought to have come from Okhotske to the east, and from Verkhneural'sk, Orenburg and other locations in the southern Ural Mountains. It was only obtained in small blocks, but these would be sliced thinly and used as veneers. A similar stone has been obtained from Saxony in Germany, which was used by the Florentine pietre dure workshops.

Ribbon jasper is the best known of the various jaspers obtained from the southern Urals and the Altai Mountains of Russia. They were worked extensively in the time of Catherine the Great, and many examples can be seen in panels, mosaics, vases and other decoration in the buildings of St. Petersburg.

GEOLOGICAL DESCRIPTION
Originally deposited as mudstone or clay, the green layers contain ferrous iron caused by reducing conditions, and the red layers are colored by the ferric iron oxide hematite, formed in oxidizing conditions. The rock was silicified by nearby igneous activity.

MAJOR USAGE
Inlay work.

Mookaite

SOURCE: Kennedy Range, Western Australia

STATUS: Actively quarried

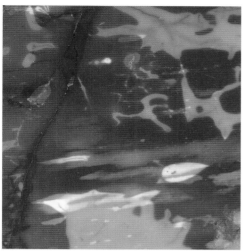

Oxf–Min 30600

It took the fossil remains of billions of minute sea creatures called radiolarians to make the Australian gem-rock known as *mookaite*, named after Mooka Creek in Western Australia, where it was first discovered.

Mookaite formed from sediments that fell to the bottom of the sea that covered part of Western Australia in early Cretaceous times. Most of the debris raining down consisted of radiolaria skeletons composed of silica, and over time this formed a hard silica rock. The remains or molds of other fossils are sometimes found, and cavities may be lined with quartz crystals. The color of *mookaite* is distributed in irregular patches, mainly cream, yellow and bright red, but also purple and brown. Some *mookaite* is opal-rich, but the most suitable for cutting and carving is composed mainly of chalcedony. Boulders in the bed of Mooka Creek were first worked commercially in the mid-1960s by the owners of the Mooka sheep station on the southwestern end of the Kennedy mountain range. Now there are a small number of licenses to extract the stone, which occurs in other nearby locations too.

GEOLOGICAL DESCRIPTION

Lower Cretaceous chert; a silicified radiolarian silt colored by iron and manganese oxides.

MAJOR USAGE

Ornaments, beads and jewelry; also popular for flintknapping.

Calcedonio di Volterra

SOURCE: Monterufoli, Tuscany, Italy

STATUS: Not quarried, but pieces still sometimes found

Oxf–Corsi 740

Flower petals and seashells showing subtle shadings of color are among the astonishingly realistic subjects depicted in Florentine pietre dure work. The stone often used to achieve these effects is called *calcedonio di Volterra.*

With its typical markings shaped like puffy clouds, *calcedonio di Volterra* was first quarried at Monterufoli in the Val di Cecina, southwest of Pomarance in Tuscany. At this site it occurs as veins, blocks and nodules with other varieties of quartz, particularly rock crystal, agate and carnelian. The color varies from pure white to yellow and brown, sometimes tinged violet or red, with delicate gradations in tone.

Quarries were opened at the end of the 16th century to supply stone for the pietre dure workshops, and yielded pieces of stone sometimes large enough for an entire tabletop. They closed during the latter half of the 19th century, but scattered blocks can still be found in the area. In 1997, the Monterufoli-Caselli Forest Nature Reserve was established and includes the site of the old quarries. It preserves the area's biological, geological and industrial heritage, so collecting is subject to certain restrictions.

GEOLOGICAL DESCRIPTION

Chalcedony and jasper formed by hydrothermal alteration of serpentinites during the formation of the Appenine mountain chain in Tertiary times. It occurs with magnesite (magnesium carbonate), which has been exploited for both industrial use and ornamental purposes.

MAJOR USAGE

Pietre dure work and other decorative uses.

Diaspri di Sicilia

SOURCE: Sicily, Italy
STATUS: No longer commercially quarried

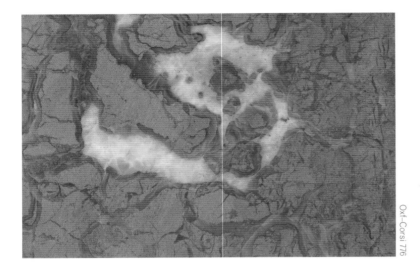

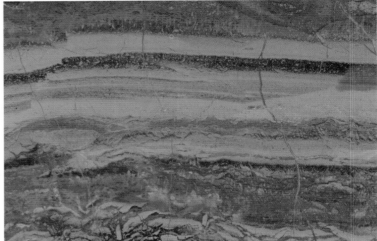

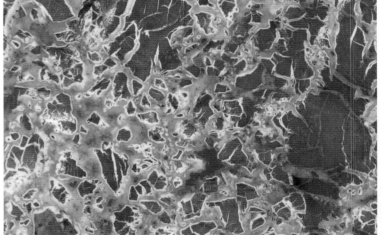

Sicilian jaspers have an amazing variety of patterns and vibrant color combinations. This is a tough stone, too, and takes a beautiful polish.

Exactly how these stones changed from ferruginous limestones in Jurassic times to hard and colorful jaspers is not well understood, but the proximity of basalt flows suggests igneous activity may be significant. The jasper is opaque and can be yellow, orange, brown, red, green or black. In the most attractive varieties, it is heavily brecciated and cemented with combinations of colorless quartz, white or translucent chalcedony, and agate. These sometimes hold tiny specks of iron oxides forming colorful haloes around the fragments. There are a considerable range of colors and patterns even within a single nodule of this stone.

The Sicilian jaspers come mainly from the province of Palermo, and particularly from the villages of Giuliana, Bisacquino, Santo Stefano Quisquina, Monreale and around the city of Palermo. They were collected as loose boulders in plowed fields. Polished vessels and other carved objects made from Giuliana jasper have been dated as early as the 12th century. The heyday of jasper production was in the late 16th and 17th centuries, when the Medici family, with their great love of ornamental stone, had quarries opened just west of the little town of Giuliana and at other locations. From this time, the jasper was used for decoration all over Italy, and was among the stones used in the pietre dure workshops in Florence *(see pages 248–49)*. In the 18th century it became fashionable to have panels of Sicilian jasper inset into carved white marble chimneypieces. The jaspers were also made into vases, knife handles *(shown right)* and other small decorative items. Today, commercial quarrying no longer takes place, but loose boulders can still be found.

GEOLOGICAL DESCRIPTION

Silicified bands and nodules in limestones. The silica may have been derived from radiolaria microfossils, from solutions associated with nearby igneous activity, or both. Brecciation, which increases toward the center of nodules, was most probably caused by shrinkage of the original mass. Cracks are resealed by quartz and chalcedony. Veinlets of yellow calcite are sometimes seen, and the relics of fossils, especially foraminifera, are not uncommon. The structures of some banded jaspers from Giuliana suggest they may have once been algal mats.

MAJOR USAGE

Architectural uses, fireplaces, ornaments, pietre dure work.

Diaspro di Barga

SOURCE: Barga, Tuscany, Italy
STATUS: No longer quarried

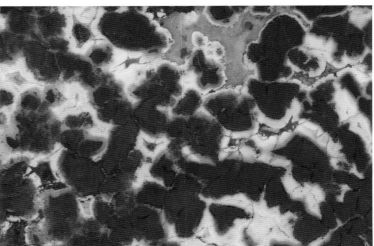

Visitors to the famous Chapel of the Princes in the Basilica of San Lorenzo in Florence may notice a rather striking blood-red and white jasper used to ornament the walls and paving.

Closer examination shows that it is a breccia of red jasper fragments, each one with a rim of pure white or pink, cemented by colorless quartz. The basilica was the parish church of the Medici family, and the Cappella dei Principi (Chapel of the Princes) is where the Grand Dukes of Tuscany are buried. It is famous for its superb pietre dure decoration.

According to geologist William Jervis, this jasper has no internal cavities or other imperfections, and takes a perfect polish. It was quarried at Giuncheto, a short distance east of the pretty hilltop town of Barga in Tuscany, but when Jervis described the stone in 1889, he noted that it had not been worked for some time because of the expense of quarrying and transportation.

Diaspro di Barga is seen in many other examples of Florentine pietre dure work, and the Opificio di Pietre Dure in Florence still has good stocks of this attractive stone. It is also used in the decoration of churches in Barga, and it can be seen in mosaics in the gardens of the 17th-century Villa Biondi near the town. In Rome, the columns in the Borghese Chapel in the church of Santa Maria Maggiore are, according to Corsi, veneered with this stone.

GEOLOGICAL DESCRIPTION
Breccia of blood-red to dark brownish red jasper fragments with an initial cementing of pink or white chalcedony, the remaining cavities entirely filled with colorless quartz.

MAJOR USAGE
Pietre dure work, veneers and mosaics.

When Grand Duke Ferdinando I de' Medici established the Opificio delle Pietre Dure in Florence in 1588, he endowed an enterprise that was to produce some of the most exquisite of all artisanry in stone—the Florentine pietre dure mosaic. The quality and artistry continue to this day with the same materials and techniques still being used.

Pictures and patterns are made from thin slices of jasper, petrified wood, porphyry, serpentinite, *lapis lazuli* and other pietre dure (hard stones, usually measuring 6 to 7 on Mohs' scale; see page 29). The local Alberese limestone and some traditional marbles are also employed. Each tiny section of stone is sawn very precisely using wire charged with abrasive powder. In intarsia, the pieces are fitted together and set into a visible backing stone, typically *paragona di Fiandra (Belgian black marble)*. In commesso the backing stone, usually slate, is completely obscured. The pieces are held in place with a warm cement made of resin and beeswax, and the surface is leveled and polished. A simple design may take weeks to complete, while more complex designs can take months, even years.

Before the Florentine workshops were established, most inlay workers plied their trade in Rome. Here, the preferred backing stone for intarsia was white *Carrara marble*, and the inlays were generally "soft" stones—marbles, alabasters and limestones, derived from ancient ruins in the city. Large tables with ornate geometric designs were commissioned by wealthy patrons, and patterns often incorporated family heraldry and symbolic emblems.

Both Florentine and Roman inlay work found a ready market among the wealthy young travelers doing the Grand Tour in the 18th and early 19th centuries. No doubt they included the Dukes of Devonshire, who commissioned their local craftsmen to create similar inlays in *Ashford black marble*. Designs were of randomly shaped pieces, regular geometric patterns or naturalistic pictures—flowers, butterflies and birds—very like those of Florentine work. At first, mostly local stones were used: *Blue John* fluorite, "alabasters," brown *rosewood marble* and *oakstone* barite, *duke's red marble* and fossil limestones. Slag glass gave a pale blue inlay, mother of pearl came from seashells, leaves were of Russian malachite or *Connemara marble*, and slender plant stems were made with a paste of marble dust, paint and gutta percha glue. European stones were introduced by the middle of the 19th century and included marbles from Siena and Carrara,

and the same greenish brown Alberese limestone from the Arno Valley near Florence that was used for leaves and stems in the Florentine work. All manner of decorative pieces from tabletops and cabinets to candlesticks, vases, paperweights and jewelry, were produced in an industry that lasted into the 1950s.

Prague, Paris, Madrid and Naples are among the other cities that had thriving centers for inlay work modeled on the pietre dure workshops of Florence, and the technique was not restricted to Europe. In India, early examples of intarsia using mother of pearl and semiprecious stones in a ground of white marble can be seen in the decoration of the Taj Mahal in Agra or the Red Fort in Delhi. Some of the most original and exciting inlay work today is produced in the United States. The range of stones now includes modern decorative minerals such as landscape jasper, sugilite, charoite and rhodochrosite, as well as *lapis lazuli*, malachite and other traditional materials. The American Masters of Stone website showcases some of the finest modern inlay work and explains how it is made.

Egyptian jasper

SOURCE: Eastern Desert, Egypt
STATUS: Not worked commercially

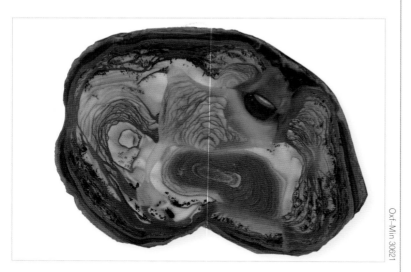

Oxf–Min 30621

Pebbles, so it seems, were a favorite souvenir for 19th-century tourists to Egypt, and many thousands of Egyptian jasper pebbles ended up in museum and private mineral collections.

These wind-eroded nodules of Egyptian jasper were found abundantly on the stonier parts of the Eastern Desert from Cairo to the Red Sea. They are banded dark brown on the outside but paler on the inside, with attractive fractures, swirls and subtle gradations of color. Sometimes they have dark dendritic markings, like trees. The finest can resemble ruin marble or modern landscape jaspers and they are colored by a similar process. Iron oxides deposited on the floor of the desert by the wind are drawn into the stones by the little water that reaches the desert. Hairline internal fractures control how the iron oxides are distributed inside the stone.

Egyptian jaspers take an excellent polish, and they were used for brooches and other jewelry, and for snuff boxes and other decorative wares. They are very commonly found in older museum mineral and rock collections.

GEOLOGICAL DESCRIPTION
Wind-eroded cherty pebbles derived from Eocene limestones, colored by fracture-controlled goethite inclusions.

MAJOR USAGE
Jewelry and small decorative items.

Landscape jasper

SOURCE: Oregon and Idaho, United States
STATUS: Commercially available

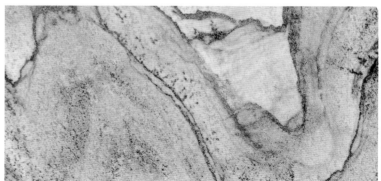

Oxf–Min 30089

Back in 1964 (so the story goes) a road repair crew, marooned by severe flooding, was quick to spot the decorative potential of boulders of rock that had been washed out from under a bridge at Biggs Canyon, Oregon.

Repairs to the highway revealed more of the remarkable stone that was to become known as *Biggs landscape jasper*, or *"picture jasper."* Word soon spread, and from then onward the stone has been avidly collected and worked by North American rock hounds.

Landscape jaspers, like the landscape marbles (see pages 100–101), are marked with yellow, brown and black oxides of iron and manganese, in patterns that resemble buildings, skies, fields and trees. Although they are composed mainly of quartz rather than calcareous siltstone, the way in which the patterns form is very similar. Compared to their calcareous counterparts, they are very much harder and take a beautiful polish.

The landscape jaspers of Oregon and Idaho were first used by Native North Americans to make tools, but their use for decorative purposes has mainly been in the last 50 years. They include the heavily patterned but now rare *Deschutes jasper* from the Deschutes River and the lightly swirled *Bruneau jasper* from Bruneau Canyon, both in Oregon. In Idaho, the *Owyhee* and *Wildhorse jaspers* and the pastel green *Willow Creek jasper* are exquisitely marked.

GEOLOGICAL DESCRIPTION
Clays and mudstones silicified by fluids emanating from lava flows. They show flow-banding, dendrites and fracture-controlled inclusions of iron and manganese oxides.

MAJOR USAGE
Carving, inlay work, jewelry.

Leopardskin jasper

SOURCE: United States, Mexico and India
STATUS: Actively quarried

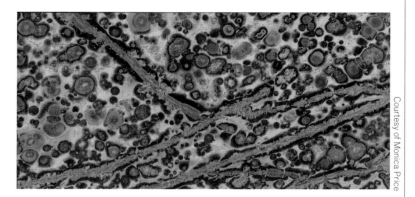

Courtesy of Monica Price

Just like the wild cat after which it is named, the typical appearance of this attractive stone is pale buff with darker brown spots and rings.

The color of *leopardskin jasper* can vary: sometimes the stone has more red, pink, yellow or green coloration. Small pieces may be entirely spotted, but larger slices show streaks and strings of spots joined together.

Leopardskin jasper is actually a rhyolite, a volcanic rock that is very rich in silica. As it cools, the silica segregates out into spherules, giving this stone its distinctive appearance. Later alteration can convert it almost entirely to fine-grained quartz, so both names, *leopardskin jasper* and *leopardskin rhyolite*, can be used. It is mined as a decorative stone at locations in California and Aguascalientes in Mexico, as well as in India and other places around the world.

GEOLOGICAL DESCRIPTION
Silicified rhyolite.

MAJOR USAGE
Spheres, eggs, obelisks, cabochons, small decorative items and jewelry.

Ocean jasper

SOURCE: Madagascar
STATUS: Commercially available

Courtesy of Monica Price

Ocean jasper is a particularly apt name for this beautiful stone because it first came from a beach outcrop that was only accessible at low tide.

Samples from Madagascar were known as long ago as the 1950s but details of the precise source were lost. In 1998, geologist Paul Obenich spent 45 days traveling the coast of Madagascar in search of the stone. He eventually located the deposit near the village of Marovato on the northwest coast of the island. He traced the deposit back from the beach and it is now mined from a tunnel in the cliff. Because there are no roads, the stone is transported for cutting and polishing by boat.

Without doubt this is one of the most attractive of the decorative jaspers to reach a worldwide market in recent decades. It is often referred to as orbicular jasper because it has a pattern of concentric circles in different colors—green, white, brown, pink and yellow. Cavities are very common and are lined with minute sparkling colorless quartz crystals. *Ocean jasper* is cut into spheres, eggs, obelisks and into decorative items such as dishes and coasters.

GEOLOGICAL DESCRIPTION
A silicified rhyolite deposit colored by trace iron silicate minerals.

MAJOR USAGE
Spheres, eggs, obelisks, cabochons and small decorative items.

Tiger's eye, hawk's eye, tiger iron

SOURCE: Northern Cape Province, South Africa, and Western Australia
STATUS: Actively quarried

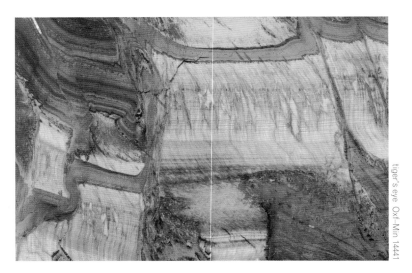

tiger's eye Oxf-Min 14441

Hawk's eye Oxf-Min 20532

An attractive play of light across the parallel fibers in these stones is known as "chatoyancy" from the French words for cat's eye. It is strikingly evident when the stone is polished.

Hawk's eye is dark grayish blue; tiger's eye is yellow and brown. Sometimes bands of both occur in the same stone or grade into one another. Quite early in the 19th century it was discovered that tiger's eye and hawk's eye are composed almost entirely of quartz. They are colored by a little crocidolite (blue asbestos), which in tiger's eye has partly altered to iron oxides.

Since the 1880s, very large quantities of tiger's eye, and lesser amounts of hawk's eye, have come from the Griquatown and Niekerkshoop areas of Northern Cape Province, South Africa. Much smaller amounts have also come from India, Australia, the United States and elsewhere. Tiger's eye was hugely popular in the 1960s and 1970s, becoming a very cheap and common semiprecious gem. Pale gray, red, green and other colors sometimes seen on the commercial market are the result of bleaching, artificial dyeing or heat-treatment. A rare and highly prized exception is known as Marra Mamba tiger's eye. It came from near Mount Brockman in the Hamersley Ranges of Western Australia and is a naturally occuring mixture of reds, blues, yellows and greens.

A more recent introduction is the stone known as tiger iron. It consists of bands of tiger's eye and hematite, sometimes with red jasper. Tiger iron comes from the Ord Ranges near Port Hedland in Western Australia.

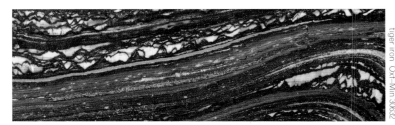

tiger iron Oxf-Min 30632

GEOLOGICAL DESCRIPTION

Veins composed of quartz intergrown with riebeckite asbestos (crocidolite) formed in quartz-rich schists of Precambrian age. These stones are often cited as classic examples of "pseudomorphism," in which one mineral—a densely fibrous vein of crocidolite—has been replaced by another—quartz—without altering the original crystal shape. Recent research has shown that the two minerals most probably formed at the same time, and that the chatoyancy is due to the presence of the asbestos crystals. In tiger's eye, the crocidolite is partially altered to hematite and goethite. Tiger iron is a banded ironstone composed of tiger's eye, hematite and jasper. It formed in Precambrian times as stromatolites, sedimentary structures built up by algal activity.

MAJOR USAGE

A very common decorative stone used for carvings, many different decorative items, jewelry, inlay work; occasionally tabletops and panels in architectural features.

QUARTZ AND OPAL

252

Silicified wood

SOURCE: Arizona, United States, and elsewhere
STATUS: Commercially available

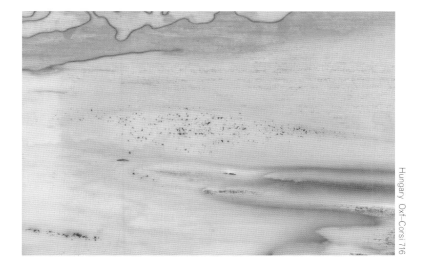

Hungary Oxf-Corsi 716

Arizona Oxf-Min 27659

Appearances can be deceptive: if wood is replaced by silica without disturbing its internal cellular structure, then the wood grain is preserved and it still looks like wood. But pick it up, and it is surprisingly hard and heavy.

The fine structure of petrified wood may be preserved so well that it is possible to say what the tree was. Most fossil wood preserved in this way was buried by volcanic ash. The ash prevents the wood decaying, and provides a rich source of silica in solution that filters through the wood, infilling cavities in its structure.

Much of the polished petrified wood sold today comes from Arizona. In late Triassic times, this was an area of swamp where huge conifer trees grew. First, flash floods toppled the trees and buried them in sediment. Then eruptions of volcanoes to the west added thick coatings of ash. The combination of rapid burial and a rich source of silica ensured excellent preservation of the wood. The petrified forest was first discovered around 1851, and from the 1870s onward, the stone was extensively exploited for making tourist souvenirs. Now, large areas are protected as part of the Petrified Forest National Park.

Silicified wood comes from many other places in the United States and around the world, notably the huge Bosques Petrificados National Monument in Argentina. A pale-colored silicified wood often used for inlay work in Europe in past centuries is said to be from Hungary.

GEOLOGICAL DESCRIPTION

Fossil wood infilled and replaced by chalcedony or opal, retaining the cellular structure of the wood. It may be colored by iron, manganese and copper minerals, and agate banding is sometimes clearly visible.

MAJOR USAGE

Sculpture, tabletops, coasters and other decorative items; inlay work.

LEFT The Petrified Forest in Arizona is littered with blocks of sicilified wood.

Precious opal

SOURCE: Červenica, Slovakia and Australia
STATUS: No longer mined in Slovakia; actively mined and quarried in Australia

Hungary Oxf-Min 1147

Australia Oxf-Min 30619

Glinting spectral colors as it catches the light, opal is rare and exquisitely beautiful. No wonder it is considered the most precious of all the varieties of silica.

Although the Native North Americans had long worked beautiful opal from Honduras and Mexico, the ancient Romans were the first Europeans to delight in this stone, obtaining it from the Slanské vrchy mountains—the most important source of this gem up to the end of the 19th century. Opal infills pores, cavities and joints in volcanic rocks near the village of Červenica. Although now in Slovakia, in its heyday of production, Červenica was in Hungary, which is why the stone is still referred to as Hungarian opal. It was extracted from surface workings until 1788, when the first underground mines were opened at Dubník and then nearby Libanka. Nuggets of pure opal were cut for jewelry. Slices of rock were polished so that the opal flashed from all the cavities and gaps. This was used for inlay work in snuff boxes, jewelry boxes and other expensive trinkets. Later in the 19th century, mining became sporadic as demand declined, ceasing completely in 1922. The reason for this lay on the other side of the world.

In Australia in the 1880s, miners searching for gold in the inhospitable outback of New South Wales found instead superb, colorful opal. More precious opal was discovered in Queensland and South Australia, and before long, new mining communities grew up. Australian precious opal is hosted in sedimentary rocks and is used mostly in jewelry. Boulder opal, in which the opal is still encased in rock matrix, is also used for small sculptures.

GEOLOGICAL DESCRIPTION

In Hungarian opal, precious opal fills cavities in Neogene andesite lava. Australian opal is hosted in Cretaceous sandstones and limestones. Opal is composed of silica and water and never forms crystals. Most opal is dull colored and looks waxy; flashes of color are only seen in precious opal. Here the silica forms neat stacks of microscopic spherules. They act like a diffraction grating, splitting white light into its spectral colors.

MAJOR USAGE

Decorative trinkets and jewelry.

Other varieties of quartz and opal

Mtorolite is a bright green chromium-bearing chalcedony, sometimes mottled white. It was discovered in chromiferous serpentinite near Mtoroshanga in Zimbabwe around 1955.

There are innumerable different agates (banded chalcedony) named after the place they are collected, and rarely of distinctive appearance. *Thunder eggs* come from several states of the United States and other places around the world. They form as spherules in silica-rich volcanic rocks, and each has a sharply angular core filled with agate. The best are sawn and polished, and are occasionally worked into decorative objects.

Of the many named varieties of jasper (another type of fine-grained quartz), *poppy jasper* from California has round splashes of brilliant red. Much Russian "jasper" from the Urals is banded green, and is silicified clay.

Besides wood, other silicified fossils can be very decorative. Sponges and corals come from locations as diverse as Hillsborough Bay, Florida, and Brighton beach in England. The well-known but misnamed *turritella agate* from Wyoming is teeming with elongate gastropods preserved in chalcedony, not *Turritella* as first thought, but the freshwater snail called *Elimia* or *Goniobasis*.

Other decorative minerals

Eye-catching in the extreme, most of the decorative minerals in this section are brightly colored or beautifully marked. They are rarely found in large quantities, which means they have little use in architecture. Instead, they are sculpted, turned into decorative items such as vases, boxes and paperweights, and used for inlay work and jewelry. These can be wonderfully ostentatious stones, and some of the finest examples are seen in churches, palaces, castles and stately homes. Visit, for instance, the State Hermitage in St. Petersburg, the art museum founded by Catherine the Great in 1764, and you cannot but admire the rich use of malachite, rhodonite, *lapis lazuli* and other semiprecious stones, and the remarkable artisanry of the Russian stoneworkers. In geological terms, some of these stones are composed of a single mineral such as malachite or fluorite. Others are made up of a mixture of minerals of which one features particularly prominently—eudialyte, charoite and sodalite are examples.

Jadeite jade

SOURCE: Myanmar (Burma), Guatemala
STATUS: Commercially available

Imperial jade Oxf-Min 13412

Oxf-Min 3207

When Hurricane Mitch tore open the Guatemalan landscape in 1998, it unlocked the long lost source of blue-green jade, a stone valued by ancient American civilizations more highly than gold.

The name "jade" has always been given to ornamental varieties of the different minerals jadeite and actinolite-tremolite. Jadeite is the rarer and more precious. It had been worked into weapons and ornaments by the Olmecs, Maya and other ancient civilizations of Mexico, Central America and the Caribbean since at least 1200–1000 BCE. They prized jade more highly than gold, but this value was not shared by the Spanish conquistadors, and over time, the location of the mines was forgotten. It was not until the 1950s that the ancient mines were rediscovered in the Motagua Valley of Guatemala. The source of the blue-green jadeite most prized by the Olmecs remained elusive until landslides caused by Hurricane Mitch in 1998 revealed huge veins of the stone.

A second important source of jadeite is in Asia. Much of the world's supply has come from Tawmaw, Hpakan and other localities in the Uru River area of Myanmar (formerly Burma). Boulders carried downstream by the river have been a rich and accessible source of the stone. Jadeite was introduced into China in the late 1700s and during the following century, surpassed the traditional nephrite jade as the most popular carving material. Artifacts made in China soon reached Europe. Commercial extraction of jadeite takes place today in both Myanmar and Guatemala.

Jadeite can be blue-green, green, white and lilac, but yellow to brown "rinds" form where the outer parts of boulders have weathered. Imperial jade is vivid green, and is particularly sought after. Jadeite is very slightly harder than nephrite; a little more dense and also more brittle.

GEOLOGICAL DESCRIPTION

Fine-grained jadeite is a pyroxene mineral formed by high-pressure-with-low-temperature metamorphic processes. Veins and masses composed almost entirely of jadeite are hosted in serpentinites and are found in very few places worldwide. Imperial jade is colored by trace chromium. Jadeite has a hardness of 6 to 7 on Mohs' scale (see page 29).

MAJOR USAGE

Ancient weapons; ornaments, carvings and jewelry.

RIGHT This headdress ornament with the head of the Jester God, Late Classic, 550–800, is made out of jadeite jade, from Guatemala.

OTHER DECORATIVE MINERALS

Nephrite jade

SOURCE: China, New Zealand, Canada, Australia
STATUS: Commercially available

Nephrite jade is tough stuff. It has a compact structure of interlocking fibers, and this makes it exceptionally durable but also ideal for carving intricate detail.

Nephrite jade is more common and less valuable than jadeite. It can be all shades of green from off-white to virtually black, but weathered surfaces are brown. Nephrite was regarded as a royal gemstone in China where it has been highly prized since at least 7000 BCE. Boulders from rivers draining the Kunlun Shan in Xinjiang Province are among the earliest sources. Despite the difficulty working such a tough material, it was carved first into ceremonial objects and weapons, and then into personal ornaments and more utilitarian items. Artifacts were traded across Asia and into Europe.

For many centuries, the New Zealand Maoris have made weapons, "hei-tikis" (pendants) and other ornaments from nephrite pebbles found on South Island, and this stone continues to be used for sculpture and tourist souvenirs. Large quantities of nephrite jade have been obtained from Cowell in South Australia since the mid-1970s, and from Polar Mountain and elsewhere in northern British Columbia, Canada, since the 1990s.

GEOLOGICAL DESCRIPTION

A fine-grained compact variety of an amphibole mineral in the actinolite-tremolite series. It is typically found as pods and veins in altered dolomitic marbles and serpentinites.

MAJOR USAGE

Ancient weapons, ornaments, carvings and jewelry.

Bowenite

SOURCE: Rhode Island, United States; South Island, New Zealand; and elsewhere
STATUS: Actively quarried

Bowenite is often called *new jade,* but this is more than misleading because it isn't new, and it is not a true jade.

An attractive green stone, bowenite was first discovered in dolomitic limestones in Dexter quarry, Lincoln, Rhode Island, by George T. Bowen in 1822—hence the name. He thought it was nephrite jade. About 30 years later it was analyzed and found to be a translucent compact form of antigorite, a serpentine mineral. It is pale to dark green or greenish yellow, and although resembling jade, it is very much softer and less durable. Despite this, it is an attractive semiprecious stone that carves well and is used to simulate jade.

Since 1966, bowenite has been the state mineral of Rhode Island. It comes from Conklin and other quarries in the Lincoln area, but has also been discovered elsewhere in the United States and in other countries. Bowenite from South Island, New Zealand, is also called *tangiwai*, the Maori word for tears. Other sources—and misnomers—are Korea (*Korean jade*), China (*Suzhou jade*) and Afghanistan.

GEOLOGICAL DESCRIPTION

Translucent compact fine-grained antigorite, a serpentine mineral. It occurs as nodules and thin beds in impure dolomitic marbles, formed by alteration of magnesium silicate minerals in the marble. It is softer than nephrite jade at 2.5 to 3.5 on Mohs' scale.

MAJOR USAGE

Used as a jade simulant in carvings, decorative items and jewelry.

Malachite

SOURCE: Ural Mountains, Russia; Katanga, Democratic Republic of Congo

STATUS: Commercially available

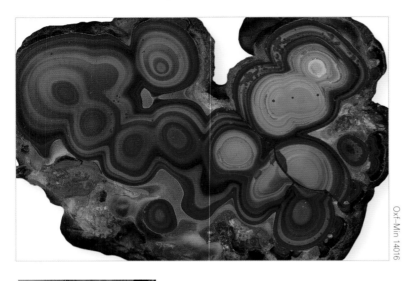

Oxf-Min 14016

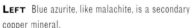

LEFT Blue azurite, like malachite, is a secondary copper mineral.
BELOW Part of the superb Malachite Room in the State Hermitage, St. Petersburg, Russia.

Bright green malachite is a very common mineral and is found all over the world, but very rarely does it form huge masses like the ones that once came from copper mines in Russia.

Malachite is always green, and when layers of needlelike crystals are packed tightly together, it appears banded with a velvety luster. Only a few locations yield masses large enough for use as an ornamental stone. Commercial working of malachite from Gumeshevsk and other copper mines of the central Ural Mountains in Russia began in earnest in the early 18th century, at first for jewelry and pigments, but as production increased, for larger decorative items and opulent architectural claddings. An exceptionally large block discovered at Mednorudyansk in 1836 was used to clad two huge columns in St. Isaac's Cathedral. The "leftovers" were then applied to pillars, mantelpieces and decorative vases in the famous Malachite Room of the State Hermitage, the czars' winter palace in St. Petersburg (you can take a virtual tour using their website). A technique known as "Russian mosaic" was developed, in which the malachite was sawn into wafer-thin slivers less than ⅛ inch (4 mm) thick and glued onto a slate or cast iron substrate. The glue was mixed with powdered malachite so it could not be easily seen. By continuing the pattern of banding across many pieces, the skilled artisans could create the impression of a single solid block of malachite.

Commercial working of malachite all but ceased in the Urals by the end of the 1870s. Arizona in the United States and Burra in South Australia have both supplied malachite for decorative purposes, but it is Katanga in the copper belt of the Democratic Republic of Congo that has been the richest source of malachite in recent years. Carvings, boxes, ornaments and jewelry are all exported worldwide.

Malachite is a copper carbonate mineral and will fizz if tested with dilute hydrochloric acid. Chrysocolla (see opposite) and azurite, another copper carbonate, are sometimes found with malachite. Azurite is bright to dark blue in color, but its association with malachite makes it easy to distinguish from lazurite (in *lapis lazuli*) and sodalite.

GEOLOGICAL DESCRIPTION

Concentric or straight-banded malachite, a copper secondary mineral that typically forms where copper deposits have weathered often within a limestone host rock. It is relatively soft, just 3.5 to 4 on Mohs' scale.

MAJOR USAGE

Sculpture, decorative items, inlay work and jewelry.

Chrysocolla

SOURCE: Arizona, United States, and southern Peru
STATUS: Commercially available

Courtesy of Monica Price

On its own this vibrantly colored mineral is far too soft for cutting and polishing, but when mixed with fine-grained quartz, it becomes a hard and wonderfully attractive semiprecious stone for lapidarists to shape and polish.

Chrysocolla is a relative newcomer among decorative stones in Europe, but it has a longer history of use in Native North American jewelry. It is a rather soft mineral that varies from bright green to greenish blue. On its own, it makes a poor decorative stone but it can also occur in small quantities in chalcedony (very fine-grained quartz) forming a hard rock that takes a beautiful polish. It is this that lapidarists refer to as "chrysocolla."

This mineral is never found in large pieces, and poorer quality stone often has many cavities patched with a dyed filler. Much chrysocolla is streaked with malachite, azurite and other copper minerals. *Eilat stone*, formerly obtained from copper mines north of Eilat in Israel, is a well known example. Today most chrysocolla-bearing decorative stones come from the copper mining districts of Arizona, and from the Acari mine, Arequipa Department and elsewhere in southern Peru, but they also occur in Mexico, the Democratic Republic of Congo and other locations around the world.

GEOLOGICAL DESCRIPTION

Crusts and compact fine-grained masses of chrysocolla, a copper secondary mineral formed by the weathering of copper deposits. Stone for cutting and carving is a natural mixture of chrysocolla and chalcedony, the very fine-grained variety of quartz.

MAJOR USAGE

Small carvings, inlay work and jewelry.

Turquoise

SOURCE: Neyshabur, Iran; southwest United States; elsewhere
STATUS: Commercially available

Oxf-Min 24644

Buyers beware! Much of the "turquoise" for sale is not the famous gem mineral loved by people across many cultures and eras.

Few ornamental stones have such a long history of use as turquoise. As far back as 3000 BCE, the ancient Egyptians made beads, scarabs and jewelry from turquoise that they mined at Serabit el-Khadem and other sites on the Sinai Peninsula. Turquoise is notable in inlay work in the burial mask of Tutankhamen. The mines near Neyshabur in Iran, still working today, have yielded arguably the finest quality turquoise for the last 2,000 years. From 200 BCE Native North Americans worked the turquoise deposits of New Mexico's Cerrillos Hills and later in California, Nevada, Arizona and Colorado. In fact most of the world's deposits lie in the southwestern United States. Turquoise has also come from Tibet, and was known to the Chinese in ancient times.

The stone is rather porous and ranges in color from light green to sky blue, although it is common for people to say "turquoise blue" to describe a certain shade of blue-green. Simulants are common and range from plastics and epoxy resins to dyed white minerals such as magnesite and howlite. Genuine turquoise is often impregnated with wax or resin to enhance its color and improve its hardness. Stones with spidery veins of brown matrix are often preferred because they looks more "natural."

GEOLOGICAL DESCRIPTION

Fine-grained compact turquoise is a copper and aluminum secondary mineral found as cavity and vein infills in aluminum-rich rocks that are altered by surface water containing dissolved copper. The stone is moderately hard, at 5 to 6 on Mohs' scale.

MAJOR USAGE

Jewelry, mosaics and small carvings.

Amazonite

SOURCE: Ilmen Mountains and Kola Peninsula, Russia; and Colorado, United States

STATUS: Commercially available

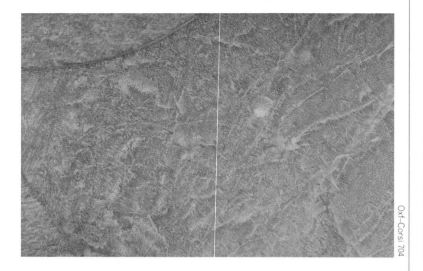

The early scientist who coined the name "amazon stone" must have been having a flight of imagination because it was never found anywhere near the Amazon River. Today, as in the past, it comes mainly from Russia.

Amazon stone is now usually called amazonite. It is the bluish green variety of a feldspar called microcline, and it is commonly streaked or flecked with white. It is rather opaque. Amazonite is a mineral found in many locations worldwide and it was used as a decorative stone by the ancient Egyptians and by early Native North Americans. During the 18th century, a major deposit was discovered in the Ilmen range of the southern Ural Mountains in Russia. This site supplied most of the amazonite used for decorative purposes until the discovery in 1876 of a rich amazonite pegmatite (igneous rock with unusually large crystals) in the Rocky Mountains of Colorado. Today, the principal source of amazonite is again in Russia, the western Keivy ridge on the Kola Peninsula. Stone suitable for cutting and polishing also comes from as far afield as Madagascar and Brazil.

GEOLOGICAL DESCRIPTION

Green microcline feldspar formed in granitic pegmatites. The green coloration is due to trace lead, and white flecks are lamellar crystal inclusions of albite feldspar. At 6 to 6.5 on Mohs' scale, it is quite a hard mineral.

MAJOR USAGE

Inlay work, vases, decorative items and jewelry.

Larimar

SOURCE: Barahona Province, Dominican Republic

STATUS: Actively mined

Polished by the Caribbean Sea, this beautiful, pale blue mineral was often encountered on beaches of the Dominican Republic. It came to be known as *larimar*.

Those beaches were in Barahona Province, near the mouth of the Bahoruco River, and in 1974, the source of the stone was located upstream in volcanic rocks near the village of Los Checheses. The discovery was not entirely new. In 1916, a local priest had opened a mine there and petitioned for rights to exploit the stone, but did not proceed for reasons lost in history. This time, the Los Chuperados mines opened successfully and now form a mass of holes and underground passages. Mining methods are primitive and the mines get ever deeper and more dangerous as miners track the altered lavas that host *larimar*.

The stone was discovered by Miguel Méndez and named after his daughter Larissa, and "mar," the Spanish for sea. It is a blue or bluish green variety of pectolite, and forms as spherules, aggregates of close-packed radiating needlelike crystals.

GEOLOGICAL DESCRIPTION

Larimar is compact fine-grained pectolite, a secondary silicate mineral infilling burned trees and other cavities in serpentinized basaltic and andesitic lavas. It is colored by trace copper, and occurs with disseminated red cuprite and green malachite. A moderately hard mineral, 5 to 7 on Mohs' scale, larimar is dissolved by hydrochloric acid and should not be acid tested.

MAJOR USAGE

Mainly used for jewelry but sometimes worked in carvings and inlays. There are some reports that the color fades on exposure to strong sunlight.

Sodalite

SOURCE: Bancroft, Ontario, Canada
STATUS: Intermittently mined

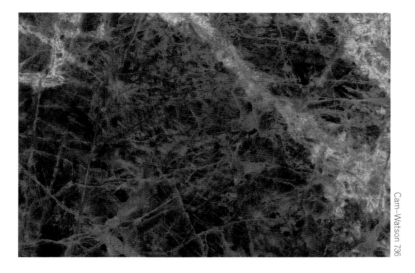

Cam-Watson 736

The sodalite, or *princess blue*, from Ontario has important royal connections. It owes much of its huge commercial success to a century-old commission by British royalty.

Sodalite is usually a rather inconspicuous mineral, but a few places around the world have rich sodalite deposits of a deep blue color. The first and most famous of these is the Princess mine near Bancroft in Ontario. Both the mine and the stone are named after Princess May of Teck, who as Duchess of Cornwall, visited Canada with her husband in 1901. They were presented with a collection of Canadian minerals including a polished sample of the blue sodalite. The Duchess admired this stone so much she asked for it to be shipped to England to decorate Marlborough House (her home in London). May went on to become Princess of Wales, and in 1910 Queen Mary, married to King George V. This royal patronage, together with an order for sodalite to decorate Brook House in London's Park Lane, the home of Sir Ernest Cassel, led to the opening of quarries for commercial working in 1906. *Princess blue* is inlaid in the floor of the Royal Ontario Museum and in the floor of St. George's Chapel, Westminster Cathedral, London. The stone has been extracted intermittently up to the present day.

Other blue sodalite rocks quarried today for architectural purposes include *sodalite blue* from Cerro Sapo, Cochabamba Department, Bolivia; *Bahia blue* from Bahia, Brazil; and *African blue* from Swartbooisdrift, Namibia. Commercially, they are classed as granites, but they are not so durable or versatile as true granites. The best quality stone, as used for smaller decorative items, can closely resemble *princess blue*.

Sodalite should not be confused with lazurite, the main blue mineral of *lapis lazuli* (see pages 262–3). Sodalite is a different, darker shade of blue, and when powdered, is colored white.

Furthermore, grains of metallic yellow pyrite commonly seen in *lapis lazuli* are never seen in blue sodalite.

GEOLOGICAL DESCRIPTION

Princess blue is sodalite, commonly veined with pink or white natrolite, and mottled black by magnetite. It forms veins and masses up to 4 feet (1.2 m) across in an altered nepheline syenite intrusion. *Bahia blue* is found in nepheline sodalite syenite. *Sodalite blue* and *African blue* both occur in carbonatites, igneous veins and dikes rich in carbonate minerals.

MAJOR USAGE

Sculpture, decorative items and jewelry. *Sodalite blue* and *Bahia blue* are used for interior architectural claddings.

LEFT AND BELOW *Princess blue* from Canada and *brèche de Kleber* from Algeria in the floor of the Chapel of the Holy Souls in Westminster Cathedral, London.

Lapis lazuli

SOURCE: Badakhshan, Afghanistan
STATUS: Actively mined

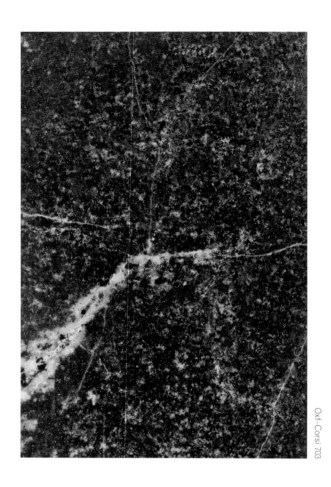

With its sparkling metallic gold "stars" set in a deep blue "sky," it is not hard to see how the precious stone known as *lapis lazuli* has captured our imagination for over 6,000 years.

A vivid blue mineral called lazurite is the main constituent of the rock called *lapis lazuli*. Sometimes it is streaked or speckled with white calcite and almost always with metallic gold pyrite— the stars in the blue night sky. It is without question a beautiful stone and was recognized as such in antiquity. The name *lapis lazuli* was first used in medieval times and comes from the Latin for stone, and "lazhward," the old Persian word for this stone and for the color blue. The ancient Persians were the first to crush and use it to make the brilliant blue pigment ultramarine.

For at least 6,500 years, *lapis lazuli* has been quarried from the remote Kokcha Valley in Badakhshan. Badakhshan was at a crossroads of European, Asian and Middle Eastern civilizations. Trade routes in ancient times passed through the Kokcha Valley, carrying *lapis lazuli* to China, where it was highly esteemed as a carving material, to the Harappan people of India, and to Pakistan and central Asia, where beads and other artifacts have been found in neolithic burials. *Lapis lazuli* was transported south and west to supply the ancient Egyptian and Mesopotamian civilizations, and later, those of the Greeks and Romans. The Roman scholar Pliny (23–79 CE) called it "sapphirus," saying it was " ... refulgent with spots like gold. It is also of an azure color, though sometimes, but rarely, it is purple."

Venetian explorer Marco Polo described the mines in 1271, but he did not visit them. *Lapis lazuli* in 18th- and 19th-century geological collections is often stated to be from Persia because the actual source was so little known; the stone merely traded in Iran. The first detailed survey of the mines, in the area of Sar-e-Sang on the east bank of the Kokcha River, was carried out by Russian geologists in the late 1960s. The district remains relatively inaccessible and politically volatile. The mines are reached only by a combination of truck, horseback and walking.

The deposits of Afghanistan are still the finest and most important in the world, but in the late 18th and 19th centuries, *lapis lazuli* was also obtained from banks of the Slyudyanka and Malaya Bystraya rivers, south of Lake Baikal in Russia. Both

Oxf-Corsi 703

BELOW Tortoises and frogs in a modern *lapis lazuli* sculpture.

OPPOSITE ABOVE A *lapis lazuli* mine high in the mountains of Badakhshan Province in Afghanistan.

OPPOSITE BELOW The rich blues of *lapis lazuli* are clearly evident in the columns and panels of the altar of St. Ignatius in the Church of Gesu, Rome.

Russian and Afghan stone have been used for decoration in St. Petersburg. Larger items such as the huge vases in the State Hermitage were made using the "Russian mosaic" technique (see page 258). Russian stone was also exported to Florence for pietre dure mosaics (see pages 248–49). Smaller deposits of *lapis lazuli* in Chile and the United States have also been worked on a commercial basis.

GEOLOGICAL DESCRIPTION

Metamorphic rock composed of blue lazurite and other feldspathoid minerals, with metallic yellow pyrite and white calcite. It is formed by contact metamorphism of limestones.

MAJOR USAGE

A wide variety of decorative uses, including inlay work and jewelry. Powdered *lapis lazuli* is bright blue and was the "ultramarine" pigment of early artists.

Labradorite

SOURCE: Canada, Finland and Madagascar
STATUS: Actively quarried

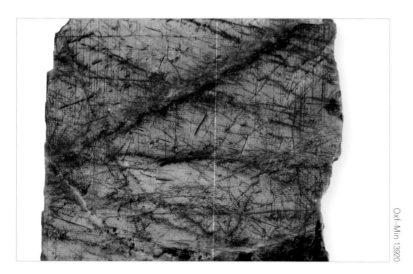

Oxf-Min 13920

Usually a dull gray mineral, labradorite magically transforms into vibrant blue, green, yellow or orange when turned in the light.

Labradorite is part of the plagioclase series of feldspars, and occurs in certain igneous rocks. After the molten rock cooled, each crystal of plagioclase started to separate out into microscopically thin layers alternately rich in calcium and sodium. Light reflecting from the different layers may be brightly colored, an interference effect very similar to that shown by a thin film of oil on water. This iridescence, sometimes termed "labradorescence," is highly decorative. Blue and green are most commonly seen; yellow, orange and red are more unusual.

Another characteristic of labradorite is plagioclase twinning. This is a feature of crystal growth visible as a series of slender, straight bands, alternately dark and light. It is often seen in plagioclase feldspars but never in the blue "labradorescent" anorthoclase (see opposite).

The first labradorite came from Paul Island on the Labrador coast of Canada in around 1770, hence the name. It was introduced by a Moravian missionary by the name of Mr. Wolfe. Since then, large quantities of iridescent stone have been obtained from the wider Nain district of Labrador. A new source was discovered during construction of fortifications in Ylämaa, southern Finland, in 1941 and since the 1980s it has been widely marketed as a gem mineral under the name *spectrolite*. Most ornamental labradorite sold today comes from quarries in Toliara Province, Madagascar. When this stone is particularly transparent it is often sold as *moonstone*.

GEOLOGICAL DESCRIPTION

Member of the plagioclase series of feldspars. Ornamental varieties occur in coarse-grained anorthosites (see page 226) and gabbroic rocks.

MAJOR USAGE

Inlay work and furniture, small decorative items and jewelry.

Labradorescent anorthoclase

SOURCE: Stavern and Ula, Vestfold, Norway
STATUS: No longer commercially available

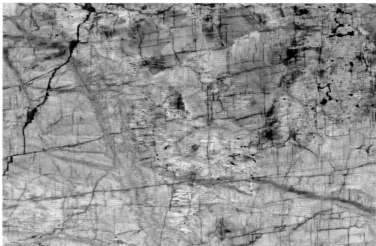

Oxf-Min 2285

It is surprising how often this beautiful stone, with its shimmering light-reflective properties, is mistaken for labradorite when encountered in inlay decoration.

Turn this dull gray mineral in the light and it shows a stunning clear light-blue or bluish green schiller, more rare and arguably more beautiful than that of labradorite.

The cause of the color is similar. Anorthoclase is a sodium-and-potassium-bearing feldspar. As it cooled, it separated out into microscopically thin layers alternately rich in the two elements. Feldspars that show compositional layering are called perthites, and when the layers are too thin to see with an optical microscope, they are known as cryptoperthites. Some cryptoperthites have a milky schiller and are known as *moonstone*. This stone, with its blue reflections, is quite different, more like labradorite, after which it is named.

Labradorescent anorthoclase comes from syenites and syenite pegmatites at Stavern, a port on the coast of Norway south of Oslo. From 1799 to 1930, Stavern was known as Fredriksvarn or Fredriksværn, and it was during this time that the local anorthoclase cryptoperthite was being used in decorative wares. That is why the locality is usually given as Stavern's old name. It was also discovered at Ula in the 1880s, now a protected site.

GEOLOGICAL DESCRIPTION
Anorthoclase cryptoperthite pegmatite from veins in an augite syenite (larvikite) intrusion.

MAJOR USAGE
Used in inlay work and tabletops.

ABOVE AND INSET
A 19th-century tabletop inlaid with labradorite. The smaller picture shows that the brilliant flashes of color (above) cannot be seen except when viewed at certain angles.

OTHER DECORATIVE MINERALS

Blue John

SOURCE: Castleton, Derbyshire, England
STATUS: Small quantities still being mined

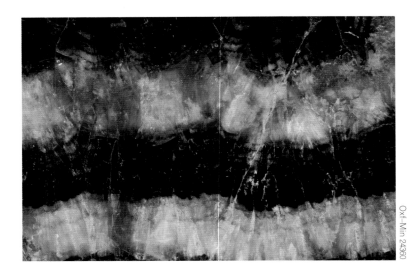

OxF-Min 24360

are purplish blue and colorless, white or iron-stained yellow. Unlike other banded fluorites, it is never green. As part of the manufacturing process, the stone is impregnated with resin to increase its strength, but still it is a remarkably fragile material and takes considerable care to work.

GEOLOGICAL DESCRIPTION

Color-banded fluorite deposited by hydrothermal processes, mainly lining or infilling ancient natural caverns in Carboniferous limestone. A rather soft mineral, it measures 4 on Mohs' scale.

MAJOR USAGE

Panels in fireplaces; vases, urns and ormolu ware; inlaid into *Ashford black marble* ware, and other decorative items; used as stained glass; jewelry today virtually its only use.

No one knows why centuries ago the elegant blue-banded fluorite from Castleton in the English Peak District was called *Blue John*. Today, items made out of this fragile mineral are highly collectible.

Mining of *Blue John* as an ornamental stone commenced sometime in the first half of the 18th century in natural caverns in Treak Cliff hill at Castleton. It is an area of Derbyshire well known as both a tourist spot and with a long tradition of lead and zinc mining. The industrialist Matthew Boulton had the stone brought to his famous Soho workshop in Birmingham and used it in ormolu (decorative metalware designed to look like gold). A mantelpiece set of candelabra, censers and a clock made for Queen Charlotte in 1770 is still in Windsor Castle. The famous architect and designer Robert Adam used *Blue John* for panels in some of his fireplaces, which can now be seen in stately homes. Many vases and examples of inlay work can also be seen in Kedleston Hall, Chatsworth House, Cavendish Museum in Castleton, Buxton Museum and Derby Museum, all in Derbyshire, England.

How the stone acquired its name is lost in history. It may be from the French, "bleu jaune," meaning blue-yellow. More probably, it is a traditional mining term, in the same way that zinc ore was called "black jack." As early as 1777, tourists were being given guided tours of the mines, and this tradition continues today at the Blue John and Treak Cliff caverns. Most of the land on which the mines are sited belongs to the National Trust, but small quantities of stone are still extracted, and used almost exclusively for making jewelry.

Blue John is a variety of fluorite that used to be known as *Derbyshire spar* (the same name as alabaster from Derbyshire). It is transparent or translucent, and has zigzag bands that

LEFT This vase of banded purple, yellow and white *Blue John* was made by Mr Vallance of Matlock around 1840. It is now in the Natural History Museum in London.

OTHER DECORATIVE MINERALS

Fluorite

SOURCE: China
STATUS: Actively quarried

Oxf–Min 29819

Common maybe, but undoubtedly colorful, fluorite is a mineral that can actually be many colors. It can even have several different colors in the same crystal.

If rows of multicolor crystals grow together to fill a cavity in the host rock, the result is a stone with bands of different colors. This can happen with fluorite

China is the principal source of the color-banded fluorite that has been used for jewelry and decorative items in the last 20 years. Much of it has come from the Deqing mine north of Mogan Mountain in Zhejiang Province. Despite the fragile nature of this mineral, it is worked into delicate thin-walled bowls and beautiful carvings. Purple, green, colorless and blue are the most common colors seen, and this stone is transparent or translucent. One of the best-known properties of fluorite is its ability to fluoresce, glowing violet-blue (or occasionally other colors) when bathed in ultraviolet light. This only happens when it contains a trace of a certain activator chemical element such as europium. As *Blue John* and most of the fluorite carved for decorative purposes do not contain the necessary activator, they do not show fluorescence.

GEOLOGICAL DESCRIPTION
Hydrothermal vein and cavity infills of color-zoned fluorite.

MAJOR USAGE
Carvings, bowls, vases and other decorative items; jewelry.

Charoite

SOURCE: Sakha (Yakutia), Russia
STATUS: Commercially available

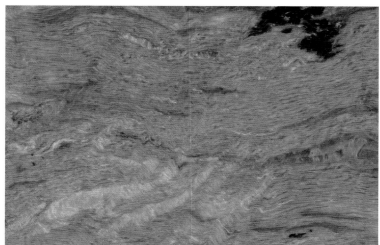

Oxf–Min 22819

In the late 1970s, a beautiful new purple decorative stone appeared in mineral shows in Europe and the United States. It was cut into gemstones and carved into vases, and remarkably it turned out to be a mineral new to science.

The mineral was called charoite after the only place it has been found, between the Chara and Olekma rivers in remote Sakha, Russia. Charoite always has a streaky or swirled appearance and is pale lilac to purple in color. It encloses grains of other minerals such as orange-brown tinaksite, dark green aegirine and creamy-white feldspar.

Charoite has been used for vases and other decorative pieces, sculpture and polished slabs for collectors. A rare use in architecture is decoration in the Aeroflot building in Paris. Deposits of this beautiful rare stone have probably been worked out, but stockpiles continue to be used for jewelry and decorative objects that are sold worldwide.

GEOLOGICAL DESCRIPTION
Charoite, a silicate mineral formed in limestone altered by fluids from a nearby syenite intrusion.

MAJOR USAGE
Vases, boxes and other decorative items, inlay work and jewelry.

Sugilite

SOURCE: Northern Cape Province, South Africa
STATUS: Small amounts still available

Oxf-Min 30633

In 1979 miners at the Wessels manganese mine in South Africa discovered a wonderful new reddish purple stone that turned out to be a rare mineral called sugilite.

Sugilite was first discovered as tiny crystals in Japan in 1944, insignificant compared with the richer more recent discovery in South Africa. The stone was quickly adopted by lapidarists (gem cutters), who compared it with turquoise in all but color.

The stone is purple tending to magenta-pink in color, and although it might be slightly banded, it never has the streaky appearance typical of charoite. The finest quality stone is very translucent, but most is rather opaque, and some so-called sugilite is actually chalcedony colored by this mineral. This is harder than sugilite and cuts particularly well, but the color is less intense. Commercial names such as *royal azel* (from the nearest town, Hotazel) and *royal lavulite* (alluding to a lavender coloration) have sometimes been used for sugilite. Not much sugilite is mined today.

GEOLOGICAL DESCRIPTION

Sugilite, a silicate mineral colored by manganese, from a metamorphosed bedded manganese ore deposit. It is moderately hard at 6 on Mohs' scale.

MAJOR USAGE

Inlay work, jewelry and small carvings.

Rhodochrosite

SOURCE: Catamarca Province, Argentina
STATUS: Commercially available

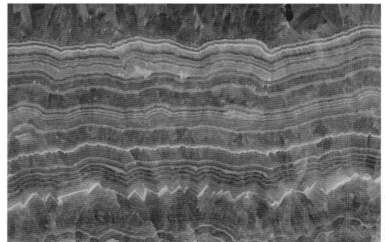

Oxf-Min 24810

Artifacts made of rhodochrosite are found in Inca burials, and it is thought the Incas once extracted silver from the metal mines that yield this exquisite pink-banded stone. This national stone of Argentina has become known as *rosa del Inca* or *Inca rose*.

The mines are at Capillitas, near Andalgalá, and extend many miles underground in the eastern foothills of the Andes. Layers of rhodochrosite infill cavities and fractures in the rock and, where there is sufficient space, form stalactites that can be up to 2 feet (60 cm) long.

It is brittle and soft, tending to be more translucent than rhodonite (see opposite). Stones of a deep cherry-red color and good translucency are considered most desirable. Different patterns are obtained depending on which direction the stone is sawn, either straight parallel bands or interconnecting concentric circles.

Mining the Capillitas deposit has always been sporadic, but large quantities of *Inca rose* have been extracted from the 1950s up to the present day. Similar banded rhodochrosite has come from the Manuelita mine, Morococha, in the Lima Department of Peru, but only in the last few years.

GEOLOGICAL DESCRIPTION

Rhodochrosite, a manganese secondary mineral, as layered cavity fills and speleothems in a sulfide ore deposit. The composition of rhodochrosite is manganese carbonate, and it will fizz weakly when tested with dilute hydrochloric acid. Measures just 3.5 to 4 on Mohs' scale.

MAJOR USAGE

Sculpture, decorative items, inlay work and jewelry.

Thulite

SOURCE: Norway and United States
STATUS: Actively quarried

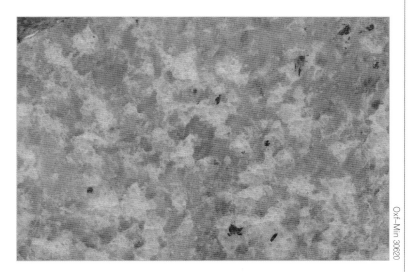

The national stone of Norway is called thulite after "Thule," an ancient name for the far north of Europe. It is found in many places in Norway and in other countries as well.

This rose-pink variety of zoisite is called thulite, or sometimes by the trade name *rosaline*. It has a granular or fibrous structure, and is often mottled with grains of colorless quartz, white calcite or yellowish green epidote. It was first discovered in Telemark, Norway, in 1820 and has since been uncovered in other places in the country. Stone for cutting and polishing is extracted at Leksvik, Nord Trøndelag. Similar stones are obtained from Western Australia; North Carolina and Washington, in the United States; and Namibia.

A hard stone, thulite is colored by trace manganese. When white grains are absent it can strongly resemble rhodonite.

GEOLOGICAL DESCRIPTION
A variety of the silicate mineral zoisite, which is colored by trace manganese. It is found as fracture fills and veins in gneisses and other metamorphic rocks. Thulite has a hardness of 6 to 7 on Mohs' scale.

MAJOR USAGE
Sculpture, decorative items and jewelry.

Rhodonite

SOURCE: Ekaterinburg, Russia and elsewhere
STATUS: Commercially available

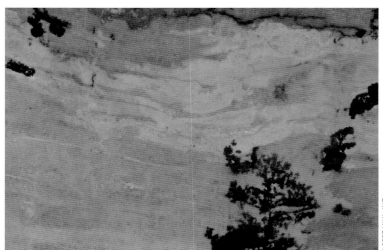

Initially this bright pink mineral was thought to be a compact form of rose quartz—and is often named as such in early stone collections. It was recognized as being a distinct mineral only in 1819.

Rhodonite was discovered in the mid-18th century in the village of Maloe Sedelnikovo, a short distance from Ekaterinberg in the Ural Mountains of Russia. Stone from this rich deposit was used to ornament the palaces of the czars: the sepulcher of Maria Alexandrovna (1824–80), Empress consort of Alexander II of Russia, in Petropavlovsky Cathedral, St. Petersburg, is made of Russian rhodonite. Another fine example is the gravestone of World War I author Henri Barbusse (1873–1935) in Père-Lachaise Cemetery, Paris.

The Russian deposits are now exhausted, but many other commercial deposits have been found worldwide. Among the most important today are those of Tamworth in New South Wales, Australia, and Vancouver Island, British Columbia, Canada. In the United States, the fine rhodonite of Cummington, Massachusetts, has been adopted as the Massachussetts state gemstone.

Rhodonite is often veined with black manganese oxides, making a striking color contrast. It is harder than rhodochrosite.

GEOLOGICAL DESCRIPTION
Nodular or bedded rhodonite, a manganese silicate mineral formed by metamorphic alteration of manganese deposits. Its hardness is 5.5 to 6 on Mohs' scale, and when pure, it will not fizz if tested with dilute hydrochloric acid.

MAJOR USAGE
Sculpture, decorative items, inlay work and jewelry.

Mention the words sculpture and stone together, and nine out of 10 people will first think of classical creations in white marble such as the statue of *Venus de Milo* sculpted in the second century BCE; *David* by Michelangelo Buonarroti, unveiled in 1504; or perhaps that well-known late 19th-century masterpiece *The Kiss* by Auguste Rodin. White marble is just one of the many different kinds of stone that lend themselves to sculpture. The choice for the sculptor depends on the appearance and physical properties of the stone.

HARDNESS

Soft stones such as steatite or alabaster (gypsum) can be scraped and carved by hand. Steatite is ideal for beginners, but alabaster is more difficult to work because it "bruises" easily, where crushed grains appear as opaque white patches. Harder stones like marble and limestone require the use of chisels. The hardest stones—porphyries, granites and many gem minerals—are nowadays carved mainly with electrical power tools. The delicacy of detail achieved by sculptors thousands of years ago is remarkable, considering they worked boulders of hard stones such as jade and chalcedony with simple hand tools charged with abrasive emery powder.

BELOW All kinds of different stones can be found in a modern sculptor's studio.

GRAIN

Both the size of grains and the way they lock together are important to the sculptor. Whether hard or soft, stones composed of minute, tightly interlocking grains can hold remarkably intricate detail, and are suitable for tiny carvings as well as larger-scale works. The stone becomes less predictable in the way it responds to carving if the grains are larger, more variable in size, do not lock together well, or if the stone has a more open, porous texture. Coarse-grained rocks are used most successfully for larger pieces.

STRUCTURAL FEATURES

Some structural features such as lamination, bedding and hairline fractures can create visual banding or planes of weakness. The challenge for the sculptor is to work with the natural structures of the stone, and not against them. Internal flaws, cleavage planes, cavities and inclusions of foreign material are more problematic. The translucency of alabaster makes it easier to spot internal planes of weakness that often beset this stone. In opaque stones, the sculptor can only evolve the design to accommodate such natural variation.

DURABILITY

The intended location for a sculpture needs to be considered. Alabasters, marbles and many serpentines are prone to etching and erosion if exposed to acid rain, and tend to be less suitable for siting

outdoors. By comparison, porphyries and granites are particularly robust and hold their appearance well in external settings. But durability is not confined to hard stones. Steatite is not readily damaged by chemical attack and works well in outside situations where it is not at risk from mechanical damage.

SIZE AND PRICE

The larger the planned sculpture, the more limited the choice of materials. Most of the gem minerals are only available in small or very small pieces, typically sold by the gram or carat (1 g = 5 ct). By comparison, rocks such as marble, porphyry and granite can be cut as huge monoliths, and are sold by the ton or kilogram. The price of stone depends on both its rarity and on the costs of quarrying and transporting it. Long distance transportation has environmental costs, which makes the use of local stones an option well worth exploring.

APPEARANCE

Translucency, color and pattern are fundamentally important in the choice of stone for sculpture. The majority of stones are opaque, but some gem minerals, alabasters and marbles are translucent. Stones can be muted in color to blend with their environment, or they can contrast with their surroundings to great visual effect. The subject of a sculpture may be suggested by the patterns and color of the rock. A classical example of this can be seen in sculptures and monuments that use oriental alabaster to recreate the folds of clothing and drapes. In abstract works, the possibilities are endless.

SCULPTURE STEP-BY-STEP

The process of turning a rough block of stone into a finished sculpture goes through a series of stages. First the shape of the sculpture is

LEFT *Icon II* (1960), a modern sculpture carved from *Carrara marble* by Dame Barbara Hepworth (1903–75), one of the foremost nonfigurative sculptors of her time.

roughed out using large chisels, a diamond-charged electric saw or an angle grinder. If the stone is hand-carved, it is worked first with points, then toothed chisels and finally, flat chisels and rondels (curved chisels). Each step reduces the ridges and furrows left by the previous one. Fine detail is added and any remaining chisel marks are removed using rasps (a coarse kind of file to scrape or abrade), "rifflers" (smaller shaped files) and different grades of abrasive paper. Finally, the stone is polished. Marbles and limestones are buffed with oxalic acid that melds the surface grains together. After washing off the acid, the stone can be finished with a commercial sealant or wax. Harder stones are worked using electrical and pneumatic tools. They are polished by buffing the stone with consecutively finer grades of abrasive, with a final finishing of sealant or wax.

Eudialyte

SOURCE: Quebec, Canada and Kola Peninsula, Russia
STATUS: Actively quarried

Oxf-Min 30623

Until recently, this ore of zirconium was rarely cut and polished for ornamental use. Now, rocks rich in deep raspberry-pink crystals of this unusual mineral are made into eye-catching jewelry and gifts.

Decorative stones rich in pink eudialyte come from two main localities, the Kipawa syenite complex in Villedieu Township, Quebec, Canada, and Mount Khibiny on the Kola Peninsula of Russia. The eudialyte from these localities is darker pink than rhodonite but has a similar hardness. It occurs as irregular crystals in a medium- to coarse-grained igneous rock, with other silicate minerals that are white, gray, black or brown in color. The finest stone is composed of nearly pure eudialyte.

GEOLOGICAL DESCRIPTION

Eudialyte, a silicate mineral that occurs mainly in rare igneous rocks called agpaitic syenites and pegmatites (coarser-grained rocks) of the same composition. It is associated with white or gray feldspar, black amphiboles and rare minerals such as pale brown agrellite (Kipawa) or dark brown astrophyllite (Khibiny).

MAJOR USAGE

Spheres, eggs and other decorative items; jewelry.

Ruby in zoisite

SOURCE: Northern Tanzania
STATUS: Commercially available, but mining is sporadic

Courtesy of Burhouse ltd

The chemical element chromium can turn some minerals red and others green. Just a small amount creates the two contrasting colors in this showy African stone, also known as *anyolite* from the local Maasai word for green.

Ruby in zoisite was originally found in various places in southern Kenya and northern Tanzania, and has been mined as a decorative stone at Mundarara mine near Longido since the late 1950s. As the name indicates, the red crystals are ruby and the green groundmass is a mineral called zoisite. The stone often has flecks of a black mineral called tschermakite. The Maasai word for green, "anya," gives this stone another name: *anyolite*. Similar material has come from India, Madagascar and the United States.

At first, *ruby in zoisite* was exported to Idar Oberstein in Germany to be worked by the skilled lapidarists there, but by the 1960s it was also being made into finished articles by Tanzanian artisans. It is a difficult stone to work because ruby is very much harder than both zoisite and tschermakite. For the artist, the challenge is to work the different constituents of the stone in a creative way.

GEOLOGICAL DESCRIPTION

Ruby, a variety of corundum, and black tschermakite (amphibole) crystals in granular zoisite. It is a chromium-rich metamorphic rock formed at high temperatures and pressures. Ruby has a hardness of 9 on Mohs' scale—much harder than both zoisite (6 to 7) and tschermakite (5 to 6).

MAJOR USAGE

Sculpture, decorative objects, jewelry.

Steatite

SOURCE: India

STATUS: Commercially available

Oxf-Min 30630

From stoneworkers in antiquity to modern lapidarists, all seem to have delighted in carving this soft, fine-grained stone. Also called soapstone, steatite may be easy to work, but it is also surprisingly durable. Dishes and jewelry thousands of years old have been discovered from Egyptian and Indian excavations.

Talc is most familiar ground up in talcum powder, but it is also the main constituent of a compact fine-grained stone called steatite. As its other name soapstone suggests, it has a distinctly slippery feel. Pure talc is white and very soft. Steatite contains varying amounts of impurities that can turn it pink, buff, red, yellow, brown, green, gray or black, and can also make it a little harder. Still, it is easily carved and takes a light polish, and this makes it a very popular medium for sculpture.

Steatite is commonly found in metamorphic rocks all over the world. It has been carved by the Shonas of Zimbabwe, Native North Americans, the Inuit of northern Canada and extensively by the Chinese. In India, it was used for making seals, beads and statuettes as far back as the Harrapan period (2500–1500 BCE), and some of the earliest Egyptian scarabs and seals were made of this stone. Today, huge quantities of inexpensive souvenirs are carved for the tourist trade in India and elsewhere in southeast Asia.

GEOLOGICAL DESCRIPTION

Massive compact talc, a silicate mineral formed by metamorphism of siliceous dolomites and alteration of serpentinites. Extremely soft, just 1 on Mohs' scale.

MAJOR USAGE

Modern sculpture; ancient artifacts.

LEFT A decorative steatite plate with cut work and inlays of shell and semiprecious stones.

Other decorative minerals

Angelite is a pale blue variety of anhydrite from Peru. It can look like *larimar,* but at 3 to 3.5 on Mohs' scale, it is much softer. Stones composed almost entirely of dumortierite can be pink, lilac or blue and come from Madagascar and elsewhere. Gaspeite is bright apple-green, a nickel-bearing carbonate mineral and is obtained mostly from Western Australia. It is a porous stone, and is treated in a similar way to turquoise. Hematite forms a metallic-gray decorative stone but the color of the powder (streak) is brownish red, and unlike magnetite, it is not magnetic. It comes from Brazil and elsewhere. Much so-called "hematite" is *hematine,* hematite powder or synthetic iron oxide mixed with epoxy resin.

Pyrophyllite is another stone used for sculpture. It is obtained from many places, including southern Africa, and is sometimes referred to as *African wonderstone.* It ranges from pink, yellow and red to green, gray or black depending on the impurities it contains. It is a little harder than talc but otherwise has similar properties.

Finding out more

ANCIENT STONES

The history of Faustino Corsi's collection is recounted by Lisa Cooke and Monica Price (1998), and sections of his treatise, *Delle pietre antiche* (1828, 2nd ed. 1833, 3rd ed. 1845), are reproduced by Dario Del Bufalo (2000) and Caterina Napoleone (2001). Raniero Gnoli's *Marmora Romana* (1971, 2nd ed. 1988) is the first major modern study, and remains an important reference. For a more up-to-date overview of the subject, consult the 643-page catalog of the exhibition *I marmi colorati della Roma Imperiale* edited by Marilda de Nuccio and Lucrezia Ungaro (2002). Images and descriptions of the stones can be seen in the books by Gabriele Borghini (1997) and Harald Mielsch (1985).

Much of the detailed literature relating to individual stones is published in conference proceedings of ASMOSIA, the Association for the Study of Marble and Other Stone in Antiquity. Egyptian stones are illustrated and described in James Harrell's website (a, b). Annamaria Giusti's book *Eternità e nobilità di Materia* (2003) contains a number of interesting essays on cultural aspects of decorative stone through history.

MODERN STONES

Published sources on stones used in more modern times (but not necessarily today) are uncommon. William (Guglielmo) Jervis wrote important accounts of the decorative stones of Italy in 1862 and 1889. John Watson's *Building Stones* (1911) and *Marbles* (1916) are highly informative about specimens in the University of Cambridge's large collection. George Merrill's *Stones for Building and Decoration* (1903) is a major reference for American stones. Mario Pieri wrote a number of books in the 1950s and 1960s which describe stones in use then. Two exquisitely illustrated books by Jacques Dubarry de Lassale, *Identifying Marble* (2000) and *Utilisation des Marbres* (2005), are good sources of information, especially about French stones. An exceptional website and rich source of information on modern stones particularly those of the United States is *Stone Quarries and Beyond* by Peggy Perazzo.

CONTEMPORARY STONES

For stones that have come into use in recent times and all those actively quarried today, Daniel Pivko has produced informative online listings of popular varieties. Other sources include trade journals, geological research papers in academic journals, and the online catalogs and specification sheets produced by quarrying companies.

Two books that give very good overviews of modern decorative stones and their uses in architecture are Frederick Bradley's *Natural Stone—A Guide to Selection* (1998) and Muriel Burton's *Designing with Stone* (1999). June Culp Zeitner's *Gem and Lapidary Materials* (1996) and R.V. Dietrich's *Gemrocks* website are particularly useful for decorative minerals. General guides to minerals, rocks and fossils, include those by A.C. Bishop, A.C. Woolley and W.R. Hamilton (2001), and Monica Price and Kevin Walsh (2004), while Paul Hancock and Brian Skinner's *Oxford Companion to the Earth* (2000) explains geological topics in an accessible way. Many museums and geological surveys now have excellent websites, see for example the account of plate tectonics given by Kious (n.d.) on the U.S. Geological Survey site. The International Commission on Stratigraphy (ICS) also has a website giving up-to-date information on geological timescales. Remember also that museum collections of decorative stones make for useful comparisons when trying to identify decorative stones, and museum curators can often help.

PRINCIPAL REFERENCES AND FURTHER READING

Alabasters and travertines

46 *Alabastro di Volterra*: Stolzuoli (c.1997); Jervis (1889) 318–326

47 *English alabaster*: Daniell (c.1960); Knowles (2005); Watson (1916) 375–382

48 *Egyptian alabaster*: Harrell (b); Lazzarini (2002) 241–243; Merrill (1893); Watson (1916) 362–364

50 *Alabastro a giaccione*: Bruno (1998); Bruno (2002); Corsi (1825) 93; Faramondi (1985) 30–31, 55

50 *Pakistan onyx marble*: SDNP (n.d.)

51 *Mexican onyx marble*: Merrill (1893); Michalzik (2001); Watson (1916)

51 *Yava onyx*: Merrill (1893); Reis (2004); Watson (1916) 369

52 *Alabastro a tartaruga*: Corsi (1845) 133; Dallan (1969) 46, 62–63

52 *Alabastro di Busca*: FNF (1939) 33; Jervis (1873) 34; Jervis (1889) 46; Corsi (1825) 101–102

53 *Alabastro di Palombara*: Bruno (2002a); Corsi (1845) 137–138; De Michelle (1979); Gnoli (1988) 225–226; Lanciani (1901) 219–229

53 *Gibraltar stone*: Gomez (n.d.); Hull (1872) 143; Watson (1916)

54 *Alabastro a pecorella*: Borghini (1997) 149–150; Chafetz (1998); Corsi (1845) 134–135; Lazzarini (2002) 244–245; Merrill (1903) 281–284; Watson (1916) 355–59

56 *Alabastro fiorito*: Borghini (1997) 142–144; Bruno (2002a); Corsi (1845) 135–136; Lazzarini (2002) 253

57 *Travertino di Civitavecchia*: Corpo Reale delle Miniere (1904) 98; Faramondi (1985) 18–19; Jervis (1889) 339–340

57 *Persian travertine*: Merrill (1893)

58 *Travertino di Tivoli*: Cappelli (1991); Corsi (1825); Doehne (1996); Jervis (1889) 354–359; Porter (1907) 17–19; TiberSuperbum (2003)

59 *Tartaro di Tivoli*: Corsi (1825) 104–106

60 *Travertino oro*: Perrier (1992)

White marbles

62 *Pentelic marble*: Corsi (1825) 16; Higgins (1996) 31–32; Korres (1995); Pensabene (2002) 207–208

63 *Parian marble*: Gorgoni (2002a); Lazzarini (2004); Pensabene (2002) 212; Watson (1916) 155–158

63 *Thasian marble*: Bruno (2002c); Koukouli ed. (1999); Pensabene (2002) 208–212

64 *White marbles of Tuscany*: Jervis (1862) 1–24; Pensabene (2002a) 212–214; Pieri (1954) 17–24; Watson (1916) 175–192

66 *Identifying white marble—filling in the jigsaw*: Gorgoni (2002); Green (2002); Lazzarini (2004)

68 *Alabama white marble*: Carpenter (2005); Merrill (1903) 204; Perazzo (a) "Alabama"; Watson (1916) 309–11

68 *Danby marble*: Conrad (2005); Corbett (2003); Merrill (1903) 231–239; Watson (1916) 336–340

69 *Colorado Yule*: McGee (1999); Merrill (1903) 208; Perazzo (a); Watson (1916) 314–5

70 *White Makrana*: Watson (1916) 258–261

Gray and black marbles and limestones

72 *Bardiglio*: Borghini (1997) 153; Jervis (1862); Jervis (1889) 260–300; Watson (1916) 192–194

73 *Greco scritto*: Borghini (1997) 237; Pensabene (2002) 220–221

73 *Ashburton marble*: Knowles (2005); Savedge Schlesinger (1968, rev.1979); Watson (1916) 19–20, 22

74 *Cherokee and Solar grey*: Day (1894); Merrill (1903) 209–211; Watson (1916) 316–318

74 *Proconnesian marble*; Borghini (1997) 252; Cramer (2002); Pensabene (2002) 203–205; Porter (1907) 87–88

75 *Cipollino nero*: Higgins (1996) 86–87; Lazzarini (1995)

75 *Bigio antico*: Borghini (1997) 158–9; Higgins (1996) 133–5; Lazzarini (1999); J.P. Getty Trust (n.d.)

76 *Nero antico, bigio morato*: Gnoli (1988) 192–195; Lazzarini (2002) 244, 265; Lazzarini (2003); Pensabene (1998)

77 *Ashford black marble*: Tomlinson (1996); Watson (1916)

77 *Irish black marble*: Feely (2002); Kinahan (1886); Lee (1888) 36–40; Rogers (2006)

78 *Belgian black marble*: Borghini (1997) 256; Cnudde (1988); Watson (1916) 84–86

80 *Champlain black*: Conrad (1990s); Merrill (1903) 239; Norton 1993

80 *Negro Marquina*: Critchley (2001)

81 *Imperial black marble*: M. White, pers. comm

81 *Marmo Portoferraio*: Corpo Reale delle Miniere (1904) 64; Corsi (1925) 55

82 *Grand antique, petit antique*: Borghini (1997) 154–156; Dubarry de Lassale (2000) 234–235, 256–257; Antonelli (2002) 272–273; Watson (1916) 115–116, 124–125; Zoppas (a) 174, 204

84 *Simulating stone—faux marble and scagliola*: Finkelstein (1997); Massinelli (c.1997)

86 *Portoro*: Jervis (1889) 258–259; Miller (1994); Seeman (1998) 58; Watson (1916) 170–171

87 *Giallo e nero di Carrara*: Corsi (1845) 112; Wirsing (1775); Gnoli

(1988) 180; Jervis (1862) 5

87 *Noir St. Laurent*: Dubarry de Lassale (2000) 262–263; Perrier (1996)

88 *King gold*: trade websites

Yellow and brown marbles and limestones

90 *Giallo antico*: Blagrove (1888) 83; Borghini (1997) 214–215; Lazzarini (2002) 243–244; Watson (1916) 271–274

92 *Giallo di Siena*: Lee (1888) 15, Watson (1916) 199–201; Jervis (1862) 24; Jervis (1889) 329–330

93 *Breccia dorata*: Borghini (1997) 170; Bruno (1999)

94 *Giallo di Verona*: Holst (1919); Pieri (1954) 40–41; Pollock (2004); Watson (1916) 80, 204

95 *Breccia nuvolata*: Lazzarini (2002a)

95 *Crema Valencia*: trade websites

96 *Giallo tigrato*: Borghini (1997) 216; Corsi (1825) 59–90; Bruno (2002) 285

96 *Breccia corallina giallastra*: Borghini (1997) 168–169; Gnoli (1971) 216

97 *Vratza*: Adams (2005); Monroe (2005)

97 *Jerusalem stone*: Anon. (2006); Reis (2002); Watson (1916) 249–250

98 *Crema marfil*: trade websites

98 *Palombino antico*: Borghini (1997) 263; Corsi (1825) 24–26; Bruno (2002) 289

99 *Alberese*: Corsi (1825) 127, 130

99 *Cotham marble*: Hamilton (1961); Mayall (1981)

100 *Landscapes in stone*: Corsi (1825) 127; Hamilton (1961); Marko (2003); McBride (2003)

101 *Pietra paesina*: Marko (2003); McBride (2003)

104 *Teakwood*: trade websites

Pink marbles and limestones

106 *Marmo del Duomo, Candoglia marble*: anon. (2005); Jervis (1889) 88–89; Watson (1916) 174–175

106 *Rosa Portogallo*: INETI (2006); Watson (1916) 209; Litos online (2006)

107 *Etowah marble*: Merrill (1903) 209–211; Watson (1916) 318–319

107 *Tennessee pink marble*: Merrill (1903) 224–230; Powell (2005); Watson (1916) 331–336

108 *Stone in a New World*: Merrill (2003); Perazzo (2006); Robinson (1890)

110 *Norwegian rose*: Melezhic (2000); Perrier (1994); Watson (1916) 205–208

110 *Cork red marble*: Nevill (1962); Rogers (2003) 63–64; Watson (1916) 53–54; Wyse Jackson (1995)

111 *Breccia corallina*: Borghini (1997) 166–167; Lazzarini (2002) 251; Lazzarini (2002a); Lazzarini (2006)

111 *Broccatellone*: Borghini (1997) 199; Lazzarini (2002) 251; Lazzarini (2002a)

112 *Cottanello*: Borgini (1997) 208; Bruno (2002) 285; Gnoli (1988) 186; Tozzi (2000)

112 *Marmo carnagione*: Corsi (1825)

113 *Breccia degli Appennini*: Corsi (1825)

113 *Rose de Numidie*: Lee (1888) 89–91; Perazzo (b); Playfair (1885); Watson (1916) 275–277

114 *Nembro rosato*: trade websites

114 *Rosa perlino*: Bosellini (1967) 46–48; Jervis (1889) 133–154; Pieri (1954) 42–43; Pieri (c.1958) 307; Valpolicella.it (2001a,b)

115 *Rosso Verona*: CPMRV (n.d.); Jervis (1889) 133–145; Pieri (1954) 44; Valpolicella.it (2001a,b); Watson (1916) 202–203

116 *Breccia pernice*: Bosellini (1967) 46–48; Jervis (1889) 143

116 *Encarnado*: Carvalho (2001); INETI (2006); Watson (1916) 210–211

117 *Adneter marmor*: Böhm (2003); Kretschmer (1986); Watson (1916) 72–74

117 *Rosso Montecitorio*: Corsi (1825) 43; Montana (1998) 55–56

118 *Rojo Alicante*: trade websites

Red and violet marbles and limestones

120 *Cipollino rosso, rosso brecciato*: Andreoli (2002); Borghini (1997) 207, 289; Gorgoni (2002); Lazzarini (2002) 248–250

122 *Rosso antico*: Borghini (1997) 288; Gorgoni (2002); Lazzarini (2002) 256; Rogers (2003) 56–57

124 *Duke's red*: Corsi (1825) 38; Chats. Acc. (1823); Tomlinson (1996) 30

124 *Griotte*: Dubarry de Lassale (2000) 94–95, 112; Merrill (1903) 332; Perrier (1996); Watson (1916) 97–98, 136, 223–224

125 *Rouge Languedoc, incarnat*: Blagrove (1888) 88; Bourrouilh (1999); De Thury (1823); Dubarry de Lassale (2000) 74–75; Dubarry de Lassale (2005); Flajs (1993); Hladil (2005); Perrier (1996); Peybernes (2004); Watson (1916) 97, 101; Zoppas (a) 180, 215–6

126 *Brèche sanguine*: Lee (1888) 89–91; Playfair (1885); Watson (1916) 274–279

126 *Breccia rossa Appenninica*: Borghini (1997) 189; Bruno (1999); Bruno (2002) 280

127 *Belgian red marbles*: Boulvain (2006); Cnudde (1998); Dubarry de Lassale (2000); Watson (1916) 88–92

127 *Breccia pavonazza*: Belli (1842) no.380; Borghini (1997) 178; Pullen (1894) 84; Gnoli (1988) 243–245

128 *Fior di pesco*: Borghini (1997) 212; Higgins (1996) 85–86; Lazzarini (2002b); Lazzarini (2002) 260–261

129 *Breccia di Settebasi, semesanto*: Borghini (1997) 192; Bruno (2002b); Corsi (1825) 108, 113–114; Corsi (1845) 148–150; Higgins (1996) 94–95; Lazzarini (1999a); Lazzarini (2002) 258–260; Porter (1907) 89

130 *Marmo pavonazzetto*: Borghini (1997) 264–265; Hamilton (1903) Ch.8; Pensabene (2002) 205–207; Porter (1907) 99–102

130 *Breccia bruna del Testaccio*: Bartelletti (2003); Borghini (1997) 164; Corsi (1825) 38, 125

131 *Breccia di Seravezza*: Bartelletti (2003); Jervis (1862) 1–22; Lazzarini (1999a); Mancini (2002); Pieri (1954); Watson (1916) 189–197

132 *Fior di pesco Apuano*: Pieri (1954) 56; Watson (1916) 194–5

Multicolored marbles and limestones

134 *Cipollino mandolato, Campan*: Antonelli (2002a); Borghini (1997) 204–205; Corsi (1845) 98; Dubarry De Lassale (2000); Dubarry De Lassale (2005); Peybernès (2004); Watson (1916) 124, 131–132

136 *Africano*: Borghini (1997) 133–135; Corsi (1825) 47–49; Corsi (1845) 99–100; Gnoli (1988) 174–178; Higgins (1996) 142; Lazzarini (2002) 250–251; Bostock (1855) bk 36 ch 8; Ward-Perkins (1966)

138 *Brèche Benou*: Dubarry de Lassale (2000) 136–137, 194–195; Zoppas (a) 143

138 *Breccia aurora*: Pieri (1954) 40; Watson (1916) 174

139 *Sarrancolin*: Blagrove (888) 109; Dubarry de Lassale (2000); Watson (1916) 134–135; Zoppas (a) 224–225

140 *Portasanta*: Borghini (1997) 285–287; Lazzarini (2002) 262–265; Porter (1907) 70–72

142 *In search of ancient quarries*: Rogers (2003); Herz (1999)

144 *Breccia di Aleppo*: Borghini (1997)161; Brindley (early 1900s); Lazzarini (2002) 262–264; Lazzarini (2003)

144 *Brèche Nouvelle*: Dubarry de Lassale (2000) 290–291; Perrier

220 *Granito rosso antico*: Harrell (a); Lazzarini (2002) 228–229; Watson (1911) 43–45

222 *Shap granite*: Knowles (2005); O'Neill (1965) 30; Scott-Smith (n.d.); Watson (1911) 20–21

222 *Rosa Porrino*: Guimaré Gutiérrez (2005)

223 *Red Peterhead granite*: Watson (1911) 26–27

223 *Balmoral granite*: Finska (n.d.)

224 *Dakota mahogany*: various web sources

224 *Baltic brown*: Finska (n.d.); Merrill (1903) 92–93

225 *Luxullianite*: Rowe (n.d.); Spalding (1999)

225 *Unakite*: Dietrich 2005; Zeitner (1996) 222

226 *Larvikite*: Dietrich (2006); Geological Museum, University of Oslo (2003); Larsen (2000)

228 *Marmo Misio*: De Vecchi (2000); Lazzarini (1998); Lazzarini (2002) 246–248

228 *Granito del Foro*: Harrell (a); Lazzarini (2002) 235–236; Peacock (1994)

229 *Orbicular granite*: Bevan (2004); Corsi (1825) 212–213; Thomas (2000)

230 *Granito della colonna*: Borghini (1997) 220; Del Bufalo (2002); Harrell (2002); Lazzarini (2002) 229–230

230 *Granito bianco e nero*: Borghini (1997); Harrell (2002a) 217; Lazzarini (2002)

231 *Granito verde antico*: Borghini (1997) 228, 232–235, Harrell (a); Lazzarini (2002) 237–238

232 *Stone in the home*: Bertoli (n.d.); Findstone (n.d.)

234 *Rustenburg*: Olivier (2005)

234 *Granito nero antico*: Borghini (1997) 224; Harrell (a); Lazzarini (2002) 229

235 *Nero Zimbabwe*: trade websites

235 *Belfast black*: Shadman (2003)

236 *Verde Ubatuba*: Draenert (n.d.); Zoppas (c) 160–161

Quartz and opal

238 *Rock crystal, smoky quartz*: Bauer (1904) 471–481; Frondel (1962); Raulet (1999); Webster (1994) 219–225; Zeitner (1996) 63–84

239 *Amethyst, citrine, rose quartz*: Bauer (1904) 481–488; Frondel 1962; Webster (1994) 225–230; Zeitner (1996) 63–84

240 *Agate, onyx*: Dietrich (2005); Pabian (2004); Pabian (2006)

242 *Moss agate*: Bauer (1904) 506–507; Harmon (2000); Pabian (2004); Zeitner (1996) 105–108

243 *Sard, carnelian*: Bauer (1904) 508–510; Frondel (1962); Zeitner (1996) 85–125

243 *Prase, plasma, bloodstone*: Bauer (1904) 488, 510–511; Frondel (1962) 218–219; Webster (1994) 234–235; Zeitner (1996) 101, 121

244 *Chrysoprase*: Bauer (1904) 497–499, Frondel (1962) 218; Webster (1994) 233–234; Zeitner (1996) 118–119

244 *Mookaite*: McLaren (n.d.); GSWA (1994)

245 *Ribbon jasper*: Bauer (1904) 501; Hintze (1915) 1476; Giusti (1992) 269–270

245 *Calcedonio di Volterra*: Brizzi (1988); Jervis (1889) 320; Marrucci (n.d.)

246 *Diaspri di Sicilia*: Jervis (1881) 193–318; Jervis (1889) 449–482; Montana (1998); Schmidt (2002)

247 *Diaspro di Barga*: Corsi (1825) 187–188; Giusti (1992) 269

248 *Inlaid stone*: Giusti (1992); Tomlinson (1993); Grundke (2004)

250 *Egyptian jasper*: Bauer (1904) 500–501

250 *Landscape jasper*: Rhodes (2006); Pabian (2004); Zeitner (1996) 131–143

251 *Leopardskin jasper*: trade websites

251 *Ocean jasper*: Hudson (2002); Hudson (2003); Mueller (2005)

252 *Tiger's eye, hawk's eye, tiger iron*: Dietrich (2005); Frondel (1962); Heaney (2003)

253 *Silicified wood*: USGS (2002); USGS (2004); Zeitner (1996) 150–167

254 *Precious opal*: Bauer (1904) 373–384; Ďuďa (1996); Ward (1997)

Other decorative minerals

256 *Jadeite jade*: Dietrich (2005); Harlow (1991); Harlow (2001); Howard (n.d.); Hughes (2000); Ward (1996); Webster (1994) 272–279; Zeitner (1996) 170–172

257 *Nephrite jade*: Dietrich (2005); Townsend (2005); Webster (1994) 267–272; Zeitner (1996) 172–175

257 *Bowenite*: Webster (1994) 275–276; Dietrich (2005)

258 *Malachite*: Bulakh (2000) chap.3; Dietrich (2005); King (2001); Webster (1994) 351–352; Zeitner (1996) 192–193

259 *Chrysocolla*: Hyrsl (2003) 254; Webster (1994) 326–327, Zeitner (1996) 117–118

259 *Turquoise*: Bauer (1904) 389–394; Watson (2002); Webster (1994) 254–263, Zeitner (1996) 182–184

260 *Amazonite*: De Graaf (n.d.); Webster (1994) 211–212; Zeitner (1996) 187

260 *Larimar*: The Larimar Museum (n.d.); Woodruff (1989); Zeitner (1996) 195–196

261 *Sodalite, Princess blue*: Steacy (1982) 202–203; Watson (1916) 393–395; Webster (1994) 374–375; Zeitner (1996) 199–200

262 *Lapis lazuli*: Bowersox (1995) 37–63; Bostock (1855) bk 37 ch 39; Bulakh (2000) chap.3; Giusti (1992) 270; Webster (1995) 263–6; Zeitner (1996) 175–7

264 *Labradorite*: Horváth (2003) 105; Ribbe (1972)

265 *Labradorescent anorthoclase*: Bauer (1904); Raade (pers.com.)

266 *Blue John*: Ford (2000); Webster (1994) 337–341

267 *Fluorite*: Ford (2000) 40; Ottens (2005) 59–60; Zeitner (1996) 190–191

267 *Charoite*: De Graaf (2006); Dietrich (2005); Konev (1993); Zeitner (1996) 215–216

268 *Sugilite*: Dietrich (2005); Shigley (1987); Webster (1994) 378–379; Zeitner (1996) 182

268 *Rhodochrosite*: Colombo (2003); Deitrich (2005); Hyrsl (2003) 249; Webster (1994) 364; Wenrich (1998) 123–124; Zeitner (1996) 197

269 *Thulite*: Webster (1994) 388; Zeitner (1996) 201

269 *Rhodonite*: Bauer (1904) 456–457; Dietrich (2005); Webster (1994) 365

270 *Eudialyte*: Britvin (1996); Wall (2003); Zeitner (1996) 284

270 *Ruby in zoisite*: Dietrich (2005); Keller (1992) 26–32; Zeitner (1996) 203–204

271 *Steatite*: Dietrich (2005); Webster (1995) 374; Zeitner (1996) 232

BIBLIOGRAPHY

Acland, H.W. & Ruskin, J., *The Oxford Museum*, Smith, Elder & Co, London, 1859

Adams, J., "Bulgarian limestone sparks global interest", *Stone World*, 1 Mar 2005, www.stoneworld.com/CDA/Archives

Andreoli, A., Berti, F., et al., "New Contributions on Marmor lassense", in L. Lazzarini, (ed.), *Interdisciplinary studies on ancient stone: Proceedings of the sixth international conference of ASMOSIA, Venice, 2000*, Ausilia, Padova, 2002, pp.13–18

Andreolli, A., Frizzi, S., et al., *Porphyry from Trentino to the world* (Progetto Europa—Canada), http://ctm.lett.unitn.it/eucanada/home.php?st=8 2003-4

Anon, "Duomo di Milano—Per il taglio dei blocchi in cava/Milan Cathedral—cutting the blocks in the quarry", *ACIMM News* (Associazione Construttori Italiani Marmo e Affini) Oct–Dec 2005, www.techstone.it/documenti/rivista/ACnews44.pdf

Anon, "2006 Prism Stone in Architecture Awards", *Stone World*, 1 July 2006, http://www.stoneworld.com/CDA/Archives

Antonelli, F. "I marmi della Gallia e dell'Iberia importati a Roma", in M. De Nuccio, et al., (eds.), *I Marmi Colorati della Roma Imperiale*, Marsilio, Venezia, 2002, pp.267–276

Antonelli, F., Gentili, G., et al., "Provenance of the ornamental stones used in the baroque church of S. Pietro in Valle (Fano, Central Italy) and commentary on their state of conservation." *Journal of Cultural Heritage* 4, 2003, pp.299–312

Antonelli, F., Lazzarini, L., et al, "Petrographic and geochemical characterization of cipollino mandolato marble from the French central Pyrénées", in J.J. Herrmann, et al., (eds.), ASMOSIA 5—*Interdisciplinary Studies on Ancient Stone—Proceedings of 5th International Conference, Museum of Fine Arts, Boston 1998*, Archetype Publications, London, 2002a, pp.77–90

Australian Museum Online 2004, "Building stones of Sydney" www.amonline.net.au/geoscience/earth/sydstones.htm

Baker, R., "Industrial History of Cumbria A–Z of industries: Slate", www.cumbria-industries.org.uk/slate.htm

Barre Granite Association, "About The Barre Granite Industry", www.barregranite.org/industry.html

Bartelletti, A. & Amorfini, A., "Le breccie policrome Apuane nell'antichà", *Acta Apuana* 2, 2003, pp.63–77

Bastogi, M. & Fratini, F., "Geologia, litologia, cave e deterioramento delle pietre fiorentine", *Memorie Descrittive della Carta Geologica d'Italia*, 2004, pp.66, 27–42

Bauer, M.H. & Spencer, L.J., *Precious stones: A popular account of their characters, occurrence and applications*, Charles Griffin & Co. Ltd, London, 1904

Belli, F., *Catalogo della collezione di pietre usate dagli antichi per costruire ed adornare le loro fabbriche dell'avv. Francesco Belli, ora posseduta dal conte Stefano Karolyi*. Roma, 1842

Bertoli, M., "Lemon Juice Test", www.findstone.com/lemonjuicetest.htm

Bevan, J., "Archaean orbicular granitoids from Boogardie, near Mt Magnet, Western Australia", in J. McPhie, et al., (eds.), *Dynamic Earth: Past, Present and Future: Geological Society of Australia, 17th Australian Geological Convention*, Abstracts 73, Hobart, 2004, p.252

Birch, R., *Sussex stones: The story of Horsham stone and Sussex marble*, Roger Birch, 2006

Bishop, A.C., Woolley, A.R., & Hamilton, W.R., *Philip's minerals, rocks & fossils*, 2nd ed., G. Philip & the Natural History Museum, London, 2001

Blagrove, G.H., *Marble decoration and the terminology of British and foreign marbles*, Crosby Lockwood and Son, London, 1888

Bonney, T.G., "Notes on some of the Ligurian and Tuscan Serpentines." *The Geological Magazine*, New Ser. Decade 26, 1879, pp.362–371

Borghini, G. (ed), *Marmi antichi*, Edizioni de Luca, Roma, 1997

Bosellini, A., Carraro, F., & Corsini, M., *Note illustrative della Carta geologica d'Italia, F. 49 Verona*, Servizio, Geologico d'Italia, Nuova Tecnica Graf., Rome, 1967

Bostock, J. & Riley, H.T., *The Natural History of Pliny*, Bohn's classical library, Henry G. Bohn, London, 1855

Boulvain, F., "Frasnian carbonate mounds from the Frasnes area, Belgium", www.ulg.ac.be/geolsed/site_MM/, 2006

Bourrouilh, R. & Bourque, P.A., "Les calcaires à stromatactis de type marbre rouge Languedoc", in M. Schvoerer, et al., (eds.), *Archéomatériaux—Marbres et Autres Roches. Actes de la IVème Conférence Internationale de l'Association pour l'Étude des Marbres et Autres Roches Utilisés dans le Passé*, CRPAA, Talence, 1999, pp.65–76

Bowersox, G.W. & Chamberlin, B.E., *Gemstones of Afghanistan*, Geoscience Press, Tucson, AZ, 1995

Bradley, F., *Natural stone: a guide to selection*, Norton, New York; London, 1998

Brard, C.P., *Minéralogie appliquée aux arts*. vol.2, F.G. Levrault, Paris, 1821

Brayley, A.W., *The History of the Granite Industry of New England, vol.2*, 1913, www.rootsweb.com/~vermont/GraniteIndustry.html

Brindley, W., "Egyptian Porphyry", *The Builder*, 12 Nov 1887, p.683

Brindley, W., "Verde antico and the old quarries."

Royal Institute of British Architects Transactions 3 (3rd series), 1897, p.267

Brindley, W. early 1900s, in M.W. Porter, *Ms catalog of the Corsi Collection*, in Oxford University Museum of Natural History

Britvin, S.N., Ivanjuk, G.J., *et al.*, "Das Chibiny-Massiv auf der russischen Kola-Halbinsel", *Lapis* 21, 1996, pp.13–30

Brizzi, G.& Meli, R., "Le pietre silicee della Fattoria di Monterufoli (Pi)." *Rivista Mineralogica Italiana* 11, 1988, pp.101–111

Bruno, M., "Su una cava d'alabastro del Circeo in località 'la Batteria' ", in P. Pensabene, (ed.), *Marmi Antichi II. Cave e tecnica di lavorazione, provenienze e distribuzione*, Studi Miscellanei 31, 1998, pp.213–222

Bruno, M., "Il mondo delle cave in Italia: Considerazioni su alcuni marmi e pietre usati nell'antichità", in M. De Nuccio, et al., (eds.), *I Marmi Colorati della Roma Imperiale, Marsilio*, Venezia, 2002, pp.277–290

Bruno, M.,"Alabaster quarries near Hierapolis, Turkey", in L. Lazzarini, et al., (eds.), *Interdisciplinary studies on ancient stone: Proceedings of the sixth international conference of ASMOSIA, Venice, 2000*, Ausilio, Padova, 2002a., pp.19–24

Bruno, M., "The quarries at Cape Latomio on Valaxa Island, Skyros (Greece)", in J.J. Herrmann, et al., (eds.), ASMOSIA 5: *"Interdisciplinary Studies on Ancient Stone," Proceedings of 5th International Conference, Museum of Fine Arts, Boston 1998*, Archetype Publications, London, 2002b., pp.27–35

Bruno, M., Conti, L., et al., "The marble quarries of Thasos: an archaeometric study", in L. Lazzarini, et al., (eds.), *Interdisciplinary studies on ancient stone: proceedings of the sixth international conference of ASMOSIA, Venice, 2000*, Ausilio, Padova, 2002c., pp.157–162

Bruno, M. & Lazzarini, L., "Discovery of the Sienese provenance of Breccia Dorata, and Breccia Gialla Fibrosa, and the origin of Breccia Rossa Appenninica", in M. Schvoerer, et al., (eds.), *Archéomatéiaux—Marbres et Autres Roches. Actes de la IVème Conférence Internationale de l'Association pour l'Étude des Marbres et Autres Roches Utilisés dans le Passé*, CRPAA: Talence, 1999, pp.77–82

Buccellati, G. & Gramaccioli, C.M., eds., *Granito di Baveno: Minerali, scultura, architettura*: University of Milan, 2003

Bulakh, A.G., "St Petersburg Stone: An Unique View of the History and Architecture of the City", http://www.geology.pu.ru/bulakh/bulakh.html, 2000

Burton, M., *Designing with stone*. Ealing Publications Ltd, Maidenhead, 1999

Cappelli, R., *Il travertino: marmo del Lazio*. Ministero per i beni culturali e ambientali: Centro europeo turismo, Roma, 1991

Carpenter, G., "Sylacauga marble world renown", *The Daily Home Online*, www.dailyhome.com/news/2005/dh-localnews-0717-gcarpenter-5g16u5539.htm, 2005

Carvalho, J., Manuppella, G., & Maura, A.C., "Portuguese ornamental limestones", www.rochas-

equip.com/objfiles/artigos/Ingles%20Calcarios%20Ornamentais%20Portugueses.pdf, 2001

CDOS—Centre for Development of Stones, "Stones of India: Nerve Centre: Rajasthan", www.stonesofindia.org/rajasthan.htm, 2002–3

Chafetz, H.S., Akdim, B., et al., "Mn- and Fe-rich black travertine shrubs: Bacterially (and nanobacterially) induced precipitates," *Journal of Sedimentary Research* 68, 1998, pp.404–412

Chats.Acc., ms., Chatsworth Accounts for 1823, in the Devonshire ms collection, Chatsworth House, Derbyshire, 1823

Cnudde, C., Harotin, J.J., & Mayot J.-P., *Stones and marbles of Wallonia*, Archives d'Architecture Moderne, Bruxelles, 1988

Colombo, F., "The polymetallic Capillitas Deposit, Catamarca, Argentina", (Abstract of the 24th Annual Tucson Mineralogical Symposium), *Mineralogical Record* 34, 2003, pp.114–115

Conrad, D. & Vanacek, D., "Industrial Minerals of Vermont: 200 Years and Going Strong: Marble", 1990s (update by Sarah King, 2005), www.anr.state.vt.us/dec/geo/marbleindustry.htm

Consorzio Ventuno, *Lapidei Ornamentali della Sardegna*, La Poligrafica Solinas, Nuoro, 2002

Cooke, L. & Price, M.T., "The Corsi Collection in Oxford", in J.J. Herrmann, et al., (eds.), ASMOSIA 5—*"Interdisciplinary Studies on Ancient Stone" Proceedings of 5th International Conference, Museum of Fine Arts, Boston 1998*, Archetype Publications, London, 2002, pp.415–420

Corbett, J.M., "The builder's reputation is safe inside Vermont's marble mountain", *Traditional Building Magazine*, Jan/Feb 2003, www.restorationtrades.com/articles/vermontmarblequarry.shtml

Corpo reale delle Miniere, *Guida all'Ufficio Geologico: Con appendice*, Tipografia nazionale di G. Bertero, Roma, 1904

Corsi, F., *Catalogo ragionato d'una collezione di pietre di decorazione*, Da' Torchj del Salviucci, Roma, 1825

Corsi, F., *Supplemento al Catalogo ragionato d'una collezione di pietre di decorazione*, Da' Torchj del Salviucci, Roma, 1827

Corsi, F., *Delle pietre antiche: trattato*, 3rd ed., Tip. di G. Puccinelli, Roma, 1845

CPMRV (Consorzio Produttori Marmo Rosso Verona), www.marmorossoverona.it/index.html

Cramer, T., Germann, K., & Heilmayer, W.-D., "Petrographic and geochemical characterization of the Pergamon Altar marble in the Pergamon Museum, Berlin", in L. Lazzarini, et al., (eds.), *Interdisciplinary studies on ancient stone: Proceedings of the sixth international conference of ASMOSIA, Venice, 2000*, Ausilio, Padova, 2002, pp.285–292

Critchley, J., "Local history set in stone", *Stone World* 10 Oct 2001, www.stoneworld.com/CDA/Archives, 2001

Cvetko Tešović, B., Gušić, I., et al., "Stratigraphy and microfacies of the Upper Cretaceous Pučišća Formation, Island of Brač, Croatia", *Cretaceous Research* 22, 2001, pp.591–613

Dallan, L., Raggi, G., et al., *Note illustrative della Carta Geologica d'Italia. Foglio 112 Volterra.*, Servizio. Geologico d'Italia, Nuova Tecnica Graf., Roma, 1969

Daniel, P., "Croatia's stone industry is expanding", *Litos*, no.59, www.litosonline.com/articles/60/ar6002e.shtml, 2002

Daniell, J.A., "Bauble making, a lost Leicestershire industry", http://us.geocities.com/oliveshark53/bauble.htm, c.1960

D'Aragona, M.G.R., "23. Statua di Matidia/Aura", in M. De Nuccio, et al., (eds.), *I Marmi Colorati della Roma Imperiale*, Marsilio, Venezia, 2002, pp.325

Day, W.C., "Stone" in *Sixteenth Annual Report of the United States Geological Survey, Part IV.—Mineral Resources of the United States, 1894, Nonmetallic Products*, www.cagenweb.com/quarries/states/ga-stone_indust_1894.html, 1894

De Graaf, M.L.D., "Mineralogy of Russia", http://maurice.strahlen.org/, 2006

De Michelle, V. & Zezza, U., "Le pietre ornamentali di Roma antica della collezione Borromeo nel Museo Civico di Storia Naturale di Milano", *Atti della Societa Italiana di Scienze Naturali e del Museo Civile di Storia Naturale, Milano*, 1979, pp.120, 67–110

De Nuccio, M., Ungaro, L., (eds), *I marmi colorati della Roma imperiale*, Marsilio, Venezia, 2002

De Thury, H., "Rapport sur l'état actuel des carrières de marbres de France", *Annales des Mines* 8, 3–96, 1823

De Vecchi, G., Lazzarini, L., et al., "The genesis and characterisation of 'Marmor Misium' from Kozak (Turkey), a granite used in antiquity", *Journal of Cultural Heritage* 1, 2000, pp.145–153

DeCampo, B., "Bethel White Granite: A classic interior/exterior material option for ageless appeal", www.churchbusiness.com/articles/637/637_111Feat6.html, 2001

Del Bufalo, D., *Marmi antiche e pietre dure*. Mario Congedo Editore, Lavello, 2000

Del Bufalo, D., "Notulae Thebaicae", in M. De Nuccio, et al., (eds.), *I Marmi Colorati della Roma Imperiale,* Marsilio, Venezia, 2002, pp.194–201

Dietrich, R.V., "Gemrocks: Ornamental & Curio Stones", www.cst.cmich.edu/users/dietr1rv/Default.htm, 2005

Doehne. E., "Travertine stone at the Getty Center", *Getty Conservation Institute Newsletter* no.1.5, www.getty.edu/conservation/publications/newsletters/11_2/news2_3.html, 1996

Dubarry de Lassale, J., *Identifying marble*, Editions H. Vial, Dourdan, 2000

Dubarry de Lassale, J., *Utilisation des marbres*. Editions H. Vial, Dourdan, 2005

Ďud'a, R., "Červenica-Dubník*", 3rd International Conference on Mineralogy and Museums, Budapest 1996, Excursion guide Field trip U3, East and Central Slovakia,* 1996

Evangelista, P. & Lazzarini, L., "La collezione ex Kircheriana di diaspri siciliani del Museo di Mineralogia alla Sapienza", in P. Pensabene, (ed.), *Marmi antichi II: cave e tecnica di lavorazione, provenienze e distribuzione*, Studi Miscellanei 31, 1998, pp.391–409

Falcone, R. & Lazzarini, L., "Note storico-scientifiche sul 'Broccatello di Spagna'", in P. Pensabene, (ed.), *Marmi antichi II: cave e tecnica di lavorazione, provenienze e distribuzione*, Studi Miscellanei 31, 1998, pp.87–97

Faramondi, S., Giardini, G., et al., *Le Collezioni dei materiali litoidi, ornamentali e da construzione del Servizio Geologico d'Italia: I litotipi della regione Lazio*, Bolletino del Servizio Geologico d'Italia Supplemento al Volume C1-1980, Instituto Poligraphico e Zecca dello Stato, Roma, 1985,

Feely, M., *Galway in stone: A geological walk in the heart of Galway,* Geoscapes, Dublin, 2002

Findstone "Forum for Advice on Care & Maintenance of Natural Stones", www.findstone.com/aw.htm

Finkelstein, P., *The art of faux*, Watson Guptill Publications, New York, 1997

Finska Stenindustri Ab "One hundred years of granite—1900–2000", http://finska.gsf.fi/

Flajs, G. & Hüssner, H., "A microbial model for the lower Devonian stromatactis mud mounds of the Montagne Noire (France)", *Facies* 29, 1993, pp.179–193

FNF (Federazione Nazionalione Fascista degli Esercenti le Industrie Estrattive), *I marmi Italiani*. Edizioni della Confederazione Fascista degli Industriale, Rome, 1939

Ford, T.D., *Derbyshire Blue John*. Landmark Publishing Ltd., Ashbourne, Derbyshire, 2000

Fraser, N.M., Bottjer, D.J., & Fisher, A.G., "Dissecting 'Lithiotis' Bivalves: Implications for the Early Jurassic Reef Eclipse", *PALAIOS* 19, 2004, pp.51–67

Frondel, C., *The system of mineralogy of J.D. and E.S. Dana. 7th ed.*, vol.3, 1962

Geological Museum Univ. of Oslo, "Larvikite—one of the world's most precious building stones", www.nhm.uio.no/geomus/nettutstillinger/Osloriften/larvikitt-eng.html, 2003

Geonord, "The Älvdalen Porphyry", www.geonord.org/shows/porph.html

Giraud, J.-D., Vittori, M., & Turco, G., "Données nouvelles sur les euphotides alpines des métagabbros à smaragdite de Corse", *Comptes rendus de l'Académie des sciences, Paris, Série II* 308, 1989, pp.51–56

Giusti, A., ed., *Eternità e nobilità di Materia.* Florence: Edizioni Polystampa, 2003

Giusti, A., *Pietre dure: hardstone in furniture and decorations*, Philip Wilson, London, 1992

Gnoli, M., "Northern Gondwanan Siluro-Devonian palaeogeography assessed by Cephalopods", *Palaeontologia Electronica*, palaeo-electronica.org/2002_2/gondwana/gondwana.pdf, 2003

Gnoli, R., *Marmora Romana*. Edizioni dell'Elefante, Roma, 1971

Gnoli, R., *Marmora Romana*. 2nd ed., Edizioni dell'Elefante, Roma, 1988

Gomez, F., "Gibraltar's Caves", www.showcaves.com/english/gb/region/GomezGibraltar.html

Gorgoni, C., Lazzarini, L., & Pallante, P., "New archaeometric data on Rosso Antico and other red marbles used in antiquity", in L. Lazzarini, et al., (eds.), *Interdisciplinary studies on ancient stone: proceedings of the sixth international conference of ASMOSIA, Venice, 2000*, Ausilio, Padova, 2002 pp.199–206

Gorgoni, C., Lazzarini, L., et al.,"An updated and detailed mineropetrographic and C-O stable isotopic reference database for the main Mediterranean marbles used in antiquity", in J.J. Herrmann, et al., (eds.), ASMOSIA 5—*"Interdisciplinary Studies on Ancient Stone" Proceedings of 5th International Conference, Museum of Fine Arts, Boston 1998*, Archetype Publications, Ltd., London, pp.115–131, 2002a

Goyal, R.S., Natani, J.V., & Chowdhary, K.D., "Marble resources of Rajasthan: An overview in the light of district resource maps by Geological Survey of India", www.cdos-india.com/papers/23%20-%20Marble%20Resources%20-%20GSI.doc

Grant, L. & Mortimer, R., "Westminster Abbey: The Cosmati Pavements", *Courtauld Institute Research Papers*, 3, 2002

Green, W.A., Young, S.M.M., et al., "Source tracing marbles: Trace element analysis with inductively coupled plasma-mass spectroscopy", in J.J. Herrmann, et al., (eds.), *ASMOSIA 5—Interdisciplinary Studies on Ancient Stone: Proceedings of 5th International Conference, Museum of Fine Arts, Boston 1998*, Archetype Publications, London, pp.132–142, 2002

Grundke, C.K., "American Masters of Stone", www.americanmastersofstone.com/, 2004

GSWA—Geological Survey of Western Australia, "Gemstones in Western Australia", www.doir.wa.gov.au/documents/gswa/gsdpap_gem.pdf, 1994

Guimaré Gutiérrez, S.R., "Una riqueza explotable", www.revistafusion.com/galicia/1999/mayo/report4-68.htm, 2005

Hamilton, D., "Algal growths in the Rhaetic Cotham Marble of Southern England", *Palaeontology* 4, 1961, pp.324–333

Hamilton, H.C. & Falconer, W., "The Geography of Strabo. Literally translated, with notes, in three volumes", www.perseus.tufts.edu/cgi-bin/ptext?lookup=Strab.+toc, 1903

Hancock, P.L. & Skinner B.J., *The Oxford companion to the Earth,* Oxford University Press, Oxford, 2000

Harlow, G.E., "Hard rock", *Natural History*, Aug 1991, pp.4–10

Harlow, G.E. & Sorensen, S.S., "Jade: Occurrence and metasomatic origin", extended abstract from International Geological Congress 2000. *The Australian Gemmologist* 21, 2001, pp.7–10

Harmon, T., *The river runs north: A story of Montana moss agate*, Tom and Cheryl Harmon, Crane, MT, 2000

Harrell, J.A. (a), "Table 1. Ancient Egyptian hardstone quarries", www.eeescience.utoledo.edu/Faculty/Harrell/Egypt/Quarries/Hardst_Quar.html

Harrell, J.A. (b), "Table 2. Ancient Egyptian softstone quarries", www.eeescience.utoledo.edu/Faculty/Harrell/Egypt/Quarries/Softst_Quar.html

Harrell, J.A. & Brown, V.M., "The oldest surviving topographical map from ancient Egypt (Turin Papyri 1879, 1899 and 1969)", *Journal of the American Research Center in Egypt*, 1992, pp.29, 81–105

Harrell, J.A. & Brown, V.M., "Rock-sawing at a Roman diorite quarry in Wadi Umm Shegilat, Egypt", in J.J. Herrmann, et al., (eds.), *ASMOSIA 5—Interdisciplinary Studies on Ancient Stone" Proceedings of 5th International Conference, Museum of Fine Arts, Boston 1998*, Archetype Publications, London, 2002, pp.52–57

Harrell, J.A. & Lazzarini, L., "A new variety of granito bianco e nero from Wadi Barud, Egypt", in J.J. Herrmann, et al., (eds.), *ASMOSIA 5—Interdisciplinary Studies on Ancient Stone: Proceedings of 5th International Conference, Museum of Fine Arts, Boston 1998*, Archetype publications, London, 2002a., pp.47–51

Harrell, J.A., Max Brown, V., & Lazzarini, L., "Breccia verde antica: sources, petrology and ancient uses", in L. Lazzarini, et al., (eds.), *Interdisciplinary studies on ancient stone: Proceedings of the sixth international conference of ASMOSIA, Venice, 2000*, Ausilio, Padova. 2002, pp.207–218

Heaney, P.J. & Fisher, D.M., "New interpretation of the origin of tiger's-eye", *Geology* 31, 2003, pp.323–326

Herz, N.,, "A history of the Association for the Study of Marbles and Other Stones in Antiquity", in M. Schvoerer, et al., (eds.), *Archéomatériaux—Marbres et Autres Roches. Actes de la IVème Conférence Internationale de l'Association pour l'Étude des Marbres et Autres Roches Utilisés dans le Passé*, CRPAA, Talence, 1999, p.6

Hewitt, J. ,"Hoptonwood stone", www.hoptonwoodstone.co.uk/, 2001

Higgins, M.D. & Higgins, R.A., *A geological companion to Greece and the Aegean*, Duckworth, London, 1996

Hintze, C.A.F., *Handbuch der mineralogie.* Verlag von Veit & Co., Leipzig, 1915

Hirth, K., *Obsidian Craft Production in Ancient Central Mexico.* University of Utah Press, Salt Lake City, 2006

Hladil, J., "The formation of stromatactis-type fenestral structures during the sedimentation of experimental slurries—a possible clue to a 120-year-old puzzle about stromatactis", *Bulletin of Geosciences* 80, 2005, pp.193–211

Holst, C.A., "The Wisconsin Capitol—Official Guide and History", 2nd ed., ftp.rootsweb.com/pub/usgenweb/wi/history/capitol/capitol01.txt, 1919

Horváth, L., "Mineral species discovered in Canada, and species named after Canadians", *Canadian Mineralogist.* Special publication 6, 2003

Howard, K.B. n.d., "Jadeite", *Gemmology Canada*, www.cigem.ca/431.html

Hudson, R., "Feeling the heat in cool Tucson, report of the 2001 Gem Show", *BC Rockhounder,* June 2001

Hudson, R., "Arizona dreaming—the Tuscson Gem Show 2003", *BC Rockhounder,* spring 2003

Hughes, R.W., Galibert, O., et al., "Burmese Jade: The Inscrutable Gem", *Gems & Gemology* 36,

pp.2–26 (in part) www.ruby-sapphire.com/jade_burma_part_1.htm & www.ruby-sapphire.com/jade_burma_part_2.htm, 2000

Hull, E., *A treatise on the building and ornamental stones of Great Britain and foreign countries*, Macmillan, London, 1872

Hyrsl, J.R., Z., "Peruvian minerals: An update", *Mineralogical Record* 34, 2003, pp.241–254

ICS—International Commission on Stratigraphy 2006. "International stratigraphic chart", www.stratigraphy.org/cheu.pdf

INETI, "Ornabase: Base de Dados do Catálogo de Rochas Ornamentais Portuguesas", http://e-geo.ineti.pt/bds/ornabase/, 2006

J. Paul Getty Trust, "Portrait Medallion of Pope Alexander VIII", www.getty.edu/art/gettyguide/artObjectDetails?artobj=1465

Jayabalan, K., Rajaram, K., & Sukumaran, G.B., "Resource Identification—Dimension Stone Granite Deposits in Various Parts of Tamil Nadu", *Indian Stone AIGSA Magazine*, www.worldstonex.com/en/InfoItem.asp?ICat=2&ArticleID=71

Jervis, G., *I tesori sotterranei dell'Italia.* vol.1, Ermanno Loescher, Turin, 1873

Jervis, G., *I tesori sotterranei dell'Italia.* vol.3, Ermanno Loescher, Turin, 1881

Jervis, G., *I tesori sotterranei dell'Italia.* vol.4, Ermanno Loescher, Turin, 1889

Jervis, W.P., *The mineral resources of central Italy: including a description of the mines and marble quarries.* Edward Stanford, London, 1862

Keller, P.C., *Gemstones of East Africa*, Geoscience Press, Phoenix, Az, 1992

Kinahan, G.H., "Economic geology of Ireland: No.II marbles and limestones" *Journal of the Royal Geological Society of Ireland (new series)* 8, 123–156, 1886

King, R.J., "Minerals explained 33: Azurite and malachite", *Geology Today* 2001, pp.17, 152

Kious, W.J. & Tilling, R.I. "This Dynamic Earth, the story of plate tectonics", U.S. Geological Survey, http://pubs.usgs.gov/gip/dynamic/dynamic.html

Knowles, K., Winterbottom, R., & Lewis, F., "Stone in Archaeology: Towards a digital resource", 2005, http://ads.ahds.ac.uk

Konev, A.A., Vorobjov, E.I., & Bulach, A., "Charoit — der Schmuckstein aus Sibirien und seine seltenen Begleitminerale", Lapis 18, 1993, pp.13–20

Korres, M., *From Pentelicon to the Parthenon: The ancient quarries and the story of a half-worked column capital of the first marble Parthenon*, Melissa, Athens, 1995

Koukouli, C., Muller, A., & Papadopoulos, S., eds., *Thasos: Matières premières et technologie de la préhistoire à nos jours: Actes du Colloque International 26-29/9/1995, Thasos, Liménaria*: Ecole Francaise d'Athenes, Athens, 1999

Kretschmer, F., *Heimatbuch Adnet—Der Marmor*, Salzburger Bildungswerk, Adnet, 1986

Lanciani, R.A., *New tales of old Rome*, Macmillan, London, 1901

Larsen, A.O., "The Langesundsfjord site: The

minerals from the Norwegian syenite pegmatites", http://home.c2i.net/aolarsen/index.html, 2000

Lazzarini, L. "Sul 'Marmo Misio', uno dei graniti più usati anticamente", in P. Pensabene, (ed.), *Marmi Antichi II. Cave e tecnica di lavorazione*, provenienze e distribuzione, Studi Miscellanei 31, L'Erma di Bretschneider, Roma, 1998, pp.111–117

Lazzarini, L., "La determinazione della provenienza delle pietre decorative usate dai Romani", in M. De Nuccio, et al., (eds.), *I Marmi Colorati della Roma Imperiale*, Marsilio, Venezia, 2002, pp.223–265

Lazzarini, L., "The origin and characterization of breccia nuvolata, marmor Sagarium, and marmor Triponticum", in J.J. Herrmann, et al., (eds.), *ASMOSIA 5—Interdisciplinary Studies on Ancient Stone, Proceedings of 5th International Conference, Museum of Fine Arts, Boston 1998*, Archetype Publications, London, 2002a., pp.58–67

Lazzarini, L., "La scoperta dell'origine chiota della Breccia d'Aleppo e di un Nero Antico, con un primo loro studio petrografico", in A. Giusti, (ed.), *Eternità e nobilità di Materia*, Edizioni Polystampa, Florence, 2003, pp.139–168

Lazzarini, L., "Archaeometric aspects of white and colored marbles used in antiquity, the state of the art", in G.M. Bargossi, et al., (eds.), *A showcase of the Italian research in Applied Petrology*, Special Issue 3 del *Periodico di Mineralogia* 73, 2004, pp.113–125

Lazzarini, L., "Quarry landscape of the month, May 2006: Vezirhan breccia quarry", www.quarryscapes.no/QLM_may_06.php, 2006

Lazzarini, L., Antonelli, F., et al., "Marmor Chalcidicum (Fior di Pesco). Source, history of use and scientific characterisation", in L. Lazzarini, et al., (eds.), *Interdisciplinary studies on ancient stone: proceedings of the sixth international conference of ASMOSIA, Venice, 2000*, Ausilio, Padova, 2002b. pp.233–240

Lazzarini, L., Masi, U., & Tucci, P., "Petrografic and geochemical features of the Carystian marble, 'Cipollino Verde', from the ancient quarries of Southern Euboea (Greece)", in Y. Maniatis, et al., (eds.), *The study of marble and other stones used in antiquity: Asmosia III, Athens: transactions of the 3rd International Symposium of the Association for the Study of Marble and Other Stones used in Antiquity*, Archetype Books, London, 1995, pp.161–169

Lazzarini, L., Pensabene, P., & Turi, B., "Isotopic and petrographic characterization of Marmor Lesbium, Island of Lesbos, Greece", in M. Schvoerer, et al., (eds.), *Archéomatériaux—Marbres et Autres Roches. Actes de la IVème Conférence Internationale de l'Association pour l'Étude des Marbres et Autres Roches Utilisés dans le Passé*, CRPAA, Talence, 1999, pp.125–129

Lazzarini, L. & Turi, B., "Characterisation and differentiation of the Skyros marbles (Greece) and the Medici's breccias (Italy)", in M. Schvoerer, et al., (eds.), *Archéomatériaux—Marbres et Autres Roches. Actes de la IVème Conférence Internationale de l'Association pour l'Étude des Marbres et Autres Roches Utilisés dans le Passé*, CRPAA, Talence, 1999a, pp.117–123

Lee, A., *Marble and marble workers, a handbook for architects, artists, etc.*, Crosby Lockwood & Son, London, 1888

Litos online, "Rosa Portuguese marble", www.litosonline.com/articles/53/ar5301e.shtml, 2006

Mancini, S., "Marmoteca 2000 Sezione dei Marmi Apuani, Nuova Catalogaziona", www.isicentry.com/Catalogo%20Marmoteca.doc, 2002

Mango, C.A., *The Art of the Byzantine Empire 312–1453*, University of Toronto Press, Toronto, 1972

Marko, F., Pivko, D., & Vratislav, H., "Ruin marble: A record of fracture-controlled fluid flow and precipitation", *Geological Quarterly* 47, 2003, pp.241–252

Massinelli, A.M., *Scagliola: l'arte della pietra di luna*, Editalia, Roma, 1997

Max Balz GMBH, "The history of the origins of the Jura limestone and of the natural slabs of Solnhofen", www.max-balz.de/englisch/3_geschichte/3_2_geologie/geologie.html

Max, M.D., *Connemara Marble and the industry based upon it*, Geological Survey of Ireland, Dublin, 1985

Mayall, M.J. & Wright, V.P., "Algal tuft structures in stromatolites from the Upper Triassic of south-west England", *Palaeontology* 24, 1981, pp.655–60

Mazeran, R. "Les brèches exploitées comme marbre dans le Sud-Est de la France a l'époque romaine", in M. Schvoerer, et al., (eds.), *Archéomatériaux—Marbres et Autres Roches. Actes de la IVème Conférence Internationale de l'Association pour l'Étude des Marbres et Autres Roches Utilisés dans le Passé*, CRPAA, Talence, 1999, pp.335–338

McBride, E.F., "Pseudofaults resulting from compartmentalized Liesegang bands: update", *Sedimentology* 50, 2003 pp.725–730

McCann-Murray, S., "A Geologic Walking Tour of Building Stones of Downtown Baltimore, Maryland", Maryland Geological Survey Educational Series No. 10, 2005, www.mgs.md.gov/esic/features/walking/index.html

McGee, E.S., "Colorado Yule marble—building stone of the Lincoln Memorial", U.S. Geological Survey Bulletin 2162, http://pubs.usgs.gov/pdf/bulletin/b2162/b2162.pdf, 1999

McLaren, A., "Mookaite: A lithic enigma", www.eskimo.com/~knapper/mookaite.htm

Melezhik, V.A. a. H., T. and Roberts, D. and Gorokhov, I.M. and Fallick, A.E., "Depositional environment and apparent age of the Fauske carbonate conglomerate, North Norwegian Caledonides", *Norges Geologiske Undersokelse Bulletin* 436, 2000, pp.147–168

Merrill, G.P., *The onyx marbles: Their origin, composition, and uses, both ancient and modern*. Government Printing Office, Washington, D.C., 1893

Merrill, G.P., *Stones for building and decoration*, 3rd ed., John Wiley/Chapman & Hall, New York/London, 1903

Michalzik, D., Fischer, R., et al., "Age and origin of the 'Mexican Onyx' at San Antonio Texcala (Puebla, Mexico)", *Geologische Beiträge Hannover* 2, 2001, pp.79–89

Mielsch, H., *Buntmarmore aus Rom im Antikenmuseum Berlin*, Staatliche Museen Preussischer Kulturbesitz, Berlin, 1985

Miller, J.K. & Folk, R.L., "Petrographic, geochemical and structural constraints on the timing and distribution of postlithification dolomite in the Rhaetian Portoro ('Calcare Nero') of the Portovenere Area, La Spezia, Italy", *Special Publications of the International Association of Sedimentologists* 21, 1994, pp.187–202

Monroe, E., "Stone sleuthing: The new US embassy", *The Sofia Echo*, 3 Mar 2005, http://www.sofiaecho.com/article/stone-sleuthing-the-new-us-embassy/id_10915/catid_29

Montana, G. & Gagliardo Briuccia, V., *I marmi e i diaspri del Barocco siciliano: Rassegna dei materiali lapidei di pregio utilizzati per la decorazione ad intarsio*, Flaccovio Editore, Palermo, 1998

Morteani, G. & Ackermand, D., "Mineralogy and geochemistry of Al-phosphate and Al-borosilicate-bearing metaquartzites of the northern Serra do Espinhaço (State of Bahia, Brazil)", *Mineralogy and Petrology* 80, 2004, pp.59–81

Mueller, E., "Ocean jasper", *Mid-Tenn Gem'ers—Newsletter of the Tennessee Gem and Mineral Society* 27, 2005, pp.5–6

Napoleone, C., *Delle pietre antiche di Faustino Corsi romano*. Franco Maria Ricci, Milano, 2001

Nevill, W.E., "Stratigraphy and origin of the Cork Red Marble", *Geological Magazine* 99, 1962, pp.481–491

Niedermayr, G., "Der Bleiberger 'Muschelmarmor'—F.X. Wulfen's 'kärnthenscher pfauenschweifiger Helmintholith'", *Carinthia II, Naturwissenschaftliche Beiträge zur Heimatkunde Kärntens* 179/99, 1989, pp.47–57

Norton, P.T., "Fossils of the Maine State Capitol", *Maine Naturalist*, 1993, www.state.me.us/legis/lawlib/fossil1.htm

NPAONBP (North Pennines AONB Partnership), "North Pennines Area of Outstanding Natural Beauty: Geodiversity Audit and Action Plan 2004–09 (Section 2)" www.northpennines.org.uk/media/pdf/h/j/GAP%20section%202.pdf, 2004

Olivier, M., "Efficiency improvement drive beginning to bear fruit", *Mining Weekly Online*, 23 Sep 2005, www.miningweekly.co.za/min/sector/opencast/?show=73625

O'Neill, H.E., *Stone for building*, Heinemann, London, 1965

Ottens, B., "Chinese fluorite", *Mineralogical Record* 36, 2005, pp.59–68

Pabian, R.K., "The Agate Page", http://csd.unl.edu/agates/agatepageintro.asp, 2004

Pabian, R.K., Jackson, B., et al., *Agates: Treasures of the Earth*, Natural History Museum, London, 2006

Pajarez-Ayuela, P., *Cosmatesque Ornament: Flat Polychrome Geometric Patterns in Architecture*, W.W. Norton, London & New York, 2001

Peacock, D.P.S., Williams-Thorpe, O., et al, "Mons Claudianus and the problem of the '*granito del foro*': a geological and geochemical approach", *Antiquity* 68, 1994, pp.209–230

Pellegris, S., "Cipollini Marbles from Toscana (Italy)", *LITOS printed edition* 66, May 2003, www.litosonline.com/articles/66/ar6602e.shtml

Pensabene, P., "Le principali cave di marmo bianco", in M. De Nuccio, et al., (eds.), *I Marmi Colorati della Roma Imperiale*, Marsilio, Venezia, 2002, pp.203–222

Pensabene, P. & Lazzarini, L., "Il problema del Bigio Antico e del Bigio Morato: contributo allo studio delle cave di Teos e di Chios", in P. Pensabene, (ed.), *Marmi antichi II: cave e tecnica di lavorazione, provenienze e distribuzione*, Studi Miscellanei 31, 1998, pp.142–173

Perazzo, P.B. (a). "Stone quarries and beyond", www.cagenweb.com/quarries/

Perazzo, P.B. (b). "Names and Origins of Stone—D", www.cagenweb.com/quarries/name_and_origion/d.html

Perrier, R., "Les roches ornementales d'Espagne.' *Mines et Carrières* 74, 1992, pp.147–158

Perrier, R., "Les roches ornementales de Norvège", *Mines et Carrières* 76, 1994, pp.85–96

Perrier, R., "Les marbres verte du Val d'Aoste", *Le Mausolée* 704, Apr 1995, pp.58–71

Perrier, R. 1996, "Les roches ornementales du Languedoc-Roussillon", *Mines et Carrières* 78, pp.65–75

Perrier, R., "Les marbres rouges de type Rosso Levanto", *Le Mausolée* no.720, Aug 1996a, pp.62–71

Peybernès, B., "Inventaire typologique et utilisation en architecture des principaux marbres du cycle hercynien des Pyrénées françaises et du SW de la Montagne-Noire", *Bulletin de la Société d'Histoire Naturelle de Toulouse* 140, 2004, pp.39–51

Pieri, M., *La scala della qualità e le varietà nei marmi Italiani.*, Ulrico Hoepli, Milano, 1954

Pieri, M., *I Marmi d'Italia. Graniti e pietre ornamentali, Seconda edizione ampliata*, Ulrico Hoepli, Milano, c.1958

Pivko, D. "The world's most popular marbles", Findstone, www.findstone.com/daniel4.htm

Pivko, D., "Natural Stones in Earth's History", *Acta Geologica Universitatis Comenianae* 58, www.fns.uniba.sk/prifuk/casopisy/geol/200358/pivko.rtf, 2003

Pivko, D., "The world's most popular granites—updated and extended to 180 granites", Findstone, www.findstone.com/daniel1.htm, 2005

Playfair, R.L., *On the re-discovery of lost Numidian marbles in Algeria and Tunis: read at the British Association (Geological Section), at Aberdeen, September 1885*, British Association, Aberdeen, 1885

Pollock, J., "Geology of the Roman Catholic Basilica of St. John the Baptist, St. John's, Newfoundland", *Geoscience Canada* 31, 2004, pp.1–10

Ponti, G., "Tecniche di estrazione e di lavorazione delle colonne monolitiche di granito troadense", in M. De Nuccio, et al., (eds.), *I Marmi Colorati della Roma Imperiale*, Marsilio, Venezia, 2002, pp.291–295

Porfyr Museet "Porfyrfakta", http://hem2.passagen.se/tommykas/

Porter, M.W., *What Rome was built with*, Henry Frowde, London and Oxford; New York, 1907

Powell, W.G., "Tennessee Marble", 2005, http://academic.brooklyn.cuny.edu/geology/powell/613webpage/NYCbuilding/TennesseeMarble/TennesseeMarble.htm

Price, M.T. (a) *The Corsi Collection*, www.oum.ox.ac.uk/collect/minpet.htm

Price, M. & Walsh, K., *Pocket Nature: Rocks and minerals*, Dorling Kindersley, London, 2005

Pullen, H.W., *Handbook of ancient Roman marbles,* John Murray, London, 1894

Raulet, S., *Rock crystal treasures: from antiquity to today,* Vendome Press, New York, 1999

Reis, M., "Supplying the world with Jerusalem Stone", *Stone World* 3 May 2002, www.stoneworld.com/CDA/Archives

Reis, M., "Rediscovering Arizona onyx", *Stone World* 5 May 2004, www.stoneworld.com/CDA/Archives

Repetti, E., *Dizionario geografico fisico storico della Toscana,* Firenze, 1833

Rhodes, D., "Biggs picture jasper: A legacy is born", *The Rock Collector* 106, 2006, pp.3–5

Ribbe, P.H., "Interference Colors in Oil Slicks and Feldspars", *Mineralogical Record* 3, 1972, pp.18–22

Robinson, E., *Holiday Geology Guide: Trafalgar Square*, British Geological Survey, Keyworth, 1996

Robinson, R.E. 1890. "In the Marble Hills (in Vermont)", *Century Magazine*, www.cagenweb.com/quarries/articles_and_books/in_the_marble_hills.html

Rock of Ages "Visitors Center and Memorial Design Studio: History", www.rockofages.com/visitors/history.html

Rogers, P., *Westminster Cathedral: From darkness to light*, Burns & Oates, London, 2003

Rogers, P., "Is this Ireland's oldest marble quarry?" *Oremus* 105, 2006, p.20

Rowe, J. "A Short History of Luxulyan Parish and The Parish Church of St. Cyriac and St. Julitta", http://homepages.rootsweb.com/~marcie/kernow/luxulyan.html

Sagar-Fenton, M. & Smith, S.B., *Serpentine*, Truran, Truro, 2005

Savedge Schlesinger, C., "The Wren Building at the College of William & Mary, Interior restoration, 1967–1968", 1968, rev.1979. www.pastportal.com/Archive/Research%20Reports/Html/RR0194.htm

Schmidt, R., "Die berühmten Jaspachate von Guiliana/Sizilien," *Lapis* 27, 2002, pp.21–28 & 33–37

Scotgaz—Gazetteer for Scotland 1995–2006. "Rubislaw quarry", www.geo.ed.ac.uk/scotgaz/features/featurefirst1485.html

Scott-Smith, "J. Shap's famous granite, and its related industry", www.ruralwebdesign.co.uk/contribute_editable/shap_history_society/shap-granite-works.htm

SDNP—Sustainable Development Networking Program Pakistan "Explore Balochistan Mineral resources", www.balochistan.sdnpk.org/mineral2.htm

Seeman, R. & Summesberger, H., *Wiener Steinwanderwege. Die Geologie der Großstadt.* Verlag Christian Brandstätter, Vienna, 1999

Shadmon, A., "Black is beautiful", *Litos*, 2003, www.litosonline.com/articles/68/ar6802e.shtml

Shigley, J.E., Koivula, J.I., & Fryer, C.W., "The Occurrence and Gemological Properties of Wessels Mine Sugilite", *Gems and Gemology* 23, 1987, pp.78–89

Spalding, A., Hartgroves, S., et al. (eds), "The conservation value of abandoned pits in Cornwall: A report for the Derelict Land Advisory Group", Cornwall County Council, 1999

Steacy, H.R., Rose, E.R., et al., "Some classic mineral localities of Southeastern Ontario", *Mineralogical Record* 13, 1982, pp.197–203

Stolzuoli, R., ed., *L'alabastro di Volterra*, Florence: Consorzio "Le Città delle Pietre Ornamentali", c.1997

The Larimar Museum, Dominican Republic, "Larimar—volcanic blue", www.larimarmuseum.com/whatis.html

The National Trust, *Farnborough Hall*, The National Trust, London, 1999

Thomas, P., "L'origene des gabbros orbiculaires: Observations de quelques roches orbiculaires et de leur gisement", www.ens-lyon.fr/Planet-Terre/Infosciences/Terrain/Echantillon/Articles/orbiculaire.html, 2000

TiberSuperbum, "Il travertino", www.tibursuperbum.it/ita/artigianato/travertino/index.htm, 2003

Tomlinson, J.M. & Ford, T.D., *Derbyshire Black Marble*, Special publication 4, Peak District Mines Historical Society, Matlock, Bath, 1996

Townsend, 2005, "Jade in Australia", www.gem.org.au/jade.htm

Tozzi, M. & Parotto, M., "The Geology of the Baroque: The Geology of the City of Rome", www.geologia.com/english/fi2004/2004_barocco.html, 2000

United States Geological Survey (USGS), "An Overview of Production of Specific U.S. Gemstones", U.S. Bureau of Mines Special Publication 14–95, http://minerals.er.usgs.gov/minerals/pubs/commodity/gemstones, 2002

United States Geological Survey (USGS), "Petrified Forest National Park: A Photographic Geology Tour", http://3dparks.wr.usgs.gov/petrifiedforest/index2.htm, 2004

Utah Geological Survey, "Building Stones of Downtown Salt Lake City, A Walking Tour", http://ugs.utah.gov/online_html/pi/pi-60/pi60pg4.htm, 2005

Valpolicella.it, "Geology", www.valpolicella.it/eng/lev1.asp?sez=territorio, 2001a

Valpolicella.it, "Marble", www.valpolicella.it/eng/lev1.asp?sez=marmo, 2001b

Viner, D., *The Iona marble quarry*. 2nd ed., New Iona Press, Isle of Iona, 1992

Von Bezing, K.L., Dixon, R.D., et al., "The Kalahari manganese field: An update", *Mineralogical Record* 22, 1991, pp.279–297

Wall, F., "Kola Peninsula: Minerals and mines", *Geology Today* 19, 2003, p.206

Ward, F. & Ward, C., *Jade*, Gem Book series / Fred Ward, Gem Book Publishers, Bethesda, MD, 1996

Ward, F. & Ward, C., *Opals*, Gem Book series / Fred Ward, Gem Book Publishers, Bethesda, MD, 1997

Ward-Perkins, W.B., "Africano marble and 'lapis sarcophagus'", in H. Dodge, et al., (eds.), *Marble in antiquity: collected papers of W.B. Ward-Perkins*, British School at Rome, London, 1992

Watson, J., *British and foreign building stones: A catalog of the specimens in the Sedgwick Museum, Cambridge*, Cambridge University Press, Cambridge, 1911

Watson, J., *British and foreign marbles and other ornamental stones: A catalog of the specimens in the Sedgwick Museum, Cambridge*, Cambridge University Press, Cambridge, 1916

Watson, M., "Turquoise—The gemstone of Tibet", The Tibetan Review, www.dharamsalanet.com/links/articles/turquoise.htm, 2002

Webster, R. & Read, P.G., *Gems: Their sources, descriptions and identification*, 5th ed., Butterworth Heinemann, Oxford, 1994

Wenrich, K.J., "Sweet Home rhodochrosite—what makes it so cherry red?" *Mineralogical Record 29*, 1998, pp.123–127

Williams, D.F. & Peacock, D.P.S., "The use of Purbeck marble in Roman and Medieval Britain", in L. Lazzarini, et al., (eds.). *Interdisciplinary studies on ancient stone: proceedings of the sixth international conference of ASMOSIA, Venice, 2000*, Ausilio, Padova, 2002, pp.135–139

Wirsing, A.L., *Marmora et adfines aliquos lapides/Abbildungen der Marmor Arten und einiger verwandten Steine*, Auf Kosten des Berlegers, Nurnberg, 1775

Woodruff, R.E. & Fritsch, E., "Blue pectolite from the Dominican Republic", *Gems and Gemology* 25, 1989, pp.216–225

Wyse Jackson, P., *The building stones of Dublin: A walking guide*. Town House and Country House, Dublin, 1993

Wyse Jackson, P., "A Victorian landmark: Trinity College's Museum Building", *Irish Arts Review* 11, 1995, pp.149–154

Zeitner, J.C., *Gem and lapidary materials: for cutters, collectors, and jewelers*. Geoscience Press, Tucson, Az, 1996

Zezza, U. & Lazzarini, L., "Krokeatis Lithos (Lapis Lacedaemonius): Source, history of use, scientific characterisation", in L. Lazzarini, et al., (eds.), *Interdisciplinary studies on ancient stone: Proceedings of the sixth international conference of ASMOSIA, Venice, 2000*, Ausilio, Padova, 2002, pp.259-264

Zoppas, B. (a), "I lapidei del Francia/French stone", in B. Zoppas, (ed.), *TRE Annual lapidei/Stone annual 5*, Antonio Zoppas Editore

Zoppas, B. (b), "I lapidei della Grecia/Greek stones', in B. Zoppas, (ed.), *TRE Annual lapidei/Stone annual 6*, Antonio Zoppas Editore

Zoppas, B. (c), "I lapidei del Brasile/Brasil stone", in B. Zoppas, (ed.), *TRE Annual lapidei/Stone annual 8*, Antonio Zoppas Editore

Index

INDEX

Picture credits

By kind permission of AA World Travel Library 109;

By kind permission of Adrian Alan Fine Art & Antiques, London
www.adrianalan.com 205R;

Alamy 24CR, /Arcaid/Richard Bryant 84BR, /Rodolfo Arpia 58-59, /BAE Inc
85, /Bildarchiv Monheim GmbH/Florain Monheim 18, /Bora 185B, /Directphoto.
org 192B, /Paul Felix 182BL, 183, /E&S Ginsberg 175B, /Imagery & Imagination
253BC, /Boris Karpinski 141BL (inset), /Philipp Mohr 22L, /Mooch Images 18R,
/plain picture/KuS 40, /pictures colour library199, /Massimo Pizzotti 187T,
/Nigel Reed 79T, /SAS 91, /Ron Scott 25 BL & BC, /Andre Seale 35T, /Swerve
108BC, /Glyn Thomas 44L, /Ernst Wrba 46L, /Wyrdlight 79B, /zefa/Guenter
Rossenbach 64L;

The Art Archive/Biblioteca Nazionale Marciana Venice/Dagli Orti 15,/Museo
Capitoline Rome/Dagli Orti 54BC, 76B/Dagli Orti 135R, /Musée du Louvre Paris/
Dagli Orti 221B, /Nicolas Sopieha 202L;

Art Directors & Trip Photolibrary /Robert Belbin 236TR, /Graham Ivory 39T,
/Helene Rogers 14, 49T 202BC, 270-271,

By kind permission of Phil Bews & Diane Gorvin www.bewsgorvin.co.uk 198BC;

By kind permission of Bowness, Hepworth Estate 271TR;

Bridgeman Art Library /Chateau de Versailles/Peter Willi 135BL, /Musée Rodin
Paris France/Philippe Galard 65BR, /National Trust Photographic Library/
Derrick E Witty, Charlecote Park UK 248-249, /Funds provided by Mrs E Hansen
in memory of Dr R Hansen, Museum of Fine Arts, Houston, Texas USA 256B;

By kind permission of Reno Carollo 69R;

Christies Images Ltd 16, 83T;

Chatsworth, The Devonshire Collection. Reproduced by permission of the
Chatsworth Settlement Trustees 150L;

Corbis 62R, /Alinari Archives/George Tatge 178B, /Beateworks/Roger Brooks
233, /Beatework/Tim Street-Porter 60R, /Remi Benali 19, /Cordaiy Photo Library

Ltd/Johnathan Smith 56B, /Kevin Fleming 23B, /Eric & David Hosking 70R,
/Paul H Kulper 121, David Lees 103, /Charles & Josette Lemars 211, /Arnaldo de
Luca 165R, /Michael Nicholson 220BC, /Douglas Peebles 33R, /Photo Images/
Lee Snider 220L, /Sygma/Vatican Pool 141B, /Nik Wheeler 92-93, /Lawson Wood
37T /Adam Woolfitt 125R;

www.decorami.com 168C;

Jeff Eden 54L;

By kind permission of Mark Godden (Albion Stone) 23T, 24TL, 24CA;

By kind permission of The Granite Shop/Jean Marie/Whirled Wyde Web 200TR;

By kind permission of David & Elizabeth Hacker 249CR;

The Holkham Estate 47R, 200TR;

By kind permission of Lorenzo Lazzarini 194B;

Marc Levoy/Stanford University 22BC;

By kind permission of Limestone Gallery 232C;

By kind permission of Lundhs Labrador 227T;

The Malachite Room/ The State Hermitage Museum 258BL;

By kind permission of Nicolai Medvedev courtesy of Harold & Erica Van Pelt
249TR;

The Natural History Museum, London 185TR, 266BR;

By kind permission of John Neilson 190L;

Gary Ombler 1, 2–3, 2TC, 2TL, 8R, 9, 10–11, 12B, 45, 46TR, 47TL, 48, 49BR,
50–51, 52, 53R, 67, 83B, 86L, 88TR, 94R, 137TR, 143C, 152C, 158B, 163TR, 167TL,
167B, 182CR, 193TL, 206L, 213TR & CR, 222TL, 225TR, 226, 227B, 229R, 237, 238T,
239TR & CR, 240–241, 242–243, 250R, 251TR, 252, 254, 255 main, 257TR, 259T,
261C, 262TL & B, 264–265, 266TL, 267TL, 272–273;

Oxford University Museum of Natural History www.oum.ox.ac.uk
2TR, 42-43, 53L, 54TR, 55, 56T, 57, 58L, 59R, 60L, 61, 62L, 63, 64-65, 68, 69L, 70L,
71, 72T&C, 73, 74-75, 76T, 77, 78TL, 80 - 81, 82, 86R, 87, 88TL, 89, 90, 92, 93TR,
94L, 95, 96-97, 98-99, 100-101, 104†TL, 105, 106TR, 107, 110-111, 112-113, 114,
115T, 116-117, 118L, 119, 120, 122L, 124, 125L, 126-127, 128T, 129, 130, 131T, 132-
133, 134, 135TL, 136, 137T, 138, 139TL, 140, 141T, 144-145, 146-147, 148-149, 150R,
151, 152T, 153, 154-155, 156-157, 158TL, 159, 160, 161T, 162, 163TL, 164, 165L, 166,
167T, 168T & CR, 169, 170T, 171, 172-173, 174TR, 176, 177T, 178T, 179T, 180-181,
184, 185TL, 186, 188-189, 190TR, 191, 192T, 193TR, 194T, 195, 196-197, 200TL, 201,
202TR, 203, 204, 205TL, 206TL, 207, 210, 212, 213TL, 214-215, 216-217, 218-219,
220TR, 221T, 222TR, 223, 224, 225TL, 228, 228TL, 230-231, 234-235, 236TL, 237TL,
239TL, 244-245, 246, 247T&C, 250L, 251L, 253T & CL, 255, 256T, 257TL, 258TL &
CL, 260, 261TL, 267TR, 268-269, /Monica T. Price 8L, 13, 21, 25, 29, 30, 32, 33, 34,
35B, 38, 39B, 49BC, 102, 115B, 122R, 131B, 139TR, 161CR, 175C, 177B, 182C, 208,
247B, 261B, 263B, /Monica T. Price/© The Devonshire Collection, Chatsworth.
Reproduced by permission of the Chatsworth Settlement Trustees 128BR,
170B, /Monica T. Price & Helen Cowdy 29, 30, /Jim Kennedy 36, 37B, /Dave
Waters 66;

By kind permission of Palazzo, Pitti, Florence, Italy 238BR;

Luke Powell 263T;

Private collection 108BL;

The Provost, Fellows and Scholars of the Queen's College Oxford 102B;

By kind permission of Eric Robinson 198BL;

By kind permission of Patrick Rogers 44BC, 123, 137B, 142-143, 143TR, 174L,
187B;

By kind permission of Marian Sava 78TR;

By kind permission of Stone Age/Parker Hobart Associates 232B;

By kind permission of www.thornhillgalleries.co.uk 139B;

Trevor Trott Photography 84CR;

By kind permission of www.westlandlondon.com 72BR;

Dean & Chapter of Westminster 209;

By kind permission of Mary White 17, 24BR;

All efforts have been made to contact copyright holders.

Acknowledgments

My research into Faustino Corsi's decorative stone collection has been in partnership with my colleague Lisa Cooke who has translated and extensively researched Corsi's *Catalogo ragionato*, and I warmly thank her for her many insights into the collection and all her support with this book. I am very grateful indeed to Kevin Walsh and Paul Ensom who have both given me valuable help with my research, and welcome feedback on what I have written. Any remaining errors are mine alone.

The Corsi research project would not have been possible without a grant from the Jerwood Foundation administered by what is now the Museums, Libraries and Archives Council. A number of experts have kindly visited Oxford to tell me more about Corsi's collection, or welcomed me to their institutions to study other decorative stone collections. I would especially like to thank James Harrell (University of Toledo, Ohio), Lorenzo Lazzarini (University of Venice), Steve Laurie (Sedgwick Museum, Cambridge), Ian MacDonald (McMarmilloyd Ltd), Maurizio Mariottini (Istituto Centrale per il Restauro/Servizio Geologico d'Italia), Patrick Rogers (Westminster Cathedral), Robert Seeman (Natural History Museum, Vienna) and David Smith (Natural History Museum, London). Information about Derbyshire stones was kindly given by Trevor Ford and Jim Rieuwerts, and I am grateful to the staff and Trustees of Chatsworth House and to Mick Cooper for access to the Chatsworth collections. My thanks to Geoffrey Holbech for permission to photograph the Farnborough Hall table, and to David and Elizabeth Hacker, Mark Godden (Albion Stone) and Eric Robinson for images and encouragement.

Working through the entire Corsi collection, I have called on the geological expertise of many of my colleagues in the Museum and the Department of Earth Sciences at Oxford, and would like to thank Martin Brasier, David Bell, Paul Jeffery, Hugh Jenkins, Jim Kennedy, Philip Powell, Kevin Walsh and Dave Waters. Norman Charnley and Steve Wyatt kindly assisted with the image of the mass spectrometer.

Most of the specimen images are of samples in the Oxford collection (prefixed "Oxf."), and I am grateful to Francesco Bernacca (Finska Stone), Michael Harris (Abingdon Stone and Marble Ltd), James Semmens (Gerald Culliford Ltd), Ian MacDonald (McMarmilloyd Ltd) and Mary White (Tennessee Valley Marble Co.) who all kindly supplied samples that are now in the Museum's collections. David Norman is thanked for permission to image samples in the fine Watson collection at Cambridge (prefixed "Camb."), and Jonathan Burhouse of Burhouse Ltd, Huddersfield, generously loaned a number of samples. Most of the specimens were scanned directly using a flat-bed scanner, and a big thank you goes to Larisa Vircavs, Christina Blackmore and Laura Cotton for doing this so well.

Finally, this book is the result of teamwork, and I would like to thank Jane Laing who started the ball rolling, James Harrison, Miranda Harvey and the team at Quintet Publishing who made it happen, and my colleagues at the Museum, friends and family who gave me so much support.